www.wadsworth.com

www.wadsworth.com is the World Wide Web site for Wadsworth and is your direct source to dozens of online resources.

At www.*wadsworth.com* you can find out about supplements, demonstration software, and student resources. You can also send email to many of our authors and preview new publications and exciting new technologies.

www.wadsworth.com
Changing the way the world learns®

About the Author

GERALD COREY is a Professor Emeritus of Human Services at California State University at Fullerton, an Adjunct Professor of Counseling and Family Sciences at Loma Linda University, and a licensed psychologist. He received his doctorate in counseling from the University of Southern California. He is a Diplomate in Counseling Psychology, American Board of Professional Psychology; a National Certified Counselor; a Fellow of the American Psychological Association (Counseling Psychology); and a Fellow of the Association for Specialists in Group Work.

Jerry received the Outstanding Professor of the Year Award from California State University at Fullerton in 1991. He teaches both undergraduate and graduate courses in group counseling, as well as courses in experiential groups, the theory and practice of counseling, and professional ethics. He is the author or co-author of 15 textbooks in counseling currently in print, 3 student videos with workbooks, and about 60 articles in professional publications. *Theory and Practice of Counseling and Psychotherapy* has been translated into the Arabic, Indonesian, Portuguese, and Chinese languages. *Theory and Practice of Group Counseling* has been translated into Chinese and Spanish.

Along with his wife, Marianne Schneider Corey, Jerry often presents workshops in group counseling. In the past 25 years the Coreys have conducted group counseling training workshops for mental health professionals at many universities in the United States as well as in Mexico, China, Germany, Belgium, Scotland, Canada, and Ireland. The Coreys also frequently give presentations and workshops at state and national professional conferences. In his leisure time, Jerry likes to travel, hike and bicycle in the mountains, and drive his 1931 Model A Ford.

Other textbooks, student manuals and workbooks, and educational videos by Gerald Corey from Brooks/Cole–Thomson Learning include:

- *Theory and Practice of Counseling and Psychotherapy,* Seventh Edition (and *Manual*) (2005)
- *Theory and Practice of Group Counseling,* Sixth Edition (and *Manual*) (2004)
- *Group Techniques,* Third Edition (2004, with Marianne Schneider Corey, Patrick Callanan, and J. Michael Russell)
- *Clinical Supervision in the Helping Professions: A Practical Guide* (2003, with Robert Haynes and Patrice Moulton)
- *Issues and Ethics in the Helping Professions,* Sixth Edition (2003, with Marianne Schneider Corey and Patrick Callanan)
- *Becoming a Helper,* Fourth Edition (2003, with Marianne Schneider Corey)
- *Groups: Process and Practice,* Sixth Edition (2002, with Marianne Schneider Corey)
- *I Never Knew I Had a Choice,* Seventh Edition (2002, with Marianne Schneider Corey)
- *The Art of Integrative Counseling* (2001)

Jerry is co-author, with his daughters Cindy Corey and Heidi Jo Corey, of an orientation-to-college book entitled *Living and Learning*, published by Wadsworth. He is also co-author (with Barbara Herlihy) of *Boundary Issues in Counseling: Multiple Roles and Responsibilities* and *ACA Ethical Standards Casebook*, Fifth Edition, both published by the American Counseling Association.

He has also made three videos on various aspects of counseling practice: (1) *CD-ROM for Integrative Counseling* (2005, with Robert Haynes); (2) *Ethics in Action: CD-ROM* (2003, with Marianne Schneider Corey and Robert Haynes); and (3) *The Evolution of a Group: Student Video and Workbook* (2000, with Marianne Schneider Corey and Robert Haynes). All of these student videos and CD-ROM programs are available through Brooks/Cole–Thomson Learning.

Have an
*INTERACTIVE,
PERSONAL
EXPERIENCE*
with counseling
theories and skills!

Introducing the
Seventh Edition
of Gerald Corey's
***Theory and Practice
of Counseling and Psychotherapy***
and its integrated suite
of teaching and learning tools

* Theory and Practice of Counseling and Psychotherapy, Seventh Edition
* Student Manual, Seventh Edition
* Case Approach to Counseling and Psychotherapy, Sixth Edition
* CD-ROM for Integrative Counseling
* The Art of Integrative Counseling

For three special and significant women in my life—

Marianne Schneider Corey, wife, valued colleague,
    insightful co-author, and best friend
Heidi Jo Corey, my daughter who is making a difference
    through her teaching of yoga
Cindy Corey, my daughter who is making an impact
    in the field of multicultural and community psychology

Case Approach to Counseling and Psychotherapy

SIXTH EDITION

Gerald Corey

California State University, Fullerton

Diplomate in Counseling Psychology,

American Board of Professional Psychology

THOMSON
™
BROOKS/COLE

Australia • Canada • Mexico • Singapore • Spain • United Kingdom • United States

THOMSON

™

BROOKS/COLE

Executive Editor: Lisa Gebo
Acquisitions Editors: Julie Martinez, Marquita Flemming
Assistant Editor: Shelley Gesicki
Editorial Assistant: Amy Lam
Technology Project Manager: Barry Connolly
Marketing Manager: Caroline Concilla
Marketing Assistant: Mary Ho
Advertising Project Manager: Tami Strang
Project Manager, Editorial Production: Katy German

Print/Media Buyer: Rebecca Cross
Permissions Editor: Kiely Sexton
Production Service: Ben Kolstad, The Cooper Company
Text and Cover Designer: Cheryl Carrington
Photo Researcher: Terri Wright
Copy Editor: Kay Mikel
Cover Image: Corbis
Printer: Webcom

For more information about our products, contact us at:
Thomson Learning Academic Resource Center
1-800-423-0563
For permission to use material from this text, submit an online request at www.thomsonrights.com

Library of Congress Control Number: 2003111398

ISBN-13: 978-0-534-55921-2
ISBN-10: 0-534-55921-2

Thomson Brooks/Cole
10 Davis Drive
Belmont, CA 94002
USA

Asia
Thomson Learning
5 Shenton Way #01-01
UIC Building
Singapore 068808

Australia/New Zealand
Thomson Learning
102 Dodds Street
Southbank, Victoria 3006
Australia

Canada
Nelson
1120 Birchmount Road
Toronto, Ontario M1K 5G4
Canada

Europe/Middle East/Africa
Thomson Learning
High Holborn House
50/51 Bedford Row
London WC1R 4LR
United Kingdom

Latin America
Thomson Learning
Seneca, 53
Colonia Polanco
11560 Mexico D.F.
Mexico

Spain/Portugal
Paraninfo
Calle Magallanes, 25
28015 Madrid, Spain

About the Contributors

JENNIFER ANDREWS, PH.D., is a faculty member in the Department of Counseling and Family Sciences at Loma Linda University. A licensed marriage and family therapist, she teaches classes that emphasize postmodern ideas and has co-authored a number of journal articles on postmodern perspectives. Dr. Andrews is a clinical member of AFTA and AAMFT as well as holding the approved supervisor designation.

Jennifer Andrews, Ph.D.

JAMES ROBERT BITTER, ED.D., is Professor of Counseling in the Department of Human Development and Learning at East Tennessee State University. He is a consultant in the areas of individual and group therapy and in the application of Adlerian principles to the counseling of children and families. Dr. Bitter is the past editor of the *Journal of Individual Psychology,* and his many publications include articles on family mapping and family constellation, created memories versus early recollections, and family reconstruction. He was associated with Virginia Satir for the last 10 years of her life.

James Robert Bitter, Ed.D.

WILLIAM BLAU, PH.D., has a private practice and teaches as an adjunct instructor at Copper Mountain College in Joshua Tree, California, and Chapman University Academic Center, Twenty-Nine Palms, California. Although his theoretical orientation is psychoanalytic, he often uses techniques from other approaches. His specialty areas include clinical biofeedback and the psychotherapy of psychotic people. Dr. Blau and his wife, Cathey Graham Blau, LCSW, BCD, work together in teaching stress management and providing couples therapy.

William Blau, Ph.D.

DAVID J. CAIN, PH.D., ABPP, received his doctorate in clinical and community psychology from the University of Wyoming. He is the founder of the Association for the Development of the Person-Centered Approach. He has served on the editorial board of several journals and is the editor of *Humanistic Psychotherapies: Handbook of Research and Practice.* Currently, Dr. Cain is the Director of the

David J. Cain, Ph.D., ABPP

David J. Clark, Ph.D.

Barbara Brownell D'Angelo, Ph.D.

Frank M. Dattilio, Ph.D., ABPP

Albert Ellis, Ph.D., ABPP

Counseling Center at United States International University and adjunct faculty in the Department of Psychology at Chapman University.

DAVID J. CLARK, PH.D., is a psychotherapist for Kaiser-Permanente Southern California, Psychiatry Department, where he is participating in a pilot project that is offering solution-oriented group therapy for brief treatment of depressed people. Dr. Clark has had a specialty in the area of addictions for more than 20 years. A licensed MFT, clinical member of the American Family Therapy Academy (AFTA), and a clinical member and approved supervisor of the American Association of Marriage and Family (AAMFT), he is currently an associate professor at Alliant International University.

BARBARA BROWNELL D'ANGELO, PH.D., a California-licensed psychologist with a behavioral orientation, taught in the Human Services Program at California State University at Fullerton and was a counselor in the Counseling Center there. Dr. D'Angelo later had a private practice in psychotherapy in Santa Ana, California.

FRANK M. DATTILIO, PH.D., ABPP, is on the faculty of psychiatry at both Harvard Medical School and the University of Pennsylvania School of Medicine. He is also a clinical psychologist in private practice. He was one of the first practitioners to apply cognitive therapy to couples and families and has authored or co-authored 11 books and more than 140 professional publications worldwide. Dr. Dattilio is also a clinical member and approved supervisor of the American Association for Marriage and Family Therapy and has been a visiting lecturer at many universities internationally.

ALBERT ELLIS, PH.D., ABPP, is the founder and director of the Albert Ellis Institute for Rational Emotive Behavior Therapy in New York. He is considered the grandfather of the cognitive behavioral approaches, and he continues to work hard at developing REBT. Dr. Ellis has published more than 700 papers in psychological, psychiatric, and sociological journals and anthologies. Dr. Ellis has authored or co-authored about 70 books and monographs. At 90 years of age, he still sees as many as 60 clients a week and gives about 200 talks and workshops to professionals each year.

KATHY M. EVANS, PH.D., is an assistant professor of Counselor Education at the University of South Carolina and is a licensed professional counselor and a licensed psychologist. Dr. Evans has taught courses in multicultural counseling and counseling theory for the past 9 years and for 11 years before that was a practicing counselor. Her research, publications, and practice have always focused on issues important to women and ethnic minority men. Recently, Dr. Evans has devoted most of her time to studying the racial, gender, and feminist identities of African American women.

Kathy M. Evans, Ph.D.

JON FREW, PH.D., is in private practice in Vancouver, Washington, and is an Associate Professor at Pacific University's School of Professional Psychology. He has published extensively in the field of Gestalt therapy and is on the editorial board of the *Gestalt Review.* Dr. Frew is co-director of the Gestalt Therapy Training Center Northwest and has conducted training workshops in the United States, Canada, and Australia.

Jon Frew, Ph.D.

WILLIAM GLASSER, M.D., is the founder and president of The William Glasser Institute in Chatsworth, California. Dr. Glasser presents many workshops each year, both in this country and abroad. His practical approach continues to be popular among a variety of practitioners and teachers. Dr. Glasser has written a number of books on reality therapy and choice theory. Some of his more recent books are *Choice Theory: A New Psychology of Personal Freedom; Counseling with Choice Theory: The New Reality Therapy;* and *Warning: Psychiatry Can Be Hazardous to Your Mental Health.*

William Glasser, M.D.

ELIZABETH A. KINCADE, PH.D., is an associate professor and coordinator of Outreach and Consultation in the Counseling and Student Development Center at Indiana University of Pennsylvania. She is a licensed psychologist, counselor, supervisor, and teacher with research and training interests in feminist theory and therapy, multicultural issues in counseling and supervision of emerging counselors. Dr. Kincade is a former president of the American College Counseling Association. She received her Ph.D. in Counseling Psychology from The Pennsylvania State University in 1989.

Elizabeth A. Kincade, Ph.D.

Arnold A. Lazarus, Ph.D., ABPP

ARNOLD A. LAZARUS, PH.D., ABPP, is Distinguished Professor Emeritus in the Graduate School of Applied and Professional Psychology at Rutgers University. Dr. Lazarus is a Diplomate in Clinical Psychology of the American Board of Professional Psychology. His writings include numerous books and professional papers. Dr. Lazarus developed the multimodal approach, a broad-based, systematic, and comprehensive approach to behavior therapy. He is considered a pioneer in developing clinical behavior therapy.

Mary Moline, Ph.D., Dr.P.H.

MARY MOLINE, PH.D., DR.P.H., is a Professor and Chair of the Department of Counseling and Family Sciences at Loma Linda University. Dr. Moline is a licensed marriage and family therapist in California. She received her Ph.D. in marriage and family therapy from Brigham Young University and her doctorate in public health from Loma Linda University. Dr. Moline has co-authored two books in the area of law and ethics. She is a clinical member and an approved supervisor of the American Association for Marriage and Family Therapy and has also taught at the graduate level for 25 years.

Gerald Monk, Ph.D.

GERALD MONK, PH.D., is the Director of the School Counseling Program and a Professor in the Department of Counseling and School Psychology at San Diego State University. Dr. Monk has published numerous articles in the areas of narrative therapy, social constructionism, and mediation, and has co-authored three books: *Narrative Therapy in Practice: The Archaeology of Hope; Narrative Counseling in Schools;* and *Narrative Mediation.* He has conducted workshops on narrative therapy and mediation in Canada, Iceland, Mexico, Austria, New Zealand, Australia, and the United States.

William G. Nicoll, Ph.D.

WILLIAM G. NICOLL, PH.D., is professor and chair of the Department of Counselor Education at Florida Atlantic University in Boca Raton, Florida. He also serves as President of the Adlerian Training Institute, Inc. Dr. Nicoll provides training in Adlerian-based interventions across the United States as well as in Europe, Asia, Latin America, and Africa. His writings focus on the applications of Adlerian brief counseling with individuals and families and with the school-related problems of children and adolescents.

DONALD POLKINGHORNE, PH.D., is a professor of Counseling Psychology at the University of Southern California and a licensed psychologist. He served as president of the Division of Theoretical and Philosophical Psychology of the American Psychological Association, as a consulting editor of the *Journal of Phenomenological Psychology,* and as a member of the editorial boards of the *Journal of Counseling Psychology* and the *Journal of Humanistic Psychology.* Among Dr. Polkinghorne's many publications are works on phenomenological research methods and existential psychotherapy and on social values.

Donald Polkinghorne, Ph.D.

PAM REMER, PH.D., is an associate professor of Counseling Psychology at the University of Kentucky and is a licensed psychologist. Dr. Remer is a feminist therapist and co-author with Dr. Judith Worell of *Feminist Perspectives in Therapy: Empowering Diverse Women.* She is a Certified Practitioner and Trainer in Psychodrama. As a therapist and educator, she specializes in women's issues and sexual assault trauma. Dr. Remer serves as an expert witness on rape trauma for criminal and civil court cases.

Pam Remer, Ph.D.

SUSAN R. SEEM, PH.D., is a faculty member in the Department of Counselor Education at the State University of New York College at Brockport and is a licensed psychologist and a national certified counselor. Her past work experience includes both college and community counseling. Dr. Seem's publications include articles on gender bias in counselor training and in clinical judgments, counseling gay and lesbian adolescents, and the consideration of gender in college counseling center practice. Dr. Seem has made numerous presentations on feminist therapy, teaching psychopathology from a feminist, multicultural perspective, and counseling centers and counselors as social change agents.

Susan R. Seem

ROBERT E. WUBBOLDING, ED.D., is Professor Emeritus of Counseling at Xavier University. He is the director of the Center for Reality Therapy in Cincinnati and also the director of training for the William Glasser Institute in Los Angeles. Dr. Wubbolding has taught reality therapy cross-culturally throughout Asia, Europe, and the Middle East and has written 10 books on reality therapy. His latest book is *Reality Therapy for the 21st Century*.

Robert E. Wubbolding, Ed.D.

CONTENTS

Preface

Case Approach to Counseling and Psychotherapy reflects my increasing emphasis on the use of demonstrations and the case approach method to bridge the gap between the theory and practice of counseling. Students in the courses I teach have found that a demonstration in class often clears up their misconceptions about how a therapy actually works. This book is an attempt to stimulate some of the unique learning that can occur through seeing a therapeutic approach in action. It also gives students a chance to work with a case from the vantage point of 11 counseling approaches: psychoanalytic, Adlerian, existential, person-centered, Gestalt, behavior, cognitive behavior, reality, feminist, postmodern, and family systems therapies.

The format of this book provides an opportunity to see how each of the various therapeutic approaches is applied to a single client, Ruth Walton, who is followed throughout the book. A feature of the text is an assessment of Ruth's case by one or more consultants in each of the 11 theoretical perspectives. Highly competent practitioners assess and treat Ruth from their particular theoretical orientation; they also provide sample dialogues to illustrate their style of working with Ruth. In certain cases I was able to enlist the founder of a theory to describe what his or her approach to working with Ruth would be. For example, William Glasser offers an assessment of Ruth in the context of choice theory and illustrates his interventions using reality therapy. Arnold Lazarus, the founder of multimodal therapy, provides an overview of how he would assess Ruth's functioning with his multimodal framework. And Albert Ellis describes his analysis of Ruth and demonstrates his style in providing rational emotive behavior therapy (REBT).

New to this sixth edition is the inclusion of postmodern approaches, in which three different therapists describe their approaches: social constructivist, solution-focused brief therapy, and narrative therapy.

The 11 theory chapters use a common format, allowing for comparisons among approaches. This format includes the guest commentary or commentaries, followed by my way of working with Ruth from that particular perspective. I discuss the theory's basic assumptions, an initial assessment of Ruth, the goals of therapy, and the therapeutic procedures to be used. The therapeutic process is concretely illustrated by client–therapist dialogues, which are augmented by process commentaries explaining the rationale for my interventions. "Questions for Reflection" at the end of each chapter help readers apply the material to their personal lives and offer guidelines for continuing to work with Ruth within each of the theoretical orientations.

Chapter 13 brings the 11 approaches together and helps students develop their own therapeutic style. I demonstrate how I would counsel Ruth in an integrated fashion by drawing on most of the therapeutic approaches. Guidelines are also provided for working with Ruth as a member of various cultural groups.

Supplementary Resources

Ideally, *Case Approach to Counseling and Psychotherapy* will be used as part of an integrated learning series I have developed for courses in counseling theory and practice. In a separate book, *The Art of Integrative Counseling*, I describe how to develop your own integrative approach to counseling and provide guidelines for acquiring a personal style of counseling practice. Ruth's case is used to illustrate this integrative perspective. *Case Approach to Counseling and Psychotherapy* can supplement the core textbook to enhance students' learning of theory by letting them see counseling in action. In the textbook, *Theory and Practice of Counseling and Psychotherapy*, 7th edition, students are given an overview of the key concepts and techniques of the 11 models of contemporary therapy. The accompanying Student Manual contains many experiential activities and exercises designed to help students apply the theories to themselves and to connect theory with practice.

A new self-study *CD-ROM for Integrative Counseling* illustrates my own integrative perspective in working with Ruth. References to the CD-ROM are given throughout this book by using an icon to help students coordinate the counseling sessions in the CD-ROM program with the topics in this book. The CD-ROM program brings together several of the therapies discussed in this book and provides concrete illustrations of my ways of working with Ruth.

Used in conjunction with this book, the CD-ROM program provides a bridge that connects theoretical perspectives with the practice of counseling.

Acknowledgments

I appreciate both the support and the challenge given by those teachers of counseling courses and clinicians who read the revised manuscript for this sixth edition and provided specific and helpful comments for improving the effectiveness of the case presentations. These people are: Mary Jo Blazek, University of Maine, Augusta; Monit Cheung, University of Houston; Beverly B. Palmer, California State University, Dominguez Hills; and Carla Washington, Florida A&M University.

Special thanks are extended to Marianne Schneider Corey, my wife and colleague, for her support and her contributions to this revision. Based on her clinical experiences as a marriage and family therapist, she went over the case of Ruth, challenging me to pay attention to subtle yet important nuances.

I am particularly indebted to those individuals who reviewed a chapter in their area of expertise and who also contributed by writing about their way of working with Ruth from their particular therapeutic perspective. Most of the original contributors updated and expanded their selections in this edition, and there are several new ones. A complete list of these contributors appears in the "About the Contributors" section.

Appreciation goes to Art Pomponio who served as a developmental editor for this project. He carefully went over all the prerevision reviews, organized themes based on the reviews, and made suggestions that were implemented in this edition.

Recognition goes to members of the staff of Thomson Brooks/Cole who have given extra time and attention to this revised edition, particularly Julie Martinez, editor of counseling. I want to acknowledge my special appreciation to Ben Kolstad, who guided the production of the book, and to Kay Mikel, the manuscript editor, whose sensitivity and editorial skills contributed in important ways to the readability and interest of this text.

Chapter 1

Introduction and Overview

 STRUCTURE OF THE BOOK

Even after reading about a theory of therapy and discussing it in class, students sometimes still have unclear notions about how to apply it. I began experimenting with asking my students to volunteer for a class demonstration in which they served as "clients." Seeing concepts in action gave them a clearer picture of how therapists use various approaches in their work. This book illustrates 11 therapies in action and shows how to selectively borrow concepts and techniques from these therapeutic approaches. In addition, I encourage you to integrate techniques that are appropriate to your client population in a style that is an expression of who you are as a person. Effective counseling combines the personality of the therapist with the technical skills that he or she employs. To apply techniques appropriately, it is essential to consider your personal style and theoretical orientation in relation to each client's unique life situation.

Before this large task of developing a personalized approach can be accomplished, however, you will need to know the basics of each of the theories and acquire some experience with these therapies. This book aims to provide a balance between describing the way therapists with a given orientation might proceed with a client and challenging you to try your hand at showing how you would proceed with the same client.

This initial chapter deals with methods of conceptualizing a case, and it provides background material on the central figure in this book, Ruth Walton. Refer to Ruth's intake form and autobiography frequently as you work with her in the 11 theory chapters. Ruth is not an actual client. I have created her by combining many of the common themes I have observed in my work with clients. However, I believe the characteristics ascribed to Ruth are representative of clients you may meet in your practice.

Ruth appears in each of the chapters on individual theories (Chapters 2-12), and in Chapter 13, which describes an integrative approach. Chapters 2 through 12 begin with commentaries by one or more "outside consultants" on Ruth's case. Each consultant was given Ruth's background information and also read my perspective on her for the theory under discussion. Then this representative wrote a section describing the following:

- The core concepts and goals of his or her therapeutic approach
- The themes in Ruth's life that might serve as a focus for therapy
- An assessment of Ruth's dynamics, with emphasis on her current life situation
- The techniques and procedures that would probably be used in counseling Ruth
- Illustrations of the therapy in action through dialogue between Ruth and the therapist

You will notice that there are two invited consultants for Chapter 7 (behavior therapy), Chapter 8 (cognitive behavior therapy), and Chapter 9 (reality therapy). For Chapter 10 (feminist therapy) three consultants work as a unified team with Ruth, which is followed up by another consultant who offers a feminist perspective in treating Ruth as a survivor of sexual assault. For Chapter 11 (postmodern approaches) there are three invited consultants, one for each of the major postmodern approaches. Thus, in Chapters 7 to 11 you have the advantage of reading two or more different styles of working with Ruth from practitioners with the same theoretical orientation.

After the guest contributors' discussion of their perspective on Ruth, I look at the basic assumptions of the approaches, make an initial assessment of Ruth, and examine the theory's therapeutic goals and procedures. The therapeutic process is made concrete with samples of dialogue between Ruth and me, along with process commentaries to provide an explanation of the direction therapy is taking. Using this model, you will see one or more expert practitioners in each theoretical orientation illustrate their way of working with Ruth. As well, I provide my own version of the theory as I draw from key concepts and selected techniques in my way of counseling Ruth.

You are encouraged to become an active learner by evaluating the manner in which the consultants and I work with Ruth from the various theoretical perspectives. You are asked to show how you would work with her as your client, using the particular approach being considered in the chapter. To guide you in thinking of ways to work with Ruth, each chapter ends with "Questions for Reflection." Besides thinking about these questions by yourself, I also suggest that you arrange to work with fellow students in small discussion groups to explore various approaches.

You can further enhance your learning by participating in a variety of role-playing exercises in which you "become" Ruth and also by participating in group discussions based on various ways of working with her. Rather than merely reading about her case, you can use various perspectives to stimulate reflection on ways in which you have felt like Ruth. In experiential practice sessions you can also draw on your own concerns in becoming the counselor. Think of as many ways as possible to use these cases as a method of stimulating introspection and providing lively class discussion.

In Chapter 13 you are encouraged to consider the advantages of eventually developing your own integrative approach and counseling style. Such an integrative, eclectic perspective of counseling entails selecting concepts and methods from various sources and theories. An integrative approach does not necessarily refer to developing a new theory; rather, it emphasizes a systematic integration of underlying principles and techniques of the various therapy systems. I encourage you to strive to build a unified system that fits you and is appropriate for the particular setting in which you practice. It is also essential that you be willing to challenge your basic assumptions, test your hypotheses as you practice, and revise your theory as you confirm or disconfirm your clinical hunches.

I demonstrate my integrative approach to counseling in the *CD-ROM for Integrative Counseling,* which shows segments of individual counseling sessions in which Ruth explores key themes in her life.[1] Throughout this book I will refer you to specific sessions in the CD-ROM program that demonstrate the application of these diverse theoretical perspectives from the initial to ending phase of therapy with Ruth. The CD-ROM and this book are ideal companions. In addition, *The Art of Integrative Counseling* also uses the case of Ruth as the central example in illustrating an integrative, eclectic approach to counseling practice.[2] This book expands on material presented briefly in Chapter 13 here, which is devoted to bringing the approaches together and illustrating how you can develop your own therapeutic style.

 # OVERVIEW OF THE THERAPEUTIC PERSPECTIVES

In the chapters to follow, the case of Ruth will be analyzed and discussed from various therapeutic perspectives. For each of these perspectives we will consider its basic assumptions, its view of how to assess clients, its goals for therapy, and its therapeutic procedures. This section presents the essence of the various approaches. As a way of laying the foundation for developing an eclectic, integrative approach, we will look for common denominators and differences among the 11 perspectives.[3]

Basic Assumptions

When therapists make initial contact with clients, their theoretical perspective determines what they look for and what they see. This largely determines the focus and course of therapy and influences their choice of therapeutic strategies and procedures. As you develop your counseling stance, pay attention to your own basic assumptions. Developing a counseling perspective is more involved than merely accepting the tenets of a particular theory or combination of theories. Your theoretical approach is an expression of your unique life experiences.

How do theoretical assumptions influence practice? Your view about the assessment of clients, the goals you think are important in therapy, the strategies and techniques you employ to reach these goals, the way you divide responsibility in the client–therapist relationship, and your view of your function and role as a counselor are largely determined by your theoretical orientation. Attempting to practice counseling without at least a general theoretical perspective is somewhat like flying a plane without a map and without instruments. But a counseling theory is not a rigid structure that prescribes the specific steps of what to do in therapeutic work. Instead, a theoretical orientation is a set of general guidelines you can use to make sense of what you are doing.

One way to approach the basic assumptions underlying the major theoretical orientations is to consider six categories under which most contemporary systems fall. These are (1) the *psychodynamic approaches,* which stress insight in therapy (psychoanalytic and Adlerian therapy); (2) the *experiential* and *relationship-oriented approaches,* which stress feelings and subjective experiencing (existential, person-centered, and Gestalt therapy); (3) the *cognitive* and *behavioral approaches,* which stress the role of thinking and doing and tend to be action-oriented (behavior therapy, rational emotive behavior therapy, cognitive therapy, and reality therapy); (4) *feminist therapy,* which stresses egalitarian relationships and social and political activism to combat oppression; (5) *postmodern approaches*, which include social constructionism, solution-focused brief therapy, and narrative therapy; and (6) *family therapy,* which stresses understanding the individual within the entire system of which he or she is a part.

Although I have separated the theories into six general groups, this categorization is somewhat arbitrary. Overlapping concepts and themes make it difficult to neatly compartmentalize these theoretical orientations. What follows is a thumbnail sketch of the basic assumptions underlying each of these 11 therapeutic systems.

Psychoanalytic Therapy   The psychoanalytic approach views people as being significantly influenced by unconscious motivation, conflicts between impulses and prohibitions, defense mechanisms, and early childhood experiences. Because the dynamics of behavior are buried in the unconscious, treatment consists of a lengthy process of analyzing inner conflicts that are rooted in the past. Therapy is largely a process of restructuring the personality; therefore, clients must be willing to commit themselves to an intensive, long-term process.

Adlerian Therapy   According to the Adlerian approach, people are primarily social beings, influenced and motivated by societal forces. Human nature is viewed as creative, active, and decisional. The approach focuses on the unity of the person and on understanding the individual's subjective perspective. Adler holds that inherent feelings of inferiority, or feeling less than one should or needs to be, initiates a natural striving toward achieving a higher, or greater, level of mastery and competence in life. Like all living organisms, humans strive throughout life to grow, evolve, and become more fully developed and capable. The subjective decisions each person makes regarding the specific direction of this striving form the basis of the individual's lifestyle (or personality style). The style of life consists of our views about others, the world, and ourselves; these views lead to distinctive behaviors that we adopt in pursuit of our life goals. We can shape our own future by actively and courageously taking risks and making decisions in the face of unknown consequences. Clients are not viewed as being "sick" or suffering from some disability or disorder needing to be "cured." Rather, they are seen as being discouraged and functioning on the basis of self-defeating and self-limiting assumptions, which generate problem-maintaining, ego-protective behaviors. Thus, clients are seen as being in need of encouragement to correct mistaken perceptions of self and others and to learn to initiate new behavioral interaction patterns. Counseling is not simply a matter of an expert therapist making prescriptions for change. It is a collaborative effort, with client and therapist actively working on mutually accepted goals and the facilitation of change at both the cognitive and behavioral levels.

Existential Therapy   The existential perspective holds that we define ourselves by our choices. Although outside factors restrict the range of our choices, we are ultimately the authors of our lives. We are thrust into a meaningless world, yet we are challenged to accept our aloneness and create a meaningful existence. Because we have the capacity for awareness, we are basically free. Along with our freedom, however, comes responsibility for the choices we make. Existential practitioners contend that clients often lead a "restricted existence," seeing few if any alternatives for dealing with life situations and tending to feel trapped or helpless. The therapist's job is to confront these clients with the restricted life they have chosen and to help them become aware of their own part in creating this condition. As an outgrowth of the therapeutic venture, clients are able to recognize outmoded patterns of living, and they begin to accept responsibility for changing their future.

Person-Centered Therapy   The person-centered approach rests on the assumption that we have the capacity to understand our problems and that we have the resources within us to resolve them. Seeing people in this light means that therapists focus on the constructive side of human nature and on what is right with people. This approach places emphasis on feelings about the self. Clients can move forward toward growth and wholeness by looking within rather than focusing on outside influences. They are able to change without a high degree of structure and direction from the therapist. What clients need from the therapist is understanding, genuineness, support, acceptance, caring, and positive regard.

Gestalt Therapy   The Gestalt approach is based on the assumption that individuals and their behavior must be understood in the context of their present environment. The therapist's task is to support clients as they explore their present experience. The fundamental method to assist in this exploration is awareness of the internal (intrapersonal) world and the external environment. Clients carry on their own therapy as much as possible by doing experiments designed to heighten awareness and to engage in contact. Change occurs naturally as awareness of "what is" increases. Interruptions in the process by which clients develop awareness and move toward contact with the environment are monitored. Heightened awareness can also lead to a more thorough integration of parts of the client that were fragmented or unknown.

Behavior Therapy   Behavior therapy assumes that people are basically shaped by learning and sociocultural conditioning. This approach focuses on the client's ability to learn how to eliminate maladaptive behavior and acquire constructive behavior. Behavior therapy is a systematic approach that begins with a comprehensive assessment of the individual to determine the present level of functioning as a prelude to setting therapeutic goals. After the client establishes clear and specific behavioral goals, the therapist typically suggests strategies that are most appropriate for meeting these stated goals. It is assumed that clients will make progress to the extent that they are willing to practice new behaviors in real-life situations. Continual evaluation is used to determine how well the procedures and techniques are working.

Cognitive Behavioral Approaches   From the perspective of rational emotive behavior therapy (REBT), our problems are caused by our perceptions of life situations and our thoughts, not by the situations themselves, not by others, and not by past events. Thus, it is our responsibility to recognize and change self-defeating thinking that leads to emotional and behavioral disorders. REBT also holds that people tend to incorporate these dysfunctional beliefs from external sources and then continue to indoctrinate themselves with this faulty thinking. To overcome irrational thinking, therapists use active and directive therapy procedures, including teaching, suggestion, and giving homework. REBT emphasizes education, with the therapist functioning as a teacher and the client as a learner. Although REBT is didactic and directive, its goal is to get people to think, feel, and act for themselves. Therapists consistently encourage and challenge clients to do what is necessary to make long-lasting and substantive change.

Other cognitive behavioral therapies share some of the assumptions of REBT. Many of these approaches assume that people are prone to learning erroneous, self-defeating thoughts but that they are capable of unlearning them. People perpetuate their difficulties through their self-talk. By pinpointing these cognitive errors and correcting them, clients can create a more fulfilling life. Cognitive restructuring plays a central role in these therapies. People are assumed to be able to make changes by listening to their self-talk, by learning a new internal dialogue, and by learning coping skills needed for behavioral changes.

Reality Therapy   Reality therapy operates from the premise that all relationship problems are in the present and must be solved in the present. Problematic symptoms are the result of clients trying to deal with a present unsatisfying relationship. Once a significant relationship is improved, the troubling symptom will disappear. Reality therapists challenge clients to consider whether their current behavior is getting them what they want. Clients are encouraged to explore their perceptions, share their wants, and make a commitment to counseling. Because clients can directly control their acting and thinking functions more than they can control what they are feeling, their actions become the focus of therapy. Clients explore the direction in which their behavior is taking them and evaluate what they are doing. They then create a plan of action to make the changes they want.

Feminist Therapy   A basic assumption of feminist therapy is that power inequalities and gender-role expectations influence individuals from a very early age. There are detrimental effects of gender socialization for both women and men, for all individuals are capable of possessing a range of characteristics and behaviors that go beyond rigid and restrictive cultural stereotypes. Therapy is conducted in a gender-sensitive manner. This includes having a positive attitude toward women and being willing to challenge patriarchal systems, empowering both women and men by helping them transcend gender socialization, and assisting women in finding their voices and discovering meaning in their lives. The therapist's role is to sensitize clients to the impact of gender, class, race, ethnicity, and other aspects in their lives. Feminist therapists are aware of the potentially destructive power dynamics in the client–therapist relationship and build mutuality into the therapeutic process. Therapy is viewed as a cooperative and collaborative relationship.

Postmodern Approaches   The postmodern approaches challenge many of the assumptions of traditional therapies. Postmodernism is marked by acceptance of plurality and the notion that individuals create their own reality. Some of the main assumptions are that people are competent and healthy, have the capacity to find their own solutions to difficulties they face, and are the experts on their own lives. The postmodern approaches have in common the basic assumption that we generate stories to make sense of ourselves and our world. People are empowered by learning how to separate themselves from their problems. Clients learn that the person is not the problem—the problem is the problem. Therapists help clients to free themselves from problem-saturated stories and open space to co-create alternative stories. In essence, clients reauthor their stories about themselves and their relationships. Therapy is a collaborative venture aimed at helping clients construct meaningful goals that will lead to a better future.

Family Systems Therapy   Family systems therapy is grounded on the assumption that the individual cannot be fully understood apart from the family system. A basic principle is that a change in one part of the system will result in a change in other parts of the system. If the family unit changes in significant ways, these changes will have an impact on the individual. Likewise, if the individual makes changes, the entire family unit will be affected. Thus, therapy involves assessing and treating an individual's concerns within the context of the interaction among family members. From a systemic perspective, being a healthy person involves both a sense of belonging to the family system and a sense of separateness and individuality. Some of the assumptions of family therapy include the notion that a client's behavior (1) may serve a function or a purpose for the family, (2) may be the result of the system's inability to function effectively, and (3) may result from dysfunctional patterns that are passed on from generation to generation. The family therapist intervenes with individual clients in ways that will enable them to deal more effectively with significant people in their lives, whether or not these other people are physically present in the therapy session.

Cultural and Individual Differences Emerging From Basic Assumptions   The contemporary theories of therapeutic practice are grounded on assumptions that are part of Western culture. Many of these assumptions are not appropriate when applied to non-Western cultures. The basic assumptions of the 11 orientations described here emphasize values such as choice, the uniqueness of the individual, self-assertion, and strengthening the ego. Therapeutic outcomes that these models stress include improving assertive coping skills by changing the environment, changing one's coping behavior, and learning to manage stress. In contrast, non-Western orientations focus on interdependence, play down individuality, and emphasize losing oneself in the totality of the cosmos.

Western therapeutic approaches are oriented toward change. Non-Western approaches focus more on the social framework than on development of the individual. The techniques associated with some of the contemporary counseling models may need to be modified when they are applied to other ethnic and cultural groups such as Asian Americans, Latinos, Native Americans, and African Americans. Seeking professional help is not customary for many client populations, and individuals will typically turn first to informal systems (family, friends, and community). Counselors should be aware of the basic assumptions underlying their theoretical orientation. In an increasingly pluralistic society, there is an ethical imperative to avoid forcing all clients to fit a mold that is not appropriate for their cultural background. Therefore, we need to learn how our assumptions influence practice.

Perspectives on Assessment

Some approaches stress the importance of conducting a comprehensive assessment of the client as the initial step in the therapeutic process. The rationale is that specific counseling goals cannot be formulated and appropriate strategies cannot be designed until a thorough picture of the client's past and present functioning is formed. In this section I describe various views of the role of assessment in therapy. I also present some ways of conceptualizing an individual case, emphasizing what information to gather during the initial stages of therapy.

Psychoanalytic Therapy   Psychoanalysts assume that normal personality development is based on dealing effectively with successive psychosexual and psychosocial stages of development. Faulty personality development is the result of inadequately resolving a specific developmental conflict. Therapists are interested in the client's early history as a way of understanding how past situations contribute to a dysfunction. This approach emphasizes the importance of comprehensive assessment techniques as a basis for understanding personality dynamics and the origin of emotional disorders. However, some analysts shy away from gathering information, preferring to let it unfold during the process of analytic therapy.

Adlerian Therapy   Assessment is a basic part of Adlerian therapy. The initial session focuses on developing a relationship based on a deeper understanding of the client's presenting concerns and accepting and valuing the client. Through this process, a sense of trust and a cooperative, collaborative therapeutic alliance evolves. The therapist begins by seeking to understand the specific concerns and issues the client brings to therapy. Also, the client's relative levels of functioning in all the basic tasks of life are explored—social, love-intimacy, occupational, and spiritual—so as to more fully understand the social context of the client's life situation. The therapist seeks to assess the client's behavioral movement in relation to others and the environment and to begin a process of striving to understand the underlying logic of the client's lifestyle. From this point, the Adlerian therapist will seek to work with the client in developing a deeper and more complete understanding of his or her basic personality structure. This involves placing emphasis on the individual's lifestyle—or the cognitive framework or schema from which the individual attempts to understand life and to make behavior choices. More specifically, the therapist seeks to ascertain the faulty, self-defeating perceptions and assumptions about self, others, and life that maintain the problematic behavioral patterns the client brings to therapy.

Some Adlerians prefer to engage in a more structured assessment process utilizing a detailed lifestyle questionnaire to gather information regarding the client's family of origin, parental relationships, sibling relationships, and family values so as to begin to see the client's perceptions of life and the context in which his or her unique style of life developed, which includes one's view of self, others, and life. Others prefer to use a more informal process, incorporating aspects of the formal lifestyle assessment (for example, family of origin information, birth order) as well as any of a variety of other assessment techniques that help to reveal the underlying cognitive framework of the client's personality. Early childhood recollections, family genograms, favorite childhood stories, family-of-origin stories, art therapy activities, and other such projective techniques can all be utilized in the assessment process by Adlerian therapists. The goal of assessment is to identify the mistaken logic in the major themes and patterns in the client's lifestyle that are connected to the present-ing issue(s). In addition to the mistaken logic in the client's lifestyle, the thera-pist also identifies assets (strengths and internal resources) the client has developed that can be drawn upon to provide a direction for the course of ther-apy and to assist the client in moving toward growth and change.

Existential Therapy   Existentially oriented counselors maintain that the way to understand the client is by grasping the essence of the person's subjective world. The primary purpose of existential clinical assessment is to understand the assumptions clients use in structuring their existence. This approach is different from the traditional diagnostic framework, for it focuses not on un-derstanding the individual from an external perspective but, instead, on grasp-ing the essence of the client's inner world.

Person-Centered Therapy   In much the same spirit as existential counselors, person-centered therapists maintain that traditional assessment and diagno-sis are detrimental because they are external ways of understanding the client. They believe (1) the best vantage point for understanding another person is through his or her subjective world; (2) the practitioner can become preoccu-pied with the client's history and neglect present attitudes and behavior; and (3) therapists can develop a judgmental attitude, shifting too much in the di-rection of telling clients what they ought to do. Focusing on gathering infor-mation about a client can lead to an intellectualized conception about the person. The client is assumed to be the one who knows the dynamics of his or her behavior. For change to occur, the person must experience a perceptual change, not simply receive data. Thus, therapists listen actively, attempt to be present, and allow clients to identify the themes they choose to explore.

Gestalt Therapy   Gestalt therapists are interested in the "backgrounds" out of which the "figures" that guide their work emerge. Many Gestalt therapists gather certain types of information about their clients to supplement the as-sessment and diagnostic work done in the present moment. Gestalt therapists attend to interruptions in the client's contacting functions, and the result is a "functional diagnosis" of how individuals experience satisfaction or blocks in their relationship with the environment.

Behavior Therapy   The behavioral approach begins with a comprehensive as-sessment of the client's present functioning, with questions directed to past learning that is related to current behavior patterns. It includes an objective appraisal of specific behaviors and the stimuli that are maintaining them. Some of the reasons for conducting a thorough assessment at the outset of therapy are these: (1) it identifies behavioral deficiencies as well as assets, (2) it provides an objective means of appraising both a client's specific symptoms and the factors that have led up to the client's malfunctioning, (3) it facilitates selection of the most suitable therapeutic techniques, (4) it specifies a new learning and shaping schedule, (5) it is useful in predicting the course and the outcome of a particular clinical disorder, and (6) it provides a framework for research into the effectiveness of the procedures employed.

Multimodal therapy, developed by Arnold Lazarus, is an example of a broad-based, systemic, and comprehensive approach to behavior therapy. It calls for technical eclecticism, but it remains firmly grounded in social learning and cognitive theory. In the multimodal orientation a comprehensive assessment process attends to each area of a client's BASIC I.D. (behavior, affect, sensation, imagery, cognition, interpersonal relationships, and drugs and biological factors). Interactive problems throughout each of these seven areas are identified, and appropriate techniques are selected to deal with each difficulty.

Cognitive Behavioral Approaches   The assessment used in cognitive behavioral therapy is based on getting a sense of the client's patterns of thinking. Attention is paid to various beliefs the client has developed in relation to certain events. Therapists are not merely concerned with gathering data about past events but are also alert to evidence of faulty thinking and cognitive distortions the client has incorporated. Once self-defeating thought patterns and beliefs have been identified, the therapeutic process consists of actively challenging these beliefs and substituting constructive ones.

Reality Therapy   Assessment of clients is typically not a formal process; psychological testing and diagnosis are not generally a part of this approach. Through the use of skillful questioning, however, reality therapists help clients make an assessment of their present behavior. They have little interest in learning the causes of clients' current problems or in gathering information about clients' past experiences. Instead, the focus is on getting clients to take a critical look at what they are doing now and then determine the degree to which their present behavior is effective. This informal assessment directs clients to pay attention to their pattern of wants, needs, perceptions, successes, and personal assets to evaluate whether their lives are moving in the direction they want.

Feminist Therapy   This approach is less than enthusiastic when it comes to traditional diagnosis. Feminist therapists criticize the current classification system for being biased because it was developed by White, male psychiatrists. Also, the classification system tends to focus on the individual's symptoms and not on the social factors that cause dysfunctional behavior. The assessment process emphasizes the cultural context of clients' problems, especially the degree to which clients possess power or are oppressed. Some assessment and treatment approaches include gender-role analysis, power analysis, assertion training, and demystification of therapy.

Postmodern Approaches   Like feminist therapy, the postmodern therapies do not emphasize assessment, diagnosis, or categorization of individuals. Postmodern therapists do not want to assume the role of judging clients or thinking and talking about them in terms of pathological categories. These therapists do not get caught up in totalizing descriptions of an individual's identity, especially if these descriptions are anchored in terms of a problem. Instead, the emphasis is placed on an individual's competencies and establishing relationships with clients whereby they become senior partners in the counseling venture. Rather than looking at what is wrong with people, this approach focuses on the client's strengths and resources.

Family Systems Therapy   In most systemic approaches both therapist and client are involved in the assessment process. Some systemic practitioners will assist clients in tracing the highlights of their family history and in identifying issues in their family of origin. The premise underlying the significance of understanding and assessing one's family of origin is that the patterns of interpersonal behavior learned there will be repeated in other interactions outside the family. Individuals may be asked to identify what they learned from interacting with their parents, from observing their parents' interactions with each other, and from observing how each parent interacted with each sibling. Clients may also identify the rules governing interactions in their family. These family precepts include unspoken rules, messages given by parents to children, myths, and secrets. Family rules may be functional or dysfunctional. Part of the assessment process will probably deal with family goals, structure (functional versus dysfunctional), decision-making processes, power structure, communication styles, history and life cycle, and multigenerational patterns that reveal a unified picture of the family's dynamics.

The Place of Assessment and Diagnosis in Counseling and Case Management

Assessment consists of evaluating the relevant factors in a client's life to identify themes for further exploration in therapy. Diagnosis, which is sometimes part of the assessment process, consists of identifying a specific category of psychological problem based on a pattern of symptoms. There are several types of diagnosis. *Medical diagnosis* is the process of examining physical symptoms, inferring causes of physical disorders or diseases, providing a category that fits the pattern of a disease, and prescribing an appropriate treatment. *Psychological diagnosis* entails identifying an emotional or behavioral problem and making a statement about the current status of a client. It includes stipulating the possible causes of the individual's emotional, psychological, and behavioral difficulties. It also entails suggesting the appropriate therapeutic techniques to deal with the identified problem and estimating the chances for a successful resolution. *Differential diagnosis* consists of distinguishing one form of psychiatric disorder from another by determining which of two (or more) diseases or disorders with similar symptoms the person is suffering from. The 2000 edition of the American Psychiatric Association's *Diagnostic and Statistical Manual of Mental Disorders, Text Revision* (DSM-IV-TR) is the standard reference for the nomenclature of psychopathology.[4]

A practitioner's view of diagnosis will depend on his or her theoretical orientation, as we have seen. For instance, psychoanalytically oriented therapists tend to favor diagnosis as one way of understanding how past situations contribute to an individual's current dysfunction. Practitioners with a behavioral orientation also favor diagnosis because they emphasize observation and other objective means of appraising both a client's specific symptoms and the factors that have led up to the person's malfunctioning. Such an assessment process allows them to employ techniques that are appropriate for a particular disorder and to evaluate the effectiveness of a treatment program. On the other side of the issue are person-centered practitioners, who maintain that diagnosis is not essential for counseling because it tends to pull therapists away from a subjective way of understanding their clients and fosters an external conception about them.

Regardless of your theoretical orientation, it is likely that you will be expected to work within the framework of the DSM-IV-TR if you are counseling in a community agency. Even if you are in private practice, you will have to provide a diagnosis on the client's claim form if you accept insurance payments for mental health services. Because you will need to think within the framework of assessing and diagnosing clients, it is essential that you become familiar with the diagnostic categories and the structure of the DSM-IV-TR.

My Perspective on Assessment

Assessment, broadly construed, is a legitimate part of therapy. The assessment process does not necessarily have to be completed during the intake interview, however, nor does it have to be a fixed judgment that the therapist makes about the client. Assessment is a continuing process that focuses on understanding the person. Ideally, assessment is a collaborative effort that is part of the interaction between client and therapist. Both should be involved in discovering the nature of the client's presenting problem, a process that begins with the initial session and continues until therapy ends. Here are some questions that are helpful for a therapist to consider during the early assessment phase:

- What are my immediate and overall reactions to the client?
- What is going on in this person's life at this time?
- What are the client's main assets and liabilities?
- What are his or her resources for change?
- To what degree does this client possess the power to change his or her situation?
- Is this a crisis situation, or is it a long-standing problem?
- What does the client primarily want from therapy, and how can it best be achieved?

- What should be the focus of the sessions?
- What major internal and external factors are contributing to the client's current problems, and what can be done to alleviate them?
- What are the cultural and systemic influences of current behavior?
- In what ways can an understanding of the client's cultural background shed light on developing a plan to deal with the person's problems?
- What are the client's beliefs and experiences pertaining to spirituality? How might these beliefs and experiences be resources that can be drawn upon in dealing with a problem?
- What significant past events appear to be related to the client's present level of functioning?
- What specific family dynamics might be relevant to the client's present struggles and interpersonal relationships?
- On what support systems can the client rely in making changes? Who are the significant people in the client's life?
- What are the prospects for meaningful change, and how will we know when that change has occurred?

As a result of questions such as these, therapists will develop tentative hypotheses, which they can share with their clients as therapy proceeds.

This process of assessment does not have to result in classifying the client under some clinical category. Instead, counselors can describe behavior as they observe it and encourage clients to think about its meaning. In this way assessment becomes a process of thinking about issues *with* the client rather than a mechanical procedure conducted by an expert therapist. From this perspective, assessment and diagnostic thinking are vital to the therapeutic procedures that are selected, and they help practitioners conceptualize a case.

Even if mental health practitioners are required to diagnose clients for administrative or insurance reasons, they are not bound rigidly to that view of their clients. The diagnostic category is merely a framework for viewing and understanding a pattern of symptoms and for making treatment plans. It is not necessary to restrict clients to a label or to treat them in stereotypical ways. It is essential that practitioners be aware of the dangers of labeling and adopt a tentative stance toward diagnosis. As therapy progresses, additional data are bound to emerge that may call for modification of the original diagnosis.

General Guidelines for Assessment   The intake interview typically centers on making an assessment and prescribing an appropriate course of treatment. As you have seen, this assessment may take various forms depending on the practitioner's orientation. For example, Adlerians look for ways in which the family structure has affected the client's development, whereas a psychoanalytic practitioner is interested in intrapsychic conflicts. I have pulled together some guidelines that might be helpful in thinking about how to get significant information and where to proceed with a client after making an initial assessment. Ten areas that are a basic part of conceptualizing an individual case are discussed here.

1. Identifying data. Get details such as name, age, sex, appearance, ethnic background, socioeconomic status, marital status, religious identification, and referral source (who referred the client, and for what purpose).

2. Presenting problem(s). What is the chief complaint? This area includes a brief description, in the client's own words, of the immediate problems for which he or she is seeking therapy. The presenting situation includes a description of the problems, how long they have existed, and what has been done to cope with them.

3. Current living circumstances. Information to collect here includes marital status and history, family data, recent moves, financial status, legal problems, basic lifestyle conflicts, support systems, and problems in personal relationships.

4. Psychological analysis and assessment. What is the client's general psychological state? For example, how does the person view his or her situation, needs, and problems? What is the client's level of maturity? Is there evidence of detrimental influences in the client's life? What are the person's dominant emotions? Is the client excited, anxious, ashamed, or angry? This phase of assessment entails describing the client's ego functioning, including self-concept, self-esteem, memory, orientation, fantasies, ability to tolerate frustration, insight, and motivation to change. The focus is on the client's view of self, including perceived strengths and weaknesses, the person's ideal self, and how the client believes others view him or her. What is the client's level of security? What ability does the person have to see and cope with reality, make decisions, assert self-control and self-direction, and deal with life changes and transitions? Standardized psychological tests of intelligence, personality, aptitudes, and interests may be used.

Another assessment procedure is the *mental-status examination*, which is a structured interview leading to information about the client's psychological level of functioning. This examination focuses on areas such as appearance, behavior, feeling, perception, and thinking. Under the behavior category, for example, the counselor making the assessment will note specific dimensions of behavior, including posture, facial expressions, general body movements, and quality of speech in the interview situation. Under the thinking category it is important to assess factors such as the client's intellectual functioning, orientation, insight, judgment, memory, thought processes, and any disturbances in thinking. The mental-status examination is also used to screen for psychosis.

5. Psychosocial developmental history. The focus here is on the developmental and etiological factors relating to the client's present difficulties. Five types can be considered: (1) precipitating factors—for example, maturational or situational stress, school entry, divorce, or death of a parent; (2) predisposing factors—for example, parent–child relationships and other family patterns, personality structure, and hereditary or constitutional factors; (3) contributory factors—for example, a current or past illness or the problems of family members; (4) perpetuating factors—for example, secondary gains such as the sympathy that a sufferer from migraine headaches elicits; and (5) sociocultural factors—that is, customs, traditions, family patterns, and cultural values.

From a developmental perspective these questions could be asked: How well has the client mastered earlier developmental tasks? What are some evidences of conflicts and problems originating in childhood? What were some critical turning points in the individual's life? What were some major crises, and how were they handled? What key choices did the client make, and how are these past decisions related to present functioning? How did the client's relationships within the family influence development? What was it like for the client to be in the family? What are family relationships like now? How are the client's cultural experiences related to his or her personality? This section might conclude with a summary of developmental history, which could include birth and early development, toilet training, patterns of discipline, developmental delays, educational experiences, sexual development, social development, and the influence of religious, cultural, and ethical orientations.

6. Health and medical history. What is the client's medical history? What was the date of the client's last consultation with a physician, and what were the results? Is there any noticeable evidence of recent physical trauma or neglect (for example, battering, welt marks, bruises, needle marks, sloppy clothing, sallow complexion)? What is the client's overall state of health? This section should include an assessment of the client's mental health. Has the client been in treatment previously for the present problem? Has there been a prior hospitalization? Has the client been taking medications? What were the outcomes of previous treatments? Is there any history of emotional illness in the family? It is important to be alert to signs that may indicate an organic basis for a client's problem (such as headaches, sudden changes in personal habits or in personality, and other physical symptoms). Regardless of the therapist's orientation, it is essential to rule out organic causes of physical symptoms before proceeding with psychotherapy.

7. Adjustment to work. What work does the client do or expect to do? How satisfied is the client with work? What is the meaning of employment to the person? Does he or she have future plans? What are the benefits and drawbacks of work? What is the client's work history? Has the person had long-term employment or a history of work problems? What is the balance between work and leisure? What is the quality of the client's leisure time? "Work" is used in the broad sense, whether or not the person receives pay for it. For instance, it would be important to inquire about a woman's satisfaction with her work as a homemaker and mother, even if she is not employed outside the home.

8. Lethality. Is the client a danger to self or others? Is he or she thinking about suicide or about hurting someone or something? Does the client have a specific plan either for committing suicide or for harming another person?

Does the client have the means available to kill him- or herself? Have there been prior attempts at self-destruction or violent behavior toward others? Is the client willing to make a no-suicide contract as a condition of beginning therapy?

   9. Present human relationships. This area includes a survey of information pertaining to spouse, siblings, parents, children, friends, colleagues, and other social ties. Included are the person's level of sexual functioning, family beliefs and values, and satisfaction derived from relationships. What are the client's main problems and conflicts with others? How does he or she deal with conflict? What support does the client get from others?

   10. Summary and case formulation. Provide a summary of the client's major defenses, core beliefs, and self-definition of current problems, strengths, and liabilities, and make an assessment. What are the major recommendations? What is the suggested focus for therapeutic intervention? This formulation might specify the frequency and duration of treatment, the preferred therapeutic orientation, and the mode of treatment. The client might be included in the assessment process as a collaborator, which tends to set the stage for a shared therapeutic venture.

   After the initial assessment of the client is completed, a decision is made whether to refer the person for alternative or additional treatment. Again, it is important to include the client in this decision-making process. If the client is accepted by the therapist, the two can discuss the assessment results. This information can be used in exploring the client's difficulties in thinking, feeling, and behaving and in setting treatment goals. Assessment can be linked directly to the therapeutic process, forming a basis for developing methods of evaluating how well the counselor's procedures are working to achieve the client's goals. Because most work settings require an intake interview, familiarity with these assessment procedures is essential.

Therapeutic Goals and Procedures

After the initial comprehensive assessment of a client, therapeutic goals need to be established. These goals will vary, depending in part on the practitioner's theoretical orientation. For example, psychoanalytic therapy is primarily an insight approach that aims at regressing clients to very early levels of psychological development so that they can acquire the self-understanding necessary for major character restructuring. It deals extensively with the past, with unconscious dynamics, with transference, and with techniques aimed at changing attitudes and feelings. At the other extreme is reality therapy, which focuses on evaluating current behavior so that the client can develop a realistic plan leading to more effective ways of behaving. Reality therapy is not concerned with exploring the past, with unconscious motivation, with the transference that clients might develop, or with attitudes and feelings. It asks the key question, "What is the client doing now, and what does the client want to be doing differently?" It assumes that the best way to change is by focusing on what one is doing and thinking. If these dimensions change, it is likely that the client's feelings and physiological reactions will also change.

Therapeutic goals are diverse and include restructuring personality, finding meaning in life, creating an I/Thou relationship between the client and the counselor, eliminating dysfunctional beliefs, helping clients look within themselves to find answers, substituting effective behaviors for maladaptive ones, correcting mistaken beliefs and assumptions, transforming gender roles and working toward gender equity, re-authoring their lives, finding exceptions to their problems, and facilitating individual differentiation from the family system. Given this wide range, it is obvious that the perspectives of the client and the therapist on goals will surely have an impact on the course of therapy and on the therapeutic interventions chosen.

Despite this diversity of goals, all therapies share some common denominators. To some degree they have the goal of identifying what the client wants and then modifying the person's thoughts, feelings, and behaviors. Although there is common ground, each theoretical orientation focuses on a particular dimension of human experience as a route to changing other facets of personality. For example, both Adlerian and cognitive behavior therapists emphasize the client's cognitions under the assumption that if they are successful in modifying beliefs and thought processes behavioral changes will follow, and feelings will eventually be modified.[5]

Selecting *therapeutic techniques,* then, depends on whether a counselor's goals are oriented toward changing thoughts, feelings, or behaviors. Psychoanalytic therapists, for example, are primarily concerned that their clients acquire *insights* into the nature and causes of their personality problems. They employ techniques such as free association, analysis of dreams, interpretation of resistance, and analysis of transference as tools to uncover the unconscious and lead to the desired insight. Gestalt therapists are interested in helping clients become more aware of their moment-to-moment *experiencing;* they use a wide range of experiments designed to intensify this experiencing of emotions. Rational emotive behavior therapists are mainly concerned that clients identify and uproot dysfunctional *thinking,* and they use a variety of cognitive (as well as behavioral and emotive) techniques. Behavior therapists are interested in helping clients decrease or eliminate unwanted *behaviors* and increase adaptive ones. Thus, they employ many procedures aimed at teaching clients new behaviors. Feminist therapists use gender-role analysis and power analysis interventions to assist clients in becoming aware of the influence of *gender socialization* on their behavior. Solution-focused brief therapists shift the focus from *problem-talk* to *solution-talk*. Narrative therapists challenge clients to *externalize their problems*, to break down problem-saturated stories, and to create a new story. Family therapists are primarily concerned with intervening with the family system as a route to *changing interactions within that system,* which will bring about changes in individuals in the family unit.

Whatever techniques you employ, it is essential to keep the needs of your client in mind. Some clients relate best to cognitive techniques, others to techniques designed to change behavior, and others to techniques aimed at eliciting emotional material. The same client, depending on the stage of his or her therapy, can profit from participating in all of these different techniques.

As a therapist, you would do well to think of ways to take techniques from all of the approaches so that you are able to work with a client on *all levels* of development. Take the case of Ruth, with whom you will become very familiar in this book. At the outset your interventions may be directed toward getting her to identify and express *feelings* that she has kept bottled up for much of her life. If you listen to her and provide a place where she can experience what she is feeling, she is likely to be able to give more expression to emotions that she has distorted and denied.

As her therapy progresses, you may well direct interventions toward getting her to think about critical choices she made that still have an influence in her life. At this time in her therapy you are likely to shift the focus from exploration of feelings to exploration of her attitudes, her *thinking processes*, her values, and her basic beliefs. Still later your focus may be more on helping her develop *action programs* in which she can experiment with new ways of *behaving*, both during the sessions and outside of them.

In addition to working with Ruth as an individual, there may be significant therapeutic value in bringing in members of her family of origin, her current family, and significant others. It could also be useful to work with Ruth as someone who has been oppressed by gender role stereotyping. Seeing Ruth as part of a system will provide another dimension that can deepen therapy. An important part of Ruth's therapy could involve encouraging social action on her part, geared to changing certain aspects of the *environment* that are contributing to her problems. It is not a matter of working with one aspect of Ruth's experiencing while forgetting about the other facets of her being; rather, it is a case of selecting a focus for a particular phase of her therapy. The challenge you will face as you encounter Ruth is how to utilize an *integrative approach* as you draw on a variety of techniques to help Ruth work through her struggles.

In working within a multicultural framework, it is especially important for counselors to use techniques flexibly. Clients should not be forced into a strict mold. Rather, techniques are most effective when they are tailored to what the individual client needs, which means therapists will have to modify their strategies. Some clients will resist getting involved in techniques aimed at bringing up and expressing intense emotions. Highly confrontive techniques may close down some clients. In such cases it may be best to focus more on cognitive or behavioral techniques or to modify emotive techniques that are appropriate for the client. Other clients may need to be confronted if they are to move. Confrontation at its best is an act of caring. It is designed to challenge clients to examine what they are thinking, feeling, and doing. Relying strictly on supportive techniques with certain clients will not provide the impetus they need to take the steps necessary to change. Techniques work best when they are designed to help clients explore thoughts, feelings, and actions that are within their cultural environment. Again, the value of bringing the client into the counseling process as an informed partner and a collaborator with the therapist cannot be overemphasized.

The remainder of this section summarizes the goals of therapy from each of the 11 theoretical perspectives along with some of the techniques commonly used by each therapeutic approach. Also addressed are these questions: When are clients ready to terminate therapy? How are the outcomes of therapy evaluated?

Psychoanalytic Therapy   The main goal is to resolve intrapsychic conflicts, toward the end of reconstructing one's basic personality. Analytic therapy is not limited to problem solving and learning new behaviors; there is a deeper probing into the past to develop one's level of self-understanding.

From the psychoanalytic perspective all techniques are designed to help the client gain insight and bring repressed material to the surface so that it can be dealt with consciously. Major techniques include gathering life-history data, dream analysis, free association, and interpretation and analysis of resistance and transference. Such procedures are aimed at increasing awareness, gaining intellectual and emotional insight, and beginning a working-through process that will lead to the reorganization of personality.

Psychoanalytic clients are ready to terminate their sessions when they and the therapist agree that they have clarified and accepted their emotional problems, have understood the historical roots of their difficulties, and can integrate their awareness of past problems with present relationships. Outcomes of therapy are subjectively evaluated, primarily by the therapist and to some extent by the client. The main criteria used to assess outcomes are the client's degree of emotional and cognitive insight and the degree to which he or she has worked through the transference relationship.

Adlerian Therapy   The Adlerian approach focuses on assisting clients to better understand how they perceive themselves, others, and life and to better appreciate their strengths and assets while avoiding the counterproductive perceptions and behaviors that have led to the development and maintenance of symptomatic behaviors in their lives. Adlerian practitioners are not bound by any set of prescribed techniques. Rather, they may employ a variety of strategies and techniques that are suited to the unique needs of their clients. The concept of social interest, Adler's criterion for mental health, further provides direction for therapeutic interventions and evaluation of the therapy process. Social interest, *gemeinschaftsgefuhl* in the original German, meaning "a community feeling," involves a sense of belonging, of being connected to one's fellow humans and one's social and occupational communities on a basis of equality and mutual value or worth. The important criterion determining the relative health or pathology of any behavior is the issue of its usefulness to others and to the larger social community. Does the behavior contribute to the well-being of both the individual *and* others, foster relationships based on mutual respect and equality in personal value while accepting our shared imperfections?

A few of the therapeutic procedures commonly employed by Adlerian therapists to facilitate growth and change include encouragement, confrontation, relabeling, cognitive restructuring, humor, paradoxical intention, interpretation, homework assignments, and teaching new behavioral skills. Adlerians stress a democratic, collaborative approach to therapy, and the client and therapist typically discuss and decide upon termination. The stress on goal alignment provides a common frame of reference from which to assess the outcomes of therapy.

Existential Therapy   The principal goal is to challenge clients to recognize and accept the freedom they have to become the authors of their own lives. Therapists confront clients on ways in which they are avoiding their freedom and the responsibility that accompanies it. The existential approach places primary emphasis on understanding clients' current experience, *not* on using therapeutic techniques. Thus, counselors are not bound by any prescribed techniques and can borrow tactics from other schools of therapy. Interventions are used in broadening the ways in which clients live in their world.

The issues of termination and evaluation are typically resolved through an open exchange between client and therapist. Clients generally make the choice to enter therapy, and it is the clients' choice and responsibility to decide when to leave therapy. If clients continue to rely on the therapist for this answer, they are not yet ready to terminate. However, therapists are given the latitude to express their reactions and views about the person's readiness for termination. The choices clients are making and the changes in their perceptions of themselves in their world are the basis for an evaluation of therapeutic outcomes.

Person-Centered Therapy   The person-centered approach seeks to provide a climate of understanding and acceptance through the client–therapist relationship that will enable clients to come to terms with aspects of themselves that they have denied or disowned. Other goals are enabling clients to move toward greater openness, trust in themselves, willingness to be a process rather than a finished product, and spontaneity.

Because this approach places primary emphasis on the client–therapist relationship, it specifies few techniques. It minimizes directive intervention, interpretation, questioning, probing for information, giving advice, collecting history, and diagnosis. Person-centered therapists maximize active listening, reflection, and clarification. Current formulations of the theory stress the full and active participation of the therapist as a person in the therapeutic relationship.

In keeping with the spirit of person-centered therapy, it is the client who largely determines when to stop coming for therapy. Likewise, the therapist assumes that clients can be trusted to determine the degree to which therapy has been successful for them. As clients increasingly assume an inner locus of control, they are in the best position to assess the personal meaning of their therapeutic venture.

Gestalt Therapy   The goal of the Gestalt approach is awareness. Clients are invited to attend to their experience of whatever aspect of their world becomes figural from moment to moment. This process of attending to present experience could lead to further integration of fragmented parts or it could lead to a different quality of contact with others. Following the client's flow of awareness can lead in many directions.

Gestalt therapists seek a dialogue with their clients and employ experiments to sharpen "what is." Out of this dialogue experiments are created that deepen a client's exploration of what becomes salient for him or her. Experiments always grow out of the phenomenological context of the therapeutic relationship, and they are done collaboratively with the client and the therapist. Clients may engage in role playing by performing all of the various parts and polarities, thus gaining greater awareness of inner conflicts. Some examples of experiments include creating a dialogue with conflicting parts of oneself, exaggeration, focusing on body messages, staying with particular feelings, reexperiencing past unfinished situations in the here-and-now, and working with dreams.

Clients are ready to terminate therapy when they become increasingly aware of what they are thinking, feeling, and doing in the present moment. When they have recognized and worked through their unfinished business, they are ready to continue therapy on their own. As with the other experiential therapies (existential and person-centered), the evaluation of therapeutic outcomes is rooted in clients' subjective experiences and perceptions about the changes that have occurred.

Behavior Therapy   The main goal is to eliminate clients' maladaptive behavior patterns and replace them with more constructive ones. Therapists identify thought patterns that lead to behavioral problems and then teach new ways of thinking that are designed to change the clients' ways of acting.

The main behavioral techniques are systematic desensitization, relaxation methods, reinforcement, modeling, assertion training, self-management programs, behavioral rehearsal, coaching, and other multimodal techniques. Assessment and diagnosis are done at the outset to determine a treatment plan. "What," "how," and "when" questions are used (but not "why" questions).

This approach has the advantage of specifying clear and concrete behavioral goals that can be monitored and measured. Because therapy begins with an assessment of baseline data, the degree of progress can be evaluated by comparing clients' behavior on a given dimension at any point in the therapy with the baseline data. Moreover, assessment and treatment occur simultaneously. Clients are frequently challenged to answer the question, "Is what we are doing in here helping you make the changes you desire?" With this information, clients are in the best position to determine when they are ready to terminate.

Cognitive Behavioral Approaches   The goal is to eliminate clients' self-defeating outlooks on life and assist them in acquiring more tolerant and rational views. Clients are taught how they incorporated self-defeating beliefs, how they are maintaining this faulty thinking, what they can do to undermine such thinking, and how they can teach themselves new ways of thinking that will lead to changes in their ways of behaving and feeling.

Typically, REBT practitioners use a variety of cognitive, affective, and behavioral techniques. Procedures are designed to get clients to critically examine present beliefs and behavior. Cognitive methods include disputing irrational beliefs, carrying out cognitive homework, and changing one's language and thinking patterns. Emotive techniques include role playing, REBT imagery, and shame-attacking exercises. A wide range of active and practical behavioral procedures are used to get clients to be specific and committed to doing the hard work required by therapy. Cognitive behavioral approaches insist on client participation in homework assignments both during and outside the therapeutic sessions. Individuals will rarely change a self-defeating belief unless they are willing to act consistently against it.

Clients are ready to terminate when they give up their *must*urbatory thinking. When they no longer badger themselves with "shoulds," "oughts," and "musts" and when they replace their irrational and self-destructive beliefs with rational and constructive ones, clients do not need further formal therapy. Therapeutic outcomes can be evaluated by looking at the specific cognitive, affective, and behavioral changes demonstrated by the client.

Reality Therapy   The goal of therapy is to help clients get reconnected with the people—both old and new—they have chosen to include in their quality worlds and to teach clients choice theory. A main therapeutic goal is to teach clients how to improve the significant relationships in their lives. Therapists help individuals find more effective ways of meeting their needs for belonging, power, freedom, and fun. The approach challenges clients to make an assessment of their current behavior to determine if what they are doing and thinking is getting them what they want from life.

Reality therapy is active, directive, and didactic. The therapist assists clients in making plans to change specific behaviors that they determine are not working for them. Skillful questioning and a variety of behavioral methods are often used to encourage clients to evaluate what they are doing. If clients decide that their present behavior is not effective, they develop a specific plan for change and make a commitment to follow through.

When clients are more effectively fulfilling their wants and needs and when they have gained (or regained) control of their world, they are ready to leave counseling. This approach has the advantage of being anchored in a specific plan for change. This plan is not nebulous, but specific, which allows for objective evaluation of outcomes.

Feminist Therapy   The major goal of feminist therapy is empowerment, which involves acquiring a sense of self-acceptance, self-confidence, self-esteem, joy, and self-actualization. Some other therapy goals are enhancing the quality of interpersonal relationships, assisting women to make decisions regarding role performances, and helping them to come to an understanding of the cultural, social, and political systems' influence on their current situation. Clients can expect more than adjustment or simple problem-solving strategies; they need to be prepared for major shifts in their way of viewing the world around them, changes in the way in which they perceive themselves, and transformed interpersonal relationships.

Feminist therapists carry out a range of information-giving functions and teaching functions. By focusing on external structures, they attempt to free clients from a "blaming the victim" stance. They are free to use techniques from many other therapy orientations, and they often employ techniques such as reframing and relabeling, bibliotherapy, advocacy, power intervention, social action, and gender-role analysis and intervention.

Feminist therapists emphasize the teaching aspects of therapy and strive to create a collaborative way of working with clients. Emphasis is placed on the demystification of the therapy process and on providing a context wherein informed consent can occur. Clients decide when they want to terminate, which usually occurs when clients feel an increased sense of personal identity and empowerment.

Postmodern Approaches   A major goal of the postmodern therapies is to create a context in which therapists co-author with clients new stories about themselves that highlight their preferred ways of being. Therapy provides the opportunity to take apart (or deconstruct) a person's dominant story that he or she brings to therapy. Clients are encouraged to rewrite their stories by taking a look at their pasts and rewriting their futures.

Postmodern therapists view the client as the expert on his or her own life. The therapist is not the expert but assumes the role of a curious, interested, and respectful partner in the therapeutic relationship. Together the client and the therapist establish clear, specific, realistic, and personally meaningful goals that will guide the therapy process. The therapist explores with clients the impact their problems have on them and how they are taking action to reduce this impact. Through the use of questions that challenge clients to separate themselves from problem identities, therapists assist clients to re-author their stories. One of the therapist's tasks is to assist clients in constructing a more appealing story line. It is essential that the story being authored in the therapy context be carried out into the social world where clients live.

Because this approach emphasizes the collaborative nature of therapy, clients are the primary agents in deciding when they have achieved their goals and when they are ready to terminate the therapeutic relationship. This approach to therapy emphasizes a time-effective format. It is appropriate to end therapy when the client finds solutions that work.

Family Systems Therapy   Depending on the specific orientation of a family systems practitioner, this approach has a variety of goals, some of which are resolving the presenting problems of the client and the family; resolving a family crisis as quickly and efficiently as possible; creating an environment where new information can be infused into a system, allowing the family to evolve on its own; restructuring a system so that autonomy by all family members is encouraged; changing the rules and patterns of interaction among family members; teaching communication skills; and teaching problem-solving skills.

A diverse range of techniques may be employed, depending on the therapist's theoretical orientation. Because the therapist joins with the family, intervention strategies are best considered in conjunction with the personal characteristics of the therapist. The central consideration is what is in the best interests of the family. Outcomes are evaluated on the basis of the particular orientation of the therapist, yet a primary criterion is the degree of relational change that occurs among members of a family. In all family therapy models, change needs to happen relationally, not just intrapsychically.

My Perspective on the Integration of Goals and Techniques
I attempt to integrate goals from most of the major theories by paying attention to changes clients want to make. My early interventions are aimed at helping clients identify specific ways in which they want to be different. Once they have formulated concrete goals, it is possible to utilize a variety of techniques that foster modification of thinking processes, feelings, and ways of behaving.

When counseling culturally diverse client populations, it is important to consider the degree to which the general goals and methods employed are congruent with the cultural background and values of clients. It is essential that both therapist and client recognize their differences in goal orientation. For example, it can be a therapeutic mistake to encourage some clients to be assertive with their parents and tell them exactly what they are thinking and feeling. A client from a Middle Eastern culture might believe it is rude to confront one's parents and that it is inappropriate to bring out conflicts. The therapist who would push such a client to be independent and to deal with conflicts within the family would probably alienate this person.

Therapists must listen to their clients and enter their perceptual world. The process of therapy is best guided by the particular goals and values of each client, not by what the therapist thinks is best. Questions therapists frequently ask of their clients are "Why are you seeking counseling from me?" "What is it that you would like to explore?" and "What is it about yourself or your life situation that you most want to change?" By staying focused on what their clients want, therapists can greatly reduce the danger of imposing their own goals on clients.

Having surveyed 11 therapy perspectives from the vantage point of their basic assumptions, views of assessment, goals of therapy, and therapeutic procedures, we are now ready to consider a specific case. As you study Ruth's case, look for ways to apply what you have just read to gain a fuller understanding of her.

 ## THE CASE OF RUTH

The themes in Ruth's life are characteristic of those of many clients I have worked with individually and, especially, in groups. As mentioned earlier, I took typical struggles from a number of clients and compiled a clinical picture of a client I call Ruth. Ruth's intake form and autobiography, reproduced here, will provide you with much of the information you need to understand and work with her. Each of the theory chapters will provide additional information. As you read the next 11 chapters, refer to this information about Ruth to refresh your memory on some of the details and themes in her life.

In addition to what is presented here, Ruth is also the subject of an interactive self-study program entitled *CD-ROM for Integrative Counseling*. See Session 1 ("Beginning of Counseling") in particular for more information on Ruth.

Ruth's Autobiography

As a part of the intake process, the counselor asked Ruth to bring the autobiography she had written for her counseling class. Although most therapists do not make it a practice to ask their clients to write an autobiography, doing so can be beneficial. It provides clients with a way of reviewing significant life experiences and gives therapists insight into their clients' self-perception. Ruth wrote:

Something I've become aware of recently is that I've pretty much lived for others so far. I've been the superwoman who gives and gives until there is little left to give. I give to my husband, John. I've been the "good wife" and the "good mother" that he expects me to be. I do realize that I need John, and I'm afraid he might leave me if I change too much. I've given my all to seeing that my kids grow up decently, but even though I'm trying my best, I often worry that I haven't done enough. When I look at my life now, I must admit that I don't like what I see. I don't like who I am, and I certainly don't feel very proud of my body. I'm very overweight, and despite my good intentions to lose weight I just can't seem to get rid of the pounds. I've always enjoyed eating and often eat too much. My family nagged me as a child, but the more they wanted me to stop, the more I seemed to eat, sometimes to the point of making myself sick. I make resolutions to start an exercise program and stick to a diet, but I've yet to find a way to follow through with my plans.

One of the things I do look forward to is becoming a teacher in an elementary school. I really think this would make my life more meaningful. Right now I worry a lot about what will become of me when my kids leave and there is just John and me in that house. I know I should at least get out there and get that job as a substitute teacher in a private school that I've wanted (and have an offer for), yet I drag my feet on that one too.

One big thing that troubles me a lot is the feeling of panic I get more and more of the time. I don't remember ever feeling that bad. Often during the day, when I'm trying to do well at school, I feel dizzy, almost like fainting, and have difficulty breathing. Sometimes I'll be sitting in class and get hot flashes, and then I sweat profusely, which is really embarrassing to me. At times my hands start to tremble, and I'm afraid that others will notice this and think I'm weird. And sometimes when I'm sitting in class or even doing shopping, my heart is racing so fast that I worry I'll die of a heart attack. Then there are times when I wake up at night with my heart beating very fast, in a cold sweat, and sometimes shaking. I feel a terrible sense of doom, but I don't know what over. I get so scared over these feelings, which just seem to creep up on me at the times I least expect them. It makes me think that maybe if I don't get better control of myself, I might go crazy.

I know that I worry about death—about my dying—a lot. Maybe I still fear going to hell. As a kid I was motivated by fear of fire and brimstone. Nine years ago I finally broke away from my strong fundamentalist church, because I could see that it was not me. Somehow, taking that philosophy class in the community college years ago got me to thinking about the values I was taught. It was the gospel, and who was I to question? So, when I was 30, I made the break from the fundamentalist religion that I had so closely lived by. I'm now attending a less dogmatic church, yet I still feel pangs of guilt that I am not living by the religion my parents brought me up with. They haven't formally disowned me, but in many ways I think they have. I know I'll never win their approval as long as I stay away from the religion that's so dear to them. But I find it more and more difficult to live by something I don't believe in. The big problem for me is that I so often feel lost and confused, wanting some kind of anchor in my life. I know what I don't believe, but I still have little to replace those values that I once lived by. I sometimes wonder if I really did discard those values, because I so often hear the voices of my parents inside my head!

As part of my college program I took a course that was an introduction to counseling, and that opened my eyes to a lot of things. One of our guest speakers was a licensed clinical psychologist, who talked about the value of counseling for people even though they are not seriously disturbed. I began to consider that maybe I could benefit from getting some counseling. Up until that time I had always thought you had to be a psycho before going to a psychotherapist. I see that I could work on a lot of things that I've neatly tucked away in my life. Yet even though I think I've almost made the decision to seek therapy, there is still this nagging fear within me, and I keep asking myself questions. What if I find out things about myself that I don't like? What will I do if I discover there's nothing inside of me? What if I lose John while I'm getting myself together? I so much want those magical answers. All my life I've had clear answers to every question. Then 9 years ago, when I became a questioner to some extent, I lost those neat answers. What if I open Pandora's box and too much comes out and I get even more overwhelmed than I already am?

What I most want from therapy is that the therapist will tell me what I have to do and push me to do it, so that I can begin to live before it's too late. The trouble is that I think I could settle for my nice and comfortable life that I have now, even though a great part of it is driving me nuts. Sure, it's boring and stale, but I don't have to make any decisions either. Then again it's uncomfortable to be where I am. But new decisions are so scary for me to make. I'm scared I'll make the wrong decisions and that in doing so I'll ruin not only my life but John's life and the future of my kids. I feel I owe it to them to stay in this marriage. I guess I'm trapped and don't see a way out. And that would be the last straw if my father ever found out that I was seeing a counselor! He'd tell me I was foolish—that all the answers to life are found in the Bible. Sometimes I wonder if I should turn my life over to God and let Him take over. I so much wish He would take over! I don't know what lies ahead. I'm afraid and excited at the same time.

Diagnostic Impressions of Ruth

While I was revising an earlier edition of this book, I had a telephone call from Michael Nystul, a professor of counseling at New Mexico State University, who told me that he was using *Case Approach to Counseling and Psychotherapy* for one of his summer courses.

"Dr. Corey," he asked, "what diagnosis would you give Ruth? My students are discussing her case, and they are interested in getting your opinion about her diagnostic category."

"Well," I replied, "I generally don't think in diagnostic terms, so I would be hard pressed to give Ruth a diagnosis."

"But if you *had* to give her a diagnosis," Dr. Nystul insisted, "what would it be?"

We exchanged our views on a possible diagnosis for Ruth. Because several possible diagnoses seemed to fit in her case, I began thinking about the process a practitioner goes through in attempting to identify the most appropriate diagnostic category for a client. I then asked several of my colleagues at the university who were familiar with Ruth's case to suggest a diagnosis. Interestingly, I got a variety of interpretations, each with a good supporting rationale. I also asked some of those who were reviewing this manuscript to give me their impressions of the most appropriate diagnostic category for Ruth. As you might suspect, there were a variety of diagnostic impressions.

At this point you are just beginning to familiarize yourself with Ruth. What would be your provisional diagnosis for Ruth? Justify the diagnosis you select on the basis of the information presented in this chapter. In learning about the various approaches to counseling Ruth in the next 11 chapters, you may find new evidence or emerging patterns of behavior that warrant modifying your

CLIENT'S INTAKE FORM

AGE	SEX	RACE	MARITAL STATUS
			Married

AGE	SEX	RACE	SOCIOECONOMIC STATUS
39	Female	Caucasian	Middle class

APPEARANCE

Dresses meticulously, is overweight, fidgets constantly with her clothes, avoids eye contact, and speaks rapidly.

LIVING SITUATION

Recently graduated from college as an elementary education major, lives with husband (John, 45) and her children (Rob, 19; Jennifer, 18; Susan, 17; and Adam, 16).

PRESENTING PROBLEM

Client reports general dissatisfaction. She says her life is rather uneventful and predictable, and she feels some panic over reaching the age of 39, wondering where the years have gone. For 2 years she has been troubled with a range of psychosomatic complaints, including sleep disturbances, anxiety, dizziness, heart palpitations, and headaches. At times she has to push herself to leave the house. Client complains that she cries easily over trivial matters, often feels depressed, and has a weight problem.

HISTORY OF PRESENTING PROBLEM

Client made her major career as a housewife and mother until her children became adolescents. She then entered college part time and obtained a bachelor's degree. She has recently begun work toward a credential in elementary education. Through her contacts with others at the university she became aware of how she has limited herself, how she has fostered her family's dependence on her, and how frightened she is of branching out from her roles as mother and wife.

    Ruth completed a course in introduction to counseling that encouraged her to look at the direction of her own life. As part of the course, Ruth participated in self-awareness groups, had a few individual counseling sessions, and wrote several papers dealing with the turning points in her own life. One of the requirements was to write an extensive autobiography that was based on an application of the principles of the counseling course to her own personal development. This course and her experiences with fellow students in it acted as a catalyst in getting her to take an honest look at her life. Ruth is not clear at this point who she is, apart from being a mother, wife, and student. She realizes that she does not have a good sense of what she wants for herself and that she typically lived up to what others in her life wanted for her. She has decided to seek individual therapy for the following reasons:

■ A physician whom she consulted could find no organic or medical basis for her physical symptoms and recommended personal therapy. In her words, her major symptoms are these: "I sometimes feel very panicky, especially at night when I'm trying to sleep. Sometimes

(continued)

HISTORY OF PRESENTING PROBLEM (*continued*)

I'll wake up and find it difficult to breathe, my heart will be pounding, and I'll break out in a cold sweat. I toss and turn trying to relax, and instead I feel tense and worry a lot about many little things. It's hard for me to turn off these thoughts. Then during the day I'm so tired I can hardly function, and I find that lately I cry very easily if even minor things go wrong."

■ She is aware that she has lived a very structured and disciplined life, that she has functioned largely by taking care of the home and the needs of her four children and her husband, and that to some degree she is no longer content with this. Yet she reports that she doesn't know what "more than this" is. Although she would like to get more involved professionally, the thought of doing so frightens her. She worries about her right to think and act selfishly, she fears not succeeding in the professional world, and she most of all worries about how becoming more professionally involved might threaten her family.

■ Her children range in age from 16 to 19, and all of them are now finding more of their satisfactions outside of the family and the home and are spending increasing time with their friends. Ruth sees these changes and is concerned about "losing" them. She is having particular problems with her daughter Jennifer, and she is at a loss about how to deal with Jennifer's rebellion. In general, Ruth feels very much unappreciated by her children.

■ In thinking about her future, Ruth is not really sure who or what she wants to become. She would like to develop a sense of herself apart from the expectations of others. She finds herself wondering what she "should" want and what she "should" be doing. Ruth does not find her relationship with her husband, John, at all satisfactory. He appears to be resisting her attempts to make changes and prefers that she remain as she was. But she is anxious over the prospects of challenging this relationship, fearing that if she does, she might end up alone.

■ Lately, Ruth is experiencing more concern over aging and losing her "looks." All of these factors combined have provided the motivation for her to take the necessary steps to initiate individual therapy. Perhaps the greatest catalyst that triggered her to come for therapy is the increase of her physical symptoms and her anxiety.

PSYCHOSOCIAL HISTORY

Ruth is the oldest of four children. Her father is a fundamentalist minister, and her mother is a housewife. She describes her father as distant, authoritarian, and rigid; her relationship with him was one of unquestioning, fearful adherence to his rules and standards. She remembers her mother as being critical, and she thought she could never do enough to please her. At other times her mother was supportive. The family demonstrated little affection. In many ways Ruth took on the role of caring for her younger brother and sisters, largely in the hope of winning the approval of her parents. When she attempted to have any kind of fun, she encountered her father's disapproval and outright scorn. To a large extent this pattern of taking care of others has extended throughout her life.

One critical incident took place when Ruth was 6 years old. She reported: "My father caught me 'playing doctor' with an 8-year-old boy. He lectured me and refused to speak to me for weeks. I felt extremely guilty and ashamed." It appears that Ruth carried feelings of guilt into her adolescence and that she repressed her own emerging sexuality.

In her social relationships Ruth had difficulty making and keeping friends. She felt socially isolated from her peers because they viewed her as "weird." Although she wanted the approval of others, she was not willing to compromise her morals for fear of the consequences.

Ruth was not allowed to date until she completed high school; at the age of 19 she married the first person that she dated. She used her mother as a role model by becoming a homemaker.

original diagnosis. This section deals with diagnostic impressions of Ruth, but this topic is revisited in each of the following 11 theory chapters. I've asked the guest contributors to give their diagnostic impressions of Ruth and to discuss how their views of diagnosis and assessment influence their practice.

Rather than identifying one specific major disorder, I will describe a number of possible provisional diagnoses that *may* be appropriate for Ruth's case. As you review the 11 different theories, consider these diagnostic classifications from the DSM-IV-TR to see which category you think best fits the case of Ruth.

Adjustment Disorder   The key feature of adjustment disorders is the development of clinically significant emotional or behavioral symptoms in response to psychosocial stresses. Some stressors may accompany specific developmental events, such as beginning school, becoming a parent, having children leave home, or failing to attain educational or career goals. There is some basis for giving Ruth a diagnosis of adjustment disorder, possibly with anxiety. She is experiencing some key developmental crises. A number of stressors are resulting in symptoms such as nervousness, worry, and fear of separation from major figures in her life. She could also be classified as adjustment disorder, unspecified, which reflects symptoms such as physical complaints, social withdrawal, or work or academic inhibition.

Panic Disorder   Individuals who have unexpected panic attacks typically describe their fear as intense and report that they feel as if they are going to die, lose control, or have a heart attack. In general, Ruth presents evidence of an anxiety disorder; specifically, her pattern of symptoms meets the diagnostic criteria for panic attack: palpitations of the heart, sweating, shortness of breath, dizziness, trembling, hot flashes and cold sweats, fear of dying, and fear of losing control or going crazy.

Dysthymic Disorder   The essential feature of a dysthymic disorder is chronic depression, which occurs for most of the day on more days than not for at least 2 years. Individuals with such a disorder often describe their condition as feeling "down in the dumps." When people experience a depressed mood, they often manifest some of the following symptoms: overeating, insomnia, low energy or fatigue, low self-esteem, difficulty making decisions, and feelings of hopelessness. At times, individuals are self-critical and view themselves as uninteresting or incapable. Ruth appears to fit this picture. She exhibits a long-term depressed mood that is part of her character but not severe enough to be considered major depression. She also manifests dependent personality traits in that she consistently puts the needs of others ahead of herself and has low self-esteem. She exhibits a number of physical complaints but does not indicate any serious physical disease necessitating surgery or other severe medical intervention.

Identity Problem   Ruth's patterns fit the syndrome of identity problem. The main features of this classification include uncertainty about long-term goals, career choice, friendship patterns, sexual orientation and behavior, moral and religious values, and group loyalties. Affected clients respond to their uncertainty with anxiety and depression and are preoccupied about their lack of a sense of self. These people doubt themselves in everyday situations. One of the most common questions asked by the person with an identity disorder is "Who am I?"

I asked two of the reviewers of *Case Approach to Counseling and Psychotherapy* to provide their diagnostic perspectives on Ruth's case. They are Dr. Michael Nystul, who was introduced earlier, and Dr. Beverly Palmer, professor of psychology at California State University at Dominguez Hills.

Dr. Nystul's DSM-IV-TR Diagnosis

The three key factors I use to facilitate the process of a differential diagnosis are onset, severity, and duration. Normally, I would explore these three issues within the context of a clinical interview, which would include a mental-status exam. In this instance, I must base my diagnostic impressions on Ruth's autobiography.

The DSM-IV-TR provides guidelines for a comprehensive assessment leading to a diagnosis. There are five categories, called axes, in the DSM-IV-TR that can be used by clinicians in formulating a treatment plan:

- **Axis I.** Clinical disorders; other conditions that may be a focus of clinical attention
- **Axis II.** Personality disorders; mental retardation
- **Axis III.** General medical conditions
- **Axis IV.** Psychosocial and environmental problems
- **Axis V.** Global assessment of functioning

As I read Ruth's autobiography, the major symptoms that stood out for me were anxiety and depression (Axis I disorders). The primary considerations for a differential diagnosis in this case appear to be an adjustment disorder with mixed anxiety and depressed mood, a panic disorder without agoraphobia, or a dysthymic disorder. For example, Ruth's diagnosis could be an adjustment disorder if (1) her symptoms (anxiety and depression) occurred within 3 months of the stressor and were resolved within 6 months of the termination of the stressor, and (2) her symptoms did not fulfill the criteria for one or more Axis I disorders such as a panic disorder or a dysthymic disorder. If her symptoms fulfilled the criteria for one or more Axis I disorders such as a panic disorder and dysthymic disorder, then those disorders would be recorded on Axis I and adjustment disorder would not be recorded.

Axis I also includes other conditions that are not mental disorders but may be a focus of clinical attention. Some of the "other conditions" that may be appropriate for Ruth include parent–child relational problem, partner relational problem, occupational problem, identity problem, and phase of life problem. I would use the clinical interview to determine if one or more of these "other conditions" would be included in Ruth's DSM-IV-TR diagnosis on Axis I.

In terms of Axis II, I would want to rule out a dependent personality disorder. The history suggests "she has fostered her family's dependence on her" and has "pretty much lived for others." If she did not meet the full criteria for a dependent personality disorder, I would record "dependent personality traits" on Axis II if I believed Ruth had prominent maladaptive personality features relating to dependency.

I would record "none" on Axis III (general medical conditions), because the history notes that a physician did not find anything medically wrong with Ruth.

Axis IV requires a listing of the psychosocial and environmental problems Ruth has experienced within the last year (or longer if she had experienced a posttraumatic stress disorder). A stressor that would be included for Ruth is discord with child. (The history suggested Ruth was having significant problems with Jennifer.) If my clinical interview suggested marital discord, that would also be included on Axis IV.

Axis V allows for the determination of Ruth's Global Assessment of Functioning (GAF). Based on DSM-IV-TR guidelines, I would estimate her current GAF to be 60, which would indicate that she has moderate symptoms or moderate difficulty in her overall psychological functioning.

Dr. Palmer's DSM-IV-TR Diagnosis   Ruth's case is difficult to diagnose because she is a person on paper rather than a person in front of me of whom I can ask questions and notice her nonverbal behavior. Yet the DSM-IV-TR category of panic disorder without agoraphobia (300.01) is the one most supported by the evidence presented. She experiences unexpected panic attacks and is worried about having additional attacks. The symptoms of a panic attack she experiences are dizziness, heart palpitations, shortness of breath, trembling, sweating, and a fear of going crazy. All of these symptoms occur within a 10-minute period and occur both at school and during the evening when she is trying to sleep. Presently, there is no evidence that she has agoraphobia (anxiety about being in a place from which escape might be difficult, which often causes the person to not want to leave her house). However, her therapist would want to monitor her for agoraphobia because recurrent panic attacks can develop into panic disorder with agoraphobia. Ruth's binge eating puts her in another DSM-IV-TR disorder: eating disorder not otherwise specified (307.50)—specifically, binge eating disorder. She reports eating more than she should when she is depressed and being very overweight. She also ate to the point of making herself sick when she was a child, and she has tried exercise and dieting but is unable to stick to either. Thus, it appears that in a discrete period of time Ruth eats an amount of food that is larger than most people would eat and that she experiences a lack of control over eating during these episodes.

Ruth has two other DSM-IV-TR conditions: a phase of life problem (V62.89) and an identity problem (313.82). She is concerned about what her life will be like after her children leave home or if she begins a professional job, and these concerns are characterized by the existential therapist as components of a midlife crisis. She is struggling with the identity issues of finding the values she does believe in and who she is apart from the expectations of others. Ruth is also having conflicts with her teenage daughter and with her husband, but it is difficult to determine whether these relational problems are causing clinically significant symptoms or significant impairment in family functioning. Thus, two other DSM-IV-TR conditions, a partner relational problem (V61.10) and a parent–child relational problem (V61.20), are probably not warranted from the evidence given.

As important as ruling *in* a particular diagnosis is ruling *out* other possible diagnoses. Ruth mentions several times that she feels "depressed" and that she eats more when she is depressed, yet there are not enough symptoms of depression to diagnose a mood disorder such as dysthymic disorder according to the DSM-IV-TR. Ruth does have low self-confidence and she does overeat, but her depressed mood and crying are not present for most of the day almost everyday for at least 2 years. Her tiredness during the day may be due to the panic attacks that make it difficult for her to sleep some nights. If she had "depression," she would feel tired even though she had had a good night's sleep, and her insomnia (typically early-morning awakening) would not be due to worrying or panic attacks. Many people use "depression" as a catch-all term to describe their present condition, but dysthymia does not fit this case as well as does an anxiety-based disorder such as panic disorder. The difference between self-diagnosis and a therapist's diagnosis is often in the degree of understanding of the psychological, social, and biological theories that are the foundation of the DSM-IV-TR categories. Of course, sometimes beneath the panic attacks and anxiety is a depression that can pop up once the panic attacks are alleviated. Another factor that must be eliminated when making the diagnosis of panic attacks is that there is no substance use or general medical condition (such as hyperthyroidism) that might cause the symptoms Ruth reports. She did have a recent checkup by a physician, which is always a wise recommendation for every therapist to make during the initial assessment.

The DSM-IV-TR is a multiaxial system of diagnosis, and so far I have given only Axis I diagnoses. Axis II is used to diagnose personality disorders or personality features that might also be the focus of treatment. Sometimes a person can have only an Axis I or only an Axis II diagnosis, but usually a person has diagnoses on both axes, and the two axes influence each other in treatment. In the case of Ruth there is no Axis II diagnosis, although she does show a few dependent personality features. As the behavior therapist says, Ruth has trouble stating her viewpoints clearly, and she often accepts projects in which she does not want to get involved. She admits dragging her feet in getting the substitute schoolteacher job she wants, which may be an indication of the dependent personality trait of having difficulty initiating projects or doing things on her own. Ruth shows only three dependent personality traits, so she does not have the full-blown picture of dependent personality disorder. The therapist also has to be careful that those traits typical of the socialization of a woman Ruth's age are not pathologized into dependent personality disorder.

Axis III is the place to indicate the results of her recent medical consultation and her problem with being overweight. Her physical condition and physical problems interact with her psychological problems reported on Axes I and II, so it is important to record them in this multiaxial system of diagnosis. For example, her being overweight affects her self-esteem, and her self-esteem affects her weight. Also, her panic attacks might be treated by medication as well as by psychological means, so health professionals from all fields need to communicate with one another. This multiaxial system is an ideal way to start this communication.

Axis IV is the place to record any social or environmental factors in Ruth's life. She reports relational problems with her daughter and with her husband, so it is on this axis that these social issues are recorded as problems with her primary support group.

The final axis, Axis V, is used to report Ruth's overall level of functioning. The usual way of recording this is by using the GAF scale. Ruth has some moderate symptoms, such as occasional panic attacks, which cause her to have some difficulty in her functioning at home, so she receives a GAF score of between 51 and 60.

One important axis is missing from the DSM-IV-TR, and that is one that records Ruth's strengths. Ruth has many strengths: she has recently pursued higher education successfully, and she has good insight into her present condition as well as a thirst for exploring her future directions. Ruth's strengths will be used in treatment just as much as will her difficulties, so it is important to have a record of them along with the DSM-IV-TR system of diagnosis.

In looking over the provisional diagnoses described here, what patterns do you see in these assessments taken as a group? Which ones do you tend to agree with the most? Why? If you do not agree with a particular diagnostic formulation, give your reasons. What are your legal and ethical responsibilities when diagnosing Ruth? Under what circumstances, if any, would you be likely to share your diagnostic impressions with her?

This section on diagnostic procedures with Ruth is necessarily brief. I encourage you to consult the DSM-IV-TR as a reference tool because it will introduce you to the categories and the labeling system that are part of the assessment and diagnostic process.

 NOTES

1. Corey, G., & Haynes, R. (2005). *CD-ROM for Integrative Counseling*. Belmont, CA: Brooks/Cole.
2. Corey, G. (2001). *The Art of Integrative Counseling*. Pacific Grove, CA: Brooks/Cole.
3. This book and *Theory and Practice of Counseling and Psychotherapy* (G. Corey, 2005, 7th edition; Belmont, CA: Brooks/Cole) have parallel coverage of the 11 theories you will be studying. As a basis for understanding the guest contributors'

presentations on working with Ruth in the chapters that follow, refer to my theory book for background information on the basic assumptions, key concepts, elements of the therapeutic process, and application and techniques for each of the theories.

4. The official guide to a system of classifying psychological disorders is the *Diagnostic and Statistical Manual of Mental Disorders,* 4th edition (compiled in 1994 with a Text Revision in 2000), by the American Psychiatric Association. The DSM-IV-TR gives specific criteria for classifying emotional and behavioral disturbances and shows the differences among the various disorders. In addition to describing neurotic, psychotic, and personality disorders, this revised edition also deals with a variety of other disorders pertaining to developmental stages, substance abuse, moods, sexual and gender identity, eating, sleep, impulse control, and adjustment.

5. In Session 3 ("Establishing Therapeutic Goals") of the *CD-ROM for Integrative Counseling,* I demonstrate my way of assisting Ruth in formulating her goals, which will provide a direction for her counseling.

Chapter 2

Case Approach to Psychoanalytic Therapy

 INTRODUCTION

In this chapter and most of the chapters to follow, before I demonstrate my way of working from each of the perspectives, you will read one or more sections written by experts in each of the theoretical orientations that illustrate their way of working with Ruth. Then I will assume the identity of a therapist from the particular orientation being considered, and, staying within the spirit of each specific approach as much as possible, I will show you my interpretation and my own style of working with Ruth. There are many differences in therapeutic style among practitioners who share the same theoretical orientation, and there is no "one right way" of practicing psychoanalytic therapy or any of the other systems. I encourage you to do your best in assuming each of the separate theoretical perspectives as you follow the case of Ruth. Doing this will help you decide which concepts and techniques you want to incorporate in your own therapeutic style.

In most of these theory chapters I am Ruth's therapist. I have read her intake form and her autobiography before meeting her for the first time. In each chapter I give an overview of the particular theory by describing (1) the basic assumptions underlying practice, (2) my initial assessment of Ruth, (3) the goals that will guide our work, and (4) the therapeutic procedures and techniques that are likely to be employed in attaining our goals. A section on the therapeutic process shows samples of our work together. It is illustrated with dialogue between Ruth and me, along with an ongoing process commentary that explains my rationale for the interventions I make and the general direction of her therapy.

It is a good practice for counselors to consult with other practitioners at times, for doing so provides them with ideas of other ways to proceed with a client. In working with Ruth, I am using this model of consultation. Background data on Ruth's case were sent to a well-known representative of each approach, who was asked: "How would you assess Ruth's case? On what themes would you probably focus? What procedures would you likely use? How would you expect the therapeutic process to unfold?" The contributions of these consultants are used to introduce each therapeutic approach. A brief biography of each of these guest consultants is provided in the *About the Contributors* section in the front of this book.

A Psychoanalytic Therapist's Perspective on Ruth

by William Blau, Ph.D.

Assessment of Ruth

Psychoanalytic Perspective and Overview of Case Material   As a psychoanalytically oriented therapist, I suspect that Ruth's background descriptions of her parents, her siblings, and herself are less than objective. Moreover, I predict that the areas of inaccuracy will turn out to be clues to the core of her personality problems. I anticipate finding that her symptoms (anxiety attacks, overeating, fear of accomplishment, panic over being 39, fear of abandonment, and so forth) can be interpreted as outward manifestations of unconscious conflicts that have their origins in childhood experiences and defensive reactions to these experiences that were necessary to her as a child. I suspect, given her intelligence and motivation, that her current exacerbation of symptoms is related to her recognition of discrepancies between what makes sense to her logically and what seems to drive her emotions and behavior. I hypothesize that Ruth is experiencing a split (a struggle between opposing dimensions of herself). This conflict is between the part of her that wants to change and the other part of her that clings to old patterns that were once necessary and have helped her maintain mental stability all her life. Although some of her defenses seem maladaptive from my perspective, I believe I cannot give her the most effective help unless I can fully understand *why* her patterns of defense seem necessary to her *now* and why, once, they were necessary to her psychological survival.

In contrast to some therapeutic practitioners, I am very interested in why Ruth thinks, feels, and behaves as she does. I have no interest in excusing her behavior or condemning others, but I believe her problems can be most fully helped by answering the "why" as well as the "what" questions regarding her life. This fundamental interest in the "whys" of an individual client's experience and behavior is a critical distinction between analytic therapy and other approaches.

Unraveling the dynamics of her history and filling in the story of her life with newly emerging memories will be an ongoing part of Ruth's treatment;

hence, this aspect of assessment is never complete although it becomes less important in the final phases of treatment.

Assessing Ruth's Suitability for Analytic Therapy   Before establishing a contract to do analytic therapy with Ruth, I would need to ascertain whether she is a good candidate for the treatment and whether she has the perseverance and resources to make this approach the treatment of choice. Assessment of her need for analytic therapy would include determining whether she wants and needs to understand the unconscious roots of her neurosis. If simply teaching her about the pathological nature of some of her behavior would lead to significant change, she would probably not need analytic therapy. Didactic approaches would suffice. I suspect, however, that Ruth does not consciously know why she reacts in symptomatic ways and that she is repeatedly frustrated when she has been given good advice by others (or by herself) but still finds the old patterns persisting.

Ruth's case history does include a number of factors suggesting that she could be a good candidate for analytic treatment. Her autobiography shows her to be a woman for whom understanding the meaning of her life is important and for whom achieving individuation is a meaningful goal. Her autobiography also shows that she has the ability to look at herself from a somewhat objective perspective. Her need for symptom alleviation is sufficient to provide strong motivation for change, yet her symptoms are not currently incapacitating.

Ruth expects that the therapist will tell her what to do with her life and take the place of her father and the God of her childhood religion. In contracting with her for treatment, I would let her know that fulfillment of her expectations is not provided by analytic psychotherapy; however, this would by no means end the issue. Despite the formal contract, I anticipate that Ruth will continue to demand that the therapist take charge of her life. This aspect of transference will be of ongoing significance in treatment. On the whole, Ruth is the sort of client for whom analytically oriented psychotherapy might be indicated.

Diagnosis   DSM-IV-TR[1] diagnosis of Ruth is of limited value, but it is necessary to ensure that physical causes for Ruth's symptoms are ruled out. Analytic therapy is more clearly indicated for some disorders than for others, and some disorders require extensive modification of technique. But traditional diagnosis is limited in that the individual's ability to form a therapeutic alliance, which is the key issue in assessment for analytic treatment, is largely independent of diagnosis. From a diagnostic standpoint the most important issues (once it has been demonstrated that Ruth is not suicidal or homicidal) would be to determine the role of organic factors in her symptomatology and to determine if she should be referred for medication.

Ruth's reported unhappiness with her life could be her way of expressing symptoms of depression that might be helped by medication in addition to psychotherapy. If she is depressed "for most of the day, for more days than not," a DSM-IV-TR diagnosis of dysthymic disorder should be considered. Her panic attacks could be related to a cardiac condition, and her "hot flashes" and other psychophysiological symptoms could have organic as well as psychodynamic origins. In DSM-IV-TR terms, Ruth meets the following diagnostic criteria:

300.01: panic disorder without agoraphobia

313.82: identity problem

Neither of these diagnostic categories, in my opinion, conveys a feeling for Ruth as she is described in her autobiography and intake form. DSM-IV-TR diagnoses tend to reify symptom clusters rather than promote understanding of the client as a person.

Panic attacks are the essential elements of the *panic disorder* diagnosis, and I would strongly consider treating these attacks initially with the cost-effective techniques of psychophysiological counseling and biofeedback rather than psychoanalytic psychotherapy. DSM-IV-TR diagnoses of panic disorder are coded as either with or without agoraphobia. I specified "without agoraphobia" because Ruth doesn't describe herself as being unduly afraid to travel or to be in crowds or similar social or confining situations.

The DSM-IV-TR category of *identity problem* is descriptive of the contents of Ruth's concerns. However, it is not a "clinical disorder" in DSM-IV-TR terms, and it minimizes the intensity of her very real suffering. The real, human Ruth presents a blending of neurotic symptoms and existential concerns.

Ruth's symptoms seem to be at a critical stage and could flower into an eating disorder, a counterphobic impulsive behavior, a generalized anxiety disorder, or a psychosomatic conversion disorder, as well as agoraphobia or a dysthymic disorder as previously discussed. Ruth's difficulties in establishing a sense of self suggest that her individuation is an important goal of treatment. I do not anticipate overtly psychotic symptoms, and her basic reality testing appears sufficiently stable that she can be expected to undergo some degree of regression in the course of treatment without danger of precipitating a psychotic break.

Key Issues and Themes in Working With Ruth

Intrapsychic Conflicts and Repression of Childhood Experiences   As a psychoanalytically oriented psychotherapist, I accept the role of detective in ferreting out the secrets of the past that are locked away in Ruth's unconscious. Although I am guided by theory to suspicious content areas, her psyche and the secrets therein are uniquely hers, and it is ultimately she who will know the truth of her life through her own courage and perceptions.

I suspect that the psychosexual aspects of Ruth's relationships with her parents (and possibly her siblings) remain key conflict areas for her, even now. In the classical Freudian model of healthy development, she would have experienced early libidinal attraction to her father, which she would eventually have replaced with normal heterosexual interests in male peers; likewise, her feelings of rivalry with her mother for her father's affection would have been replaced with identification with her mother. In the ideal model, moreover, she would have experienced rebellion against parental constraints, particularly during the developmental period associated with toilet training and also in adolescence.

In reality Ruth appears to have superficially avoided normal rebellion and to have repressed her sexuality except for adopting a wifely role with the first man she dated. Although she followed the format of using her mother as role model and having children by an acceptable husband, she apparently abdicated in the struggles of sexuality, rebellion, and identification, leaving these conflicts unresolved. Her conscious recollections of her parents are of a rigid, fundamentalist father and a "critical" mother. I would be interested in knowing what these parents were really like, as perceived by Ruth in childhood. How did her father handle his feelings for his children? Did his aloofness mask strongly suppressed incestuous feelings that she intuitively sensed? Were these ever acted out?

A Freudian view of her father's harsh reactions to Ruth's "playing doctor" would emphasize the Oedipus/Electra aspects of this father–daughter encounter. Her father's refusal to speak to her for weeks after this incident suggests jealousy rather than simply moral rejection of childhood sexual activity. This suspicion is supported by the parentally imposed isolation of the children that delayed dating until after high school. Ruth's attempts to win her father's approval by supplanting the role of her mother (in caring for her younger siblings) is also consistent with these Oedipus/Electra dynamics. Ruth internalized her father's overtly negative attitude to sexuality.

If these hypotheses are correct, a theme in therapy will be Ruth's reexperiencing of the sensual aspects of her attachment to her father and his response to her. As she is able to first "own" these feelings and memories and then to relinquish the fantasy of fulfillment with her father, she can become open to an adult relationship in which her sexuality is appreciated rather than scorned or distorted.

Although there is no direct evidence of sexual abuse in the case material, the family dynamics are such that there is the possibility of actual incestual acts by the father, the memories of which have been repressed by Ruth. Even more likely is the pattern wherein the father's incestuous feelings were not overtly acted out but were so intense that he developed defenses of reaction formation and projection, labeling her sexuality (rather than his) as reprehensible. The jealous response of Ruth's mother is consistent with either of the above patterns of paternal behavior, but the mother's response is more patho logical (and more pathogenic) if actual abuse occurred.

Oedipus/Electra feelings by both parent and child are considered part of normal development. However, intense conflicts and guilt regarding these feelings or experiences are very common in clients seeking counseling or psychotherapy, and all too often actual molestation is eventually determined to have occurred.

Regardless of the details of the actual memories and buried feelings unearthed in therapy, the analytic therapist is alert for indications of psychological traumas in the client's early life, psychic wounds that may be associated with a family *secret* that the client has needed to protect from exposure through suppression, denial, and repression. The probability of a secret being at the heart of Ruth's neurosis is increased by the indication in the case material that she was socially isolated and that her lack of relationships outside the family was enforced by the parents, at least in terms of dating. The entire family may have lived with their unspoken secrets in relative isolation. Although incestuous themes in one form or another are the most common secrets unearthed, other "unthinkable" secrets may be at the center of the repression—namely, the hidden mental illness, homosexuality, or alcoholism of a family member.

To what extent is Ruth bringing themes from her family of origin to her present family? She defines her husband only by what he is not (her father) and by his potential to reject her (as her father had rejected her). Does she know the man she married at all, or is he merely a stand-in for the real man in her life? Is her husband's apparent rejection of her attempts at personal growth a facet of his personality, or is he being set up? Her reaction to her daughter Jennifer may very likely be related to her own failure to rebel. Acceptance and nurturance by Ruth of the suppressed child-rebel aspect of herself may well improve her relationship with her daughter.

Symptoms and Psychodynamics

A psychoanalytic approach views psychological symptoms as active processes that give clues to the client's underlying psychodynamics. Some acute symptoms are valuable in that they alert the client that something is wrong. Other symptoms, particularly when chronic, may be extremely resistant to intervention and may severely impair or even threaten the life of the client.

Ruth's symptoms (assuming that organic factors are absent or minimal) suggest compatibility with psychoanalytically oriented therapy. I would use analytic theory to help Ruth understand the role of anxiety in her life and the methods she uses to control her anxiety. I view Ruth's current existential anxiety as related to these issues: Her early training by her parents clearly made individuation (in the object-relations sense) a very scary proposition for her; hence, any attempt toward individuation is anxiety provoking. She is, therefore, terrified not only of acting impulsively but also of acting independently. She hopes to make her own choices in life but also hopes that her therapist will make her decisions for her.

Ruth's symptom of overeating probably gratifies her need for affection, but a psychoanalytic approach to this symptom would also explore its developmental origin. Oral gratification is the primary focus of libidinal energy in the earliest stage of development. Symptoms associated with this stage can appear if the client suffered deprivation during this period. If this is the case, the adult tends to be fixated on getting the satisfaction never adequately obtained during the childhood stage.

Ruth's weight problem also has psychodynamic meaning. Being overweight may lead to her feeling sexually unattractive and, therefore, less likely to be faced with dealing with her sexuality. Ruth's increasing difficulty in leaving home suggests a fear of meeting others who might threaten the stability of her marriage. This symptom is consistent with the dynamics of her being overweight.

The exacerbation of physical symptoms and anxiety are cited in the background information as being the catalyst for Ruth's seeking therapy at this time. A psychoanalytic approach to these symptoms would explore the "secondary gain" associated with each symptom. A symptom is expected to include elements from both sides of an intrapsychic conflict. For instance, a headache might serve to keep her sexually distant from her husband while also providing a pretext for avoiding social contacts that might threaten the marriage.

Analytic therapy provides a means for treating Ruth's symptoms, but only in the context of broader treatment of her psychological problems. Some symptoms can be treated directly, and at lesser expense, by nonanalytic therapies. When the client desires insight as well as symptom relief or when the "secondary gain" of the symptom leads to either failure of the direct approach or to the substitution of a new symptom for the old one, analytic therapy is indicated. Ruth gives evidence of multiple symptoms and of a desire to examine her life. Hence, consideration of analytic therapy rather than a symptom-focused behavioral approach is reasonable.

Ruth might also consider the alternative of brief therapy. I consider brief analytic therapy a specialty area in which selected clients opt to focus on highly specific goals. Although it shortens the duration of treatment, it also modifies the therapeutic contract and places stringent demands on client and clinician alike. Brief therapy as a specialty should not be confused with arbitrary restrictions on the length of treatment imposed by managed care. Such restrictions are generally inconsistent with insight-oriented analytic therapy. Insight in analytic therapy typically requires the client to experience therapeutic regression and the "working through" of distortions in the context of the therapeutic relationship, processes that cannot be terminated prematurely without danger of psychological harm to the client.

The therapy described in the remainder of this section includes a mixture of supportive and insight techniques. Hence, if it were necessary to limit Ruth's treatment to a fixed number of sessions, I would modify my approach to emphasize supportive interventions and minimize regressive techniques. Supportive therapy could be of value to Ruth, even within the constraint of an arbitrarily limited number of sessions, particularly if she could resume treatment periodically as needed. Ruth and I must agree on any limitation to the number of sessions at the onset of treatment, and it is my responsibility to ensure any limitation is understood throughout therapy.

Open-ended treatment, in which a third-party payor periodically approves or rejects additional sessions, is incompatible with both insight-oriented and supportive analytic therapy. Terminating therapy at the whim of an outside agency can be highly deleterious to the client. Such a termination is experienced as abandonment at best, and it may be equated unconsciously with betrayal or even malevolence on the part of the therapist.

Treatment Techniques

Psychoanalytically Oriented Psychotherapy Versus Psychoanalysis   The treatment approach I propose for Ruth is psychoanalytically oriented psychotherapy rather than psychoanalysis. This choice does not indicate a theoretical disagreement with the methods of classic analysis; psychoanalytic psychotherapy is a form of analytic treatment that has advantages and disadvantages compared with classical psychoanalysis. In classical analysis the analyst adopts a "blank-screen" approach in which expressions of the real analyst–client relationship are minimized to promote development of the client's transference relationship with the analyst. Transference leads the client to react to the analyst as if he or she were a significant person from the client's past life.

Psychoanalytic therapy does *not* require the blank-screen approach, is less frustrating to the patient, allows the therapist more flexibility in technique, is less costly, may be shorter in duration, and provides "support" for the patient's least maladaptive defenses. Hence, it is often the treatment of choice. The drawbacks of analytic psychotherapy as compared with psychoanalysis are directly related to the advantages. The variations in technique lead to a lowering of expectations, as many aspects of the client's personality will remain unanalyzed due to elimination of the blank screen and the consequent intrusion of aspects of the "real" relationship between therapist and client of their "as-if" transference relationship. If, for example, Ruth is in analysis with me, free-associating from the couch, and she states her belief that I disapprove of some feeling or behavior of hers, I can be reasonably sure that she is reacting to me as if I were some other figure in her life. In contrast, if she makes the same assertion in face-to-face psychotherapy, my actual nonverbal behavior (or prior self-disclosure of any sort) may have given her valid clues to my actual (conscious or unconscious) disapproval of her feelings or behavior. I can never know the exact degree to which her response is a transference response as opposed to a response to my "real" behavior in our "real" relationship. In psychoanalytically oriented psychotherapy with Ruth, I must keep in mind that every aspect of our interaction will have a mix of "real" and "as-if" components. To the degree that I participate in the "real" relationship by providing support, by giving advice, or by sharing an opinion or personal experience, I am limiting my ability to maintain an analytic stance to the material she presents.

Although significant therapeutic work is possible using this model, I must be very sensitive to the meanings Ruth will attribute to my "real" interactions with her. If I disapprove of a particular act or intention of hers, for example, I can reasonably expect her to assume that I approve of all her reported acts or intentions to which I have not expressed disapproval. Thus, although I am free to use the "real" as well as the "as-if" relationship in making therapeutic interventions, I am not free to vacillate in my therapeutic stance without risk of doing harm.

The Therapeutic Contract   I form as clear a therapeutic contract as possible with Ruth, explaining the goals, costs, and risks of the treatment as well as briefly describing the methods and theory of psychotherapy. As a psychoanalytic therapist, I believe the economics of treatment, both in terms of financial arrangements and also in the investment of time and energy in therapy, cannot be separated from the process and outcomes of therapy. Thus, I make my expectations regarding payment explicit, including the analytic rule that fees are charged for canceled sessions. This contractual clarity regarding fees has therapeutic implications in that Ruth's obligation to me for my services is specified at the outset of treatment. Thereafter, she can feel free of any additional requirement to meet my needs, and I can interpret any concerns that she does express about my needs in terms of the "as-if" relationship.

A treatment schedule of two or three sessions per week, each session lasting 50 minutes, is typical for psychoanalytically oriented therapy. Any planned vacations in the next 6 months or so, by either Ruth or me, should be noted, and therapy should not commence shortly before a vacation.

Other aspects of the contract include confidentiality (and its limitations), the degree to which I am available for emergencies or other between-session contacts, and an admonition to generally avoid making major life decisions during the course of treatment. The latter "rule" for clients in analysis is relevant to Ruth. She indicates that she wants a therapist to make decisions for her, and I have some concern about the possibility of her leaping to decisions while experiencing regression in the course of treatment.

Free Association   Free association is a primary technique in psychoanalysis and is the "basic rule" given to clients. In my therapy with Ruth I emphasize the technique of free association at certain times, such as when she comments that she doesn't know what to talk about. However, we have verbal interaction in addition to her free associations, even in the early phases of therapy. I often instruct her to express her associations to her dreams, to elements of her current life, and to memories of her past life, particularly new memories of childhood events that emerge in the course of treatment.

Dreams, Symptoms, Jokes, and Slips   Dreams are considered the "royal road" to the unconscious, and I encourage Ruth to report her dreams and to associate to them. As an analytically oriented therapist, I conceptualize each of her dreams as having two levels of meaning, the manifest content and the latent meaning. Analytic theory postulates that each dream is a coded message from her unconscious, a message that can be interpreted so as to understand the unconscious wish that initiated the dream and the nature of the repression that forced the wish to be experienced only in disguised form. Hypotheses about the latent meaning of dream symbols can be derived from theory, but the actual interpretation of her dream elements is based on her own unique associations to her dream symbols.

In addition to dreams, the hidden meanings inherent in Ruth's symptoms are subject to analysis. Her presenting symptoms, manifestations of resistance, memories, and spontaneous errors (slips of the tongue) are clues to her underlying dynamics. The wordplay involved in slips of the tongue is meaningful, as may be any intentional joke or pun made or recalled by her in a session.

Interpretations of Resistance and Content   My initial interpretations are of resistance, and I follow the rule of interpreting the resistance Ruth presents relative to a content area before actually interpreting the content. I recognize that every accurate interpretation is an assault on her defenses, and I know that she will react to the interpretation as a threat to her present adjustment. Hence, in choosing the timing of a particular interpretation, I am guided by her readiness to accept it as well as by my sense of its accuracy. I also follow the general rule that more inferential interpretations should be made in the later stages of therapy after a therapeutic alliance and trust have been established. Early interpretations should be minimally inferential, often only noting a correspondence. For example, commenting to Ruth that she wrote less in her autobiography about her mother than she did about her father is much less inferential than interpreting her overeating as a defense against sexuality.

Many interpretations, particularly in the later stages of therapy, relate to her transference reactions and are geared to helping her work through childhood-based conflicts in the context of her therapeutic relationship with me. This brief dialogue begins with the here-and-now and ends with an insight about the past:

Ruth: I worry I'm just hiding in my therapy. It's an indulgence; I should be using your time to fix my problems, not just to talk about anything I like.
Therapist: What's being hidden here?
Ruth: That I'm not really working. I tell myself I'm going to a doctor's appointment, but you just listen, and I just play around with my thoughts.
Therapist: Is it OK to play here, at your doctor's appointment?
Ruth: Of course not. This is work; we're not playing. You wouldn't see me if I were here to play, Dr. Blau.
Therapist: There was a time when your father didn't speak to you for weeks.
Ruth: That was about playing doctor too! Do I still think it's sinful to explore? My dad would be shocked at some of the thoughts I've explored here.
Therapist: How would he react?

Ruth: He'd be. Oh, I just remembered how he looked then. He got red in the face and stammered. His brow got sweaty. He punished me for my sin.

Therapist: For whose sin?

Ruth: Maybe for his own. I hardly knew anything about sex when he decided I was bad; maybe his thinking about me being sexual made him feel guilty or something.

Therapist: But you're the one who got punished.

Ruth: Yeah. I got punished for what he thought and felt, not for what I actually did.

In this example I follow a hunch that Ruth's concern about "playing" at her "doctor's" appointment might have associations to the childhood incident when she was punished for "playing doctor." Her acceptance of this association sets the stage for the final interpretive exchange and insight.

Even the best interpretations are only hypotheses that are presented to the client for consideration. Premature interpretations can be harmful, even if correct. As a therapist, I keep an open mind about the meaning of Ruth's thoughts, feelings, memories, dreams, and fantasies, and I rarely make interpretations about the actuality of past events, imagined or remembered. Although I use my hunches to promote the process of freeing repressed memories, I do not treat my hunches about the past as if they were facts to be imposed on the client's reality.

Transference and Countertransference   Ruth's experience in therapy is both gratifying and frustrating. It is gratifying in that we spend each hour focusing on her life. Her needs, hopes, disappointments, dreams, fantasies, and everything else of importance to her are accepted as meaningful, and she need not share center stage with anyone else. It is her hour, and I listen to everything without criticizing her or demanding that she see anything my way or do anything to please me. My sustained, active attention to and interest in her are different from any other interpersonal interaction. Other people in her life insist on wanting things from her, or they want to criticize her, or at the very least they expect her to be as interested in them as they are in her.

But the sessions are also frustrating. Ruth wants help, and all I seem to do is listen and occasionally ask a question or comment on what she has said. Do I like her? Or am I only pretending to be interested because that's what I am paid for? When, she wonders, will the therapy start helping? When will she find out how to resolve her issues about her marriage and her boring life?

Given this mixture of gratification and frustration, it is not surprising that Ruth begins to see *me* as a source of both of those emotions. Moreover, it is not surprising that she will "transfer" onto me attributes of others in her life who have been sources of gratification and frustration to her. Hence, she begins to react to me as if I were her father, mother, or other significant figure.

The permissiveness of the sessions also allows Ruth to regress—to feel dependent and childlike and to express her thoughts and feelings with little censorship. I take almost all the responsibility for maintaining limits; she need only talk. Her regression is fostered to the degree that I maintain the classic analytic stance, and it is ameliorated to the degree that I interact with her in terms of our "real" relationship—for example, by expressing empathy.

Ruth's past haunts her present life and interpersonal relationships, and to an even greater degree it haunts her relationship with me. But the distortions projected onto me exist in a controlled interpersonal setting and, therefore, are amenable to interpretation and resolution. The therapeutic session provides a structure in which the nature of her conflicts can be exposed and understood, not only in the sense of intellectual insight but also in the analysis of their actual impact on her perceptions and feelings about me and the therapeutic relationship.

The therapeutic relationship provides gratification and frustration for the therapist as well as for the client. My therapeutic task includes monitoring not only the content of the sessions but also my feelings that grow out of this relationship. There are aspects of Ruth that I like and others that I dislike. I find her dependency both appealing and irritating. I enjoy the positive attributes she projects onto me, and I experience some hurt when she projects negative attributes onto me. Nevertheless, I must minimize indulgence in these reactions and concentrate instead on ensuring that my participation consistently promotes her self-understanding and individuation. Although she is free to demand anything and everything from me, I must deny myself almost all the rewards of a "real" relationship with her.

Understanding the theory of therapeutic techniques helps me keep my perspective, as does recollection of my own therapy. The therapy I have received is useful to me in understanding the psychotherapeutic experience from the client's point of view, and it helps me understand some of my conflicts that could impair my effectiveness as a therapist. Nevertheless, my adherence to the ideal role is imperfect. To some extent I inadvertently let my feelings and conflicts distort my perceptions of Ruth. My distortions include my projecting onto her attributes of significant figures in my own life; I experience countertransference. Although I can minimize countertransference, it can never be eliminated. Therefore, to minimize the negative impact of my countertransference on Ruth's treatment, I monitor my feelings about her and my reactions toward her, and I periodically discuss my treatment of her, including these feelings, with a trusted colleague. Voluntary consultation about my feelings and interventions is, in my opinion, an effective method for assessing and minimizing deleterious effects of countertransference. If I find myself uncomfortable discussing a particular aspect of Ruth's treatment, I suspect that countertransference is at work. Consultations must be conducted so as to protect her confidentiality; this usually includes her releasing of the information and my altering information about her identity during the consultation.

My scrutiny of my countertransference reactions to Ruth may be of value in helping me understand her; often my unconscious reactions to a client give clues to that patient's dynamics and to the reactions that others have to the patient. Countertransference can be used in the service of the therapy if it can be understood and controlled. Monitoring my own countertransference feelings serves as a major source of clinical information about the client. If I were to find my countertransference to be having a significant negative effect on Ruth's treatment, I would, after consultation, enter therapy myself and either refer her to a colleague or continue to treat her under supervision.

Some aspects of countertransference may be partially inseparable from the conscious motivation of the therapist to engage in the arduous work of psychotherapy. As I work actively with Ruth to break the spell cast on her in her past, I apply my understanding of the nature of the spell and of the "magic" needed to break it. As I engage in this struggle, I run the counter-transference risk of becoming invested in the hero role, thereby fostering her dependence and prolonging her regression. But to some extent I have opted for this role by choosing the profession of psychotherapist. Thus, by participating in Ruth's life as the hero she has dreamed of, I am fulfilling my own not-so-unconscious needs. But if I am to stay a hero in the sense of being a good therapist, I must renounce the role of hero to Ruth at precisely the moment in therapy in which I have released her from the past's constricting spell.[2]

 ## JERRY COREY'S WORK WITH RUTH FROM A PSYCHOANALYTIC PERSPECTIVE

If you are using the *CD-ROM for Integrative Counseling*, refer to Session 10 ("Transference and Countertransference") and compare what I've written here with how I deal with transference and countertransference.

Basic Assumptions

As I work with Ruth within a psychoanalytic framework, I am guided by both the psychosexual perspective of Sigmund Freud and the psychosocial perspective of Erik Erikson. My work with Ruth is also influenced to some extent by contemporary psychoanalytic trends, which are often classified in terms of ego psychology and object-relations theory. I am moving beyond Freud to illustrate that contemporary psychoanalysis is an ever-evolving system rather than a closed and static model.

The *psychosexual* theory, as seen in traditional Freudian psychoanalysis, places emphasis on the internal conflicts of an individual during the first 6 years of life. This theory assumes that certain sexual and aggressive impulses are repressed during these formative years, because if they were to become conscious, they would produce extreme anxiety. Although these memories and experiences are buried in the unconscious, they exert a powerful influence on the individual's personality and behavior later in life.

The *psychosocial* theory, developed primarily by Erikson, emphasizes sociocultural influences on the development of personality. It assumes that there is a continuity in human development. At the various stages of life, we face the challenge of establishing an equilibrium between ourselves and our social world. At each crisis, or turning point, in the life cycle we can either successfully resolve our conflicts or fail to resolve them. Failure to resolve a conflict at a given stage results in fixation, or the experience of being stuck. It is difficult to master the psychosocial tasks of adulthood if we are psychologically stuck with unresolved conflicts from an earlier period of development. Although such a failure does not necessarily doom us to remain forever the victim of fixations, our lives are, to a large extent, the result of the choices we make at these stages.

The more recent work in the *psychoanalytic approach* is represented by the writings of Margaret Mahler, Heinz Kohut, and Otto Kernberg, among others. Contemporary psychoanalytic practice emphasizes the origins and transformations of the self, the differentiation between the self and others, the integration of the self with others, and the influence of critical factors in early development on later development. Predictable developmental sequences are noted in which the early experiences of the self shift in relation to an expanding awareness of others. Once self–other patterns are established, they influence later interpersonal relationships. Human development can best be thought of as the evolution of the way in which individuals differentiate self from others. One's current behavior is largely a repetition of the internal patterning established during one of the earlier stages of development.

In viewing Ruth's case, I make the assumption that her early development is of critical importance and that her current personality problems are rooted in repressed childhood conflicts. Borrowing from Kohut's thinking, I surmise that she was psychologically wounded during childhood and that her defensive structure is an attempt to avoid being wounded again. I expect to find an interweaving of old hurts with new wounds. Thus, I pay attention to the consistency between her emotional wounding as a child and those situations that result in pain for her today. Much of our therapeutic work is aimed at repairing the original wounding.

I make many of these assumptions before meeting a client. The psychoanalytic perspective on the developmental process provides me with a conceptual framework that helps me make sense of an individual's current functioning. Although I do not force my client into this theoretical mold, I do make certain general assumptions about the normal sequence of human development.

Assessment of Ruth

This assessment is based on a few initial sessions with Ruth, her intake form, and her autobiography. Her relationships with her parents are critically important from a therapeutic standpoint. She describes her father as "distant, authoritarian, and rigid." My hunch is that this view of her father colors how she perceives all men today, that her fear of displeasing her husband is connected to her fear of bringing her father displeasure, and that what she is now striving to get from her husband is related to what she wanted from her father. I expect that she will view me and react to me in many of the same ways she responded to her father. Through this transference relationship with me, Ruth will be able to recognize connecting patterns between her childhood behavior and her current struggles. For example, she is fearful of displeasing her husband, John, for fear he might leave. If he did, there would be a repetition of the pattern of her father's psychological abandonment of her after she had not lived up to his expectations. She does not stand up to John or ask for what she needs out of fear that he will become disgruntled and abandon her. She is defending herself against being wounded by him in some of the same ways that she was wounded by her father.

From a psychosexual perspective I am interested in Ruth's early childhood experiences in which she developed her views pertaining to sexuality. Her father's response when he caught her in an act of sexual experimentation needs to be considered as we work with her present attitudes and feelings about sex. As a child and adolescent, Ruth felt guilty and ashamed about her sexual feelings. She internalized many of her father's strict views of sexuality. Because her father manifested a negative attitude toward her increased sexual awareness, she learned that her sexual feelings were evil, that her body and sexual pleasure were both "dirty," and that her curiosity about sexual matters was unacceptable. Her sexual feelings became anxiety provoking and were thus rigidly controlled. The denial of sexuality that was established at this age has been carried over into her adult life and gives rise to severe conflicts, guilt, remorse, and self-condemnation.

Viewing Ruth from a psychosocial perspective will shed considerable light on the nature of her present psychological problems. Ruth never really developed a basic trust in the world. As an infant, she learned that she could not count on others to provide her with a sense of being wanted and loved. She did not receive affection throughout her early childhood, a deprivation that now makes it difficult for her to feel that she is worthy of affection. The task of early childhood is developing *autonomy,* which is necessary if one is to gain a measure of self-control and any ability to cope with the world. In Ruth's case she grew up fast, was never allowed to be a child, and was expected to take care of her younger brother and sisters. Although she seemed to be "mature" even as a child, in actuality she never became autonomous.

From the contemporary psychoanalytic perspective, Ruth will not feel truly independent until she feels properly attached and dependent. This notion means that to be independent she must allow herself to depend on others. Ruth, however, never felt a genuine sense of attachment to her father, whom she perceived as distant, or to her mother, whom she viewed as somewhat rejecting. For Ruth to have developed genuine independence, she would have needed others in her life whom she could count on for emotional support. But this support was absent from her background. During the school-age period she felt inferior in social relationships, was confused about her gender-role identity, and was unwilling to face new challenges. During adolescence she did not experience an identity crisis because she did not ask basic questions of life. Rather than questioning the values that had been taught to her, she compliantly accepted them. In part, she has followed the design established by her parents when she was an adolescent. She was not challenged to make choices for herself or to struggle to find meaning in life. In her adulthood she managed to break away from her fundamentalist religion, yet she could not free herself of her guilt over this act. She is still striving for her father's approval, and she is still operating without a clearly defined set of values to replace the ones she discarded. A major theme of Ruth's life is her concern over how to fill the void that she fears will result when her children leave home.

Psychoanalytic theory provides a useful perspective for understanding the ways in which Ruth is trying to control the anxiety in her life. She readily accepted her parents' rigid morality as one of her primary ego defenses because it served the function of controlling her impulses. Further, there is a fundamental split within her between the "good girl" and the "bad girl." Either she keeps in control of herself and others by doing things for them, or she gets out of control when she enjoys herself, as she did when she was "playing doctor." She feels in control when she takes care of her children, and she does not know what she will do once they leave home. Coupled with this empty-nest syndrome is her ambivalence about leaving the security of the home by choosing a career. This change brings about anxiety because she is struggling with her ability to direct her own life as opposed to defining herself strictly as a servant of others. This anxiety will be a focal point of therapy.

Goals of Therapy

The goal of our analytically oriented work will be to gradually uncover unconscious material. In this way Ruth will be able to use messages from the unconscious to direct her own life instead of being driven by her defensive controls. Therapy is aimed at promoting integration and ego development. The various parts of her self that she has denied will become more connected. The ideal type of identity is an autonomous self, which is characterized by self-esteem and self-confidence and is capable of intimacy with others.

Therapeutic Procedures

I suspect that a major part of our work will entail dealing with resistance, at least at the start of therapy. In spite of the fact that Ruth has come to therapy voluntarily, any number of barriers will make her progress slow at times. She has learned to protect herself against anxiety by building up defenses over the years, and she will not quickly surrender them. As we have seen, some of her primary defenses are repression and denial. The chances are that she will have some ambivalence about becoming aware of her unconscious motivations and needs. Merely gaining insight into the nature of her unconscious conflicts does not mean that her therapy is over, for the difficult part will be exploring and working through these conflicts.

I expect that I will become a significant figure in her life, for I assume that she will develop strong feelings toward me, both positive and negative. She will probably relate to me in some of the same ways that she related to her father. Working therapeutically with this transference involves two steps. One is to foster this development of transference; the second consists of working through patterns that she established with significant others in her past as these feelings emerge toward me in the therapy relationship. This second step is the core of the therapy process. *Working through* refers to repeating interpretations of her behavior and overcoming her resistance, thus allowing her to resolve her neurotic patterns. Although I do not use a blank-screen model, keeping myself mysterious and hidden, in this type of intensive therapy the client is bound to expect me to fulfill some of her unmet needs. She will probably experience again some of the same feelings she had during her childhood. How she views me and reacts to me will constitute much of the therapeutic work, for this transference material is rich with meaning and can tell Ruth much about herself.

In addition to working with Ruth's resistances and with any transference that develops in our relationship, I will probably use a variety of other techniques to get at her unconscious dynamics. Dream analysis is an important procedure for uncovering unconscious material and giving her insight into some areas of unresolved problems. I will ask her to recall her dreams, to report them in the sessions, and then to learn how to free-associate to key elements in them. Free association, a major procedure in our therapy, involves asking her to clear her mind of thoughts and preoccupations and to say whatever pops into her head without censoring, regardless of how silly or trivial it may be. This procedure typically leads to some recollection of past experiences and, at times, to a release of bottled-up feelings. Another major technique at my disposal is interpretation, or pointing out and explaining to Ruth the meanings of behavior manifested by her dreams, her free-association material, her resistances, and the nature of our relationship. Timed properly, these interpretations (or teachings) can help Ruth assimilate new learning and uncover unconscious material more rapidly. This, in turn, will help her understand and deal with her life situation more effectively.

The Therapeutic Process

The crux of my therapeutic work with Ruth consists of bringing her past into the present, which is done mainly through exploring the transference relationship. My aim is to do more than merely facilitate recall of past events and insight on her part; instead, I hope that she will see patterns and a continuity in her life from her childhood to the present. When she realizes how her past is still operating, character change is possible, and new options open up for her.

Elements of the Process   After Ruth has been in therapy for some time, she grows disenchanted with me because she does not see me as giving enough. For instance, she becomes irritated because I am not willing to share anything about my marriage or my relationships with my children. She says that I give her very analytical responses when she is simply trying to get to know something about me personally. She complains that she is the one doing all the giving and that she is beginning to resent it. Here is a brief sample of a session in which we talk about these feelings.

Ruth: I want you to be more of a real person to me. It feels uncomfortable for you to know so much about me when I know so little about you.

Jerry: Yes, it's certainly the case that I know a lot more about your life than you know about mine and that you're more vulnerable than I am.

Ruth: Well, you seem so removed and distant from me. You're hard to reach. This is not easy for me to say . . . uhm . . . I suppose I want to know what you really think of me. You don't tell me, and I'm often left wondering what you're feeling. I work hard at getting your approval, but I'm not sure I have it. I get the feeling that you think I'm bad.

Jerry: I wonder if you have felt this way before?

Ruth: Well, ah . . . you know that I always felt this way around my father. No matter what I did to get his approval, I was never really successful. And that's sometimes the way I feel toward you.

I am consciously not disclosing much about my reactions to Ruth at this point because she is finally bringing out feelings about me that she has avoided for so long. I encourage her to express more about the ways in which she sees me as ungiving and unreachable and as not being what she wants. It is through this process of exploring some of her persistent reactions to me, I hope, that she will see more of the connection between her unfulfilled needs from the past and how she is viewing me in this present relationship. At this stage in her therapy Ruth is experiencing some very basic feelings of wanting to be special and wanting proof of it. By working over a long period with her transference reactions, she will eventually gain insight into how she has given her father all the power to affirm her as a person and how she has not learned to give herself the approval she so much wants from him. I am not willing to reassure her because I want to foster the expression of this transference.[3]

Process Commentary   I am not working with Ruth from the perspective of classical psychoanalysis. Rather, I am drawing from psychosocial theory and from concepts in the newer psychoanalytic thinking, especially from Kohut's work. I direct much of our therapy to the exploration of Ruth's old issues, her early wounding, and her fears of new wounds. The bruises to her self that she experiences in the here-and-now trigger memories of her old hurts. Especially in her relationship with me, she is sensitive to rejection and any signs of my disapproval. Therefore, much of our therapeutic effort is aimed at dealing with the ways in which she is now striving for recognition as well as the ways in which she attempted to get recognition as a child. In short, she has a damaged self, and she is susceptible to and fearful of further bruising. We discuss her attachments, how she tried to win affection, and the many ways in which she is trying to protect herself from suffering further emotional wounds to a fragile ego.

Much of Ruth's work involves going back to early events in her life—recalling them and the feelings associated with them—in the hope that she can be free from the restrictions of her past. She comes to realize that her past is an important part of her and that some old wounds will take a long time to heal.

One of the major ways Ruth gains insight into her patterns is by learning to understand her dreams. We regularly focus on their meanings, and she free-associates to some symbols. She has a very difficult time giving up control and simply allowing herself to say freely whatever comes to mind in these sessions. She worries about "saying the appropriate thing," and we examine this material in the sessions. Dream work is one of the major tools to tap her unconscious processes.

Ruth also discovers from the way she responds to me some key connections between how she related to significant people in her life. She looks to me in some of the same ways that she looked to her father for approval and for love. I encourage her recollection of feelings associated with these past events so that she can work through the barriers preventing her from functioning as a mature adult.[4]

 QUESTIONS FOR REFLECTION

As you continue working with the therapeutic approaches described in this book, you will have many opportunities to apply the basic assumptions and key concepts of each theory to your own life. Some of these questions for reflection will assist you in becoming involved in a personal way. Other questions are designed to give you some guidance in beginning to work with Ruth. They are intended to help you clarify your reactions to how the consultant and I worked with Ruth from each of the therapeutic perspectives. Select the questions for reflection that most interest you.

1. Dr. Blau emphasizes the importance of understanding the "whys" of a client's experience and behavior. What advantages and disadvantages do you see in this focus?

2. Blau suggests that the psychosexual aspects of Ruth's relationships with her parents, and possibly her siblings, still represent key conflict areas in her present behavior. In what ways may her early experiences be having a significant impact on her life today? How might you explore these dynamics with her?

3. Do you share the emphasis of this approach on the importance of Ruth's father in her life? How might you go about exploring with her how conflicts with her father are related to some of her present conflicts?

4. What is one of the most significant themes (from the analytic perspective) you would focus on in your sessions with Ruth?

5. In what ways would you encourage Ruth to go back and relive her childhood? How important is delving into the client's early childhood in leading to personality change?

6. What defenses do you see in Ruth? How do you imagine you would work to lessen these defenses?

7. Blau discusses the importance of both the therapist's "real" relationship and the "as-if" relationship with Ruth. How might you differentiate between her transference reactions and her "real" reactions to you?

 NOTES

1. The source for the DSM-IV-TR is as follows: American Psychiatric Association (2000). *Diagnostic and statistical manual of mental disorders,* 4th edition, Text Revision. Washington, DC: Author.

2. Here Dr. Blau discusses his views of working with Ruth's transference and makes important comments pertaining to his ability and willingness to recognize, monitor, and deal with his own potential countertransference. If you are using the *CD-ROM for Integrative Counseling,* refer to Session 10 ("Working With Transference and Countertransference") to see my perspective on these issues.

3. Again, if you are using the *CD-ROM for Integrative Counseling,* refer to Session 10 ("Transference and Countertransference") and compare what I've written here with how I deal with transference and countertransference.

4. For a more detailed treatment of psychoanalytic theory, see G. Corey (2005), *Theory and Practice of Counseling and Psychotherapy* (7th edition; Belmont, CA: Brooks/Cole). The basic concepts introduced in William Blau's work with Ruth and in my version on psychodynamic work with Ruth are covered comprehensively in Chapter 4 (Psychoanalytic Therapy).

Chapter 3

Case Approach to Adlerian Therapy

An Adlerian Therapist's Perspective on Ruth

by James Robert Bitter, Ed.D. and William G. Nicoll, Ph.D.

Introduction

Jerry Corey consulted with us on the case of Ruth and asked for our help conducting a thorough initial interview and developing a summary of impressions based on this initial interview. This initial interview generates a relatively clear picture of the client in relation to what Adler called the *life tasks* of (a) friendship and social relations, (b) work and occupation, and (c) love, intimacy, and sexuality. We also provided a lifestyle assessment, including a summary of the family constellation, a record of early recollections, and an interpretation of Ruth's pattern of basic convictions. We use a modified form of Adlerian counseling that we call *Adlerian brief therapy*.[1]

Lifestyle information in this process is often collected and interpreted by two therapists, using a technique called *multiple therapy*.[2] The client is initially interviewed by one therapist, who then presents the data to a second therapist. The client experiences social interest in the very structure of therapy. The model of two therapists cooperating in a single effort is often therapeutic in and of itself.

This section provides a detailed and comprehensive assessment of Ruth's early background and her current functioning. We hope you will continue to use this material as you work with her case in other chapters. We begin with our narrative summaries from a general diagnosis and lifestyle assessment.[3] We co-construct these summaries with the client based on an interviewing model delineated in the *Individual Psychology Client Workbook*, which was developed by Robert L. Powers and Jane Griffith.[1] Here, we have provided some minimal data and our initial summaries from our assessment process. We follow these summaries with a process outline of *Adlerian brief therapy* and an example of its application with Ruth.

The Initial Interview

In addition to the information presented in Chapter 1 in Ruth's autobiography and intake interview, Ruth also indicated that she was the oldest of four children who are ordered as follows: Ruth, age 39, living with her husband in California; Jill (–4), age 35, an architect living in Chicago; Amy (–6), age 33, a social worker and homemaker in California; and Steve (–9), age 30, a clerk in a shipping office who still lives at home with Ruth's parents.

Ruth believes she is the one who is most affected by her unhappiness. Her family is kind and understanding. Ruth was a homemaker and mother until her children became adolescents. She then entered college part time and obtained a bachelor's degree. Through her contacts with others at the university she has become aware of how she has limited herself, how she has fostered her family's dependence on her, and how frightened she is of branching out from her roles as mother and wife. Ruth responded to questions about the three life tasks in the following way.

Love and Intimacy   "I have had only one relationship. John and I started going out after I graduated from high school. We got married, and we've been together ever since. John says he had been interested in me for a long time before we went out. He had seen me in church. We met formally at a church social. He stayed with me for a whole day. We talked, and he listened to everything I said. He was very attentive. When he walked me home, he asked if we could go to a movie. I said yes, and my parents didn't object. John was strong-minded, knew what he wanted, and had goals and dreams. I liked his dreams, especially since they included me. He was always calm and never seemed to get angry. He's still very patient, the way I think men should be. He's the only man I ever dated, but he has been good to me.

"I think being feminine means that you are caring and nurturing and give a great deal of yourself to others. You have to be able to balance family, which is your responsibility, and community. There is always a lot to do. I think being feminine also means that you're attractive to men. I do really well at the first part, but I doubt that I'm attractive to men, especially with the weight I've put on.

"John hardly ever complains, but he would probably like to have sexual relations more often. I never really enjoyed sex that much. It's OK, I mean, but I don't get in the mood as often as John. If I have any complaint, it's that I would like to make more decisions in the family and even for myself, but I would probably botch it up.

"If I could have anything going better in this area, I would like to feel more feminine and appreciated and loved. I would like to feel comfortable doing things for myself without feeling as if I'm letting John down or, worse, losing him."

Work and Occupation   "I have worked all my life in the home: first, my father's home and now, my own home. I have taken care of children and a home since I was a young teenager. I have occasionally done some volunteer work, but very little really. There's so much to do with the children and John. What I like most about being a homemaker, or housewife, is when people like what I do for them. Sometimes, though, it feels as if the kids don't even notice. They just expect everything. John notices more. I notice all the things that never get done, especially now that I'm getting my teaching credential. I guess school is my work for the moment. It's still hard, but I like it more than I liked high school. I'm learning a lot, but it takes a lot of time and energy, and I'm way behind at home.

"I want very much to finish my certification as a teacher and to teach in an elementary school, third grade. I want to help students who have a hard time."

Friendship and Community   "I have developed some good friends recently at school. I feel that school is really a turning point for me, both for work and for having people I can talk to. My classes have helped me meet people who really seem to like me and with whom I feel really comfortable, just talking.

"Most of my friends are women, but I don't have very many friends. I maybe have one or two long-term friends, but I have shared more with college friends than I have with my long-term friends. I guess people like it that I listen pretty well. I'm interested in what people have to say. I'm not a leader by any stretch of the imagination, but I like to be a part of things.

"I think when people first meet me, they think I'm not much; but after they get to know me, they know that I'm dependable and that I care about people. I think I make a good friend, but this is new for me.

"Oh, I also know people who work around John, but we don't socialize with them much, and I don't know what they think of me. I'm not nearly as community-oriented as my mother was.

"I would like to see the friendships I have started at school really grow and develop. I would like to have some of them as fellow teachers and get to work in the same school. That would be great, to have a friend just down the hall."

Our Summary   From this information, we developed a summary of our initial impressions. The summary is written in the third person to allow Ruth to stand back from her experience and to see herself through a narrative that puts her life in context and shows its dynamic movement.

Ruth has presented herself for therapy at a potential turning point in her life. She has spent many years doing what she began preparing to do early in life. Ruth, the oldest of four children, was drafted into caring for her brother and two sisters at a young age. She used her mother as a role model of a "good homemaker" and continued her work when she married her husband, John. John and Ruth have four children, who are now adolescents. When her children became teenagers, she decided to seek work where she would continue to feel needed. Returning to school, she completed a bachelor's degree and is seeking a teacher's certificate. College and her fellow students opened a whole new world to Ruth. She began to see many new possibilities for herself, including a place in the world as a professional teacher and as a person with many more friends than she has been used to having. She is feeling both excited by the new possibilities and worried about losing the people and world she has known all her life.

Ruth feels pulled by both worlds; she is experiencing a conflict between satisfying her needs in the occupational life task and her needs in the family-intimacy life task. In one world (school), the opportunities seem limitless and exciting and full of promise, even if new and somewhat overwhelming and risky. In the other world (home), her life is safe, known, familiar, and predictable, and she knows exactly what she needs to do to succeed and to feel safe and secure. She wants both worlds to fit together, but she is not always sure how to make that happen. She also wants to perform *perfectly* in both worlds. Even though part of her knows that the demand for perfection at both home and school is impossible, she has not let herself off the hook. Mostly, she wants everyone involved to be happy with her and, above all to avoid displeasing anyone. She wants John to be happy; she wants her children to be happy; she wants her instructors to be happy; she wants her new friends to be happy; and last, and least, she wants herself to be happy. When she cannot figure out how to make it all happen, she often finds herself becoming worried, anxious, and depressed. When she doesn't have time to become worried, anxious, or depressed, she settles for dizziness, headaches, heart palpitations, sleeplessness, and other physical disturbances, which act as a message to her family and herself that she needs some rest and needs some care.

Ruth has put everyone else in life first. She comes from a family in which at least one other child achieved success easily, and she found it hard to please her mother and father. She could not guess what would make them happy, and she feared their disapproval and rejection. The family atmosphere was strict and controlled, and she found her place by caring for children and others in the way that she believed women were supposed to do. It is hard for her to put herself first at this point in life without fearing she will do something wrong, displease her husband and family, and thereby risk losing everything.

Ruth has a well-defined set of goals for therapy:

- Deal with the physical and emotional symptoms that express the conflict and demands she feels in her life.
- Find a balance between seeking what she wants and maintaining what she has.
- Get help with at least one daughter, whose rebellion acts as a constant reminder of "what can happen if Mom is not ever-present and vigilant."

- Discover what she can make of herself and her life with opportunities opening up and time running out. She is, after all, 39 years of age and "losing it" . . . fast!

Ruth's Lifestyle Assessment

The Family Constellation   During a lifestyle assessment, Ruth described her father as devoted to his work. When she was young, he was stern, and he was an authority figure in the community. He was respected and righteous. He was also cool and detached. With Ruth, he was often distant, strict, and ungiving. He was rather aloof from all of the children and insisted on respect. Jill is his favorite child; he likes her accomplishments.

With regard to discipline, he would yell at the children, or he would withdraw from a misbehaving child totally and not talk to the child for weeks on end. Ruth felt scared and, at times, disowned.

Ruth doesn't know what nationality her dad is, but she knows he is the oldest of four boys, and he came from a religious family. It was assumed early in his life that he would be a minister, and he prepared for it all his life. His family was poor, but always got by, and they were always proud.

Ruth's mother was a hard worker; she rarely complained out loud. She was very proper, always did the right thing, and was quite dignified. She was proud of her role as a minister's wife. She was self-sacrificing. She would go without so that her husband or the kids could have the things they needed. She would even give up things for herself so that people in the church could have food or clothing or shelter.

It was very important to Ruth's mother that the children maintain a good image in the church and the community. As unselfish as she could be, she was emotionally ungiving, very serious, not very happy (or so it appeared), and very strict with the children.

She was devoted to seeing that the children grew up right, but she was not personally involved in their lives unless they got in trouble. Her favorite child is Steve. He could do no wrong in her eyes. She did not want any of the children to bring shame on the family, and she wanted all of them to be hard workers.

Ruth's mother is Scots-Irish. She was also poor when she was little. She was the youngest of three girls, and she was the only one to marry. "She always told us how lucky she was to have a Christian life."

Ruth's parents have a stiff and formal relationship. Very little affection was demonstrated, and they rarely laughed. They did not argue: mother stood behind whatever father said or did. Ruth wanted to make them happy, but it was not an easy task.

Ruth's paternal grandmother took an interest in her. She seemed to understand Ruth, and she would often talk to Ruth and give her good advice. She was the one who first approved of John.

Ruth's description of her siblings can be drawn as follows:

Sibling Array

Ruth (39)   Responsible, hard-working, organized, dedicated, capable, trustworthy, self-critical, undemanding, scared, unable to please either parent. I was lonely: I felt useful and needed; I wanted approval from my folks; I was a good girl, and I took care of my sister and brother.

Jill (–4)   Bright, pretty, accomplished, conforming, well-behaved. Got along with Dad; got along fairly well with Mom. Jill was the most like me; she was good and was successful at life. Things came more easily to her. She won honors at school.

Amy (–6)   Immature, demanding, the family "troublemaker"; admiring of me, hard-working, independent. In trouble with Dad, and tried to please Mom, without success. Amy was the most different from me; she seemed irresponsible by comparison.

Steve (–9)   Pampered, overprotected, in trouble with Dad but protected by Mom. Got Mom's attention. Sensitive, argumentative with me, not too accomplished. Steve was also different from me; in Mom he found a shelter from life.

In Ruth's childhood neighborhood, Ruth and her siblings were mostly absent; she didn't play much. Children from church were sometimes invited to the house, but mostly siblings worked or played with one another, if at all. She didn't have any real friends of either sex: just her brother and sisters.

Ruth was expected to do well in school. It was hard for her. She had to work at it all the time. Even when she worked hard, she sometimes didn't do very well. Math and sciences were the hardest for her. English and history were her best subjects. She liked to read, and that helped. She would get so nervous when she was doing math or science that she couldn't concentrate. The teachers generally liked her (with one or two exceptions), but they always felt that she was not living up to her potential, and that's what they told her parents. She didn't socialize with other kids much. She was quiet and kept to herself. Other kids thought she was "weird."

When Ruth was 6 years old, she reports: "My father caught me 'playing doctor' with an 8-year-old boy. He lectured me and refused to speak to me for weeks. I felt guilty and ashamed." Ruth reached adolescence with minimal information from her mother, father, or peers. She remembers being scared at 12 when menarche occurred. "I didn't know what was happening. My mother gave me the things I needed and a booklet to read." She was not allowed to date until she completed high school; at age 19 she married the first person she dated. "I was lucky to find a good man. All I knew was my mother's version of how to be a good homemaker."

From Ruth's lifestyle information, we were able to co-construct with Ruth a narrative summary of the meaning she attached to her family constellation and family life. This summary constitutes a retelling of Ruth's life story with an emphasis on the meaning and patterns associated with her current life experiences.[5]

Our Summary   Ruth is the oldest of four children, raised in a family where hard work and perfection were the expected standard; unfortunately, as she learned early in life, hard work was no guarantee that perfection could be achieved. Even after a huge effort, the slightest mistake could lead to a rebuke or a rejection that was deeply felt, leaving her lonely, cautious, and scared. Thus, Ruth approaches life with an emphasis on seeking to always do the "right" thing as she perceives others to define it while guarding against doing anything wrong, displeasing others and thereby inviting their rejection and loss of affection.

Her father set a masculine guiding line that was characterized by a harsh, strict, stern, and angry persona; his every stance was authoritarian, critical, and religiously perfectionistic. Indeed, her father was such a dominant authority in her life that it was easy for her to confuse God-fearing with father-fearing. Like a female version of Cain in the Bible, she was locked in a struggle for approval in which she would never be good enough and her sister Jill could do no wrong. The struggle to please her father gradually settled into strategies for avoiding his displeasure, and fear became the operative motivator in her life.

Ruth's mother set a feminine guiding line that was characterized by a serious devotion to principle, righteousness, duty, and her husband. Her behavior suggested that life was filled with hard work and sacrifice, a burden that women should suffer quietly, with dignity, and without complaint. Although she provided for the children's physical and spiritual needs, she did little to provide relief from the harsh stance that her husband took in the world.

Only Ruth's grandmother provided her with a different role model for womanhood. She demonstrated that it was possible for women to be interested in, involved with, and caring toward others.

The family atmosphere was characterized by formality and stiffness, a rigid consistency and discipline in which frivolity and, indeed, happiness were out of place. The family values included were hard work, perfectionism, and a belief that appearances were extremely important. No crack in the architecture could be tolerated.

Under her father's regime, Ruth felt it was impossible for her to match the privilege and talent that was extended to Jill, her younger sister by 4 years. Jill was the accomplished, approved of, and rewarded child; the combination of Ruth's mistakes and Jill's favored position rendered mythical the notion that hard work was its own reward—or even that it would ultimately pay off. Ruth formed an alliance with Amy, an equally disfavored and hard-working sibling; they were the children who would struggle through a hard life together. Amy looked up to Ruth, but she was not about to suffer her father's tyranny quietly or respectfully. Her rebellion became the only sure way she had to establish her independence.

In her father's kingdom the subservient queen birthed a prince, who stole her heart. Because no mere boy could hope to compete with the stature of the king, Steve entered into and accepted the protection of the queen. He became both spoiled and helpless in her care. In this way he avoided the family demands for hard work and perfectionism while putting the most powerful of the family members in his service.

Ruth's favorite childhood story, *Cinderella,* provides further insight into her lifestyle themes and can be used as a metaphor in therapy to focus on her rules of interaction, the basic convictions underlying her presenting issue. Like Cinderella, Ruth hoped that hard work, a pleasing personality, and patience would one day be rewarded with a prince who would discover her true beauty behind the ashes of a hard life. She lived in fear and captivity, serving the needs of others but longing to be free to fly. When the first prince came along, Ruth slipped on the slipper and moved out. Leaving with a prince is not the same as flying free, however, and she is still searching for a way to get off the ground but fearful that by doing so the prince will become the rejecting stepmother as was her father.

In a world where men are powerful and women serve, her hope of becoming a minister, strong and powerful like her father, seems an unrealistic fantasy. To teach in an elementary school, however, offers her a position of significance in the lives of young people entrusted to her care and her own special world not too far from the safety of the castle of the "good" prince. Even a good prince can become displeased: Ruth's approval rating has always been and is now only as good as her last accomplished deed and as fleeting as her next discovered error. Entry into a new and different world must be balanced with the needs and demands of the old; she senses that it would not do for her to risk what is known and familiar in pursuit of what is unknown, risky, and possibly reserved only for men or the women favored by them.

Record of Early Recollections   Within an Adlerian lifestyle assessment, early recollections function as a projective technique. Each individual recounts 6 to 12 early memories that are chosen by the person to reflect images of self, others, the world and, sometimes, ethical convictions. Early recollections are like little stories with morals (as in Aesop's fables) that serve as meaning-markers in the person's life. As such, early memories always reveal more about the person in the present than they do about the person's past. Indeed, sometimes an early memory is "real" to the person but can easily be shown to be historically inaccurate or even impossible.

To be useful as a projective device, our directions must remain minimal and neutral. We start by asking Ruth to think back to when she was very little (before the age of 9) and to tell us one thing that happened one time. In Ruth's interview, she is able to provide just five early recollections.

1. **Age 3.** "I remember my father yelling at me and then putting me in another room because I was crying. I don't remember why I was crying, but I know I was scared, and after he shouted, I was petrified."
   Most vivid moment: father yelling
   Feeling: scared, petrified

2. **Age 4.** "I was in church, talking with a boy. My mother gave me dirty looks, and my father, who was conducting the service, gave me a stern lecture when we got home."

> *Most vivid moment:* the looks parents gave me
> *Feeling:* scared and confused

3. **Age 6.** "An 8-year-old neighbor boy and I had our clothes off and were 'playing doctor' when my father caught us in my bedroom. He sent the boy home and then told me in a cold and solemn voice that what I had done was very wrong. He did not speak to me for weeks, and I remember feeling very dirty and guilty."

> *Most vivid moment:* being caught by my father
> *Feeling:* scared, "bad," and guilty

4. **Age 7.** "I remember my second-grade teacher saying that I was not doing well in school and that I was going to get a bad report card. I tried so hard to do well because I didn't want to bring home bad grades. This teacher didn't like me very much, and I couldn't understand what I had done wrong. I thought I was trying my best. I was scared."

> *Most vivid moment:* the teacher telling me I was getting a bad report card
> *Feeling:* scared

5. **Age 8.** "I was in a church play, and I worked for months memorizing my lines. I thought I had them down perfect. My parents came to the play, and for a time I was doing fine, and I was hoping they would like my performance. Then toward the end I forgot to come in when I was supposed to, and the director had to cue me. My mistake was apparent to my father who later commented that I had spoiled a rather good performance by my lack of attention. I remember feeling sad and disappointed, because I had so hoped that they would be pleased. And I don't recall my mother saying anything about the play."

> *Most vivid moment:* father commenting on my mistake
> *Feeling:* embarrassed

Our Summary   These memories represent Ruth's convictions as she is now, so we summarize her position and stance in the first person. In many ways, the summary expresses Ruth's commentary on her life experiences.

"I live in a man's world that is often harsh, uncaring, and frightening. Helplessness and emotion will not be tolerated in this world and will lead to being separated from it. In a man's world women must not speak, not even to other men. The rebuke of authority is both immediate and frightening. Men and their world are never available to women. A woman is wrong to want to know about men or explore them. Dabbling in a man's world can lead to banishment and total exile.

"Only achievement counts in the real world. No amount of hard work can make up for a lack of performance. No amount of pleasing can win over someone who is against you. Significant people always find out about mistakes: the most important people always seem to be present when a lack of attention leads to an error that ruins even a good effort. To err in the real world is embarrassingly human; to forgive is against policy."

From this summary, we fashion this list of basic convictions that serve as interfering ideas in Ruth's quest for a rich and fulfilling life:

- The power and importance of men are exaggerated, as is her fear of their disapproval. Pleasing seems to her the best route to safety in a man's world, but it leaves her unsure of her own identity and in constant fear of rejection.
- The inevitability of mistakes and failure is exaggerated and feared; the slightest human errors are to be avoided: 100% is passing, 99% is the start of creeping failure.
- Doing the right thing, being "good," is required just to survive; doing the wrong thing signals impending doom: caution is always warranted in an unpredictable world.
- Murphy's Law governs: What can go wrong will go wrong.
- Hard work is always demanded but will not necessarily produce the desired results or achievements.

Adlerian Brief Therapy With Ruth

Adlerian counseling has evolved substantially over the last six decades since Adler's death in 1937. Many different models have borrowed from Adler's Individual Psychology concepts and have been integrated with Adlerian therapy. Even under the umbrella of Adlerian psychotherapy, different approaches to clinical practice currently coexist. Despite differences in style, all Adlerians share a focus on understanding lifestyle, the individual's socially constructed pattern of living, and a commitment to holistic, systemic, and teleological assessments and treatment. We have successfully applied the Adlerian brief therapy model to our work with individuals, couples, and families.[6]

Five points define our therapeutic process: (a) time limitation, (b) focus, (c) counselor directiveness and optimism, (d) symptoms as solutions, and (e) the assignment of behavioral tasks. The two of us differ to some extent on the relative emphases that should be given to a definitive time limitation, counselor directiveness, and the assignment of behavioral tasks. We both agree, however, that *focused work* will tend to keep therapy brief, that nonorganic *symptoms are the client's solution* to a personal problem, and that *motivation modification* is the goal when both directive interventions and behavioral tasks are used.

Integrating a time limitation into therapy reflects the reality that we meet people in the middle of their lives, and we will say "goodbye" to them in the middle of their lives. We enter into a contract with our clients that suggests we can make a difference in each other's lives in a relatively short period of time. There is optimism in the contract, a belief in the client's ability to change, grow, and improve her or his life situation. For the time we will be meeting, our focus is on being fully present for our clients. While we do not always define exactly the number and duration of sessions with a client, when we do, we are able to work more quickly, staying focused on desired outcomes.

Clarity of focus and practice is the central element that limits time in therapy. For the Adlerian brief therapist, two goals guide every session. First, the therapist seeks to develop a systemic, holistic understanding of the person in treatment. This is most often accomplished by some form of formal or informal lifestyle assessment process that seeks to elicit individual patterns and motivations and the rules of interaction that govern the individual's idiosyncratic patterns of perceiving, behaving, and coping. Second, the therapist wants to know what the individual wants from therapy: Toward what goals will they work together? Effective work requires that the therapist balance both goals. We ask ourselves recurrently: "Where are we going . . . and with whom?"

The process within sessions often resembles a meeting of minds and hearts. While both of us (Jim and Bill) recognize that "therapeutic relationship" and "client change" are intimately connected, Jim's focus emphasizes relational qualities in therapy (PACE) whereas Bill tends to organize his work around strategies for change (BURN). For a look at how the two of us think about therapist-client interactions, see Table 3-1.

Human beings have goals. They act purposefully and in goal-motivated patterns based on the interpretations they make about self, others, and life (their worldviews). A teleological understanding "makes sense" out of symptoms, patterns of behavior, feelings, convictions, values, and beliefs. A teleological orientation illuminates the client's present and intended future: today and the rest of our lives. In this sense, the past is merely a remembered (and often revised) context generated by the person in support of current goals and purposes. Real change, second-order change, always follows from some form of motivation modification, a reorientation of client interpretations regarding the circumstances that brought him or her to therapy.

Adlerian brief therapists want to co-develop (with clients) functional solutions, expand limited choices, and create new possibilities. We want to activate underutilized resources—both internal and external. Actually, it is often possible to accomplish these therapeutic goals in a single session. Whether in one session or 12, making a difference in clients' lives requires the therapist to pay attention to the flow of therapy as well as to the unique understandings that arise from that therapy.

The Flow of Adlerian Brief Therapy

Figure 3-1 presents a structural map for the flow of therapy that we adapted from Dreikurs's holistic approach to psychotherapy.[7] We use the word *flow* to indicate a fluid and dynamic movement, one that eschews mechanistic steps or stages. Indeed, there is nothing in the arrangement of the flow of the session that cannot be rearranged to fit the needs of the client or the therapy session.

TABLE 3-1   Two Levels of Focus Within Adlerian Brief Therapy

Jim's Focus	Bill's Focus
Jim likes to bring his attention to the rhythm of the therapeutic experience. This reflects his work with Virginia Satir and Erv and Miriam Polster and a focus on experiential therapy.	Bill first listens to the "how" of behavior, especially what people do and what they feel. Next, Bill listens for the "what for," or the purpose or functions of behavior. Finally, Bill works with the client to reveal the "whys" of behavior and the rules of interaction.
Purpose: Since every interaction, as well as every thought, feeling, and behavior, has a purpose, what is the purpose of what is happening right at this moment in therapy? What motivates the patterns that make up the person's life? What purpose do feelings serve? What meaning is attached to living?	*Behavior redescription:* Clients, and counselors, often adopt the language of pathology, a language of possession: for example, "I am bipolar." "I have an anxiety disorder." By adopting a language of use, we move the client to focusing on behavioral interactions. We ask: When was the last time this occurred? What did you do? How did you feel? Who else was affected? What did they do? How did you respond?
Awareness: Awareness is the alpha and omega of experience. What awareness does the client enjoy? What experiences are blocked from client awareness? What meaning is lost? What purpose is served? How is awareness related to contact with others?	*Underlying rules:* Careful attention to the client's answers opens an avenue to the purpose(s) that symptoms may serve. The sequence of behaviors and interactions also begins to suggest the rules the person uses to function in life, to cope, and to maintain stability.
Contact: What is the quality of contact between the therapist and the client? What kind of contact does the client make with others in her or his life, with the environment, and with oneself? What purpose is served by the contacts the client makes? How can contact augment client awareness? Which awarenesses would augment contact?	*Reorientation:* The therapist seeks a cognitive shift in the client's understanding of self and symptoms. Adlerians use tentative disclosures of purpose, reframing of rules and experience, relabeling concepts, paradox, and even humor. The therapist seeks to shift the client's "private logic" to common sense.
Experience: What is the quality of life experience the person brings to therapy? Is it a thin life or one thick with meaning? Is it a fascinating or interesting life story? What experience exists between therapist and client? Would an experiment (only one form of experience) lead to a fuller appreciation of life and other experiences available to the person?	*New behavioral rituals:* Real change takes place *between* sessions, not *in* sessions. Rituals are regular, repeated actions that reaffirm and maintain new possibilities. We ask: What is the client going to do? What strategies and interventions will encourage the client to take "real" steps in his or her own behalf? How can the therapist use self to align with and augment client functioning?

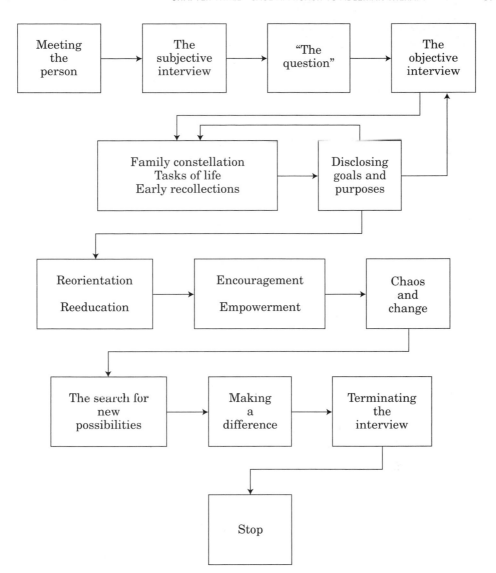

FIGURE 3-1   The Flow of Adlerian Brief Therapy

Meeting the Person   The first contact we have with a client may be by phone or through a referral. We recognize that coming to therapy can be challenging, and we want to facilitate a smooth transition. We want the client to feel welcome. While client concerns are often rehearsed and tend to surface quickly, Adlerian brief therapists focus initially on the *client-as-a-person*. Through mutual respect, genuine interest, and even fascination, we hope the client will experience our full presence. This presence, real contact with the client, is supported even in the first few minutes of therapy by the use of our five senses. What the therapist sees, hears, and experiences, perhaps in the touch of a handshake, is especially important.

The Subjective Interview   Being fully present provides the client with the support that is needed to tell her or his unique story. Empathic listening, interest, and fascination enable the therapist to follow the client closely, staying with the next most interesting question or development. This concentration on *the next* brings focus to the interview and encourages a depth of disclosure and understanding between counselor and client. A client who can clearly articulate what is important to her or him has already begun to take some control of self and life. Toward the end of this part of the interview, Adlerian brief therapists ask: "Is there anything else you feel I should know to understand you and your concerns?"

During the subjective interview, motivational and behavioral patterns in the person's life begin to emerge. At first tentatively, Adlerian counselors begin to hypothesize about what works for the client. How do the patterns in a person's life reflect the individual's rules of interaction? How do the patterns and rules directly contribute to maintaining the concerns that are being identified? And in what way might the stated concerns actually be the person's best current solution to life's demands?

"The Question"   Based on Dreikurs's[8] formulation of "The Question," Adlerians attempt to differentiate organic symptoms or problems from ones that are psychogenic. Initially phrased by Adler[9] and later reframed by Dreikurs, The Question is: "What would you be doing, what would change, if you didn't have these symptoms or problems?" or "How would your life be different if you didn't have these issues, concerns, or problems?" When the answer is: "Nothing would be different, except the symptoms would be gone," then we suspect the problem is probably physiological—even if it is masquerading as a psychological complaint. When the client indicates that life, work, friendships, or family would improve, we immediately suspect that the problem serves the purpose of helping the client retreat from the challenge of these life tasks.

When Ruth was asked "The Question," she said she would be happy at home and at work. She would have a job as an elementary school teacher and would work with a third-grade class. She would have energy for her children's activities and those of her husband, and she would see her family more often. Her answer suggests that she lives in doubt about her worth and value, and she fears possible failure and disapproval when she faces the test of her worth in the real world. Can she make it in the world of work as an elementary school teacher? Does she have a right to work and also be happy at home? Can she ever do enough for her husband and children to feel really loved by them? When Ruth faces these questions, she begins to doubt herself and her abilities, and her symptoms enable her to retreat from the answers she most fears.

The Objective Interview   The objective interview is essentially a lifestyle assessment of the client. We want to create a holistic picture of the individual, including information about when the problem or concern started, precipitating events, medical history, present or past medications, social history, and the reasons the person is seeking therapy. The most important aspects of the objective interview, however, started with the early systemic work of Adler: the development of narratives related to family constellation; the life tasks of friendships, occupation, and intimacy; and early recollections.

The concepts of *family constellation,* the *tasks of life,* and *early recollections* are part of the practice of Adlerian therapy. Each of these areas of investigation will produce life stories that, taken together, yield patterns of living and coping: they "make sense" of the client's concerns. Listening to the client's interpretation of the place she or he holds in the family also helps us understand the client's overall sense of place in the world. The individual's experience of life's demands or tasks allows us to uncover client strengths, perceived weaknesses, and most important, coping styles. Early recollections reveal the person's convictions about self, others, life, the world and, sometimes, even ethics. They also can reveal the client's stance in relation to the therapeutic relationship and the therapist.

Disclosing Goals and Purposes   Adlerians introduce goals and purposes as part of a meaningful dialogue about symptoms, behaviors, feelings, values, and convictions. Most goals and purposes function out of the client's awareness at a nonconscious level. To make goals conscious and explicit is to already change client process. Behavior is enacted in social engagements, and assessing the results of social interactions is the surest way to formulate a hypothesis or guess about an individual's motivation. When such disclosures follow from a clarity of focus obtained in the subjective and objective interviews, they often elicit a recognition reflex in the person.

Reorientation and Reeducation   Adlerian therapists use the concepts of reorientation and reeducation to emphasize that treatment is an educative process; it is about helping the client to change direction, cope more effectively, and meet life with a new understanding. Rather than merely decreasing or eliminating symptoms, Adlerian brief therapy aims at augmented social-emotional competence and mental health. We want clients to have a sense of belonging and a sense of being valued in their community as an antidote to isolation and withdrawal: we want to increase community feeling and *social interest*. While we do not have specific outcomes for therapy in mind before we meet the client, we believe that some general conditions can be identified that are better for human life: to think rationally, to feel fully within the human experience, to greet the world with optimism and hope, to have courage and confidence, to make a contribution, to have a sense of humor, to have friends and to be a true friend, and to be interested in the well-being of others.

Encouragement and Empowerment   Encouragement and empowerment are the foundation for all change through therapy. Adlerian counselors believe that courage follows from a sense of empowerment and that empowerment results from rediscovering the individual's internal and external resources. The discovery of strengths gets one through the difficult times and prepares the way for new possibilities. Functional solutions and real change are the result of facing life's challenges with courage rather than in retreat.

Chaos and Change   Change is seldom easy. It requires the person to move from what is familiar and known to what is unfamiliar and unknown. Disorientation and chaos are the most common experiences one has when change happens too fast or when the requirements are overwhelming. When a client is in chaos, the therapist must remain steady and focused if she or he is to help the client refocus. Careful and often delicate, small movements are needed during this time. We remind our clients that they are not alone—and not without strengths. We hold them *only* to decisions that can be implemented immediately, leaving longer-range issues for later.

The Search for New Possibilities   New possibilities tend to emerge rather than be created. They are what follows when a tight therapeutic focus is connected to the client in what we call "the relational present": the experience of being together with the therapist. In general, client-generated possibilities are more useful than therapist-generated possibilities, because they reinforce a sense of personal strength, courage, and capability in the client. Still, when the relationship has been caring and collaborative throughout, most clients will accept therapist suggested options and prescriptions calmly and with hope.

Making a Difference   Adlerian counselors want to make a difference in the lives of their clients. In a single session, that difference may be only a small shift in understanding, a new clarity about patterns or meaning, an emotional realization, or a small experiment designed for more useful interactions. As therapists, we ask ourselves: "If I had only one session to be helpful in this person's life, what would I want to accomplish? And what would they want me to accomplish?" There is never any guarantee that a future session will occur.

Terminating the Interview   Terminating an interview session is merely an interruption of therapy. Of necessity, any therapeutic relationship, no matter how intense the involvement, is time-limited. Each session is followed by separation, the space in which clients may actually enact the new possibilities of their lives. In the beginning, these separations may be only days or a week, but over time, they will evolve into separations of months—or even years. Still, the relationship is always available and reconnection is only a phone call away. In this sense, we do brief, intermittent therapy, and we treat our therapy as a way-station in the ongoing journey through the client's life. The professional counselor–client relationship is never terminated but, rather, interrupted much like the relationship with one's physician or dentist; wherein we find ourselves returning when we require further assistance.

In the case of Ruth, the data for the initial interview and the lifestyle assessment were collected by Jim, her primary therapist. Those data were then presented to and discussed with Bill while Ruth listened and acted as a collaborating or clarifying agent to the discussion. The two therapists then generated their initial summaries, including *the pattern of basic convictions* and *the interfering ideas*. The session ended with the two therapists listening to Ruth give her initial impressions of the ideas and information contained in the summaries. Written copies of the summaries were sent to her the following day, so that she could read them before the next session.

Reviewing the Previous Session   Following this multiple therapy session, Ruth met with Jim alone. After they greeted each other, they began this discussion.

Jim: What was the last session like for you?

Ruth: I was really amazed. The summaries that you came up with seemed just like me. Then when they came in the mail, I read them, and I wondered if my family knew me as well as I feel the two of you do.

Jim: So what was it like for you to have two therapists instead of one?

Ruth: It was very interesting. I was surprised that the two of you disagree sometimes. I liked the way you disagreed and stayed friends and didn't get mad or anything. That's hard for me. I don't like to disagree with John. [*Pause*] I think I'm afraid he'll get mad at me.

Jim: What does he get mad at you about?

Ruth: I know John pretty well, I guess, and there's not much we disagree about—except my schooling.

Jim: If I were to hazard a guess based on what we learned in the lifestyle assessment, I would guess that there may be quite a lot you have not directly asked your husband—or even your children—because you were concerned about displeasing them. Does that fit you? Do you find yourself "guessing," trying to read their minds so you won't upset them?

Ruth: Yes, I know I do that a lot.

Jim: What did you notice when Bill and I disagreed?

Ruth: Well, the two of you were just fine. You just listened, and then you asked me what I thought.

Jim: Actually, I was quite pleased that you and Bill had come to an understanding that I had missed. If we were all alike in the world, there wouldn't be much use in talking, would there? Do you think John would enjoy hearing your opinion even if it was different from his?

Ruth: Maybe.

Jim: I think you would really like to know what John thinks about your lifestyle summaries, and no amount of guessing is going to be the same as really hearing from him. The worst that might happen is that he wouldn't agree with them.

Here, in a relatively early session, the therapist uses the cooperation and mutual respect modeled in therapy to encourage Ruth to take a small chance with her husband. If she actually asks John to look at her lifestyle summaries and share his opinion with her, there will be some material for the next session whatever his response or her reaction to the response may be.

A Small Reeducation During Multiple Therapy

Near the end of Ruth's counseling experience, she again meets with Bill and Jim together. This time the focus is on her value when she is engaged in meaningful work and when she is not. An early recollection is used to mark change and growth in her therapy.

Bill: Ruth, it's good to see you again. How long has it been? About 2 months or so since I last sat in with the two of you? How have things been going?

Ruth: I think our work together has been very good. We had some sessions that included John, and I really feel that he's supporting me in all of the transitions I'm making. In recent weeks, I walk away from here, and I sometimes wonder if I am doing enough in therapy. Much of what we talk about now seems so easy to me. I'm not leaving as I used to—practically exhausted and sure that I was working through a lot of stuff.

Jim: This is interesting. We haven't really talked about this before. How was it for you when you left here last time?

Ruth: Well, I think we did some good work together in that I learned something about staying with change in my life even when the going gets tough, but it was not actually hard to learn that. I used to leave here wondering if I would ever figure myself out. Last time, I felt, well, I can do what I need to do.

Bill: When I listen to Ruth, Jim, there's an idea that is repeated over and over. It's something like "Anything worth doing requires very hard work. Without the hard work, Ruth may doubt whether she is doing anything worthwhile." Did I get that right, Ruth?

Ruth [*With a look of recognition on her face*]: I think you did. That's been one of my beliefs since childhood.

Bill: Yes, it may have been, but I think we're inviting you to reconsider that notion. It may be a mistaken notion, especially now that you're older and more competent. Things do come easier to people as they gain competence.

Ruth: Maybe I have this therapy thing figured out.

Jim: My experience of you is that you have a lot of things figured out. There's been a lot of progress since you started about 9 months ago.

Bill: Let's try something—another early recollection. Ruth, see if you can think back to a time when you were very young. Something happened one time . . .

Ruth: Very young? Well, I remember something in second grade. Is that OK?

Bill: Yes, that's fine. You were about 7 or 8?

Ruth: Seven, I think. I was asked by a neighbor to help her little girl learn colors, because she was in kindergarten. Her mother had colored four squares in the driveway with chalk. I think her name was Jan, the little girl, and we played all afternoon, bouncing a ball from one color to another. Her mother later told my mother that I had made all the difference in the world.

Bill: What stands out about that story. And how did you feel?

Ruth: The look of pride on my mother's face when she told me what Jan's mother had said. I like making a difference in someone's life.

Jim: It's a great memory! There's not an ounce of hard work in it. And it's a great early recollection for a future teacher to have. Can you sense how different this memory is from the ones you reported when you first came to see us?

Ruth: I don't actually even remember the early recollections I gave you originally. Is this one different?

Bill: Very different. I was just looking at them here in your file. I think the next time you get together with Jim, you should go back and review where you were when you started and where you are now.

A change in one's early recollections is not uncommon when change has also happened in one's life. The change may not be dramatic, as in a completely new memory. Sometimes, it is a shift in emphasis: something new stands out, or the client's reaction is different than originally reported. In Ruth's new memory here she is "making a difference" in someone's life (social interest), and she is now focused more on her own competence and experiencing the appreciation of others for her work. This is a significant change in her sense of belonging and a great place for a new teacher to start.

 ## JERRY COREY'S WORK WITH RUTH FROM AN ADLERIAN PERSPECTIVE

With the detailed information about Ruth derived from the initial interview, the lifestyle assessment, and the sample therapy sessions provided by Drs. Jim Bitter and Bill Nicoll, I will continue counseling Ruth from an Adlerian orientation. In the following section, I demonstrate the Adlerian slant on working with Ruth regarding her mistaken beliefs.

Session 6 ("Cognitive Focus in Counseling") of the *CD-ROM for Integrative Counseling* illustrates Ruth's striving to live up to expectations and to measure up to perfectionistic standards. I draw upon Adlerian concepts in this particular therapy session with Ruth.

Basic Assumptions

As an Adlerian therapist I view my work with Ruth as teaching her better ways of meeting the challenges of *life tasks*. One assumption that will guide my interventions with her is that although she has been influenced by her past, she is not necessarily molded by it. This premise of self-determination leaves little room for a client to take the role of a passive victim. I assume that Ruth has the capacity to influence and create events. What is crucial is not what she was born with but what she is choosing to make of her natural endowment.

Ruth's childhood experiences are of therapeutic interest to me. They are the foundation and early context for the social factors that contributed to her psychological development. True to the Adlerian spirit, I function as a therapist on the belief that it is not her childhood experiences in themselves that are crucial; rather, it is her *attitude* toward these events. Since these early influences may have led to the development of *faulty beliefs* and assumptions in her style of life, I will explore with her what it was like at home as she was growing up. Our focus will be on understanding and assessing the structure of her family life, known as the family constellation, and her earliest recollections (both of which were reported in detail in the previous section by Drs. Bitter and Nicoll).

Because I operate from a phenomenological stance (dealing with the client's subjective perception of reality), I will want to find out how she views the major events and turning points of her life. I assume that she has created a unique style of life that helps to explain the patterns of her behavior. My attention will be on how she has developed her distinctive behaviors in the pursuit of her life goals.

Assessment of Ruth

Adlerian therapists typically use the lifestyle questionnaire in making an initial assessment of the client and in formulating the goals and directions for therapy. This questionnaire gathers information about the client's childhood experiences, especially as they relate to family influences, birth order, relationships of each of the other family members, early memories, and other relevant material that will provide clues about the social forces influencing the client's personality formation. (Drs. Bitter and Nicoll drew heavily from the framework of Adlerian lifestyle assessment, so I will not repeat that discussion here.)

Goals of Therapy

The four major goals of an Adlerian approach to therapy with Ruth correspond to the four phases of the therapeutic process. These goals are (1) to establish and maintain a good working relationship between Ruth and me as equals, (2) to provide a therapeutic climate in which she can come to understand her basic beliefs and feelings about herself, (3) to help her reach insight into her mistaken goals and self-defeating behaviors through a process of confrontation and interpretation, and (4) to assist her in developing alternative ways of thinking, feeling, and behaving by encouraging her to translate her insights into action.

Therapeutic Procedures

One of the aims of Ruth's therapy is to challenge her to take risks and make changes. Throughout the entire process *encouragement* is of the utmost importance. My assumption is that with encouragement Ruth will begin to experience her own inner resources and the power to choose for herself and to direct her own life. Encouragement begins with the therapist's acceptance and valuing of the client as he or she is; appreciating that the client is functioning in the best way possible given the client's current view of self, life and others. By now, Ruth will ideally have challenged her self-limiting assumptions and will be ready to put plans into action. Even though she may regress to old patterns at times, I will ask her to "catch herself" in this process and then continue to experiment with and practice new behavior.

Throughout her therapy I will use a variety of techniques aimed primarily at challenging her cognitions (beliefs and thinking processes). Adlerians contend that first comes thinking, then feeling, and then behaving. So, if we want to change behavior and feelings, the best way is to focus on Ruth's mistaken perceptions and faulty beliefs about life and herself. Drawing on a variety of techniques, some borrowed from other modalities, I will use confrontation, questioning, encouragement, assigning of homework, interpretation, making suggestions, and any other methods that can help her begin to change her vision of herself and her ability to behave in different ways.[10]

The Therapeutic Process

The process of Adlerian therapy can be understood by recalling some basic ideas from contemporary psychoanalytic therapy. There is a link between these two approaches, especially on the issue of looking at how early patterns are related to our present personality functioning.

Elements of the Process

Uncovering a Mistaken Belief   Ruth and I have been working together for some time, and she is beginning to see striking parallels between the role she assumed as an adolescent, by becoming the caretaker of her sisters and brother, and her contemporary role as "supermother" to her own children. She has discovered that for all of her life she has been laboring under the assumption that if she handled herself unselfishly, she would be rewarded by being acknowledged and feeling a sense of personal fulfillment. As a child she wanted to be loved, accepted, and taken care of emotionally by her father, and she has worked very hard at being the perfect wife and the devoted mother to her own children. In this way she hopes to relate to her husband so he will love and accept her. Still, she has never really felt appreciated or emotionally nurtured by him, and now she is realizing that she has built her life on a personal mythology: If people loved her, she would be worthwhile and would find happiness through her personal sacrifices.

Helping Ruth Reach Her Goals   At this time in Ruth's therapy we are exploring some other options open to her. Lately we have been talking a lot about her goals and about her vision of herself in the years to come. Ruth talks about feeling selfish that she is going to school since this means that she has less time to give at home. Ruth becomes aware that the guilt often stops her from reaching the goals that are meaningful to her. For part of our counseling session we explore some of Ruth's mistaken notions that get in the way of her doing what she would like to be doing.

Ruth: I keep feeling I shouldn't be at school and should be at home. John keeps telling me how much he and the kids miss me. If only I could stop feeling that I should be the dedicated mother and wife!

Jerry: You say that John keeps telling you how much he and the kids miss you. It's really very nice to be missed; but you interpret his meaning to be "Ruth, you should stay at home. You're displeasing everyone."

Ruth: That's true. That's what I think he believes.

Jerry: Well, it may be a mistaken notion you have. You could check it out. You could ask John what *he* means when he says he misses you. Maybe all he means is that he loves you [*Pause*], and believes that the kids love you too. You could ask.

Ruth: Asking John how he really feels about my school and career and what I'm doing is extremely hard. [*Pause*] He could tell me that he hates my school and career goals and they're threatening our relationship. But I think I am willing to give it a try.

I am hoping that Ruth, by confronting a mistaken notion, will find the courage to check a lifelong idea against a current reality. She will be scared to be sure. Without some fear there is no need for courage. A week passes, and Ruth returns.

Ruth: Guess what? John and I talked. We both cried. He was afraid that I wouldn't need him anymore. Afraid of losing *me*! Can you believe it? But he didn't want me to stop school.

Jerry: I'm very happy for you. What a treat to have a real risk work out so well for you.

Ruth: When John talked about the kids wanting their mother home, I started to feel guilty all over again. But at least now I notice those times when my guilt stops me and I'm working at not letting guilt control me.

Jerry: Good! At this point in your life, guilt is a habit. Like any habit, it takes time to change it. For now you're catching yourself when guilt is getting in your way. Eventually I suspect that you will be able to control your guilt instead of it controlling you.

From here we proceed to look at a week of Ruth's time and how she might balance personal needs with the needs of others. Planning special time for her family maintains Ruth's sense of belonging and her real need for social interest without short-circuiting the gift of time her family is giving her for school.

It also provides her with a structure by which she can devote her full attention to the tasks or people at hand: quality time in both cases.

Process Commentary My major aim in our sessions is to both encourage and challenge Ruth to consider alternative attitudes, beliefs, goals, and behaviors. By seeing the link between her mistaken beliefs and her current feelings and behaviors, she is able to consider options and change. She takes some big risks in approaching her husband. Given her history with and interpretation of men, she risks a harsh, rejecting rebuke. What she gains, however, is an increased sense of her worth and value to this important man in her life. She also gains in courage and confidence.

Once Ruth has made some new decisions and modified her goals, I teach her ways in which to challenge her own thinking. At those times when she is critical of herself, I provide encouragement. Partly because of my faith in her and my encouragement, she comes closer to experiencing her inner strength. She becomes more honest about what she is doing, and she augments her power to choose for herself instead of merely following the values she uncritically accepted as a child.

A most important ingredient of the final stages of Ruth's therapy is commitment. She is finally persuaded that if she hopes to change, she will have to set specific tasks for herself and then take concrete action. Although she attempts to live up to what she believes is the role of the "good person," she eventually develops increased tolerance for learning by trial and error, and with this she becomes better at "catching herself" when she repeats ineffective behavior.[11]

 # QUESTIONS FOR REFLECTION

1. As you review the basic features of a lifestyle assessment (family constellation, early recollections, basic convictions and interfering ideas) of Ruth, what associations do you have with your own childhood experiences?

2. As you think about your own family of origin, what most stands out for you? After reflecting on your early experiences in your family, attempt to come to some conclusions about the ways in which these experiences are operating in you life today.

3. What are three of your earliest recollections? Can you speculate on how these memories might have an impact on the person you are now and how they could be related to your future strivings?

4. List what you consider to be the major "basic mistakes" in your life. Do you have any ideas about how you developed these mistaken perceptions about yourself and about life? How do you think that they are influencing the ways in which you think, feel, and act today?

5. From what you learned about Ruth through the lifestyle assessment, what aspects of her life might you want to give the primary focus? What

themes running through her life lend themselves especially well to Adlerian therapy?

6. One of the goals of Adlerian therapy is to increase the client's social interest. Can you think of ways in which you could work with Ruth to help her attain these goals?

7. Ruth describes herself as coming from a middle-class family. They were fundamentalist Christians, and the family values involved doing right, working hard, and living in a way that would reflect well on the family. Considering this background, how well do Adlerian concepts and therapeutic procedures fit for Ruth? How would the Adlerian approach fit for her if she were an Asian American? Latina? African American? Native American?

8. What major cultural themes do you see in Ruth's case? How would you address these themes using an Adlerian framework?

 ## NOTES

1. See the following sources for a full discussion of Adlerian brief therapy: Bitter, J. R., & Nicoll, W. G. (2000). Adlerian brief therapy with individuals: Process and practice. *Journal of Individual Psychology, 56*(1), 31–44; Bitter, J. R., Christensen, O. C., Hawes, C., & Nicoll, W. G. (1998). Adlerian brief therapy with individuals, couples, and families. *Directions in Clinical and Counseling Psychology, 8*(8), 95–112; Nicoll, W., Bitter, J. R., Christensen, O. C., & Hawes, C. (2000). Adlerian brief therapy: Strategies and tactics. In J. Carlson & L. Sperry (Eds.), *Brief therapy strategies with individuals and couples* (pp. 220-247). Phoenix: Zeig/Tucker; Sonstegard, M. A., Bitter, J. R., Pelonis-Peneros, P., & Nicoll, W. G. (2001). Adlerian group psychotherapy: A brief therapy approach. *Directions in Clinical and Counseling Psychology, 11*(2), 11–24.
2. Multiple therapy is discussed in: Dreikurs, R., Shulman, B. H., & Mosak, H. H. (1982). *Multiple therapy: The use of two therapists with one patient.* Chicago: Alfred Alder Institute.
3. Based on material in Powers, R. L., & Griffith, J. (1987). *Understanding life style: The psycho-clarity process.* Chicago: AIAS; Shulman, B. H., & Mosak, H. H. (1988). *Manual for lifestyle assessment.* Muncie, IN: Accelerated Development.
4. *The Individual Psychology Client Workbook (with supplements),* by Robert L. Powers and Jane Griffith, © 1995 by the Americas Institute of Adlerian Studies, Ltd. 600 North McClurg Court, Suite 2502A, Chicago, IL 60611-3027.
5. For a more complete discussion on this topic, see Disque, J. G., & Bitter, J. R. (1998). Integrating narrative therapy with Adlerian lifestyle assessment: A case study. *Journal of Individual Psychology, 54*(4), 431–450.
6. Adlerian brief therapy is dealt with in detail in these two sources: Bitter, J. R., Christensen, O. C., Hawes, C., & Nicoll, W. G. (1998). Adlerian brief therapy with individuals, couples, and families. *Directions in Clinical and Counseling Psychology, 8*(8), 95-112; Bitter, J. R., & Nicoll, W. G. (2000). Adlerian brief therapy with individuals: Process and practice. *Journal of Individual Psychology, 56*(1), 31–44.
7. Dreikurs, R. (1997). Holistic medicine. *Individual Psychology, 53*(2), 127–205.
8. Ibid.

9. Adler, A. (1964). *Problems of neurosis: A book of case histories* (P. Mairet, Ed.). New York: Harper & Row. (Original work published 1929)

10. Here I demonstrate the Adlerian slant on working with Ruth cognitively, especially regarding her mistaken beliefs. Session 6 of the *CD-ROM for Integrative Counseling* reflects Ruth's striving to live up to expectations and to measure up to perfectionistic standards.

11. In Session 13 ("Evaluation and Termination") of the *CD-ROM for Integrative Counseling,* I encourage Ruth to make concrete plans regarding where she wants to go now that therapy has ended. For a more detailed treatment of Adlerian theory, see G. Corey (2005), *Theory and Practice of Counseling and Psychotherapy* (7th edition). The basic concepts introduced by Jim Bitter and Bill Nicoll in their assessment of Ruth are covered comprehensively in Chapter 5 (Adlerian Therapy). Also see G. Corey (2005), *Student Manual for Theory and Practice of Counseling and Psychotherapy* (7th edition). This manual contains a lifestyle assessment that you can take as an exercise. Completing the inventory will help you understand the comprehensive approach to assessment of Ruth used by Drs. Bitter and Nicoll in this chapter.

Chapter 4

Case Approach to Existential Therapy

An Existential Therapist's Perspective on Ruth

by Donald Polkinghorne, Ph.D.

Introduction

Practitioners who approach psychotherapy from an existential perspective emphasize the client's personal responsibility for creating his or her own existence. Existential thought holds that people are essentially different from the rest of nature in that they have the capacity for self-direction and voluntary behavior. People need not exist as passive objects buffeted about by instinctual needs, environmental stimuli, or social pressures. The role of the therapist working with a client in an existential crisis is to provide assistance and support for the client's efforts to take control of his or her own existence. The force of client change comes from the self's thrust toward authenticity, and the instrument of change is the client's will. The therapist is not the cause of change, nor does the therapist's use of techniques bring it about. The client's primary need during this process of self-formation is a counseling relationship with an experienced person who empathetically understands his or her struggles and supports the client's efforts to claim his or her own life. Such understanding and support require therapists who are skilled in helping clients move through obstructions to change and experiment with expressing their new power and freedom.

Initial Assessment

The sources of the distress that lead clients to seek counseling are varied. A clinical assessment lets counselor and client come to an understanding of the covert source of the manifest symptoms. Ruth's symptoms include psychosomatic complaints of dizziness, hot flashes, and difficulty in breathing. Her other symptoms are feelings of depression, crying over trivial matters, occasional feelings of panic, sporadic difficulties in leaving her house, and a general dissatisfaction with her life. Because she reported that a physician could not find an organic basis for her symptoms, I will explore other possible sources.

Given the information reported in her intake form and autobiography, I tentatively explore with Ruth the possibility that the source of her distress may be an existential crisis. Her intake form reports that "she is not really sure who or what she wants to become" and that "she would like to develop a sense of herself apart from the expectations of others." Also, the variety of symptoms she is experiencing, the time she has been experiencing them, and the lack of a specific stressor lead me initially to rule out a particular life event as the source of her distress. Focusing on existential themes is not necessarily appropriate for all clients. The purpose of my assessment work with Ruth is to determine if the source of her distress is the lack of personal meaning reflecting an existential crisis. If this is the case, counseling work with her that emphasizes life's existential issues will be therapeutically the most effective and productive.

The judgment about which possible source or sources of distress should be first explored in the therapy work is a mutual project and involves collaborative decision making by Ruth and me. Also, assessment is not finished after the initial focus of therapy is chosen; rather, we return to it repeatedly. As therapy progresses, our stress on the selected source may prove to be unproductive or incorrect, and a reexploration of the possible source may be necessary. At times, changes in the area of work may occur because the initial focus was too shallow or too deep.

Work focusing on an existential crisis as the source of manifest symptoms explores the deepest levels of Ruth's existence and requires that she reexamine the assumptions that have governed her actions and self-identity. As a result, our assessment work includes more than a judgment about the source of her symptoms; it also requires an inventory of her personal strengths, social supports, and willingness to undertake the rigors of self-examination. Ruth has demonstrated personal fortitude, by enrolling in college after years away from school, and perseverance and intelligence, in completing her degree. We have to explore whether her motivation is limited to the removal of her distressing symptoms or includes a desire to take control of her self-definition and life direction. We also have to examine what social support is available to Ruth if she undertakes the process of existential change. I try to determine if her belief that her husband and children would not support her in this change is accurate. I also explore other possible sources of support, such as close friends in whom she can confide. The purpose of this part of the assessment is to understand which areas of her personal and social strengths will be available and to tentatively determine the pace and sequence of our therapeutic work.

When employed appropriately, DSM-IV-TR descriptors serve as a shorthand vocabulary for discussing particular aggregations of symptoms, but it is inappropriate to employ these terms to classify people. Although clients seek counseling because of the distress of their symptoms, it is the *person*, with his or her unique history and interpretative meaning structure, with whom we work. Counselors working in an existential mode are not antagonistic to the use of DSM-IV-TR descriptors to designate a symptom complex as long as the integrity of the client's personhood is maintained.

From a DSM-IV-TR perspective, I believe Ruth's complex of symptoms most closely fits under the designation identity problem. Although her distress and impairment in physical functioning, her career indecision, and the deterioration of her family relationships are painful, they do not appear severe enough to be classified as a mental disorder. Thus, her symptoms are better classified as one of the "other conditions that may be a focus of clinical attention." The focus of clinical attention in her case will be on her uncertainty about her long-term goals, career choice, and friendship patterns. The source of an identity problem is often an existential crisis, and therapy that addresses a client's existential themes is most appropriate. I believe this is Ruth's situation.

Goals of Therapy

The primary goal of existential therapy is to help clients lead more authentic lives. This means assisting them in taking charge of their life, helping them choose for themselves the values and purposes that will define and guide their existence, and supporting them in actions that express these values and purposes. From my initial assessment these goals seem appropriate for Ruth's therapy.

Therapeutic Procedures

The existential method shares with other psychotherapeutic approaches the use of basic counseling skills such as attending to clients' descriptions of their experience rather than assuming to know what they have experienced, reflecting rather than distorting their meaning, and reassuring rather than judging them. This approach to counseling is not technique driven, nor can it be identified by a specific set of techniques. Different existential counselors use different procedures that they have found personally of help in enabling their clients to move through the course of authentic self-generation.

This does not mean that existential therapists are eclectic in the sense of managing a collection of techniques developed by the various theoretical schools of counseling. Also, they are not eclectic in the sense of being nontheoretical and guided by the pragmatic criterion of "doing whatever works to relieve the symptom." The various techniques existential therapists use are chosen to serve the goals of existential therapy.

The most important therapeutic procedure in existential counseling is developing an authentic relationship in which therapist and client are fully present to each other without the protective shields of scripted roles and social mandates. In addition to serving as a guide in establishing this special kind of relationship, the existential therapist uses a wide variety of other procedures in working with clients. Most of these fall under the rubric of *talk therapy*, including (1) questioning; (2) interpretation—for example, using an existential term to name a feeling the client is experiencing; (3) reframing—for example, redescribing a client's statement "I can't do that because a friend would not approve" as "I choose to give responsibility and control of my actions to my friend"; (4) confronting or challenging; and (5) supportive encouragement.

An array of other procedures are available to existential therapists. I sometimes ask clients to create imaginative scenarios. For example, I ask them to imagine alternative actions they could have taken in a situation and then explore what responses another person might have made and consider how they would have felt if the imagined action had been undertaken. I also ask clients to report particularly impressive dreams. In addition, I make use of rehearsals, or role playing, and homework assignments. Finally, because movement toward an authentic life can be confusing to the client's family, and because the understanding and support of family members can make an important contribution to the person's progress in therapy, I often ask clients if I could include the spouse or other loved ones in a meeting.

These examples are drawn from my work with clients and are representative only of my personal style. They are not necessarily used by other counselors who do existential therapy. The general purpose of such procedures is to help clients reflect on their experiences and achieve greater self-knowledge. The particular purpose is to help clients achieve insight into the sources of authority that stand behind their self-definition and values.

The Therapeutic Process

Ruth comes for counseling after 2 years of confusion, depression, neurotic anxiety, inability to sleep, and a range of psychosomatic complaints. An actual therapeutic process does not move smoothly through a sequence of steps to its conclusion. Rather, it has stops and starts and returns to previously worked-through areas and then goes forward again to further steps. Nevertheless, there is a general developmental sequence through which existential therapy advances. Sufficient progress in one area of concern lays the groundwork for developments in the next area. The sequence through which the sessions usually progress is (1) establishing a therapeutic relationship, (2) identifying the problem and setting the therapeutic goal, (3) analyzing the existential source of the symptoms, (4) developing a commitment to create an existentially authentic life, and (5) manifesting an authentic existence.

Elements of the Process
Establishing a Therapeutic Relationship   The first step in existential therapy, as it is in most counseling approaches, is to establish a therapeutic alliance in which clients experience the therapist as someone who empathetically understands their distress and accepts them as a person. In the first sessions I expect Ruth to test my responses to disclosures she offers to determine how safe it is for her to reveal "darker" fears and desires. I resist moving through this

"check-out" beginning phase too quickly. She needs enough experience with me as a person to know that she can disclose the parts of her self (such as her "selfishness") that she has learned are unacceptable and that have produced withdrawal and condemnation from others. Before she can venture into the deeper layers of her self, she needs to accept that the relationship with me is different from the ones she has previously experienced; I am not her father and will not respond to her as he has. In the relationship we are creating, it will be safe for her to experiment with new behavior and self-definitions; I will not abandon her if she displeases me. I also need to convey that I support her impulse to make changes in her life and will use my experience to assist her in accomplishing these changes. During the initial sessions, I relate that her journey will be a difficult one and that there will be periods when the struggle no longer seems worth it; I am, however, committed for the long run and will see it through with her.

In existential therapy the therapeutic relationship becomes a model of the authentic relationships Ruth will be able to establish with her family members as she takes control of her life. There are no "magic words" that I can speak to create a therapeutic relationship. An authentic relationship is the prerequisite resource for work on existential issues. Attending to its development and maintenance will occupy my work with Ruth throughout our time together. It is not something that can be built and then forgotten. We will have to return repeatedly to deal with issues that might erode the special type of therapeutic encounter we have developed. I expect that my content work with Ruth will follow the order that generally occurs in existential therapy. The work in the first phase, identifying the problem and setting the therapeutic goal, overlays the period of the initial development of the therapeutic relationship and provides the content of our discussions during the time in which the relationship is growing.

Identifying the Problem and Setting the Therapeutic Goal   I begin by asking Ruth to recount the distress she is feeling and to describe what she hopes to accomplish in our therapeutic work. I use this time to appraise my initial assessment, which was based on her intake form and autobiographical statement. Although her subsequent life events may have pushed new concerns to the forefront, I assume that the basic issues in her life have not changed much. The concerns I expect her to report remain those of feeling lost, stuck, and confused about the direction of her life. Her hope is that therapy will help her find the right direction for her life and get her started moving in that direction.

I also expect that she is continuing to experience a variety of manifest psychosomatic symptoms. I explore with her the severity of these neurotic symptoms. I want to determine whether she is so distraught or depressed that she is not able to begin the existential tasks of reflective self-exploration. If her symptoms are too severe, we will postpone the existential work until their intensity is lessened. If it is necessary to address her symptoms directly before moving on, I will instruct her in methods for anxiety reduction and, if I judge it to be necessary, will refer her for possible prescription of psychiatric medications. I use her demeanor in the sessions and her descriptions of her symptoms to judge her capacity to begin the existential therapy. If it appears that the symptoms are not so severe as to limit her performance outside therapy significantly, I do not want to suppress, disguise, deny, or mute her feelings with medications. She needs to have access to her feelings for the reflective work of existential therapy to be effective.

The first move in this portion of the therapy is for me to suggest an interpretation of the reason she is experiencing her symptoms. The context and manner in which I propose the interpretation is crucial. Before employing this interpretative move in the therapy, I wait until Ruth is signaling the question "Why am I feeling this way?" I do not say merely, "Your problem is that you're in an existential crisis and need to take charge of your life." I approach the interpretation as a process that begins as a soft and tentative suggestion from me:

Therapist: Other clients I've worked with who had similar concerns and symptoms found that they were experiencing a developmental crisis in which the ways they behaved in the past were no longer satisfying.

Assuming that Ruth comes to the recognition that her "old" self is no longer working for her, I introduce the idea that our therapeutic task is to build a "new" self that will not produce the symptoms that are part of her present life. I explain that other clients have found that constructing a new self is a difficult task and have drawn on their reserves of strength and courage. I explain that the therapeutic journey will take up to a year of work. During this portion of the therapy we are negotiating an explicit goal for our work together. If she agrees to work with me toward this existential goal, I describe the phases through which therapy will move. I ask her to consider before our next meeting whether she wants to commit herself to this goal. This will be a crucial session, in which we make an explicit agreement to proceed with the phases of the existential work. This agreement will serve as the context and backdrop for our sessions. We will recall this commitment and the agreed-on destination many times during the succeeding sessions.

Analyzing the Existential Source of the Symptoms   Having recognized that the old way of being is no longer working and that the goal of our work together is to build a new self, Ruth begins the specific existential portion of her therapy. I start by asking her to talk about her experience of herself. I ask her to explore what things she does that make her feel guilty and to recall when she has done things she disliked because it was proper for a person like her to do them. We gradually construct a picture of the values and rules Ruth has used up to this time to guide her actions.

Therapist: Why do you do things that you feel you don't want to do? Why did you rush home to prepare the family's meal when you wanted to stay at school and attend a special lecture?

I want Ruth to become aware of and be able to describe the content of the expectations that have controlled her life. After developing an explicit awareness of these commands, we move to a discussion of the extent of their power. Ruth recognizes that these expectations have operated in a forceful way in her life, producing compliant and obedient behavior. I ask her to consider their power to control her behavior when she continues to perform as a "good mother" and "good wife" even though this behavior is no longer consistent with what she wants to do. In our work in this phase I emphasize that we are not judging the "goodness" or "badness" of the expectations that have been part of her self; rather, we are concentrating on becoming aware of what the expectations were and of the extent of their power over her. By making judgments at this time about her internalized commands, I may prompt Ruth into defensive diversions such as this:

Ruth: Yes, but being a good wife is appropriate; are you saying I should be a bad wife?

After this analysis of the expectations that have guided Ruth's behavior, I ask her to consider the source of these expectations:

Therapist: Where do you think you got these ideas about how you should behave? How did you come to hold the idea that for you to be a good person you had to do these things?

I propose that for most people these ideas originate with their parents. This is the occasion for us to explore her childhood relations with her parents. I ask her to link her present notions of the proper way to behave with the memories she has of edicts given by her parents. I ask her to recollect salient incidents in her childhood that were particularly formative.

We focus on the relationship with her minister father. She has described him as being especially forceful in molding her values and implanting an image of the kind of person she was to be. I ask her to consider her vulnerability as a child to her father's criticisms and her need to become the kind of person he wanted her to be. I urge her to reexperience the feelings she had when he expressed his scorn and disapproval and then withdrew from her because she hadn't done what he wanted. She is asked to return imaginatively to the situation of certain remembered events—for example, the time she was caught by her father "playing doctor," and the time she took over caring for her brother and sisters to earn her parents' acceptance. Re-creating and reexperiencing these powerful childhood experiences may bring forth deep emotional responses from Ruth, and I need to be accepting and supportive of her during these sometimes painful and sorrowful moments.

The purpose of these imaginative re-creations and any cathartic experiences they bring is for Ruth to gain some emotional distance from these formative childhood experiences. This distance opens these experiences to reflective analysis, and the analysis allows her to recognize that the directives that have governed her behavior have their origin in her childhood efforts to gain her parents' acceptance. They also allow her to recognize that these directives continue to control her life and that the criteria she uses to judge her worth are powerful remnants of her parents' criteria.

We pause in the therapy to tease out the details of the ideas she uses to decide what to do and to judge her "goodness" or "badness." We consider the positive and negative ideals that motivate her behavior. On the positive side we explore the ramifications of what it means for her to be a "good girl" and a "good wife," and we consider what is behind her drive to perform like a "superwoman." She describes a "good girl" in terms that are consistent with her father's conservative values and with her mother's belief in the appropriateness of the gender-based, socially mandated role of a housewife. On the negative side we investigate her notion of "being selfish" and the "badness" connected to this notion:

Ruth: People who do what they want to are selfish, and selfish people come to a bad end. If I do what I want, my husband and children will no longer love me, and they'll probably abandon me.

Next, the therapy moves to a discussion about Ruth's success in living up to these ideals. I ask her to recognize the advantage to her of having clear ideas about how she should behave and which directions her life should take. I want her to acknowledge that she has done well in fulfilling the expectations that have guided her life: her career choice, her parenting efforts, and her sexual behavior have all fulfilled the images she had about who she should be. I point out to her that some people lose the clarity of their life direction during the turmoil of adolescence. She, however, seems to have retained into adulthood the images she first adopted in her childhood. I ask her to reflect on any rebellious efforts during her adolescence and on her decision to marry at a relatively young age to the first boy she dated. We are trying to uncover whether she made any tentative moves toward new possibilities and different directions for her life. The purpose of this part of the therapeutic work is to deepen Ruth's understanding of the early development of her self-image and the reasons for its resiliency and potency in controlling her life. We are also trying to locate any previous attempts to question the adequacy of these controlling ideas.

In this phase of therapy, we focus on the more contemporary events in Ruth's life and the crisis she has been experiencing. I offer the interpretation that she is undergoing new growth as a person and that the ideals that have controlled her life are becoming constricting and suffocating. I suggest that these ideals have served her as a protective garment sheltering her from the uncertainty of what she should do with her life. In recent years the garment has started to unravel, and it is no longer sufficient to protect her. The process of unraveling was begun through the pull of the inevitable events of her personal existence: The esteem she had received from her children was disrupted by their adolescence, her role of mother was ending as the children were soon to leave home, her physical attractiveness was waning, and her 39th birthday brought her to a stage of life in which she recognized her vulnerability to death. I introduce the terms old self and new self at this time to provide a language for us to use to distinguish the self she has been from the self she can become.

I ask Ruth to describe her decision to go to college and to consider a career as a teacher. I want to learn if this decision was merely a continuation of her old self-directions and was an instance of being a "good girl" or if it was the beginning of the move to break away from the constraints of her old self-images. Because of the significance she gave in her intake interview to her experience in her counseling course, I ask her to describe the insights she gained in the course. I suspect that this course was a catalyst in beginning or accelerating the unraveling of her old self. At this time I suggest to her that in her present condition her old self is no longer intact and powerful enough to give clear direction to her life, and she has no new vision of self to replace the old. She is in between selves.

I introduce the idea of existential guilt, proposing that the feeling of emptiness she is experiencing is a call to take charge of her life and to choose a new self that incorporates what she wants to be. I concede the powerful pull she is experiencing to put things back together as they were before—that is, to reinstate the stable relationship she had with her old self before her life events called this relationship into question. She seems, however, to accept that she cannot easily return to her old self; that is, she can't put the broken old self back together. I also admit the attractiveness of having me provide her with a substitute set of directions. I propose that these choices will not eliminate her feelings of lack of control; that is, she will continue to experience existential guilt. I help her understand that her existential guilt is a reminder that she cannot continue to avoid the obligation to decide what a worthy life will be for her and to begin to form her life in that direction.

I do not pass over the difficulty of change and grant that fear accompanies any attempt at personal change. I ask Ruth to share her fears about moving on to a new self. She has expressed various concerns about making changes in her life. She has also said that she is afraid she will make the wrong decisions and that she may discover there is nothing inside her. I need to communicate that I understand the power and reality of these fears but that I am also aware of her strengths and the courage she has shown in returning to school and in the reflective work of therapy. I need her to accept that I will be with her and provide support if she decides to continue with our journey. This is a time to review and renew the therapeutic goal of self-creation that we decided on at the beginning of therapy.

Up to this point in our work together, Ruth has achieved some clarity about the reasons for her present condition and a readiness to move to the constructive work of therapy—the construction of her new self. What previously operated covertly in her life has been brought into awareness, and she has gained some freedom from the control of the old self.

Reconstruction of the Self   The task for this phase of the therapy will be for Ruth to begin deciding what kind of life she will live in the future. Existential thought maintains that the authentic self is the consequence of a process of creativity, not of discovery. The authentic self is a personal construction that is the result of a person's conscious choice of values and purposes. Existentialism holds that living authentically means being true to one's own evaluation of what is a worthy existence.

In moving into this phase of therapy, I have to help Ruth recognize and understand the feelings of existential anxiety that appear when she becomes aware that she is responsible for deciding who she will be. When she fully realizes that she need not continue to be her old self and is free to decide what she wants to become, she begins to experience the unease of floating without being tied down by the guidelines of parental expectations and social requirements. I need to help her recognize the difference between these new feelings, which accompany her experience of open possibilities, and her previous feelings, which accompanied her experience of closed possibilities. Before, she felt tied down and afraid of not beginning "to live before it is too late." Now, she feels responsible to act without required guidelines. I help her accept the light-headedness of existential anxiety and support her in not prematurely shutting down her self-creative process. A method for avoiding responsibility for one's own existence is to give control over it to some other person or to adopt a mandated social script.

The next step for Ruth and me is the actual work of self-reconstruction. I ask her to imagine herself on her deathbed, looking back at what she has done with her life, to assist her in discerning what kind of life she considers worthwhile and meaningful for her. I ask her to create several scenarios of what she wants to be like and wants to be doing in 5 years, and I ask her to decide which ones she most wants to have happen. We examine the implied values of these choices to develop options for her consideration. These exercises lead to asking Ruth to decide tentatively what direction she wants to pursue in her life and whether such a direction will be vital and ultimately valuable for her. I remind her that one of the options she can consider is a life direction that retains the values that are part of her old self. The difference, however, is that these values will now be ones she has freely chosen, not ones she adopted out of fear of rejection and abandonment. Whatever directions she chooses, they need to be those to which she can commit herself and devote her life.

After Ruth makes some first attempts at deciding the values and purposes that will define her new self, we begin an exploration of the implications of these choices. Because her choices will change the way she lives her life, we develop thought experiments of what it will be like to live as her new self. Although these reflective exercises begin to affect the actual choices she is making in the world, we attempt to keep the therapy discussions ahead of the changes she is acting out in the world outside the therapy environment.

Existentialist thought emphasizes that we are beings-in-the-world. We do not exist as disconnected and encapsulated beings; instead, we are engaged with and relate to our selves, to others, and to the physical environment. We have the capacity to "stand out" from these relationships and to choose how we will engage in them, but we cannot avoid the engagement. In our therapeutic work Ruth has been "standing out" from her engagement with the world and has been reflecting on the values she wants to have guide her future relations. We now move the therapy to considerations of how her tentatively chosen values will affect her relations with her own self, with her body, and with other people.

I ask Ruth to focus first on what it will be like for her to relate to her self as a person responsible for her own actions. She will have to consult her own values to decide what she should do. She will no longer act or perform simply because it is what others expect of her or because that is what someone of her sex and age does in this society. We explore her readiness to take on the burden of being the source of her own behavior. I ask her to create scenarios in which the newly chosen convictions guide her actions. We explore the feelings that arise in the imaginative playing out of the new behavior.

Because of the importance religion has had in Ruth's life and because of the continuing pressures her father exerts, I ask her to consider what she will decide about the religious dimension of herself. In the process of her self-creation, the source of her religious beliefs has to be transferred from her father to her own self. I ask her to distance herself from her father's beliefs and to reflect on what, given the freedoms of her self-creation project, she will choose as her own beliefs. We take time to examine how her chosen religious beliefs will relate to and complement the values and purposes she is choosing for her new self. I ask her to consider whether there are inconsistencies between the values and religious beliefs she is proposing. For her new self to serve as her source of personal power and authority, its values and purposes need to be integrated. It is possible that Ruth will need to spend time harmonizing her chosen religious beliefs and her chosen life directions. If so, we will work through any tensions between these two dimensions of her self.

Another area for exploration with Ruth is the implications of her newly chosen direction for her relationships with her family. As in the previous explorations, I ask her to tease out the controls that are leftover parts of her old self. We again use imaginative exercises in considering how becoming her new self will affect her relationship with her family. I ask her to imagine what she would do if she were free from having to conform to the stereotypical social roles of wife and mother. I also ask her to imagine what relationships she would have with her family members if she were in charge and could begin to develop them from scratch. We examine these scenarios for the values she would like to have guide her relations with her family. We also consider how these family values fit with the emerging choices she is making about the purpose and direction she wants for her life. I ask her to consider what changes in her relations to her family members are implied by the new self she is creating. I suggest that she concentrate on changes in her own behavior instead of on how she would like the other family members' behavior to be different. I remind her that her authority extends only to re-creating her own self, not the selves of others. We focus extended attention on her relationship to her husband and their marriage. The marriage bond can be threatened during a period of personal change in one of the partners. This is the time I ask Ruth if she would like to bring her husband to one of our sessions. She has expressed concern that if she changes he may leave her. I ask her to share with him her vision of what their marriage will be like if her relationship to him is guided by the ideals of her new self. She and I explore what she might do to contribute to making this vision of her marriage a reality in her newly forming life.

I ask Ruth to concentrate on the implications of her emerging self for her career. She has trained to be a teacher and yet has expressed that she is afraid to begin because she might fail. We review these feelings, and if they are still present, we reflect on their source. I remind her that in her self-creation she is free to choose her career, whether homemaker, teacher, or something else. I ask her to examine the implications of her emerging values for her career choice.

In this step of therapy Ruth has begun the constructive process of self-creation. She has examined the implications of her decisions for the purposes and values she is choosing to guide her existence. We have examined how these choices may bring about changes in her various relations. She has started to actualize her possibility for living an authentic existence. She has begun to change her actions to reflect her newly chosen values. Up to this point, the therapy has focused on having her gain insight into her situation and on having her choose the values that will guide her life. She and I are only halfway on the journey to having her existence become an expression of authenticity. The next phase will change the focus from gaining insight and making choices to changing her life activities. We will now focus on manifesting her authenticity in her daily life.

Manifesting an Authentic Existence   Deciding to change in a therapy setting and actually changing how one is in the world are different processes. The previous phases of therapy have been preparatory. Ruth's determination of what it is that has ultimate value for her is not an end in itself; it is only a prelude for her living these new values and engaging in the life process of creating her authentic existence. Our goal in this phase is to enable her to find ways to implement her chosen life purposes in practice.

This final phase of Ruth's therapy concentrates on helping her put into practice behaviors that express the values she has chosen for her new self. Manifesting the self she has decided to become in the previous parts of the therapeutic work is not a simple task. During this phase of the therapy, we use the sessions to review the attempts Ruth has made during the week to enact her new values. We also decide on specific actions that represent further steps in authenticity and assign them as homework to be done during the following week. I ask her to report on her successes and failures in meeting the challenge to become what she has determined she wants to be. This is a time of experimentation with new behaviors, and at times these new actions will be awkward and will not appropriately reflect the values they were meant to express. At other times, circumstances and social forces will interfere with her resolve and produce results she didn't intend.

Through the course of this part of the therapy, Ruth's confidence grows. She has settled into the new definition of her life and has learned how to manifest this definition in practice. The therapy work has accomplished its goal, and she is ready to live a life based on directions she has chosen for herself. It is time to draw our sessions to an end. Because of the intensity and depth of our work, we express the realization that it is to end soon by feelings of sadness and loss. I need to anticipate the coming separation and use part of our final sessions to recognize and acknowledge the appropriateness of the alarm she may feel about continuing her growth toward authenticity without our regular meetings. I have to be aware of my own feelings of sadness over the loss of our times together, times in which she has opened her self to me and has shared the despair and joy of her struggle. My task is to let go, and hers is to move away.

Process Commentary   By the time the therapeutic process has ended, Ruth and I have been working together for a year. She has made significant changes in her life, gaining control of her existence and setting the directions that will guide her future. The fears, indecisiveness, and neurotic symptoms with which she began therapy have receded, and she is actively engaged in life tasks that are consistent with the directions she has chosen. I have noticed significant differences in her. She is more vibrant and animated; she is more sure of herself and has taken a more assertive role in our interactions.

I have accompanied Ruth on her difficult journey to a more authentic existence. During the journey we have experienced times of despair as well as times of joy. There have been times when it seemed that progress had stopped and we could not go on, and other times of breakthrough and rapid advancement. She has come to trust me enough to share her deepest fears and embarrassments as well as her pride and happiness in her achievements. Our relationship has deepened, and my care and concern for her have intensified. I have grown in my appreciation of her courage and tenacity.

During our work together, Ruth has aimed her life in newly chosen directions and has begun to act in accord with these directions; she has also begun to feel at home in her new self. Although she will continue to make adjustments in her life direction, I believe Ruth will stay on the path of self-creation. Living her new life, however, will be a continuous struggle.

She will have to make compromises and agonize over decisions, but these will now be in the context of a personal commitment to her own values. She will continue to have life projects that require her attention: the quality of her relationship with her husband and the productivity of her occupational involvement. She will have episodes when she doubts her personal authority to be the creator of her life purpose, and she will experience the untethered feelings of existential anxiety. I believe Ruth's response to these episodes will be to accept these feelings as attendant experiences of personal freedom. I do not believe she will revert to her old way of being by turning over the decisions about who she will be to the voices and commands of others.

I invite Ruth to continue to meet with me on a less frequent basis, perhaps every other month. These meetings will be occasions for checking in and talking about the challenges she is confronting in her continuing work toward authenticity. I expect us to suspend these meetings after about a year.

JERRY COREY'S WORK WITH RUTH FROM AN EXISTENTIAL PERSPECTIVE

In the *CD-ROM for Integrative Counseling*, Session 11 ("Understanding How the Past Influences the Present"), I demonstrate some ways I utilize existential notions in counseling Ruth. We engage in a role play where Ruth becomes the voice of her church and I take on a new role as Ruth—one in which I have been willing to challenge certain beliefs from church. This segment illustrates how Ruth explores finding new values. In Session 12 ("Working Toward Decisions and Behavioral Changes") Ruth solidifies the process of making new decisions, which is also an existential concept.

Basic Assumptions

The existential approach to counseling assumes that the relationship the therapist establishes with the client is of the utmost importance in determining how successful therapy will be. Therapy is not something that I do to the person (in this case, Ruth); I am not a technical expert who acts on a passive client. I view therapy as a dialogue in the deepest and most genuine sense, an honest exchange between Ruth and me. We will be partners traveling on a journey, and neither of us knows where it will end. At times we will not even have a clear idea of where we are heading. She and I may both be changed by the encounter, and I expect that she will touch off powerful associations, feelings, memories, and reactions within me. My hope is to understand her world from a subjective viewpoint and, at the same time, to let her know my personal reactions to her in our relationship.

Initial Assessment of Ruth

Ruth appears to be a good candidate for existential therapy. She is courageous enough to question the meaning of life and to challenge some of her comfortable, but dull, patterns. She is facing a number of developmental crises, such as wondering what life is about now that her children are getting ready to leave home. As she begins to expand her vision of the choices open to her, her anxiety is increasing. The process of raising questions has led to more questions, yet her answers are few. She is grappling with what she wants for herself, apart from her long-standing definition of herself as wife and mother. A major theme is posed by the question "How well am I living life?" One of Ruth's strengths is her willingness to ask such anxiety-producing questions. Another of her assets is that she has already made some choices and taken some significant steps. She did diverge from her fundamentalist religion, which she no longer found personally meaningful; she is motivated to change her life; and she has sought out therapy as a way to help her find the paths she wants to travel.

Goals of Therapy

The purpose of existential therapy is not to "cure" people of disorders; rather, it is to help them become aware of what they are doing and to encourage them to act to make life-changing decisions. It is aimed at helping people like Ruth get out of their rigid roles and see more clearly the ways in which they have been leading a narrow and restricted existence. The basic purpose of her therapy is to provide her with the insights necessary to discover, establish, and use the freedom she possesses. In many ways Ruth is blocking her own freedom. My function is to help her recognize her part in creating her life situation, including the distress she feels. I assume that as she sees the ways in which her existence is limited she will take steps toward her liberation. My hope is that she can create a more responsible and meaningful existence.

Therapeutic Procedures

As an existential therapist, I do not rely on a well-developed set of techniques. Instead, I focus on certain themes that I consider to be part of the human condition, and I emphasize my ability to be fully present with Ruth by challenging her and by sharing my reactions with her as they pertain to our therapeutic relationship. My role is to help Ruth clarify what it is that brought her to me, where she is right now, what it is she wants to change, and what she can do to make these changes happen. I will borrow techniques from several therapies as we explore her current thoughts, feelings, and behaviors within the current situations and events of her life.[1]

When we deal with her past, I will encourage Ruth to relate her feelings and thoughts about past events to her present situation. Here are some of the questions I might pursue with her, any of which we might eventually explore in therapy sessions:

- In what ways are you living as fully as you might? And how are you living a limited existence?

- To what degree are you living by your own choices, as opposed to living a life outlined by others?
- What choices have you made so far, and how have these choices affected you?
- What are some of the choices you are faced with now? How do you deal with the anxiety that is part of making choices for yourself and accepting personal freedom?
- What changes do you most want to make, and what is preventing you from making them?

In essence, Ruth is about to engage in a process of opening doors to herself. The experience may be frightening, exciting, joyful, depressing, or all of these at times. As she wedges open the closed doors, she will also begin to loosen the deterministic shackles that have kept her psychologically bound. Gradually, as she becomes aware of what she has been and who she is now, she will be better able to decide what kind of future she wants to carve out for herself. Through her therapy she can explore alternatives for making her visions become real.

The Therapeutic Process

At this point in her therapy Ruth is coming to grips more directly with her midlife crisis. She has been talking about values by which she lived in the past that now hold little meaning for her, about her feelings of emptiness, and about her fears of making "wrong" choices. Here are some excerpts from several of our sessions.

Elements of the Process

Helping Ruth Find New Values   In a later session Ruth initiates her struggles with religion:

Ruth: I left my religion years ago, but I haven't found anything to replace it. I'm hoping you can help me find some new values. You have so much more experience, and you seem happy with who you are and what you believe in. On my own I'm afraid I might make the wrong decisions, and then I'd really be messed up.

Jerry: If I were to give you answers, that wouldn't be fair to you. It would be a way of saying that I don't see you as capable of finding your own way. Maybe a way for you to begin is to ask some questions. I know, for me, one way of getting answers is to raise questions.

Ruth: I know that the religion I was brought up in told me very clearly what was right and wrong. I was taught that once married, always married— and you make the best of the situation. Well, I'm not so willing to accept that now.

Jerry: How is that so?

Ruth: Sometimes I'm afraid that if I stay in therapy I'll change so much that I'll have little in common with John, and I may eventually break up our marriage.

Jerry: You know, I'm aware that you've somehow decided that your changes will cause the breakup of your marriage. Could it be that your changes might have a positive effect on your relationship?

Ruth: You're right, I haven't thought about it in that way. And I guess I've made the assumption that John won't like my changes. I more often worry that what I'm doing in therapy will eventually make me want to leave him, or he might want to leave me. Sometimes I have an impulse to walk away from my marriage, but I get scared thinking about who I'd be without John in my life.

Jerry: Why not imagine that this did happen, and for a few minutes talk about who you would be if John weren't a part of your life. Just let out whatever thoughts or images come to your mind, and try not to worry about how they sound.

Ruth: All my life I've had others tell me who and what I should be, and John has picked up where my parents and church left off. I don't know what my life is about apart from being a wife and a mother. What would our kids think if John and I split up? How would it affect them? Would they hate me for what I'd done to the family? I know I'm tired of living the way I am, but I'm not sure what I want. And I'm scared to death of making any more changes for fear that it will lead to even more turmoil. John and the kids liked the "old me" just fine, and they seem upset by the things I've been saying lately.

Jerry: In all that you just said, you didn't allow yourself to really express how you might be different if they were not in your life. It's easier for you to tune in to how the people in your life might be affected by your changes than for you to allow yourself to imagine how you'd be different. It does seem difficult for you to fantasize being different. Why not give it another try? Keep the focus on how you want to be different rather than on the reactions your family would have to your changing.

Dealing With Ruth's Anxiety   Ruth has trouble dealing with change. There is immediate anxiety whenever she thinks of being different. She is beginning to see that she has choices, that she does not have to wait around until John gives her permission to change, and that others do not have to make her choices for her. Yet she is terrified by this realization, and for a long time it appears that she is immobilized in her therapy. She will not act on the choices available to her. So I go with her feelings of being stuck and explore her anxiety with her. Here is how she describes these feelings.

Ruth: I often wake up in the middle of the night with terrible feelings that the walls are closing in on me! I break out in cold sweats, I have trouble breathing, and I can feel my heart pounding. At times I worry that I'll die. I can't sleep, and I get up and pace around and feel horrible.

Jerry: Ruth, as unpleasant as these feelings are, I hope you learn to pay attention to these signals. They're warning you that all is not well in your life and that you're ready for change.

I know that Ruth sees anxiety as a negative thing, something she would like to get rid of once and for all. I see her anxiety as the possibility of a new starting point for her. Rather than simply getting rid of these symptoms, she can go deeply into their meaning. I see her anxiety as the result of her increased awareness of her freedom along with her growing sense of responsibility for deciding what kind of life she wants and then taking action to make these changes a reality.

Exploring the Meaning of Death   Eventually we get onto the topic of death and explore its meaning to Ruth.

Ruth: I've been thinking about what we talked about before—about what I want from life before I die. You know, for so many years I lived in dread of death because I thought I'd die a sinner and go to hell for eternity. I suppose that fear has kept me from looking at death. It has always seemed so morbid.

Jerry: Why don't you talk about areas of your life where you don't feel really alive. How often do you feel a sense of excitement about living?

Ruth: It would be easier for me to tell you of the times I feel half dead! I'm dead to having fun. Sexually I'm dead.

Jerry: Can you think of some other ways you might be dead?

I am trying to get Ruth to evaluate the quality of her life and to begin to experience her deadness. After some time she admits that she has allowed her spirit to die. Old values have died, and she has not acquired new ones. Ruth is gaining some dim awareness that there is more to living than breathing. It is important that she allow herself to recognize her deadness and feel it as a precondition for her rebirth. I operate under the assumption that by really experiencing and expressing the ways in which she feels dead she can begin to focus on how she wants to be alive, if at all. Only then is there hope that she can learn new ways to live.

Process Commentary   Ruth's experience in therapy accentuates the basic assumption that there are no absolute answers outside of herself. She learns that therapy is a process of opening up doors bit by bit, giving her more potential for choices. This process happens largely because of the relationship between us. She becomes well aware that she cannot evade responsibility for choosing for herself. She learns that she is constantly creating herself by the choices she is making, as well as by the choices she is failing to make. As her therapist I support her attempts at experimenting with new behaviors in our sessions. Our open discussions, in which we talk about how we are experiencing each other, are a new behavior for her. These sessions provide a safe situation for her to extend new dimensions of her being. At the same time, I teach Ruth how she might use what she is learning in her everyday life. She risks getting angry at me, being direct with me, and telling me how I affect her. We work on ways in which she might continue this behavior with selected people in her environment.

One of my aims is to show Ruth the connection between the choices she is making or failing to make and the anxiety she is experiencing. I do this by asking her to observe herself in various situations throughout the week. Through this self-observation process Ruth gradually sees some specific ways in which her choices are directly contributing to her anxiety. My goal in working with Ruth is not to eliminate her anxiety; rather, it is to help her understand what it means. From my perspective, anxiety is a signal that all is not well, that a person is ready for some change in life.

Perhaps the critical aspect of Ruth's therapy is her recognition that she has a choice to make. She can continue to cling to the known and the familiar, even deciding to settle for what she has in life and quitting therapy. Or she can also accept the fact that in life there are no guarantees, that in spite of this uncertainty and the accompanying anxiety she will still have to act by making choices and then living with the consequences. Ruth chooses to commit herself to therapy.[2]

 ## QUESTIONS FOR REFLECTION

1. What life experiences have you had that could help you identify with Ruth? Have you shared any of her struggles? Have you faced similar issues? How have you dealt with these personal struggles and issues? How are your answers to these questions related to your potential effectiveness as her therapist?

2. What are your general reactions to the ways in which Dr. Polkinghorne and I have worked with Ruth? What aspects of both of these styles of counseling might you carry out in somewhat the same manner? What different themes might you focus on? What different techniques might you use?

3. Compare this approach to working with Ruth with the previous approaches, psychoanalytic therapy and Adlerian therapy. What major differences do you see?

4. How might you work with Ruth's fears associated with opening doors in her life? Part of her wants to remain as she is, and the other part yearns for a fresh life. How would you work with this conflict?

5. Using this approach, how would you deal with Ruth's fears related to dying? Do you see any connection between her anxieties and her view of death?

6. What are your thoughts and feelings about death and dying as they apply to you and to those you love? To what extent do you think you have explored your own anxieties pertaining to death and loss? How would your answer to this question largely determine your effectiveness in counseling a person such as Ruth?

7. What are some of the other existential themes mentioned in this chapter that have personal relevance to your life? How do you react to the question "Can therapists inspire their clients to deal with their existential concerns if they have not been willing to do this in their own lives?"

 ## NOTES

1. In Session 9 ("An Integrative Focus") of the *CD-ROM for Integrative Counseling*, I illustrate what I am describing in my existential way of working with Ruth. As an existential therapist, I am free to draw techniques from many therapeutic modalities as an avenue of exploring with Ruth current situations and events of her life.

2. For a more detailed treatment of the existential approach, see G. Corey (2005), *Theory and Practice of Counseling and Psychotherapy* (7th edition). The basic concepts introduced by Dr. Polkinghorne in his assessment and treatment of Ruth are covered comprehensively in Chapter 6 (Existential Therapy). Also see G. Corey (2005), *Student Manual for Theory and Practice of Counseling and Psychotherapy* (7th edition). The combination of the textbook and manual will flesh out the existential perspective in my work with Ruth demonstrated in this chapter.

Chapter 5

Case Approach to Person-Centered Therapy

A Person-Centered Therapist's Perspective on Ruth

by David J. Cain, Ph.D., ABPP

Introduction

Assessment and diagnosis are viewed as ongoing processes by the person-centered therapist, not as formal procedures undertaken at the beginning of psychotherapy. The word *diagnose* is derived from a Greek word that means "to know" or "to discover." In my view, therapy is basically a process of self-discovery whose critical components are intrapersonal and interpersonal learning. The therapist's primary function is to facilitate learning in the client. Thus, the client's discovery of personal knowledge about self is much more relevant than what the therapist knows about the client or the psychiatric disorder the client is viewed as experiencing.

As a person-centered therapist, I would not undertake any formal assessment with a client unless the client requested it, nor would I attempt to establish a DSM-IV-TR diagnosis for the client. In more than 25 years as a practicing psychotherapist, I have found the practice of formal diagnosis to be fraught with more liabilities than assets. Although an extensive discussion of the pros and cons of diagnosis is beyond the scope of this book, I will mention what I believe to be some of the most significant limitations.

First, I have not found that establishing a diagnosis helps much with treatment. The DSM-IV-TR system of diagnosis does not provide treatment guidelines. With few exceptions (for example, exposure and cognitive restructuring for anxiety problems), the bulk of psychotherapeutic research has shown that all established approaches have roughly equivalent success with a wide variety of problems.

Second, all diagnostic categories are inevitably reductionist in that they reduce clients and their experiences to a list of symptoms. In reality there is considerable variability among individuals with the same diagnosis.

Third, the uniqueness of each person tends to be lost in the diagnostic process because the emphasis is placed on common characteristics. It is a biological and psychological fact that each person is unique. The act of categorizing tends to constrict the therapist's conceptual understanding of the client and de-emphasizes the importance of individual differences and the complexity of the person.

Fourth, diagnosis overly emphasizes what is wrong with clients and gives relatively little attention to their strengths and resources.

And, finally, a diagnosis is made primarily from an external point of view (that of the clinician) rather than from the internal frame of reference of the client. Clients generally have relatively limited participation in the determination of their diagnosis, even though they are the best authorities on their experience.

I find that dimensions of the person other than diagnostic symptoms are more important in understanding and responding therapeutically to my client. Among the most relevant dimensions are the client's self-concept and worldview; incongruencies between the self-concept, behavior, and experience; the capacity to attend to and process experience, especially affect; learning style and ability to learn from experience; comportment or characteristic manner of living; implicit and explicit personal goals and strivings; a sense of purpose and personal meaning; and the sense of being grounded, whole, and integrated.

In my experience a critical endeavor of the client is the definition ("Who am I?") and redefinition of the self ("Who am I becoming?"). This process is facilitated by the therapist's and client's openness to the client's experience and its personal meaning and is hindered by limited diagnostic formulations of the client's psychopathology. In the optimal case, diagnosis is a continuous process of self-learning in which the client remains receptive to all sources of experience and relevant information. In contrast, diagnostic categorization on the part of therapists may create a false sense of security about what they "know" about the client and limit their creativity and adaptability in responding therapeutically. The danger here is that therapists may begin to interact with a static category rather than an evolving being, thus limiting their range of perceptions and variety of therapeutic responses and, consequently, the client's potential for change.

The essential purpose of assessment is to enable the client to develop relevant and meaningful personal knowledge, especially knowledge about the "self" and how the self-concept affects behavior. One of the major factors that makes therapy "person-centered" is the responsibility placed on the client for self-direction. Although I may play a significant role in helping the client explore her- or himself, the client is more likely to be affected by, and to put to use, personal experiences and learning that are self-discovered. The excitement and deep satisfaction that come from self-exploration and self-discovery are potent factors that engage the client in the therapeutic process.

Assessment of Ruth

In working with Ruth I will be especially attentive to how she views her *self*, including aspects that are evident and those that are implicit and unclear but forming. Several components of Ruth's self-concept emerge from her autobiography. In her own words Ruth identifies herself as the "good wife" and the "good mother" that "he [John] expects me to be." Thus, she strongly identifies herself with the roles of wife and mother, but she has defined and attempted to fulfill these roles in the image her husband wishes. By allowing her husband to define what she is and should be (if she is to be accepted), she has abdicated her role and power in defining the person she is and in making personal choices about her life. She has allowed her husband to determine her conditions of worth, and she lives in fear that if she does not live up to his conditions "he might leave me." Ruth's tendency to mold herself for others is a pervasive aspect of her functioning. As she says, "I've pretty much lived for others so far . . . I've been the superwoman who gives and gives." Defining herself as a giving and caretaking person are, of course, aspects of herself in which Ruth takes pride, and understandably so. At the same time, defining herself in this relatively narrow manner limits her view of what she might become.

Until she was 30, Ruth's identity and value system were strongly influenced by the fundamentalist religion of her parents, especially her father. She feared that she would be rejected by her parents if she did not live up to their expectations of who she should be. She states, "They haven't formally disowned me, but in many ways I think they have. I know I'll never win their approval as long as I remain away from the religion that's so dear to them." Ruth is intent on pleasing others, even at the cost of sacrificing her own needs and identity. In a real sense she is selfless, without a clear sense of who she is or can become. Some of the basic questions she is likely to address in therapy are "What do I want?" "What kind of person do I want to be?" "How do I want to live?" and "Can I be this person and maintain a good relationship with my husband and family?"

Other aspects of Ruth's self-concept are more peripheral. An important clue to her self-concept is the view she has of her body and its many symptoms. However she defines herself, it is important to realize that the self is embodied, that it is contained in and functions through a body. Thus, an essential part of her sense of herself has to do with how she sees and feels about her body. At present she views her physical self as overweight and unattractive. In her words: "I don't like what I see. I don't like who I am, and I certainly don't feel proud of my body." Ruth experiences many disturbing bodily symptoms that adversely affect her sense of her physical self. A large part of Ruth's manner of being is dominated by fear, anxiety, panic, and a sense that many daily life events and ongoing concerns are overwhelming. She is afraid that she will die. These fears and anxieties seem to manifest themselves in various forms of bodily symptoms (namely, insomnia, heart palpitations, headache, dizziness, and crying spells). Quite literally, much of Ruth's life is *sickening*—depressed, fearful, constricted, and avoidant.

Although Ruth feels some pride and satisfaction in being a caretaker, this role also results in ambivalence and dissatisfaction. She experiences considerable conflict over who she is, what she believes, and how she is living. By her own admission, she doesn't like who she is, her overweight body, and the fact that her life is devoid of any joyful or meaningful activity apart from her roles as wife and mother.

A potential aspect of her identity is that of a teacher, but she has not yet incorporated this role into her self-structure. She imagines that teaching will be fulfilling, but as yet she places her own desires behind those of her family. Her religious beliefs and values are changing and are in conflict with her earlier fundamentalist views. Other aspects of Ruth's identity will emerge during the course of therapy.

Ruth's future is vague and tentative. She is dimly aware of the person she might become, yet she is fearful that pursuing her interests and needs and developing her own identity will result in her losing her husband and family. But she has not given up. In recent years she has become a "questioner" and holds onto the glimmer of hope that she can "begin to live before it's too late." There is a yearning in Ruth to be more than she is—to expand herself and her life possibilities. She is entering a transitional phase in her life with considerable trepidation.

Key Issues

A key issue with Ruth is the incongruence between the person she is and the selves that are "trying" to emerge, though hesitantly and cautiously. Her incongruence manifests itself in a variety of ways—as cognitive dissonance, in her many physical symptoms, and in anxiety and stress—all of which have the tendency to impel her toward the solution of her discomfort. Her depression and physical symptoms tell her that something is wrong with her life, but fear is her main obstacle to becoming a more autonomous, fuller, and more gratified person. Fear of the loss of her husband's and children's support and love render her hesitant to move from the safety of her current life, but her dissatisfaction with it and herself are drawing her forward.

A basic assumption of the person-centered therapist is that the human organism has a natural tendency to manifest its potential. Carl Rogers described the *actualizing tendency* as people's inherent inclination to develop all of their capacities: to differentiate, to expand, and to become more autonomous. This tendency for people to move in directions that maintain and enhance themselves can be deterred, however, by motives that interfere with their ability to

manifest their growth needs. At such times they may fail to differentiate between actions that are gratifying (such as being liked) and those that develop
their potential (namely, standing up for their values).

Ruth feels somewhat secure in her present life, even though it is boring
and unfulfilling in terms of personal growth and meaning. Her capacity to
move forward is limited by her lack of trust in her judgment ("I'm scared I'll
make the wrong decisions") and resourcefulness ("I'm trapped and don't see a
way out"). As a consequence, she is inclined to look to others (God, husband,
her therapist) for guidance and direction.

Paradoxically, Ruth is as much afraid of living as she is of dying. The an-
ticipation of change terrifies her because it threatens the limited security and
stability she experiences in her family and current lifestyle. Yet there are hopeful signs. Ruth is restless, dissatisfied, and afraid that her life is slipping by.
She has a fragile desire for a better life and a tenuous vision of what she might
become. She is "excited and afraid at the same time." If she can listen to the
inner voices of her feelings and attend to the distress signals of her body, Ruth
will begin to see more clearly who she is and what she wants and, in the
process, will begin to find her own voice and path.

Therapeutic Process and Techniques

As I anticipate working with Ruth, my primary focus is on the quality of the
relationship I hope to provide for her. My desire is to allow myself to be curious about her and receptive to anything she would like to share about herself
and her life. To the best of my ability, I will be fully present and listen carefully to what she says while being sensitive to how she presents herself, including her nonverbal and implicit messages. As much as possible, I hope to
leave any preconceptions and hypotheses I may have about her behind and to
attend to her with fresh ears and eyes. It is my desire to create a trusting, supportive, safe, and encouraging atmosphere in which Ruth will experience me
as genuinely interested in her, sensitive to her feelings, nonjudgmental, and
accurately understanding of her expressed and intended meanings. I hope to
communicate my belief in her resourcefulness and my optimism about her
capacity to learn what she needs to learn and move forward in her life. If I am
successful in these endeavors, Ruth will listen to herself, learn from her experiences, and effectively apply her learnings.

Any specific techniques, methods, or responses I may use will be dictated
by Ruth's therapeutic needs and what best fits her at a given time. Because I
view Ruth as a collaborator in the therapeutic process, I will take my cues
from her regarding how I might best respond at the moment. At times I may
collaborate more directly with Ruth to determine what might be helpful or
check directly with her to ascertain if what I'm doing is helpful, trusting that
she knows best how I can serve her at a given time. A variety of therapeutic
techniques might be employed on Ruth's behalf with her participation in
choosing the approaches that she feels might be most helpful. Careful listen-

ing and accurate understanding of my client's overt and tacit meanings always precede the introduction of therapeutic techniques or exercises. My basic question in employing any technique is, "Does it fit?"

One important aspect of my role is as a facilitator of learning. Life is constantly teaching us important lessons about ourselves, about others, and about life in general. At times, I view my role as helping my client "learn how to learn." My style of responding to Ruth will reflect my attempt to adapt to her personal learning style, which often can be inferred through observation.

Finally, I will be myself in the relationship. Thus, Ruth will have a good sense of who I am as a person. Consequently, she will experience my sense of humor, my openness and directness, and my serious and playful sides. She will find that I can be provocative and challenging as well as quietly attentive and gentle as she undertakes her personal journey. She will also see the pleasure I feel in working with her and seeing her become the person she wishes to be.[1]

The Beginning Phase of Therapy   I anticipate that Ruth will tend to be tentative as therapy begins, perhaps starting with her general sense of dissatisfaction with her life, herself, and her physical symptoms. She may find the relatively nondirective nature of our interaction somewhat disconcerting at first, preferring that I lead her in the "right" direction, ask questions, advise her on what she "should" do, and "push" her to do it. However, I believe she will gradually perceive that my reluctance to direct or advise her is based on my trust in her ability to determine her own direction and find a course of action that fits her. My message is, "This is your life, and you are the author of its future." I am confident that Ruth will discover that she has more personal strengths and resources than she is aware of at present.[2]

The beginning phase of therapy goes as follows:

Therapist: I'm interested in hearing anything you would like to share about yourself—anything that's troubling you—whatever is on your mind.

Ruth: Right now the thing that's bothering me the most is my weight. Whenever I get anxious or depressed, I tend to overeat. Lately I've gained about 10 pounds. I feel fat and dumpy. I hate the way I look.

Therapist: You sound angry with yourself for your eating and your appearance.

Ruth: I am. And my husband likes me better when I'm thinner. I've been trying to diet, but I just can't seem to stick with it.

Therapist: You're not pleasing your husband or yourself. And I guess you're getting discouraged about whether you're able to lose weight.

Ruth: It's not just losing weight. It's accomplishing anything I set out to do. I just can't seem to follow through. Usually I get off to a good start, but as soon as something goes wrong, I get discouraged.

Therapist: And when you get discouraged you . . . ?

Ruth: I start to give up and get depressed.

Therapist: And when you get depressed you . . . ?

Ruth: Eat.

Therapist: So you eat to ease those feelings.

Ruth: I guess so.

Therapist: If your feelings could talk, what might they say?

Ruth: I think they would say "You can't do anything right."

Therapist: Pretty harsh words.

Ruth: I do tend to get down on myself when I start to falter. Sometimes I think I need someone else to push me to accomplish my goals.

Therapist: Sometimes you'd just like someone to help you get through the tough times.

Ruth: I'm almost 40 and I'm still not sure what I want to do, much less if I can do it. I'd like to be a teacher, but my husband wants me to stay home and take care of him and the kids. I like being a mother and a wife, but I feel that life is passing me by.

Therapist: So there's a sense of urgency in your life. Life is moving on and, although you think you'd like to teach, you don't trust yourself to stick to it or your diet or anything else. And when you have a setback, you get discouraged and wish someone else could get you to stick to your goals. To ease the pain you eat. And all this is complicated by your fear that if you do teach you may alienate your husband.

Ruth: That about says it.

Process Commentary   What quickly emerges are the emotions that impair Ruth's progress. She is fearful that she will fail, becomes angry and self-critical when she does, and then, depressed and discouraged. She attempts to assuage these feelings by eating, only to find herself dissatisfied by her weight and herself again. Although she seems to like teaching and experiences some success at it, she is not yet clear that this career choice is right. Nor is she willing to take a step that might disrupt her family. As her therapist, I hope to enable her to view her feelings as "friendly" aspects of herself that can help her develop a greater sense of clarity, direction, and confidence in her endeavors. So we continue.

Therapist: So what do you make of all that?

Ruth: I guess I do wish I could depend on someone else to help me when I'm stuck. I've always depended on my parents or John for guidance. I did break away from my church several years ago, but I don't think my parents will ever understand that or accept my beliefs about religion. John couldn't understand why I wanted to finish college and be a teacher. He thinks I should be happy being a homemaker and a mother.

Therapist: I guess you long to be understood and supported by your parents and husband, but sometimes they just don't. What makes sense to you doesn't always make sense to them. Yet you'd still like their approval and backing.

Ruth: I'm such a wimp. Sometimes I think I'll never be able to do what I believe in without worrying about what someone else thinks.

Therapist: What is clear is that what people think of you *does* matter—often a great deal. Then you feel like a wimp when you let others' opinions of you become more important than your own. But you did change your religious convictions, and you did finish college. You sometimes do finish what you start, and do what you really want to do, despite others' misgivings.

Ruth: Well, I do feel good about those things. It took me forever to finish college, but I did. And I think I did a pretty good job in my student teaching. I guess there's no reason I should expect them to agree with me. They have their own ideas about what is right.

Therapist: And so do you.

Ruth: Yes, I think I do. I'm pretty sure I want to be a teacher.

Process Commentary   Ruth's dissatisfaction with her need for approval is becoming evident. When her self-initiated religious changes and completion of college are acknowledged and affirmed by the therapist, Ruth begins to see herself more positively apart from the views of others. She is beginning to recognize that she can give herself the credit she deserves for her accomplishments.

As therapy progresses, Ruth becomes increasingly aware of the incongruence she experiences between the person she is and the person she yearns to be. It is likely that she will feel guilty about what she perceives as selfishness when she attends more to her own needs, and she is fearful that her marriage and family will be disrupted. As Ruth expands and modifies her perceptual field, however, she comes to believe that her desires and goals are as deserving of attention as those of her family.

The Middle Phase of Therapy   Ruth may, at some point, wish to bring her husband into her therapy sessions to address the conflict she feels over taking a course of action that displeases him or her children. Whether John is supportive of her change or not, she will have to wrestle with her own conflict about doing what she wants and becoming a more separate, independent person. Her marriage will probably go through a dramatic transition if she pursues her hopes. It may improve as she becomes a fuller person or become more conflicted if her husband is threatened by her development.

The middle phase of therapy highlights these ideas:

Ruth: John and I had another fight last night. He wants me to spend more time with him and the kids and less time with my friends and at the new church I've been attending. I feel a little guilty about being away from home more, but I really like some of the new people I've met.

Therapist: You feel torn between allegiances to your family and yourself.

Ruth: Yes. I love my kids and John, and I like taking care of them. But there's more that I want to do. And besides, the kids are old enough now to take care of themselves more. In fact, Rob just moved out last week, and Jennifer has started in a community college. Susan and Adam are involved in lots of activities at the high school. And John is involved in his bowling two nights a week. So it's not as if they need me around all the time.

Therapist: As you see that they have lives of their own, it seems that your family needs you less than they did. Or maybe you need them less as you have begun to do more things that are important to you.

Ruth: I think it's a little of both. I got a lot of satisfaction from making sure they were happy—you know, being a good mother and wife. But I realize that sometimes I got too involved and didn't let them do more for themselves because I wanted them to need me. Now I kind of like taking more time for myself. The kids are basically OK. Even Jennifer has begun to settle down. She just had to realize that when I said "no" I meant "no," not "maybe." She doesn't always like some of my rules, but she's more accepting of limits.

Therapist: Being a good mother and wife was very important to you, but sometimes you become more involved than you need to be. Now you've become clearer about the kind of mother you want to be and that includes setting limits and sticking to them. And you're less worried about how they'll ever survive without you.

Ruth [*laughs*]: Yeah, I must have thought I was supposed to be Mother Teresa or something. Actually, the kids aren't the problem. John is. He's having a hard time accepting the ways I've changed. He's used to having me spend more time with him and do little things for him that I don't have as much time to do now. Sometimes he complains that I'm not as interested in him as I used to be, or he just sulks. I think I've spoiled him, and he's having a hard time adjusting.

Therapist: Having a life of your own is risky to you and threatening to John. You seem to be struggling with your feelings about John.

Ruth: I am. But I'm not sure what I feel. Sometimes I think he's acting like a big baby. At other times I feel sorry for him. Or sad.

Therapist: What seems to be the main feeling?

Ruth: Kind of sad and annoyed. Doesn't make sense.

Therapist: Notice where in your body the feeling seems to be located.

Ruth: Mostly in my stomach.

Therapist: Can you describe the sensation in your stomach?

Ruth: Kind of queasy and scared.

Therapist: A queasy, scared feeling?

Ruth: Yeah.

Therapist: Just pay attention to that feeling for a while. See if there's a word or maybe an image that seems to fit that queasy, scared feeling.

Ruth: It's kind of like the panicky feelings I get sometimes.

Therapist: Panicky. Stay with it.

Ruth: It's like the feeling I get when I'm scared that I can't handle something. Sort of being afraid that I'll be overwhelmed.

Therapist: Um Hm. Scared. Overwhelmed.

Ruth: What comes to mind is the fight I had with my parents over leaving the church. I knew it was the right thing, but I was terrified of losing their support.

Therapist: So it's more like terrified.

Ruth: Like I'm frightened of having to be on my own. Like being abandoned! That's it.

Therapist: Abandoned. A sense that you're on your own and there's no one there to support you.

Ruth: Exactly. When I left the church, my parents were utterly disapproving of me. Whenever I wanted to do something they disapproved of, they would become distant and sometimes wouldn't even speak to me. It's the same with John. When I'm a good wife and focus my life around him and home, he's happy with me. But when I started doing things that meant a lot to me—like teaching and developing new friends—well, he got sulky and pulled away. So I guess I've been feeling abandoned by him too. It all makes sense.

Therapist: That seems to fit. Afraid of being abandoned and a bit sad for John.

Ruth: Yes, it all makes sense.

Process Commentary   Ruth is beginning to become more separate from her family, though she remains involved with them and concerned about their well-being. She is more acceptant and tolerant of the reality that taking care of her needs and desires may, at times, displease other family members. Ruth is also learning to allow her husband and her kids to take care of themselves more.

During the latter segment of this interview, Ruth was encouraged to focus on a feeling that was initially unclear. Using a process called experiential focusing, Ruth was encouraged to pay attention to where and how her feeling manifested itself in her body. Through a series of steps, Ruth was able to clarify the feeling and understand its relationship to her panic states and primary relationships. Such insights as these are often quite powerful because they clarify the way the problem is carried bodily. It's as if the body knows what's wrong in a more profound way than can be articulated verbally. As the problem is processed physically and cognitively, the insight derived has a convincing ring of truth. More important, Ruth has learned a process that will be invaluable in helping her make sense of her experience.

Later in the therapy, Ruth continues addressing her marriage and its personal meaning.

Ruth: I feel badly about taking more time for myself, but John has things to do on his own. And we still spend a lot of time together. It's just that he doesn't think I need him as much as I used to, and I think he feels insecure about this.

Therapist: Maybe you don't need him as much as you used to?

Ruth: Hmm. Well, I'm not sure. I think maybe I needed him to need me more than I do now. And now he seems to want me to need him the way I used to. I think he doesn't feel as important to me as he did. He is important. But for different reasons. Now, I want us to be friends and more like equal partners. Before, he was more like my father—more controlling and demanding. It was as if he didn't think I could do anything without having him to guide me. And I guess I did let him take charge more then because I was so terrified of doing things on my own. In my mind he was more the head of the house. Now, I'm a little more confident and . . . well, I guess I don't want to need him like a little girl needs her parents. It's more like I want his advice when I ask. What I really want is his *support*.

Therapist: You've changed and grown quite a bit. Earlier in your marriage you wanted and allowed John to take charge more. You felt then that you needed his guidance because you weren't able to make decisions for yourself. And you became extremely anxious when John would withdraw and sulk. Now, as your confidence has grown, you want someone who will offer advice when you ask him but support you in your choices. Instead of a father, you want an equal partner.

Ruth: Yes! That's what I want. I want John to see that I'm different from him and to appreciate me for the person I am. When I want his input on something, I want him to understand that I may or may not do what he suggests. I think he still thinks that when I ask his opinion it means I'll do things his way. No wonder he gets frustrated or hurt sometimes. I think I need to make it clear that his ideas do matter to me but if I don't follow his suggestion it doesn't mean that I don't value him. I just want to do things my own way sometimes.

Process Commentary   Ruth is growing stronger and more independent. She is clearer about the kind of relationship she wants with her husband and able to see her husband more objectively. As Ruth has progressed in therapy, she is beginning to see herself in a more positive and differentiated way. She is feeling more power and control in her life and will probably become more assertive. More of her satisfaction will be derived from her work and interests apart from, but not excluding, her roles of mother and wife. As she learns to listen to the messages of her feelings and her body, she will identify her needs more clearly and draw on her resources more effectively to satisfy them. Her depression, anxiety, and physical symptoms should diminish as Ruth learns to identify and effectively address the sources of her conflicts. Gradually, she will learn that there is someone in her life on whom she can always depend—herself.

The Final Phase of Therapy   Here is a sample dialogue of the final phase of our therapy:

Ruth: Things have settled down a lot with John. Although it's been a difficult adjustment for him, he seems to accept me more the way I am now.

Therapist: And how are you now?

Ruth: I think the main thing is that I feel a lot more independent. I still want my family and friends to like me and approve of what I do, but it's OK if they don't. The main thing is that I feel good about me, at least most of the time.

Therapist: You sure look better—more confident and settled. Your sense of independence and your ability to trust your decisions have made you stronger.

Ruth: I am. And I feel pretty good most of the time. Once in a while I'll get a panicky feeling, but I've learned to pay attention to my feelings, understand what the problem is, and take care of it. Last week I was real anxious about my younger daughter, Susan. I didn't like the guy she's been going out with, and I told her why. Well, she insisted on seeing him, and I didn't know what to do. I talked it over with John, and we decided to let her continue to see this guy as long as we knew where she was and she made curfew. I think the main thing that helped me was realizing that she has pretty good judgment.

Therapist: Sounds like you've learned to trust your feelings and your judgment and to tolerate your anxiety about Susan because you trust her. Maybe you haven't done such a bad job as a parent. You and John also seem to be working together more as parents—more as partners.

Ruth: Believe me, it hasn't been easy. It's still hard to sleep until I hear that door open when she comes home, but nothing awful has happened so far. As for John and me, most of the time we work out our differences. We still fight occasionally, but I don't worry anymore that he'll leave me. Even when I get stubborn about something he disagrees with, he tries to see my point of view.

Therapist: You've found that you can tolerate your anxieties much better than you thought you could. It seems, too, that you and John can deal with your differences without them becoming fatal.

Ruth: You know, I actually think he likes me better the way I am now. I may be harder to live with in some ways, but I'm not so dependent and scared. I'm more fun now, and John likes that. I like me a lot better too.

Therapist: You've become more of the person you've been struggling to be. There's a lot to like in you.

Process Commentary   Ruth now views others' acceptance and liking as desirable though not necessary to her well-being. More important, she has learned to like herself and feel at peace with who she is. She is more confident about herself as a wife and mother and is more able to tolerate the inevitable anxieties of parenting.

The process of person-centered therapy can be conceived of as a rebirth of the self, with the therapist serving as midwife. Many clients who seek therapy are conflicted about who they are and how they are living. Their sense of self lacks clarity and is often viewed in terms of important roles (namely, daughter, mother, wife, student) that are largely defined by their culture and significant others. To the degree that we buy into these roles, we tend to move away from and lose a sense of our natural inclinations and tendency to actualize our potential in a manner consistent with our true selves. In an attempt to find acceptance and approval and avoid conflict with others, especially with those most important to us, we try to bend and shape ourselves in a manner that often leaves us feeling incongruent, dissatisfied, conflicted, and at odds with ourselves and with others.

Person-centered therapy, as is evident in Ruth's case, provides the client with an opportunity to experience one's self and life in a clearer, more differentiated, and grounded manner. This process is assisted enormously by the therapist's ability to capture the essence of the client's experience, especially the person's current view of self, worldview, and explicit and implicit needs, goals, and strivings. The therapist helps the client recognize that his or her experiences are the basis for critical learning and the creation of personal knowledge, meaning, and choice about how one might live and who one might become. One of the critical processes of therapy is enabling clients to develop confidence in their perceptions, judgments, and sense of knowing. Because both affective and rational ways of knowing have strengths and limitations, a goal of person-centered therapy, as I conceive it, is to enable clients to draw effectively from both ways of knowing. When their knowledge of feelings is congruent with their rational knowledge, clients will usually experience a sense of clarity, peace, and confidence in their learning. They will often respond to such moments with comments like "Yes, that's it" or "That feels right." The cognitive and affective realms have been integrated, and they feel freer to act on their learning.

As Ruth became clearer about what she wanted in her life—as mother, wife, and individual—and began to re-create herself, she also realized that this choice required that she stand up for herself and sometimes take a position that not all others would like, support, or approve. The therapist's genuine acceptance and affirmation help Ruth free herself from beliefs and feelings about how she "should" live. I believe Ruth learned to face life's most basic challenge: to be herself and find a way to live with others that allows her to maintain self-respect and integrity while accepting the reality that being herself will sometimes bring conflict with others.

Concluding Comments

A misconception about client-centered psychotherapy is that it is inevitably long-term therapy. It is not. In fact, like many therapeutic approaches, person-centered therapy is often effective in 10 sessions or less, and many clients have benefited from a single session. Therapies that are directive are thought to be briefer because they employ more teaching and guiding techniques. Such therapies assume that the therapist knows how to help the client relieve symptoms rapidly. In my view, such approaches fail to appreciate fully the resources and inherent wisdom in clients.

Although it may take a bit longer to help Ruth tap her own resources, find her own direction, and learn how to move forward, "slower may be faster." As

Ruth learns how to process her experiences more effectively, she also develops attitudes and skills that can enable her to become more self-sufficient. The confidence Ruth gains from learning to trust her own experiences and decision-making capacity enables her to feel more grounded, centered, and optimistic.

Both personal and therapeutic experiences have convinced me that feeling understood and accepted by important others is conducive to our well-being. Regardless of one's therapeutic approach, the desire to hear our clients and to enter into their experiential world is almost inevitably helpful and never harmful.

 # JERRY COREY'S WORK WITH RUTH FROM A PERSON-CENTERED PERSPECTIVE

It is clear that David Cain views the therapeutic relationship as the core of the therapeutic process. In the *CD-ROM for Integrative Counseling* I provide a concrete illustration of how I also view the therapeutic relationship as the foundation for our work together. See Session 1 ("Beginning of Counseling"), Session 2 ("The Therapeutic Relationship"), and Session 3 ("Establishing Therapeutic Goals)" for a demonstration of these principles as they pertain to the person-centered approach.

Basic Assumptions

From a person-centered perspective I view counseling as being directed at more than merely solving problems and giving information. It is primarily aimed at helping clients tap their inner resources so that they can better deal with their problems, both current and future. In Ruth's case I think I can best accomplish this goal by creating a climate that is threat-free, one in which she will feel fully accepted by me. I work on the assumption that my clients have the capacity to lead the way in our sessions and that they can profit without my directive intervention. I assume that three attributes on my part are necessary and sufficient to release Ruth's growth force: genuineness, acceptance and positive regard, and empathy. If I genuinely experience these attitudes toward Ruth and successfully communicate them to her, she will decrease her defensive ways and move toward becoming her true self, the person she is capable of becoming. Therapy is not so much a matter of my doing something to Ruth as it is establishing a relationship that Ruth can use to engage in self-exploration and ultimately find her own way.

Assessment of Ruth

In talking to Ruth I can see that she is disappointed with where she is in life and that she is not being herself around her friends or family. Her therapy is based on this concern.

As I review Ruth's autobiography, I see her wondering: "How can I discover my real self? How can I become the person I would like to become? How can I shed my phony roles and become myself?" My aim is to create an atmosphere in which she can freely, without judgment and evaluation, express whatever she is feeling. If she can experience this freedom to be whatever she is in this moment, she will begin to drop the masks and roles that she now lives by.

Goals of Therapy

My basic goal is to create a therapeutic climate that will help Ruth discover the kind of person she is, apart from being what others have expected her to be. When her facades come down as a result of the therapeutic process, four characteristics will likely become evident: (1) her openness to experience, (2) a greater degree of trust in herself, (3) her internal source of evaluation, and (4) her willingness to live more spontaneously. These characteristics constitute the basic goals of person-centered therapy.

Therapeutic Procedures

When clients begin therapy, they tend to look to the therapist to provide direction and answers. They often have rigid beliefs and attitudes, a sense of being out of touch with their feelings, a basic sense of distrust in themselves, and a tendency to externalize problems. As therapy progresses, they are generally able to express fears, anxiety, guilt, shame, anger, and other feelings that they have deemed too negative to incorporate into their self-structure. Eventually, they are able to distort less, express feelings previously out of awareness, and move in a direction of being more open to all of their experience. They can be in contact, moment by moment, with what they are feeling, with less need to distort or deny this experience.

The Therapeutic Process

Elements of the Process   During the early stages of her therapy, Ruth does not share her feelings but talks instead about externals. To a large degree she perceives her problems as being outside of herself. Somehow, if her father would change, if her husband's attitude would change, and if her children would present fewer problems, she would be all right. During one of our early sessions, Ruth wonders whether I will be able to really understand her and help her if she does share her feelings.

Exploring our Relationship   Ruth lets me know how difficult it is for her to talk personally to me, and she tells me that it's especially uncomfortable for her to talk with me because I'm a man. I feel encouraged because she is willing to talk to me about her reservations and to bring some of her feelings toward me out in the open.[3]

Ruth: I've become aware that I'm careful about what I say around you. It's important that I feel understood, and sometimes I wonder if you can really understand the struggles I'm having as a woman.

Jerry: Well, I like it that you're willing to let me know what it's like for you to attempt to trust me. I hope that you won't censor what you say around me, and I very much want to understand you. Perhaps you could tell me more about your doubts about my ability to understand you as a woman.

Ruth: It's not what you've said so far, but I'm fearful that I have to be careful around you. I'm not sure how you might judge me or react to me.

Jerry: I'd like the chance to relate to you as a person, so I hope you'll let me know when you feel judged or not understood by me.

Ruth: It's not easy for me to talk about myself to any man; all of this is so new to me.

Jerry: What is it that you think I'd have a hard time understanding about you as a woman? And you might want to talk more about what makes it difficult to talk to me.

Ruth: So far, no man has ever been willing to really listen to me. I've tried so hard to please my father and then to please John. I suppose I wonder if you can understand how I depended so much on my father, and now on John, to give me a feeling that I'm worthwhile as a woman.

Jerry: Even though I'm not a woman, I still know what it feels like to want to be understood and accepted, and I know what it's like to look to others to get this kind of confirmation.

It is important that we pursue what might get in the way of Ruth's trust in me. As long as she is willing to talk about what she is thinking and feeling while we are together in the sessions, we have a direction to follow. Staying with the immediacy of the relationship will inevitably open up other channels of fruitful exploration.

Becoming Aware of Feelings   In a later session Ruth talks about how hard it is for her to really experience her feelings. She is not very aware of the nature of her feelings because she blocks off any feelings that she deems inappropriate. She does not permit herself to freely accept the flow of whatever she might be feeling. Notice how she puts it:

Ruth: It's hard for me to feel. Sometimes I'm not sure what it is that I feel.

Jerry: From moment to moment you're not aware of what feelings are flowing inside of you.

Ruth: Yeah, it's difficult enough for me to know what I'm feeling, let alone express it to someone else.

Jerry: So it's also hard for you to let others know how they affect you.

Ruth: Well, I've had lots of practice in sealing off feelings. They're scary.

Jerry: It's scary not knowing what you're feeling, and it's also scary if you know.

Ruth: Sort of . . . When I was a child, I was punished when I was angry. When I cried, I was sent to my room and told to stop crying. Sometimes I remember being happy and playful, only to be told to settle down.

Jerry: So you learned early that your feelings got you in trouble.

Ruth: Just about the time I start to feel something, I go blank or get confused. It's just that I've always thought that I had no right to feel angry, sexual, joyful, sad—or whatever. I just did my work and went on without complaining.

Jerry: You still believe it's better to keep what you feel inside and not express feelings.

Ruth: Right! And I do that especially with my husband and my children.

Jerry: It sounds as if you don't let them know what's going on with you.

Ruth: Well, I'm not so sure they're really that interested in my feelings.

Jerry: It's as if they really don't care about how you feel. [*Ruth begins to cry.*] Right now you're feeling something. [*Ruth continues crying, and there is a period of silence.*]

Ruth: I'm feeling sad and hopeless.

Jerry: Yet now you're able to feel, and you can tell me about it.

In this interchange it is important for Ruth to recognize that she can feel and that she is able to express feelings to others. My acceptance of her encourages her to come in contact with her emotions. This is a first step for her. The more difficult task is for Ruth to increasingly become aware of and share her emotions with the significant people in her life.

Exploring Ruth's Marital Problems   In another session Ruth brings up her marital difficulties. She explores her mistrust of her own decisions and her search outside of herself for the answers to her problems.

Ruth: I wonder what I should do about my marriage. I'd like to have some time to myself, but what might happen to our family if I made major changes and nobody liked those changes?

Jerry: You wonder what would happen if you expressed your true feelings, especially if your family didn't appreciate your changes.

Ruth: Yes, I guess I do stop myself because I don't want to hurt my family.

Jerry: If you ask for what you want, others are liable to get hurt, and there's no room in your life to think both about what's good for others and what's good for yourself.

Ruth: I really didn't realize that it had to be either them or me. It's just that at 39 I'm just now thinking about who I am. Perhaps it's too late for me to question what I have in my relationships.

Jerry: Well, I don't know that there's a given time when we should ask such questions. I feel excited for you and respect you for asking these questions now.

Ruth: What I know is that my life has been very structured up to this point, and now all this questioning is unsettling to me and is making me anxious. I wonder if I want to give up my predictable life and face the un-known. I get anxious thinking about how my husband and kids will be if I keep making changes. What if they don't like my changes and it upsets them?

Jerry: I'm touched by what you're saying, and I remember some of my own struggles in facing uncertainty. When you say you're anxious, it would help me to understand you better if you could tell me some of the times or situations in which you feel this anxiety.

Ruth: Sometimes I feel anxious when I think about my relationship with John. I'm beginning to see many things I don't like, but I'm afraid to tell him about my dissatisfactions because I don't want him to get angry.

Jerry: Would you be willing to tell me some of the specific dissatisfactions you have with John?

Ruth then proceeds to talk about some of the difficulties she is experiencing with her husband. I also encourage her to share with me some of the impulses that frighten her. I am providing a safe atmosphere for her to express some new awarenesses without reacting judgmentally to her. I also give her some of my personal reactions to what she is telling me. Then I ask her if she talks very often with John in the way she is talking with me. I am receptive to her and wonder out loud whether he could also be open to her if she spoke this way with him. We end the session with my encouraging her to approach him and say some of the things to him that she has discussed in this session.

Process Commentary   We proceed with how Ruth's fear of others' anger keeps her from asking for what she really wants in her life. She then begins to seek answers from me, not trusting that she knows what is best for herself. Ruth thinks I have the experience and wisdom to provide her with at least some answers. She continues to press for answers to what she should do about her marriage. It is as though she is treating me as an authority who has the power to fix things in her life. She grows very impatient with my unwillingness to give her answers. As she puts it, she is convinced that she needs my "validation and approval" if she is to move ahead.

We return to an exploration of Ruth's feelings toward me for not giving her more confirmation and not providing reassurance that she will make correct decisions. She tells me that if I really cared about her I would give her more direction and do more for her than I am doing. She tells me that all I ever do is listen, that she wants and expects more, and that I am not doing my job properly. I let her know that I do not like her telling me what I am feeling about her. I also tell her that I do care about her struggle but that I refuse to give her answers because of my conviction that she will be able to find answers within herself. I hope she will learn that I can be annoyed with her at times yet not reject her.

Ruth continues to risk sharing more of her feelings with me, and with my encouragement she also begins to be more open with her family. Gradually, she becomes more willing to think about her own approval. She demands less of herself by way of being a fixed product, such as the "perfect person," and allows herself to open up to new experiences, including challenging some of her beliefs and perceptions. Slowly she is showing signs of accepting that the answers to her life situation are not to be found in some outside authority but inside herself.

Although it is not easy for me to refuse to provide answers and direction for Ruth, I believe that to do so would imply a lack of faith in her capacity to find her own way. Therefore, I do not rely on techniques, nor do I fall into the trap of being the guru. We focus on Ruth's feelings about not trusting herself, and she explores in depth the ways in which she is discounting her ability to take a stand in many situations.[4]

 QUESTIONS FOR REFLECTION

1. Knowing what you do of Ruth, how would it be for you to develop a therapeutic relationship with her? Is there anything that might get in your way? If so, how do you think you would deal with this obstacle? To what degree do you think you could understand her subjective world?

2. Dr. Cain indicates that he would not undertake any formal assessment or attempt to establish a DSM-IV-TR diagnosis for a client unless the client requested it. In working with Ruth, he emphasizes her self-assessment and her own definition of her problems. What are your thoughts about excluding formal assessment strategies before engaging in a therapeutic relationship? Do you believe Ruth is able to make a valid self-assessment?

3. Cain says, "If she can listen to the inner voices of her feelings and attend to the distress signals of her body, Ruth will begin to see more clearly who she is and what she wants and, in the process, will begin to find her own voice and path." To what degree do you agree with this assumption? How does your answer influence the way you would work with Ruth?

4. In the therapeutic relationship with Ruth, Cain's interventions were based mainly on listening and accurately responding to what she says. He did not make directive interventions but attempted to stay with her subjective experiencing. What kind of progress do you see her making with this approach?

5. Ruth confronted me with her doubts about my ability to understand her as a woman. Do you think she would do better to see a female therapist? Would you recommend that I suggest a referral to a woman, especially since she brought up her concerns about my being a man? Do you think a male therapist would have a difficult time understanding her world and her struggles as a woman?

6. Ruth mentioned that it was especially difficult to trust a man and that she felt judged by men. How could you work with this theme therapeutically from a person-centered perspective?

7. With both this approach and existential therapy, the client–therapist relationship is central, and the focus is on clients' choosing their way in life. Do you agree that Ruth has this potential for directing her life and making wise choices? Would you be inclined to let her select the topics for exploration, or might you suggest topics? Would you be more directive than either Cain or I was?

 NOTES

1. In David Cain's work with Ruth, he clearly views the therapeutic relationship as the core of the therapeutic process. The *CD-ROM for Integrative Counseling* provides a concrete illustration of how I also view the therapeutic relationship as the foundation for our work together. See the first three sessions: "The Beginning of Counseling," "The Therapeutic Relationship," and "Establishing Therapeutic Goals."

2. If you are using the *CD-ROM for Integrative Counseling,* compare David Cain's assumptions about his client's capacity to tap her internal resources with my interventions at the beginning phase of counseling.

3. In this section of my work with Ruth I encourage her to explore our relationship, especially her reservations about talking about herself. What I describe here is similar to what is depicted in the *CD-ROM for Integrative Counseling,* Session 2 ("The Therapeutic Relationship"). What are some ways that I am attempting to build trust with Ruth?

4. For a more detailed treatment of the person-centered approach, see G. Corey (2005), *Theory and Practice of Counseling and Psychotherapy* (7th edition). Chapter 7 (Person-Centered Therapy) provides a foundation to understand Dr. Cain's work with Ruth from a person-centered perspective.

Chapter 6

Case Approach to Gestalt Therapy

A Gestalt Therapist's Perspective on Ruth

by Jon Frew, Ph.D.

Introduction

Gestalt therapy is practiced with a theoretical foundation grounded in field theory, phenomenology, and dialogue. Individuals are inseparable from the environments they inhabit. Gestalt therapists are interested in the ongoing relationship between the individual and the environment (also referred to as the "field"). Phenomenology involves seeking an understanding based on what is given, obvious, or comprehensible through the senses rather than on interpretations or meanings defined objectively by the observer. The therapist encourages the client to describe, not explain, experience and to attend to moment-to-moment awareness of elements of the field. The emphasis is on the subjective world as the client perceives it.

Gestalt therapy has adopted Martin Buber's dialogical philosophy of relationship to capture the spirit of the I/Thou relationship between therapist and client.[1] The healing that occurs in psychotherapy is a result of the quality of the meeting that occurs between client and therapist. Practicing in a dialogical manner, Gestalt therapists attempt to be fully present, convey to the client that they comprehend and accept the other's experience, and vigilantly attend to the impact of each intervention made.

The goal of Gestalt therapy is, quite simply, the restoration of awareness. The essential method involves following the aspects of the client's experience of self and of environment that become figural or salient for the client. Gestalt therapists will selectively bring aspects of their own moment-to-moment experience, what is figural for them, into contact with the client. In Gestalt therapy, we are not trying to get anywhere or make something in particular happen. Rather, our work is designed to heighten the client's awareness of the present moments as they unfold. Change occurs through attention to what is, not by striving toward preordained objectives.[2]

Assessment of Ruth

Gestalt therapy emphasizes healthy functioning and interruption in healthy functioning. As such, therapists do not use the language of "pathology," or "normal" and "abnormal." Instead, individuals are viewed as having the capacity to self-regulate and to develop in their dealings with the various environments they encounter throughout life. Contact with the environment can be satisfying or interrupted in a variety of ways. Gestalt therapists' assessment involves examining the process that occurs as the individual interacts with self and environment.

Instead of a DSM-IV-TR diagnosis, the Gestalt therapist assesses to determine a "functional diagnosis." The need–fulfillment cycle is one model used to assess a client's level of functioning in two primary and related areas: To what degree is the client aware of self and environment, and can the client move into contact with aspects of the environment in ways that meet needs, achieve self-regulation, and promote growth and change? The need–fulfillment model outlines a "cycle of experience," which begins with physical or emotional sensations and proceeds through awareness (a sharpened sense of meaning), excitement, action, and toward contact with the environment. A functional diagnosis allows the Gestalt therapist to assist clients to understand exactly how they experience interruptions in the natural process of need identification and fulfillment. This is eminently more useful to clients than telling them they are dysthymic or have panic attacks or have an adjustment disorder.

Assessment is an ongoing process embedded in the dialogue between client and therapist (not separate from or occurring before the therapy itself). Gestalt therapists assess in two ways.

First, hypotheses are formed as the therapist listens to clients talk about their lives outside the therapy session. For example, from Ruth's autobiography we learn that she is frequently flooded with powerful sensations (panic, dizziness) that do not lead to a sharpened awareness that could move Ruth into contact with her environment. Instead, she translates her sensations of fear into worry patterns about dying or losing control, and that cycle of experience ends without closure. The panic attacks continue because Ruth is unable to move from the sensation level into some type of action (for example, talking about her anxiety with another) and contact. Ruth also sets goals in her life, such as losing weight or getting a job, which she then resists taking action to reach. She imagines that if she were different she would be happier, or in Gestalt therapy terms "be in more satisfying contact with the environment." The interruption may be that Ruth is "putting the cart before the horse." She is defining an action that is not grounded in the earlier steps in a cycle of experience (sensation, awareness, excitement) that would begin with who Ruth is, not with who she wants to become.

The second and primary way the Gestalt therapist assesses clients' level of awareness and contacting style is by attending to how clients are in contact with the therapist in the therapy session itself. Clients' diminished awareness and ways of making or interrupting contact will become manifest in the relationship with the therapist. The therapy relationship becomes a key vehicle for clients to learn more about how they experience themselves and how they can bring that awareness into contact with the therapist.

Gestalt therapy is practiced in both brief and longer-term contexts. The client's functional diagnosis can be determined relatively quickly through history taking and attending to the client's level of awareness and the quality of contact made in the therapeutic relationship. In a brief therapy model, the therapist supports the client's understanding of his or her characteristic ways of diminishing awareness and contact using the need–fulfillment cycle as a tool to aid in this understanding. Clients can do homework assignments between sessions and continue to examine their own awareness and contacting processes after the therapy is complete. In a longer therapy model, anachronistic patterns of contacting, which are artifacts of past creative adjustments, are examined and shift with more intensive and sustained support from the Gestalt therapist.

Key Issues and Themes

From her autobiography, certain key issues emerge about how Ruth makes contact with her environment. For much of her life Ruth has concentrated on what others want or expect her to be. Operating in that mode has taken Ruth away from paying attention to what she wants from others. Satisfactory contact begins with attention to self—what one is experiencing at the moment and what one is drawn toward in the environment. The payoff for Ruth in living for others has been security. By avoiding herself, she has kept others around her. She fears change in general and attending to her own wants and desires in particular because that could rupture the confluence with others on which she has come to depend. She has already lost her parents. She fears that any further demonstration of her needs and wants could drive her husband away.

The dread and doom of her anxiety experience could very well be a manifestation of this conflict between Ruth's natural inclination to begin to pay more attention to herself and what she needs from others and the learned but unaware response to block those kind of awarenesses, fearing they could lead to being abandoned and left unable to care for herself.

These points are drawn from her autobiographical information and must be viewed as purely hunches until the therapy with Ruth begins. The themes we will actually work with must arise in the session, within the dialogue between Ruth and the therapist, not from clever interpretations in the therapist's head.

Therapeutic Interventions

Gestalt therapy proceeds by watching and listening to clients as they describe what it is like to be in their experience as they sit with you during a therapy session. Assessment, "diagnoses," and identification of themes and issues follow from practicing in the phenomenological and dialogic way. In this dialogue with Ruth, my goals are to assist Ruth in identifying a "figure" or an experience that becomes salient for her, to heighten her awareness of that experience, and to explore how she might make contact with me about that figure of interest.

Therapist: What are you aware of, Ruth, as we begin today?

Ruth: Recently I've become aware that I live for others. I give and give until there is little left to give.

Therapist: How is it for you to give so much?

Ruth: Exhausting and frustrating. The expectations and demands of my husband and children never end, and I never feel like I am doing enough.

Therapist: What do you notice as you tell me this?

Ruth: I don't understand your question.

Therapist: You have been telling me about how much you give to others and how tiring that is. What are you experiencing right now?

Ruth: Well, I'm not tired.

Therapist: Take a minute and check in with yourself.

Ruth [*After a minute*]: I realize I don't do this very often.

Therapist: What are you discovering?

Ruth: I feel a little nervous, but it's different from the anxiety and panic I get.

Therapist: Pay attention to the nervousness and tell me what you can about it.

Ruth: My stomach is fluttering, and I have lots of energy in my legs and arms. I did some theatre in college, and this feels like those moments before I would go on stage.

Therapist: From your description and the way you look right now, it sounds like you might be excited.

Ruth: Yeah, that fits—excited and apprehensive. I realize I don't know exactly what will happen next.

Therapist: You are looking at me very intently. Are you aware of that?

Ruth: I am now [*Fidgets in her chair and looks away*]. Do you have any ideas about how I can stop giving so much?

Therapist: I don't have any idea about that at this moment, Ruth. Tell me what you are aware of now.

Ruth: When you pointed out how I was looking at you, I got scared.

Therapist: Scared?

Ruth: Yeah, a wave of anxiety came over me.

Therapist: And now?

Ruth: Now I am having trouble looking at you. It's more comfortable to look out the window.

Therapist: Would you be willing to experiment for a few minutes?

Ruth: Sure, if you think it would help. What should I do?

Therapist: You agree to experiment without any information about what I have in mind?

Ruth: Sounds like me. I agree to a lot before I know what I'm getting into. To be honest, I'm not sure I want to experiment. What would be the objectives of this experiment?

Therapist: Experiments in Gestalt therapy don't have any particular preset goals. The purpose would be to help you learn more about yourself.

Ruth: Actually, I like the idea of not having goals. I never seem to reach the ones I set in my life.

Therapist: The experiment I am proposing would be to try switching back and forth between eye contact with me and looking away . . . to see what happens for you in each mode.

Ruth: That sounds easy enough. I would like to try it. [*Ruth spends more time looking away from the therapist at first but gradually increases time in eye contact.*]

Therapist [*After several minutes*]: So what do you notice?

Ruth: Looking away is easier, more comfortable. When I look at you, the anxiety returns.

Therapist: You are looking at me now. How is this for you?

Ruth: Like I said, I feel anxious, edgy [*She pauses, takes a deep breath*]. Actually, right now I feel lost and confused. I get this feeling a lot.

Therapist: Finish this sentence for me. Right now I'm lost and confused because _____.

Ruth: . . . because I know you must want something from me, but I don't know what it is. I know how to be a good mother and wife, but it's not clear what I should do here.

Therapist: I saw something shift in your expression. Did you notice that too?

Ruth: Yeah, the feeling has changed.

Therapist: What's going on now?

Ruth [*With a look of mild surprise*]: I'm frustrated. No, that's not all of it. I'm angry. Huh! [*She smiles*]

Therapist: You seem amused by that.

Ruth: It's different. I never get angry except at myself.

Therapist: And this time?

Ruth: I'm angry at you.

Therapist: Will you say that again, and look at me when you do?

Ruth: Another experiment? OK, I'll try. "I'm angry at you for not telling me what you want from me."

Therapist: What happens as you say that to me?

Ruth: I feel good, energized, and even powerful. [*Ruth sits silently, looking relaxed and content; then she looks away and begins to fidget.*]

Therapist: Where did you go?

Ruth: Images of my husband and father came in. I'm angry at them too. I don't know exactly what they want from me either. [*Ruth's expression changes again; she is quiet and tears begin.*]

Therapist: What's happening now?

Ruth: I'm so caught up in giving to others that I don't get what I want. I wouldn't know where to start to find out.

Therapist: We could start here. Is there anything you want from me now?

Ruth: When I started therapy with you, I wanted you to tell me what I should do.

Therapist: And now?

Ruth: I want you to be interested in how I feel and the things I think about.

Therapist: Look at me again Ruth. What do you see?

Ruth: I see a kind face, soft eyes. I see interest, even concern and care. It's very comfortable for me now to have this eye contact.

Process Commentary Experienced basketball players talk about "letting the game come to them." They use this phrase in contrast to "forcing the action" or "trying to make something happen." Practicing Gestalt therapy in a dialogic, phenomenological way is very similar. Therapists take their time, follow their clients' lead, and let the dialogue unfold without rushing or pushing for results.

I began the session by inviting Ruth to check in with herself as she talked about issues in her life. That intervention brings her into the present moment and brings her to the awareness that she rarely attends to her immediate experience. The next several interchanges follow a cycle of experience as Ruth identifies a sensation that leads to an awareness and a sense of excitement about what will happen next.

A contact boundary phenomenon (or interruption) occurs at this point that is a key theme in Ruth's life. Instead of carrying on into action and contact that would be anchored in what Ruth wants, she scans the "field" (the environment) to ascertain what is wanted from her at that moment. When I point out how intently she is looking at me, her anxiety level increases, and she deflects by changing the subject.

I suggest an experiment. Notice how the experiment emerges "organically" from the moment-to-moment dialogue between us. She was already looking at me and looking away. The experiment simply allows us to explore that behavior more intentionally. As Ruth experiments with eye contact, the figure or theme of our session comes into sharper focus. When she looks at me, she experiences a set of feelings related to an assumption that I want something from her and that she doesn't know how to find out what it is.

Ruth's assumption that I want something from her could be defined as a projection, one of the boundary disturbances delineated in Gestalt theory. Typically, a Gestalt therapist would respond to this projection by requiring Ruth to own her own experience. When Ruth said that, I did not want anything from her. I could tell her that, to clarify the boundary condition, but I chose not to make that clarification. Instead, I stayed with Ruth's ongoing experience. As she perceived me as wanting something from her, what was that like for her?

Allowing Ruth to run with her perception of me as wanting something from her led her to another awareness. She was angry at me—and others—for not being clear about what I wanted. A brief experiment directed the anger outward rather than to her typical style of self-criticism. Telling me she was angry at me seemed to complete a cycle of experience (there are many in any therapy session). Ruth acted on the environment, and her contact with me led to a momentary sense of contentment. As that "figure" reached completion, another emerged. Ruth realized that she doesn't attend to what she wants. Invited to do that as we end the session, she identifies a specific want—my interest in her—and through eye contact sees accurately (without projection) that I am interested.

Like all of us, Ruth has characteristic ways of organizing and making meaning out of her moment-to-moment experience of herself and her environment. These ways of making sense out of experience are frequently shaped more by past experiences than by present needs and opportunities. The present moment is accessed through awareness, which is explored through the therapist's active interest in Ruth's ongoing experience.

As Ruth attended to herself and to contact with the therapist, one of her characteristic ways of perceiving relationships formed into an awareness. She saw the therapist as wanting something from her. As the session progressed, that figure eventually shifted to what she wanted from the therapist. This session demonstrates how change occurs through attention to "what is" and how the exact nature of change cannot be aimed for or predicted by a Gestalt therapist.

What Ruth perceives others to want from her and what she wants from others is a key theme, and I believe it will reappear in future sessions. Ruth's inclination to organize her experience of others as having expectations of her she must meet represents a creative adjustment she once made when the field conditions supported that interpretation and her efforts to give to others were reinforced. This probably began in relation to her parents and church. Currently, her relationships with her husband, children, and college professors replicate those same field conditions.

As my therapy relationship with Ruth proceeds, I continue to encourage her to be aware of her moment-to-moment experience. Present awareness, by definition, will counter her tendency to operate on automatic pilot in relationship to me and others. Ruth will continue to learn, as she did in this session, how to accurately assess the present situation. Eventually, Ruth will be able to apply this ability to be in the present to other relationships in her life.[3]

JERRY COREY'S WORK WITH RUTH FROM A GESTALT PERSPECTIVE

In my version of Gestalt work with Ruth I watch for cues from Ruth about what she is experiencing in the here-and-now. By attending to what she is expressing both verbally and nonverbally, I suggest experiments during our sessions. In the *CD-ROM for Integrative Counseling*, Session 7 ("Emotive Focus in Counseling"), I demonstrate how I create experiments to heighten Ruth's awareness. In this particular session I employ a Gestalt experiment, asking Ruth to talk to me as if I were John. During this experiment, Ruth becomes quite emotional. You will see ways of exploring emotional material and integrating this work into a cognitive framework as well.

Basic Assumptions

Approaching Ruth as a Gestalt therapist, I assume that she can deal effectively with her life problems, especially if she becomes fully aware of what is happening in and around her. My central task as her therapist is to help her fully experience her being in the here-and-now by first realizing how she is preventing herself from feeling and experiencing in the present. My approach is basically noninterpretive; instead, I will ask Ruth to provide her own interpretations of her experiences. I expect her to participate in experiments, which consist of trying new ways of relating and responding.

Our sessions will focus on whatever aspect of Ruth's experience is figural. I will attend to the themes (or figures) that emerge for Ruth and follow her lead when she brings up unfinished business from her past and indicates that she want to work on certain themes. Because these feelings are not fully expressed in awareness, they linger in the background and are carried into Ruth's present life in ways that interfere with effective contact between Ruth and others. Her awareness is bound to lead to changes in her interpersonal contacting. A basic premise of Gestalt therapy is that by experiencing conflicts directly, instead of merely talking about them, clients will expand their own level of awareness and integrate the fragmented and unknown parts of their personality.

Assessment of Ruth

Ruth has the capacity to live fully as an integrated person. The difficulties in Ruth's life resulted in creative adjustments, which allowed her to survive and function in past environments. As a Gestalt therapist, I work with Ruth to examine the ways in which she is presently "stuck."

Ruth has never learned that it is acceptable to have and to express feelings. True, she does feel a good deal of guilt, but she rarely expresses the resentment that she likely feels. Any person who is as devoted to others as she is probably feels some resentment at not having received the appreciation she believes is due her. Ruth does not allow herself to get angry with her father, who has punished her by withholding his affection and approval. She does not experience much anger toward John, despite the fact that here again she does not feel recognized. The same is true for both her sons and daughters. Ruth has made a lifetime career out of giving and doing for her family. She maintains that she gets little in return, yet she rarely expresses how this arrangement affects her. It appears that Ruth is keeping all of these feelings locked inside herself, and this is getting in the way of her feeling free. A lot of Ruth's energy is going into blocking her experience of threatening feelings, sensations, and thoughts. Our therapy will encourage her to express her moment-by-moment experience so that her energy is freed up for creative pursuits instead of being spent on growth-inhibiting defenses.

Goals of Therapy

My goal is to provide a context in which Ruth can expand her awareness of what is going on within herself and also how she interacts with others. With awareness Ruth will be able to recognize denied aspects of herself and proceed toward the reintegration of the many facets within herself. Therapy will provide the necessary intervention to help her gain awareness of what she is thinking, feeling, and doing in the present. As Ruth comes to recognize and experience blocks to maturity, she can begin experimenting with different ways of being.

Therapeutic Procedures

I draw heavily on interventions aimed at intensifying here-and-now experiencing. These techniques are designed to help Ruth focus on what is going on within her body and to accentuate whatever she may be feeling. In this sense I am active in my sessions with Ruth. However, I take my cues from her, largely by paying attention to what she is saying both verbally and nonverbally. It is essential that I work within the context of what emerges for Ruth as we talk with each other rather than imposing my agenda of what I think Ruth should explore. From these cues I pick up from Ruth, I create experiments that enable her to heighten whatever she is experiencing.

Some of the experiments that Ruth might carry out may entail giving expression to unexpressed body movements or gestures, or they may involve talking in a different tone of voice. I may ask her to experiment with rehearsing out loud those thoughts that are racing through her—ones she usually keeps to herself. Ruth will be invited to try new behavior and see what these experiments can teach her. If Ruth learns how to pay attention to whatever it is she is experiencing at any moment, this awareness itself can lead to change.

Jerry: Ruth, as we sit here, what are you aware of?

Ruth: I'm having a hard time knowing what I want to talk about today. There are so many things going on, and I want to cover everything. I'm impatient and want to get well quick.

Jerry: I can appreciate wanting to do a lot in a short time. Let me suggest that you sit for a few moments and listen to yourself. What is it that you'd most want for this hour?

Ruth: I just keep feeling guilty over all that I haven't been, especially as a mother. Right now I'm feeling pretty sad because of all the mistakes I've made with my kids.

Jerry: Does one of your children particularly stand out for you?

Ruth: Jennifer! She's on my mind so much. No matter what I try, nothing seems to work. I read books on parenting and that doesn't help. I just feel so guilty!

Jerry: Ruth, rather than telling me about how guilty you feel over not having been the mother you think you should have been to Jennifer, how about simply listing all the ways that you feel this guilt?

Ruth: Oh, that's not hard—there are so many ways! I feel guilty because I haven't been understanding enough, because I've been too easy on her and haven't set limits, because I've been away at college when she needed me during her difficult years. And in some ways I feel responsible for the problems she is faced with—I could go on!

Jerry: So go on. Say more. Make the list as long as you can. [*I am encouraging her to say aloud and unrehearsed many of the things she tells herself endlessly in her head. She continues to speak of her guilt.*]

Ruth [*Letting out a deep sigh*]: There! That's it!

Jerry: And what is that sigh about?

Ruth: Just relief, I suppose. I feel a little better. I just had a flash. You know, I resent Jennifer for expecting me to be the perfect mother. After all, I've gone out of my way for all of my kids. But Jennifer never gives me a clue that I do anything right by her.

Jerry: And what is it like for you to acknowledge that you resent the expectation that you have to be the perfect mother?

Ruth: Well, now I'm feeling guilty again that I have such negative feelings!

I am aware that Ruth is not going to rid herself forever of her guilt. If she does not let her guilt control her, however, she can make room for other feelings. Based on Ruth's bringing up her resentment, which I suspect is related to her guilt, I propose the following experiment:

Jerry: If you're willing to go further, I'd like you to repeat your list of guilts, only this time say "I resent you for . . ." instead of "I feel guilty over . . ."

Ruth: But I don't feel resentment—it's the guilt!

Jerry: I know, but would you be willing to go ahead with the experiment and see what happens?

Ruth [*After some hesitation and discussion of the value of doing this*]: I resent you for expecting me to always be understanding of you. I resent you for demanding so much of my time. I resent you for all the trouble you got yourself into and the nights of sleep I lost over this. I resent you for making me feel guilty. I resent you for not understanding me. I resent you for expecting affection but not giving me any.

My rationale for asking Ruth to convert her list of guilts into a list of resentments is that doing so may help her direct her anger to the sources where it belongs, rather than inward. She has so much guilt partly because she directs her anger toward herself, and this keeps her distant from some people who are significant to her. Ruth becomes more and more energetic with her expression of resentments.

Jerry: Ruth, let me sit in for Jennifer for a bit. Continue talking to me, and tell me the ways in which you resent me.

Ruth [*Becoming more emotional and expressive*]: It's hard for me to talk to you. You and I haven't really talked in such a long time. [*Tears well up in her eyes.*] I give and give, and all you do is take and take. There's no end to it!

Jerry: Tell Jennifer what you want from her.

Ruth [*Pausing and then, with a burst of energy, shouting*]: I want to be more like you! I'm envious of you. I wish I could be as daring and as alive as you. Wow, I'm surprised at what just came out of me.

Jerry: Keep talking to Jennifer, and tell her more about how you're feeling right now.

With Ruth's heightened emotionality she is able to say some things to Jennifer that she has never said but has wished she could. She leaves this session with some new insights: Her feelings of guilt are more often feelings of resentment; her anger toward Jennifer is based on envy and jealousy; and the things she dislikes about Jennifer are some of the things she would like for herself.

Exploring the Polarities Within Ruth   In later sessions Ruth brings up the many ways she feels pulled in different directions. What emerges for her is all the expectations that her parents had for her and the many expectations others still have for her. She reports that she doesn't always want to be the "perfect person." She resents having to be so good and never being allowed to have fun. As she talks, what comes to her awareness are the polarities within her that seem incompatible. We continue working with some of the splits within Ruth's personality. My aim is not to get rid of her feelings but to let her experience them and learn to integrate all the factions of her personality. She will not get rid of one side of her personality that she does not like by attempting to deny it, but she can learn to recognize the side that controls her by expressing it.

Ruth: For so many years I had to be the perfect minister's daughter. I lost myself in always being the proper "good girl." I'd like to be more spontaneous and playful and not worry constantly about what other people would think. Sometimes when I'm being silly, I hear this voice in my head that tells me to be proper. It's as if there are two of me: one that's all proper and prim and the other that wants to be footloose and free.

Jerry: Which side do you feel most right now, the proper side or the uninhibited side?

Ruth: Well, the proper and conservative side is surely the stronger in me.

Jerry: I have an idea of an experiment that I'd like you to try. Are you willing?

Ruth: Why not? I'm ready to work.

Jerry: Here are a couple of chairs. I'd like you to sit in this chair here and be the proper side of you. Talk to the uninhibited side, which is sitting in this other chair.

Ruth: I wish you would grow up! You should act like an adult and stop being a silly kid. If I listened to you, I'd really be in trouble now. You're so impulsive and demanding.

Jerry: OK, how about changing and sitting in the chair over here and speaking from your daring side? What does she have to say to the proper side over there?

Ruth: It's about time you let your hair down and had some fun. You're so cautious! Sure, you're safe, but you're also a very, very dull person. I know you'd like to be me more often.

Jerry: Change chairs again, talking back to the daring side.

Ruth: Well I'd rather be safe than sorry! [*Her face flushes*]

Jerry: And what do you want to say back to your proper side?

Ruth [*Changing chairs*]: That's just your trouble. Always be safe! And where is this getting you? You'll die being safe and secure.

This exchange of chairs goes on for some time. Becoming her daring side is much more uncomfortable for Ruth. After a while she lets herself get into the daring side and chides that old prude sitting across from her. She accuses her of letting life slip by, points out how she is just like her mother, and tells her how her being so proper stops her from having any fun. This experiment shows Ruth the difference between thinking about conflicts and actually letting herself experience those conflicts. She sees more clearly that she is being pulled in many directions, that she is a complex person, and that she will not get rid of feelings by pretending that they are not inside of her. Gradually, she experiences more freedom in accepting the different parts within her, with less need to cut out certain parts of her.

A Dialogue With Ruth's Father   In another session Ruth brings up how it was for her as a child, especially in relation to a cold and ungiving father. I ask her not merely to report what happened but also to bring her father into the room now and talk to him as she did as a child. She goes back to a past event and relives it—the time at 6 years old when she was reprimanded by her father for "playing doctor" with a friend. She begins by saying how scared she was then and how she did not know what to say to him after he had caught her in sexual play. So I encourage her to stay with her scared feelings and to tell her father all the things that she was feeling then but did not say. Then I say to Ruth:

Jerry: Tell your father how you wish he had acted with you. [*As Ruth talks to her father, she strokes her left hand with her right hand. At a later point I hand her a pillow.*] Let yourself be the father you wished you had, and talk to little Ruth. The pillow is you, and you are your father. Talk to little Ruth.

Ruth [*This brings up intense feelings, and for a long time she says nothing. She sits silently, holding "Ruth" and caressing her lovingly. Eventually, some words follow.*]: Ruth, I have always loved you, and you have always been special to me. It has just been hard for me to show what I feel. I wanted to let you know how much you mattered to me, but I didn't know how.[4]

Process Commentary   During the time that Ruth is doing her work, I pay attention to what she is communicating nonverbally. When she asks why I "make so much fuss over the nonverbals," I let her know that I assume that she communicates at least as much nonverbally as through her words. As she is engaged in carrying on dialogues with different parts of herself—with her daughter and with her father—she feels a variety of physical symptoms in her body. For example, she describes her heart, saying it feels as if it wants to break; the knots in her stomach; the tension in her neck and shoulders; the tightness in her head; her clenched fists; the tears in her eyes; and the smile across her lips. At appropriate moments I call her attention to her body and teach her how to pay attention to what she is experiencing in her body. At different times I ask her to try the experiment of "becoming" her breaking heart (or any other bodily sensation) and giving that part of her body "voice."

When Ruth allows herself to speak for her tears, her clenched fists, or her shaking hands, she is typically surprised by what her body can teach her. She gradually develops more respect for the messages of her body. In the same manner we work with a number of her dreams. When she feels free enough to become each part of a dream and then act out her dreams, she begins to understand the messages contained in them.

Ruth exhibits some resistance to letting herself get involved in these Gestalt experiments, but after challenging herself and overcoming her feelings of looking foolish, she is generally amazed at what comes out of these procedures. Without my interpretations she begins to discover for herself how some of her past experiences are related to her present feelings of being stuck in so many ways.

A theme that emerges over and over in Ruth's work is how alive material becomes when she brings an experience into the present. She does not merely intellectualize about her problems, nor does she engage in much talking about events. The emphasis is on participating in experiments to intensify whatever she is experiencing. When she does bring a past event into the present by actually allowing herself to reexperience that event, it often provides her with valuable insights. Ruth does not need interpretations from me as her therapist. By paying attention on a moment-to-moment basis to whatever she is experiencing, Ruth is able to see the meaning for herself.

Ruth's awareness is, by itself, a powerful catalyst for her change. Before she can hope to be different in any respect, she first has to be aware of how she is. The focus of much of her work is on *what* she is experiencing at any given moment, as well as *how*. Thus, when she mentions being anxious, she focuses on *how* this anxiety is manifested in a knot in her stomach or a headache. I focus her on here-and-now experiencing and away from thinking about *why*. Asking why would remove Ruth from her feelings. Another key focus is on dealing with unfinished business. Business from the past does seek completion, and it persists in Ruth's present until she faces and deals with feelings that she has not previously expressed.

 ## QUESTIONS FOR REFLECTION

1. Dr. Frew describes an assessment process that grows out of an I/Thou dialogue between Ruth and himself. What do you think of this approach to assessment?

2. Frew maintains that in Gestalt therapy the interventions are based on observing and listening to what is in the client's present awareness. He takes his time, follows Ruth's lead, and lets the dialogue unfold without rushing or pushing for results. What are your thoughts about using this approach to designing therapeutic interventions?

3. Gestalt interventions are useful in working with the splits and polarities within a person. As you can see, Ruth has problems because she is not able to reconcile or integrate polarities: dependent versus independent, giving to others versus asking and receiving, and the need for security versus the need to leave secure ways and create new ways of being. Are you aware of struggling with any of Ruth's polarities in your life now?

4. Can you think of some ways to blend the cognitive focus of Adlerian therapy with the emotional themes that are likely to emerge through Gestalt work with Ruth? Provide a few examples of how you could work with her feelings and cognitions by combining concepts and methods from the two approaches.

5. What main differences do you see between the way Frew worked with Ruth (as a Gestalt therapist) and the way Cain worked with her (as a person-centered therapist)? What about the differences in the way I counseled Ruth from these two perspectives?

6. Think about Ruth as being from each of the following ethnic and cultural backgrounds: Native American, African American, Latino, and Asian American. How might you tailor Gestalt experiments in working with her if she were a member of each of these groups? What are some of the advantages and disadvantages of drawing on concepts and interventions from Gestalt therapy in working with cultural themes in her life?

7. What specific areas of unfinished business are most evident to you as you read about Ruth? Do any of her unexpressed feelings bring to awareness any of your own business from the past? What potential unresolved areas in your own life might interfere with your ability to work effectively with Ruth? How might you deal with these feelings if they came up as you were counseling her?

NOTES

1. For a discussion of the dialogical philosophy of relationship, see M. Buber (1970), *I and Thou* (Scribner's).

2. For a more detailed discussion of the key concepts of Gestalt therapy, see G. Corey (2005), *Theory and Practice of Counseling and Psychotherapy* (7th edition). Chapter 8 (Gestalt Therapy) outlines the basic elements of the therapeutic process.

3. R. Hycner & L. Jacobs (1995), *The Healing Relationship in Gestalt Therapy: A Dialogic/Self Psychology Approach* (Gestalt Press) is an excellent resource for understanding contemporary Gestalt therapy, which is based on a meaningful dialogic relationship between client and therapist. The authors address issues that are at the core of the therapeutic relationship.

4. The *CD-ROM for Integrative Counseling* has a vivid illustration of the power of Gestalt experiments. In Session 11 ("Understanding How the Past Influences the Present"), Ruth symbolically talks to her father. I ask her to bring the past event to life by talking directly to her father as the scared 6-year-old child.

Chapter 7

Case Approach to Behavior Therapy

A Multimodal Behavior Therapist's Perspective on Ruth

by Arnold A. Lazarus, Ph.D., ABPP

Introduction

Multimodal therapy is a broad-based, systematic, and comprehensive approach to behavior therapy that calls for technical eclecticism (that is, the use of effective techniques regardless of their point of origin). The multimodal orientation assumes that clients are usually troubled by a multitude of specific problems, which should be dealt with using a wide range of specific techniques. Whenever feasible, therapists should select empirically supported treatments of choice for specific disorders. The comprehensive assessment, or therapeutic modus operandi, attends to each area of a client's BASIC I.D. (B = behavior, A = affect, S = sensation, I = imagery, C = cognition, I = interpersonal relationships, and D = drugs and biological factors). Discrete and interactive problems throughout each of the foregoing modalities are identified, and appropriate techniques are selected to deal with each difficulty. A genuine and empathic client–therapist relationship provides the soil that enables the techniques to take root.

Multimodal Assessment of Ruth

In Ruth's case more than three dozen specific and interrelated problems can be identified using the diagnostic, treatment-oriented BASIC I.D. methodology.

Behavior

fidgeting, avoidance of eye contact, and rapid speaking

poor sleep pattern

tendency to cry easily

overeating

various avoidance behaviors

Affect

anxiety

panic (especially in class and at night when trying to sleep)

depression

fears of criticism and rejection

pangs of religious guilt

trapped feelings

self-abnegation

Sensation

dizziness

palpitations

fatigue and boredom

headaches

tendency to deny, reject, or suppress her sexuality

overeating to the point of nausea

Imagery

ongoing negative parental messages

residual images of hellfire and brimstone

unfavorable body image and poor self-image

view of herself as aging and losing her looks

inability to visualize herself in a professional role

Cognition

self-identity questions ("Who and what am I?")

worrying thoughts (death and dying)

doubts about her right to succeed professionally

categorical imperatives ("shoulds," "oughts," and "musts")

search for new values

self-denigration

Interpersonal relationships

unassertiveness (especially putting the needs of others before her own)

fostering her family's dependence on her

limited pleasure outside her role as mother and wife

problems with children

unsatisfactory relationship with her husband (yet fear of losing him)

looking to the therapist for direction

still seeking parental approval

Drugs and biological factors

overweight

lack of an exercise program

various physical complaints for which medical examinations reveal no organic pathology

Like Jerry Corey, I typically don't think in diagnostic terms. Indeed, a multimodal clinician sees the range of problems across the BASIC I.D. as the "diagnosis." It does not make sense to me to present one particular diagnosis. Many of the labels contained in the DSM-IV-TR would seem to apply to Ruth. These include:

300.4: dysthymic disorder

300.01: panic disorder

309.28: adjustment disorder with mixed anxiety and depressed mood

V61.1: partner relational problem

313.82: identity problem

If forced to pick one of these labels, I would say that adjustment disorder with mixed anxiety and depressed mood comes closest to covering her main difficulties.

Selecting Techniques and Strategies

The goal of multimodal therapy is not to eliminate each and every identified problem. Rather, after establishing rapport with Ruth and developing a sound therapeutic alliance, I would select several key issues in concert with her. Given the fact that she is generally tense, agitated, restless, and anxious, one of the first antidotes might be the use of relaxation training. Some people respond with paradoxical increases in tension when practicing relaxation, and it is necessary to determine what particular type of relaxation will suit an individual client (for example, direct muscular tension–relaxation contrasts, autogenic training, meditation, positive mental imagery, diaphragmatic breathing, or a combination of methods). I have no reason to believe Ruth would not respond to deep muscle relaxation, positive imagery, and self-calming statements.

The next pivotal area is her unassertiveness and self-entitlements. I will employ behavior rehearsal and role playing. Our sessions will also explore her right to be professional and successful. Cognitive restructuring will address her categorical imperatives and will endeavor to reduce the "shoulds," "oughts," and "musts" she inflicts on herself. Imagery techniques may be given prominence, and her homework assignment may include using a particular image over and over until she feels in control of the situation. For example, I may ask Ruth to picture herself going back in a time machine so that she can meet herself as a little girl and provide her alter ego with reassurance about the religious guilts her father imposed.

Therapist: Can you visualize yourself stepping into a time machine and traveling back in time to meet up with yourself as a very young child?

Ruth: OK, I think I can do that.

Therapist: How far back in time would you like to travel? At what age would you wish to meet up with your alter ego, your much younger self?

Ruth: I see myself as a 10-year-old child.

Therapist: The special time machine and you are now journeying back into the past. [*Pause*] Now, please imagine yourself stepping out of the machine, and there you see a little girl. It is you, Little Ruth, at 10 years of age. She looks up at you but does not realize that she is looking at her adult self. But this Little Ruth senses something very special about you, and she will pay close attention to whatever you say to her. [*Pause*] Picture yourself giving Little Ruth a hug. [*Pause*] Now, what would you like to tell her about your father's preachings?

Ruth: [*Big Ruth tells Little Ruth that her father is thoroughly misguided and not to heed the religious guilt he is imposing on her.*]

Most people resonate with this imagery and, with considerable emotion, they narrate the supportive, corrective, reparative, and encouraging points they would share with their alter ego. If they do not spontaneously go there, the therapist will prompt them in this direction. After 5 or 10 minutes (depending on how engrossed they remain in the image) clients are asked to reenter the time machine and go forward until they step out into the present. Many people have found this to be a robust and helpful procedure, and it can be practiced at home several times a day as well as in therapy sessions. The active mechanism behind this procedure is presumed to be a form of desensitization and cognitive restructuring.

If Ruth and her husband agree to it, some marital counseling (and possibly some sex therapy) may be recommended, followed by some family therapy sessions aimed at enhancing the interpersonal climate in the home. Indeed, if Ruth becomes a more relaxed, confident, assertive person, John and her children may need help to cope with her new behaviors. Moreover, I can try to circumvent any attempts at "sabotage" by him or the children.

If Ruth feels up to it, I will teach her sensible eating habits and will embark on a weight reduction and exercise regimen. Referral to a local diet center may be a useful adjunct.

As a part of the assessment process, I ask Ruth to fill out the 15-page Multimodal Life History Inventory.[1] This process enables me to detect a wide range of problems throughout the BASIC I.D. The following dialogue ensues:

Therapist: On page 12 of the questionnaire, you wrote "no" to the question "Do you eat three well-balanced meals each day?" and also to the question

"Do you get regular physical exercise?" And on page 15, you wrote that you frequently drink coffee, overeat, eat junk foods, and have weight problems.

Ruth: Maybe I should go on a diet again.

Therapist: Well, the problem with going on a diet is that people soon come off it and gain weight, perhaps even more weight than they lost. I think the goal is to develop sensible eating patterns. To begin with, I have a list of foods a nutritionist gave me, stuff that we should avoid eating or cut down on. [*The list contains mainly foods with a high fat content, especially those with saturated fats, as well as foods with a high sugar content.*] For starters, would you be willing to take it home and see how many of these items you can cut out of your diet?

Ruth: Certainly.

Therapist: I wonder if we could make a pact?

Ruth: About what?

Therapist: That you would agree to take a brisk 1- to 2-mile walk at least three times a week.

Ruth: I can do that.

Therapist: By the way, there's an excellent diet center in your neighborhood. They have a program in which they train people to understand food contents and to easily calculate the amount of fiber and calories you require. They also run support groups. It's often easier to develop new eating habits when you're part of a group instead of trying to do it on your own.

Ruth: Yes, I know the place you mean. I've often thought of going there. Do you really think it would be a good idea?

Therapist: Yes, I really do.

Therapy Sessions With Ruth

After I draw up Ruth's Modality Profile (BASIC I.D. chart), the clinical dialogue proceeds as follows:

Therapist: I've made up a list, under seven separate headings, of what your main problems seem to be. For example, under behavior I have the following: fidgeting, avoidance of eye contact, rapid speaking, poor sleep pattern, tendency to cry easily, overeating, and various avoidance behaviors.

Ruth: That's what I do; they're all correct. [*Pause*] But I'm not exactly sure what you mean by "various avoidance behaviors."

Therapist: Well, it seems to me that you often avoid doing things that you'd like to do; instead, you do what you think others expect of you. You avoid following through on your plans to exercise and to observe good eating habits. You avoid making certain decisions.

Ruth: I see what you mean. I guess I'm a pretty hopeless case. I'm so weak and panicky, such a basic coward, that I can't seem to make up my mind about anything these days.

Therapist: One thing you seem to be very good at and never avoid is putting yourself down. You sure won't feel helpless if you start taking emotional risks and if you're willing to speak your mind. What does that sound like to you?

Ruth: Are you asking me if I'd like to be more outgoing and less afraid?

Therapist: That's a good way of putting it. What do you think would happen if you changed in that regard?

Ruth: I'm not sure, but I certainly don't think my father would approve.

Therapist: And how about your husband?

Ruth [*Looking downcast*]: I see what you're getting at.

Therapist: Would you agree that you first tended to march to your father's drum and then handed most of the control over to your husband? [*Ruth is nodding affirmatively.*] Well, I think it's high time you become the architect and designer of your own life.

Ruth does not feel overwhelmed, so I discuss the other items on her Modality Profile. If she had showed signs of concern ("Oh my God! I have so many problems!"), I would have targeted only the most salient items and helped her work toward their mitigation or elimination.

Whenever feasible, I select data-based methods of treatment. Thus, in dealing with her panic attacks, I first explain the physiology of panic and the fight-or-flight response. Emphasis is placed on the distinction between adaptive and maladaptive anxiety. For example, anxiety is helpful when it prompts Ruth to study for an exam, but it is maladaptive when its intensity undermines her performance. Her anxiety reactions are examined in terms of their behavioral consequences; secondary affective responses (such as fear of fear); sensory reactions; the images, or mental pictures, they generate; their cognitive components; and their interpersonal effects. In each instance I apply specific strategies. Behaviorally, for example, I encourage her to stop avoiding situations and instead to confront them. In the cognitive modality, she is enjoined to challenge thoughts like "I must be going crazy!" or "I'm going to die!" and to replace them with these self-statements: "My doctor confirmed that I'm physically healthy." "Being anxious won't make me crazy!" Because so many people who suffer from panic tend to overbreathe (hyperventilate), I teach Ruth how to breathe more slowly and use her diaphragm, thereby dampening her physical symptoms. The adjunctive use of drug therapy such as the new generation of antidepressants may also be considered, especially if her progress is unduly slow.

It is usually important to deal with "pivotal events"—critical incidents or significant memories that seem to play a central role. Thus, in an effort to extinguish the guilt and proscriptions associated with her father's general remonstrations, especially the way he berated her for "playing doctor," I would employ the time travel method discussed earlier.

Therapist: Let's use that time machine method again. It will probably counteract several painful memories.

Ruth: That's OK with me.

Therapist: Good. First just relax in the chair for a few moments? [*Pause*] Let your body feel pleasant and at ease. [*Pause*] Can you close your eyes and imagine that we have that time machine and this time it will take you back to visit yourself at the age of 6? [*Pause*] You step into the device, and you step out and see 6-year-old Little Ruth. The 39-year-old Ruth, you at present, looks at the 6-year-old Ruth, 33 years into the past. [*Pause*] Can you picture that?

Ruth [*Nods affirmatively*]: Oh yes, I see her all right.

Therapist: What is she doing?

Ruth: She's holding a rag doll in her right hand and sucking two fingers of her other hand.

Therapist: Can you tell if your visit to her has come before or after her father caught her playing doctor?

Ruth [*Pausing*]: Judging by the guilty look in her eyes, it must be after.

Therapist: Now Little Ruth looks at you, at 39-year-old Ruth. She doesn't realize that you really are her, 33 years into the future, a grown woman, a wife, a mother, Little Ruth all grown up. But she senses something special about you, and she feels very close to you and trusts you. Can you get into that image?

Ruth [*Softly*]: Yes.

Therapist: Good. Now what do you want to say to Little Ruth?

Ruth: First, I want to tell her not to buy into all that stuff about religion, the gospel, and all that guilt [*Pause*].

Therapist: Talk to her, explain it to her. She'll hear you. She'll listen to you.

As this dialogue continues, Ruth is encouraged to offer her 6-year-old alter ego some good advice, encouragement, and nonjudgmental insights.

Ruth becomes deeply involved and grows very emotional, especially when challenging the painful notions and events that have tended to haunt her. At the end of the exercise I ask Ruth to step into the time machine again and to travel forward into the present. A detailed discussion then ensues, and Ruth experiences reparative effects.

A Conjoint Session With Ruth and John

The treatment trajectory depends mainly on Ruth's readiness for change (for example, her willingness to take risks, be assertive, and challenge her dysfunctional thoughts) and the extent to which her husband is invested in keeping her subservient. John feels threatened by Ruth when she starts expressing and fulfilling herself, and conjoint sessions are essential to persuade him that he will be better off in the long run with a wife who feels personally satisfied rather than bitter, frustrated, and bored. Thus, I suggest to her that she encourage John to attend at least one therapy session with her. I tell her that I intend to go out of my way to bond with John so as to gain his compliance. In this connection, I have the following dialogue with Ruth and John:

Therapist [*Addressing John*]: Thank you for agreeing to meet with me. As you know, I've been trying to help Ruth overcome various fears and anxieties, and I believe she has made considerable headway. But now we're at a point where I need your input and assistance. I wonder if we can start by hearing your views on the subject.

John [*Glancing at Ruth*]: What do you want to know?

Therapist: Quite a number of things. I'd like to know how you view her therapy, whether you think it was or is necessary, and if you think she has been helped. I'd like to hear your complaints about Ruth—after all, no marriage is perfect.

John [*Addressing Ruth*]: Can I be perfectly honest?

Ruth: John, that's why we're here.

Therapist: Please be completely frank and above board.

John: What do I call you?

Therapist: Let's not be formal or stuffy. Call me Arnold.

John: Well, Arnold, the way I see it is that Ruth has bitten off more than she can chew. Things were pretty good until she decided to go to college. I don't think she can manage a career and a home. It's putting too much pressure on her. I mean, you know, I think if you take things away from the family, everyone suffers. It's not as if she needs to work for the money. Heck, I've always made enough to support my family.

Therapist: That's very important. Have things changed for the worse inside the family since Ruth started studying? Has she neglected you and the kids? Is the family suffering?

John: Well, not exactly. I mean, Ruth's always been a good wife and a devoted mother. But [*Pause*] I don't quite know how to put it. [*Pause*]

Therapist: Perhaps you're reacting to a feeling inside of yourself that there's the potential for some sort of penalty or withdrawal . . . that something will be taken away from you.

John: Yeah, maybe.

Therapist: You're facing a turning point that many families encounter. The job of mothering is virtually done. Let's see. Your four children are now 19, 18, 17, and 16 years old. So the energy Ruth had to expend in taking care of them in the past must be replaced by something else. Now that the kids are almost grown up, she has more time on her hands. Her full-time homemaking has now become a part-time activity. As Ruth approaches 40, it seems that she needs to become more than a wife and mother. Not less, but more. It would be a mistake for her to do anything that would damage or undermine her relationship with you and the children. Let's say she aspired to become an executive who would spend 60 hours a week at work. Then there would be big trouble.

John [*Smiling*]: You can say that again!

Therapist: Well, if she works as an elementary schoolteacher, the time that she used to devote to caring for your kids would be put to constructive use. But if she just hung around at home, you'd soon have a bitter, resentful, and frustrated woman on your hands. What would she do with all that free time except become a royal pain in the neck? Does that make sense?

John: I guess I see what you're getting at.

Therapist: Besides, let's face it. Even though you make good money, with four kids to put through college, a bit of extra cash won't hurt. [*Talking to Ruth*] I hope you don't mind too much that John and I have been talking about you as if you weren't in the room. I meant no disrespect, but I really wanted to touch base with him.

Ruth: No, I understand. May I ask something?

Therapist [*Ironically*]: Only if you get down on bended knee.

Ruth [*Smiling*]: The 6-year-old strikes again! [*Turning to John*] John, have I ever neglected you or the children?

John: Like I said, you've been a good wife and mother.

Therapist: Now the question is whether you can continue being a good wife and mother and also become a good teacher.

A follow-up session with Ruth after the conjoint meeting commences as follows:

Therapist: I'm curious to know if our threesome meeting seemed to have any positive effects. What do you think we accomplished?

Ruth: It's hard to tell. I mean John came away saying that you made sense, which I think is a very good sign. He seemed quite comfortable with you.

Therapist: Well, I hope that the "sense" I made adds up to getting him to realize that if you don't work but function as a full-time homemaker now that the children have grown up it will be to everyone's detriment. I want you, from time to time, to underscore that point. We need John to become fully aware that there's a positive payoff, a definite advantage for him if you work, and that it's in no way a reflection of his earning capacity. As I told him, the extra money will be useful, but it's not essential. Can you gently but firmly make those points over and over?

Ruth: I think that's what's needed for John to feel OK about it.

Therapist: And you? Do you feel OK about it? You've expressed quite a bit of conflict over this issue.

Ruth: I'm still afraid of many things, and I'm still not entirely confident that I can succeed.

Therapist: Well, should we look into this now?

Ruth: Susan—she's my 17-year-old—has me a little upset over an incident that occurred. Can we discuss this first?

Therapist: Sure.

Concluding Comments

The initial objective was to gain permission from "Big Daddy John" for Ruth to pursue a career. If John seemed motivated to enter couples therapy with a view to improving their marriage—really getting to know and appreciate each other, enhancing their levels of general and sexual communication—this would be all to the good. It would not surprise me if he also elected to seek personal therapy for some of his insecurities. As a multimodal therapist, I would expect to encounter no difficulties in treating Ruth individually, Ruth and John as a couple, and John as an individual.

The multimodal approach assumes that lasting treatment outcomes require combining various techniques, strategies, and modalities. A multimodal therapist works with individuals, couples, and families as needed. The approach is pragmatic and empirical. It offers a consistent framework for diagnosing problems within and among each vector of personality. The overall emphasis is on fitting the treatment to the client by addressing factors such as the client's expectancies, readiness for change, and motivation. The therapist's style (for example, degree of directiveness and supportiveness) varies according to the needs of the client and the situation. Above all, flexibility and thoroughness are strongly emphasized. I very much believe in "bibliotherapy" and would urge Ruth to read my user-friendly self-help book, *The 60-Second Shrink: 101 Strategies for Staying Sane in a Crazy World*. I might also give her a copy of my book, *Marital Myths Revisited: A Fresh Look at Two Dozen Mistaken Beliefs About Marriage*, as a gift.[2]

Most therapists would probably find Ruth capable of being helped and relatively easy to treat. Unlike some clients with severe personality disturbances, she displays no excessive hostility, no intense self-destructive tendencies, and no undue "resistance," and her interpersonal style appears to be collaborative rather than belligerent or contentious. Nevertheless, if one treats only two or three modalities (which is what most nonmultimodal counselors address), several important problems and deficits may be glossed over or ignored, thereby leaving her with untreated complaints that could have been resolved and with a propensity to relapse (for example, revert back to her timid, conflicted, anxious, depressed, and unfulfilled modus vivendi).

In this era, when brief therapy is the order of the day, instead of focusing or dwelling on one or two so-called pivotal issues (which is what many time-limited counselors attempt to do), multimodal therapists would address one major problem from each dimension of the BASIC I.D.[3] In Ruth's case, if we had only 6 to 10 sessions in which to work, the following issues might be selected:

Behavior: Address her avoidance response.

Affect: Implement anxiety-management techniques.

Sensation: Teach her self-calming relaxation methods.

Imagery: Use positive self-visualizations.

Cognition: Try to eliminate categorical imperatives ("shoulds," "oughts," and "musts").

Interpersonal relationships: Administer assertiveness training.

Drugs and biology: Recommend a sensible nutrition and exercise program.

The multimodal maxim is that breadth is often more important than depth. The clinician who sinks one or two deep shafts is likely to bypass a host of other issues. It is wiser to address as broad an array of problems as time permits. Through a "ripple effect," a change in one modality tends to generalize to others, but the greater the number of discrete problems that can be overcome, the more profound the eventual outcome is likely to be.[4]

Another Behavior Therapist's Perspective on Ruth

by Barbara Brownell D'Angelo, Ph.D.

Introduction

Behavior therapy encompasses a wide variety of specific techniques, including biofeedback training, assertiveness training, desensitization, operant conditioning, modeling, and role playing. The common thread running through these techniques is a focus on finding solutions to current behavioral problems and complaints. The client identifies a specific complaint and, together with the therapist, devises a plan to address it. There is little mystery in the behavioral approach. In addition, since the treatment goals are well defined, it becomes clear early in the therapeutic process how well the therapy is progressing. The therapist's task is to fine-tune the program with constant attention to whether it is working. The behaviorist asks "what," "when," and "how" questions rather than "why" questions.

Basic Assumptions and Their Application

Behavior therapists make six basic assumptions.

1. Assessment is an ongoing process in behavioral therapy. It begins with the client's complaint, which is then analyzed to determine its antecedents and consequences. The client keeps a record of the frequency and intensity of occurrences, and this becomes the tool in devising a therapeutic plan and in deciding whether the therapy is working.

2. The therapeutic relationship is a source of powerful reinforcement and is essential if treatment is to succeed. The therapist must be supportive, attentive, and engender a feeling of confidence and trust in the client.

3. The major focus is on the present rather than the past. When the past is discussed, the emphasis is on discovering how it applies to the current situation.

4. Attention is directed toward observable behavior, although this can include not only actions but also feelings and thoughts. Anything that is identifiable, discernible, and quantifiable is fair game.

5. Therapist and client together conduct a careful evaluation of the antecedents and consequences of a behavior to determine how best to set up a program of behavioral change. Creativity is crucial because each person

presents a unique challenge, and the most effective combination of techniques must be fine-tuned for each individual.

6. The client is encouraged to try new behaviors and, together with the therapist, to devise plans to put the program into effect. During the sessions, the therapist may model the desired behavior, role-playing with the client, and may ask the client to practice the new behavior in the neutral office setting prior to trying it out in real life.

Let's look at how these assumptions can be applied in counseling Ruth.

Assessment   Traditional diagnostic categories are rarely useful to the behavior therapist because there is no direct relationship between the diagnosis and a specific treatment. The therapist may be required to submit a diagnosis, however, for the client to qualify for insurance to defray part of the cost of therapy or as a requirement of a managed care program. In such cases the diagnosis is made but is not a factor in decisions on treatment. There may also be unintended ramifications for clients should they be pinned with a diagnosis of mental disorder. The ethical issues involved with such diagnoses should be fully studied and understood to preclude clients from suffering future consequences. For example, disability, life, and health insurance plans may consider such diagnoses as negative factors in determining future eligibility for insurance.

Given these cautions, if Ruth chooses to participate in a third-party reimbursement process and if a formal diagnosis is required by her insurance carrier, I think that an *adjustment disorder* is most fitting in her case. She evidences clinically significant emotional or behavioral symptoms in response to stressors such as having her children leave home, completing graduate school, and securing a teaching position.

As a behavior therapist, I rely on Ruth for direction by asking what is motivating her to seek therapy. I want to know from her which of her issues are causing her the most discomfort. Rather than theorizing about hidden meanings, I directly ask her what she would like to change.

Therapist: Tell me what brings you here today.
Ruth: I've been in therapy before, and it helped me a lot. I guess I had thought I could use what I'd learned and didn't need any more help.
Therapist: And now you're not so sure.
Ruth: Yeah, I'm just not following through on trying to get a job, and I'm feeling more and more upset with myself in general.
Therapist: What bothers you about this? Not having a job or the feeling of being upset?
Ruth: Both. I hate moping around, but I feel in my heart that if I got moving on a plan I wouldn't be so depressed. Then, too, I'm afraid if I really did get a job I couldn't be there for my family.
Therapist: It sounds as if you're not sure what you really want for yourself.
Ruth: You're right. I keep flip-flopping.

Therapist: OK. It's important that I understand how you see things. Before we look at this in more detail, could you tell me if you're concerned about any other issues?

Ruth: Well, yes. I was doing great on my weight-control program. I lost almost 12 pounds. And then I just stopped exercising and started stuffing again. I've already gained half of it back.

Therapist: So after initially being successful, you're finding yourself backsliding.

Ruth: Sad but true. I started to feel guilty about not getting breakfast for John and the kids. The exercise class was at eight in the morning, so I just dropped out.

Therapist: Your children.

Ruth: Four of them. They're all teenagers.

Therapist: And they expect you to make breakfast for them.

Ruth: Not really. But if I don't, then they'd just skip it altogether.

Therapist: It sounds as if you're carrying the full weight of responsibility for your family.

Ruth: I always have. I've always put their needs ahead of mine. It seems I can never find the time or energy to do anything I want to do—I mean, just for me.

Ruth touches on several specific areas she would like to target: getting a job, losing weight, and changing her role as supermom. Upon further discussion, it becomes clear that most of her difficulties are a result of her relationships with her husband and children. Her continuous sacrificing for them has created in her a reservoir of resentment, which has, in turn, immobilized her.

Therapist: Let me try to summarize what you've been saying. You would like to start putting yourself first, for a change.

Ruth: Yes, but I don't want to feel guilty about it.

Therapist: I understand. That's something we'll want to work on. This week, though, I'd like you to do some record-keeping. It'll give us a good idea of what's really going on.

Ruth: You want me to write things down?

Therapist: Yes. We'll need some very concrete information to help us get a handle on this. Here's a small binder, divided into two sections. Let's write the day of the week at the top of each page. Now, whenever you do something for yourself, or do something that you really, truly want to do, write it down here. Whenever you do something for your husband or your children, describe it on this page. Also, make a note next to each entry about your feelings related to each episode. OK?

Ruth: All right. I think this is going to be interesting.

Ruth has identified her major complaint, but we don't know enough about it yet. After a week of keeping track, she will have a good record of the extent of the problem, and we will be on our way toward designing a program to deal with it. A second benefit of data collection is that her motivation is being put to a test. If she returns the following week with a blank binder and a bushel of excuses, I will wonder if she is truly motivated to make changes. A final reason for asking her to record her interactions is that it will give her a feeling of accomplishment and a sense that she is taking some positive action.

The Therapeutic Relationship   Regardless of the therapeutic approach, the chemistry between therapist and client must be right if progress is to be made. Ruth has benefited from previous therapy, and she therefore has a positive expectation about seeking help. During the first session, we discuss her experiences with her previous therapist and her current expectations.

Therapist: You said you benefited from your previous therapy. Can you tell me what was particularly helpful?

Ruth: [*She then tells me what she found useful in her therapy and we have a dialogue about this.*]

Focus on the Present   I want to concentrate on Ruth's current life and to encourage changes in the present. However, the past contains valuable lessons for the present, and we will therefore call on past experiences when necessary. A consistent pattern of self-denial characterizes Ruth's daily life. Even she was surprised to recognize the extent of it. At this point, I wish to determine the nature of the problem as she currently experiences it. I am not interested in searching for causative factors in her childhood but basically want to know "what is going on" with her today.

Ruth: Well, here it is—my week in review.

Therapist: You started on Tuesday. Let's see what you've got here.

Ruth: It started bright and early on Tuesday. Adam needed cotton balls for a school project, so I drove across town to the all-night grocery. Then I made breakfast and packed lunches for everyone but Jennifer. She snubs brown-bagging.

Therapist: This brought you to 9 o'clock in the morning.

Ruth: Yes. I don't waste time. Then I cleaned up after everyone. I hate to say it, but I couldn't stand the messes in Susan's and Adam's rooms, so I picked up there too.

Therapist: And what were you feeling when you were in their rooms?

Ruth: I guess I felt disgusted . . . ticked off. I mean they're 16 and 17 years old, for heaven's sake. I felt like a servant, a totally unappreciated servant at that.

Therapist: No wonder. Balanced against these 26 entries on Tuesday, there was nothing that you did for yourself.

Now that Ruth is aware of the degree to which she sacrifices for her family and ignores her own needs, we want to begin thinking about making changes. I ask her for some ideas of what she might find enjoyable and ask her to recall activities from her past that gave her pleasure.

Therapist: This is a good time to do some brainstorming. Let's write down some of the things you think you might enjoy doing. Does anything come to mind?

Ruth: I used to sing in the choir. They say I have a pretty decent voice.

Therapist: OK, let's write, "Join the church choir."

Ruth: And right after John and I married, we went on long walks together. I remember that as having been fun.

Therapist: Good. Keep going. What else do you remember that was enjoyable?

Ruth: I used to love taking pictures and arranging them in artistic collages. I haven't done that in years.

Therapist: This is a nice start. You've come up with several things. During the next several days, keep your mind alert to ideas you can add to the list and jot them down. We'll go over them at our next meeting and make some selections.

Attention Directed to Observable Behavior   Ruth has observed and recorded interactions with her family. In addition, she made notes on her thoughts and feelings about these interactions as they took place. Midway through the second session, we discuss some alternative behaviors she might try, but we also need to address the thoughts and feelings that are causing her such discomfort.

Ruth: This week I found myself getting overly concerned if all my kids were having breakfast. Of course, I put it on my shoulders to make sure they all ate. If I thought I could leave the family to their own devices, I would.

Therapist: Certainly it is important that your children have breakfast. But is this totally your responsibility?

Ruth: Unfortunately, I tell myself if they don't eat I am not doing my job!

Therapist: Let's try something. Close your eyes for a minute and imagine you've just set breakfast out for your family and you're getting into the car, heading for class.

Ruth: OK. Now what?

Therapist: Let this image become as real as possible to you, and tell me what you're saying to yourself.

Ruth: I'm saying, "What if Adam doesn't eat what I've put out for him?"

Therapist: All right. Now, tell me what you're feeling.

Ruth: A knot in my stomach . . . kind of a constricted feeling in my chest. I hate that feeling.

Therapist: OK. Now, just as an experiment, I'd like you to say—aloud: "I've done more than enough for them this morning. Adam will eat what he needs." Would you repeat that statement five times, and put some intensity into it.

Ruth repeats the statement aloud, and then I instruct her to repeat it silently until it seems natural to her. After several repetitions, I ask Ruth to focus on her feelings. After working on her feelings, further practice is desirable. I may also suggest that she take a step toward trying out a new behavior.

Therapist: Now, how do you feel about setting out breakfast for John and the kids and going to the exercise class? Is this something you'd be willing to do one time this week?

Ruth: I'll think about it and tell you how it goes next week. OK?

Therapist: Good. See you then.

Analyzing Antecedents and Consequences   One of Ruth's short-term goals is to resume her morning exercise class. I want to assist her by making it easy for her to succeed and ensuring that she will feel positive about the experience. Setting the stage for success—arranging favorable antecedents—is crucial to carrying out the plan.

Then we work together to structure Ruth's situation so that she will find it easy to attend the exercise class. A related strategy is to build in as many rewards as possible. This is done by ensuring that the consequences of a behavior are rewarding.

Trying Out New Behaviors   The therapy session provides a neutral setting where behaviors can be practiced without risk. Ruth needs assistance in developing a more assertive stance with her family. One aspect of assertiveness training involves learning new behaviors by way of role playing. In a role-playing exercise I pretend I am John and ask Ruth to talk to me as she would if I were John. Then we switch roles. Ruth takes on John's role, and I demonstrate a more assertive stance so that Ruth can consider alternative behaviors. Finally, we switch roles again, and Ruth practices relating to me as John in more assertive and effective ways.

Concluding Comments

Ruth is an exceptionally motivated client with positive expectations about the value of therapy. She shows willingness to take suggestions and follows through on homework assignments. These qualities are especially crucial if behavior therapy is to be effective because the burden of change is squarely on the shoulders of the client.

Maladaptive behavior develops over many years, beginning in early childhood, and continues to cause problems throughout an individual's life. Therefore, we must have patience when we encounter a person like Ruth because her behaviors are deeply entrenched. We cannot expect to erase the effects of years of maladaptive behaviors with a few suggestions. Rather, we should expect that she will cling to familiar patterns of behavior as she slowly comes to accept new ways of thinking and being.

As a behavior therapist I need to be somewhat eclectic to be effective. The focus is on overt behaviors but also includes thought patterns and emotions. All of these can be articulated and therefore manipulated by the client. Ruth was aware of the strong emotional reactions she felt when she put her own needs before her family's. Unless we address these powerful emotions, we set ourselves up for failure.

It is also important that Ruth have realistic expectations regarding therapy. Permanent change will not come immediately, and she should expect that living well is truly a lifelong process. This doesn't mean that therapy lasts forever. Therapy is seen as an aid in helping her establish more rewarding patterns of behavior. After 10 or 15 weekly sessions, I would recommend her tapering off to monthly meetings. This allows Ruth to become increasingly self-sufficient while guaranteeing therapeutic support for as long as she truly needs it. As she begins to obtain rewards from her positive changes, she will come to depend on her own abilities. My hope for Ruth is that she will learn more effective coping skills that will translate into improved relationships and greater self-acceptance.

JERRY COREY'S WORK WITH RUTH FROM A BEHAVIORAL PERSPECTIVE

In the *CD-ROM for Integrative Counseling*, Session 8 ("Behavioral Focus in Counseling"), I demonstrate a behavioral way to assist Ruth in developing an exercise program. It is crucial that Ruth make her own decisions about specific behavioral goals she wants to pursue. This applies to my attempts to work with her in developing methods of relaxation, practicing assertive skills, and designing an exercise plan.

Basic Assumption

A basic assumption of the behavioral approach is that therapy is best conducted in a systematic manner. Although behavior therapy includes a variety of principles and therapeutic procedures, its common denominator is a commitment to objectivity and evaluation.

Assessment of Ruth

I very much like beginning with a general assessment of a client's current functioning. This assessment begins with the intake session and continues during the next session if necessary.

Ruth and I come up with two problem areas on which she wants to focus. First, she feels tense to the point of panic much of the time and wants to learn ways to relax. Second, from the standpoint of her interpersonal relationships, she does not have the skills to ask for what she wants from others, she has trouble expressing her viewpoints clearly, and she often accepts projects she does not want to get involved in.

Goals of Therapy

The general goal of behavior therapy is to create new conditions for learning. I view Ruth's problems as related to faulty learning. The assumption underlying our therapy is that learning experiences can ameliorate problem behaviors. Much of our therapy will involve correcting faulty cognitions, acquiring social and interpersonal skills, and learning techniques of self-management so that she can become her own therapist. Based on my initial assessment of her and on another session in which she and I discuss the matter of setting concrete and objective goals, we establish the following goals to guide the therapeutic process:

- Learn and practice methods of relaxation
- Learn stress management techniques
- Learn assertion training principles and skills

Therapeutic Procedures

Behavior therapy is a pragmatic approach, and I am concerned that the treatment procedures be effective. I will draw on various cognitive and behavioral techniques to help Ruth reach her stated goals. If she does not make progress, I must assume much of the responsibility because it is my task to select appropriate treatment procedures and use them well. As a behavior therapist, I am continually evaluating the results of the therapeutic process to determine which approaches are working. Ruth's feedback in this area is important. I will ask her to keep records of her daily behavior, and I will expect her to become active to accomplish her goals, including working outside the session.

I expect that our therapy will be relatively brief, for my main function is to teach Ruth skills she can use in solving her problems and living more effectively. My ultimate goal is to teach her self-management techniques so that she will not have to be dependent on me to solve her problems.

The Therapeutic Process

Elements of the Process   The therapeutic process begins with gathering baseline data on the specific goals Ruth has selected. In her case much of the therapy will consist of learning how to cope with stress and how to be assertive in situations calling for this behavior.

Learning Stress Management Techniques   Ruth indicates that one of her priorities is to cope with tensions more effectively. I ask her to list all the specific areas that she finds stressful, and I discuss with her how her own expectations and her self-talk are contributing to her stress. We then develop a program to reduce unnecessary strain and to cope more effectively with the inevitable stresses of daily life.

Ruth: You asked me what I find stressful. Wow! There are so many things. I just feel as if I'm always rushing and never accomplishing what I should. I feel pressured so much of the time.

Jerry: List some specific situations that bring on stress. Then maybe we can come up with some strategies for alleviating it.

Ruth: Trying to keep up with my schoolwork and with the many demands at home at the same time. Dealing with Jennifer's anger toward me and her defiance. Trying to live up to John's expectations and at the same time doing what I want to do. Getting involved in way too many community activities and projects and then not having time to complete them. Dealing with how frazzled I feel in wearing so many hats. Feeling pressured to complete my education. Worrying that I won't be able to find a good teaching job once I get my credential. How's that for starters?

Jerry: That's quite a list. I can see why you feel overwhelmed. We can't address all of them at once. I'd like to hear more about what being in these stressful situations is like for you. Tell me about one of these situations, and describe what you feel in your body, what you're thinking at the time, and what you actually do in these times of stress. [*I want to get a concrete sense of how she experiences her stress, what factors bring it about, and how she attempts to cope with it.*]

Ruth: Well, I often feel that I wear so many hats—I just have so many roles to perform, and there's never enough time to do all that's needed. I often lie awake at night and ruminate about all the things I should be doing. It's awfully hard for me to go to sleep, and then I wake up in the morning after hours of tossing and turning feeling so tired. Then it's even harder for me to face the day.

Jerry: Earlier you mentioned that you have panic attacks, especially at night. I'd like to teach you some simple ways to use the relaxation response just before you go into a full-scale attack. You'll need to identify the cues that appear before a panic attack. I'd then like to teach you some simple and effective relaxation methods. Instead of wasting time lying there trying to sleep, you could be practicing a few exercises. It's important that you practice these self-relaxation exercises every day, for 20 minutes.

Ruth: Oh my! That's 20 minutes of one more thing I have to cram into my already busy schedule. It may add to my stress.

Jerry: Well, that depends on how you approach it.

We talk at some length because I am afraid Ruth will make this practice a chore rather than something she can do for herself and enjoy. She finally sees that it does not have to be a task that she does perfectly but is a means of making life easier for her. I then teach her how to concentrate on her breathing and how to do some visualization techniques, such as imagining a very pleasant and peaceful scene. Then, following the guidelines described in Herbert Benson's book *The Relaxation Response*, I provide her with these instructions:[5]

Jerry: Find a quiet and calm environment with as few distractions as possible. Sit comfortably in a chair and adopt a passive attitude. Rather than worry about performing the technique, simply let go of all thoughts. Repeating a mantra, such as the word *om,* is helpful. With your eyes closed, deeply relax all your muscles, beginning with your feet and progressing up to your face. Relax and breathe.

A week later, Ruth tells me how difficult it was to let go and relax.

Ruth: Well, I didn't do well at all. I did practice every day, and it wasn't as bad as I thought. But it's hard for me to find a quiet place to relax. I was called to the phone several times, and then another time my kids wanted me to do their wash, and on and on. Even when I wasn't disturbed, I found my mind wandering, and it was hard to just get into the sensations of feeling tension and relaxation in my body.

Jerry: I hope you won't be too hard on yourself. This is a skill, and like any skill it will take some time to learn. But it's essential that you block off that 20 minutes in a quiet place without disturbances.

Ruth and I discuss how difficult it is for her to have this time for herself. I reinforce the point that this is also an opportunity to practice asking others for what she wants and seeing to it that she gets it. Thus, she can work toward another of her goals: being able to ask for what she wants.

Learning How to Say No   Ruth tells me that she has been a giver all of her life. She gives to everyone but finds it difficult to ask anything for herself. We have been working on the latter issue, with some success. Ruth informs me that she does not know how to say no to people when they ask her to get involved in a project, especially if they tell her that they need her. She wants to talk about her father, especially the ways in which she thinks he has caused her lack of assertiveness. I ask her to recall a recent time when she found it difficult to say no and to describe that scene.

Ruth: Last week my son Adam came to me late at night and expected me to type his term paper. I didn't feel like it at all because I had had a long and hard day, and besides, it was almost midnight. At first I told him I wasn't going to do it. Then he got huffy, and I finally gave in. But what could I do?

Jerry: You could have done many things. Can you come up with some alternatives?

I want Ruth to search for alternative behaviors to saying yes when it is clear that she wants to say no. She does come up with other strategies, and we talk about the possible consequences of each approach. Then I suggest some behavioral role playing. First, I play the role of Adam, and she tries several approaches other than giving in and typing the paper. Her performance is a bit weak, so I suggest that she play Adam's role, and I demonstrate at least another alternative. I want to demonstrate, by direct modeling, some behaviors she does not use, and I hope that she will practice them.

As the weeks progress, there are many opportunities for Ruth to practice a few of the assertive skills she is learning. Then she runs into a stumbling block. A PTA group wants her to be its president. Although she enjoys her membership in the group, she is sure that she does not have time to carry out the responsibilities involved in being the president. In her session she says she is stuck because she doesn't know how to turn the group down, especially since no one else is really available.

We again work on this problem by using role-playing techniques. I play the role of the people pressuring her to accept the presidency, and I use every trick I know to tap her guilt. I tell her how efficient she is, how we are counting on her, how we know that she won't let us down, and so on. We stop at critical points and talk about the hesitation in her voice, the guilty look on her face, and her habit of giving reasons to justify her position. I also talk with her about what her body posture is communicating. Then we systematically work on each element of her presentation. Paying attention to her choice of words, her quality of voice, and her style of delivery, we study how she might persuasively say no without feeling guilty later. As a homework assignment, I ask her to read selected chapters of the book *Your Perfect Right*, by Alberti and Emmons.[6] There are useful ideas in this book that she can think about and practice between our sessions.

The next week we talk about what she has learned in the book, and we do some cognitive work. I especially talk with her about what she tells herself in these situations that gets her into trouble. In addition to these cognitive techniques, I continue to teach Ruth assertive behaviors by using role playing, behavioral rehearsals, coaching, and practice.

Process Commentary   In this approach Ruth is clearly the person who decides what she wants to work on and what she wants to change. She makes progress toward her self-defined goals because she is willing to become actively involved in challenging her assumptions and in carrying out behavioral exercises, both in the sessions and in her daily life. For example, she is disciplined enough to practice the relaxation exercises I have taught her. She learns how to ask for what she wants and to refuse those requests that she does not want to meet, not only by making resolutions but also by regularly keeping a record of the social situations in which she was not as assertive as she would have liked to be. She takes risks by practicing in everyday situations those assertive skills she has acquired in our therapy sessions. Although I help her learn how to change, she is the one who actually chooses to apply these skills, thus making change possible.

 # QUESTIONS FOR REFLECTION

1. What are your thoughts about Dr. Lazarus's multimodal approach to assessment as a way to begin therapy?

2. What are some of the features you like best about Lazarus's approach? about Dr. D'Angelo's approach? about my approach in working with Ruth? What are some of the basic similarities you see in these three behavioral approaches? What are some basic differences in style? How might you have proceeded differently, still working within this model, in terms of what you know about Ruth?

3. Lazarus succeeded in getting Ruth to agree to take a brisk walk at least three times a week. As a behavior therapist, how would you deal with her if she told you that she had not kept her agreement to carry out her exercise?

4. What is your reaction to both Dr. D'Angelo's and my attempts to get Ruth out of therapy as fast as possible so that she can apply self-management skills on her own? What skills can you think of to teach her so that she can be more self-directed?

5. In what ways did Lazarus work with Ruth's past in helping her understand her present condition? Do you think that for change to occur in her current situation she must go back to her past and work out unfinished business? Explain.

6. What are your reactions to the manner in which Lazarus conducted the conjoint session with Ruth and John? If you were conducting such a behaviorally oriented session, what homework might you suggest to them as a couple? Do you have any suggestions for specific behavioral assignments for each individual?

7. Identify some specific coping skills that D'Angelo taught Ruth. Assuming that you were to teach her some new skills in dealing with her problems, how might you help her if she were to backslide by getting stuck in some old patterns?

8. Using other behavioral techniques, show how you might proceed with Ruth if you were working with her. Use whatever you know about her so far and what you know about behavior therapy approaches to show in what directions you would move with her.

 NOTES

1. For detailed information on the Multimodal Life History Inventory, see A. A. Lazarus & C. N. Lazarus (1991), *Multimodal Life-History Inventory*. Champaign, IL: Research Press. This is a comprehensive inventory that allows for an assessment of a wide range of problems throughout the BASIC I.D.

2. See A. A. Lazarus & C. N. Lazarus (1997), *The 60-Second Shrink: 101 Strategies for Staying Sane in a Crazy World*. Atascadero, CA: Impact Publishers. This self-help book deals with a range of topics including thinking yourself healthy, building successful relationships, handling anxiety and stress, managing your weight, and communicating effectively. It makes a good companion for therapy clients. See also A. A. Lazarus (2001), *Marital Myths Revisited: A Fresh Look at Two Dozen Mistaken Beliefs About Marriage*. Atascadero, CA: Impact Publishers. This book makes a good adjunct for couples who are in marriage counseling.

3. For a more detailed description of the BASIC I.D., see A. A. Lazarus (1997), *Brief but Comprehensive Psychotherapy: The Multimodal Way*. New York: Springer. This is an excellent source of techniques and procedures for brief interventions. Lazarus shows how to deal with the whole person by developing assessments and treatment interventions for all the modalities of human experience.

4. For an overview of multimodal therapy, see G. Corey (2005), *Theory and Practice of Counseling and Psychotherapy* (7th edition). Chapter 9 (Behavior Therapy) describes the unique features of multimodal therapy as an assessment and treatment approach.

5. Refer to H. Benson (1976), *The Relaxation Response*. New York: Avon. This is a readable and useful guide to developing simple meditative and other relaxation procedures. Particularly helpful are the author's summaries of the basic elements of meditation (pp. 110–111) and methods of inducing the relaxation response (pp. 158–166).

6. See R. E. Alberti & M. L. Emmons (2001), *Your Perfect Right: A Guide to Assertive Behavior*, 8th edition. San Luis Obispo, CA: Impact Publishers. Therapy clients will learn about the principles and techniques of assertion training from this popular book. It is clearly written, with many examples of ways of acquiring assertive skills.

Chapter 8

Case Approach to Cognitive Behavior Therapy

A Rational Emotive Behavior Therapist's Perspective on Ruth

by Albert Ellis, Ph.D., ABPP

Introduction

REBT assumes that people like Ruth do not get disturbed by the unrealistic and illogical standards they learned (from their family and culture) during their childhood. Rather, they largely disturb themselves by the dogmatic, rigid "musts" and commands they creatively construct about these standards and values and about the unfortunate events that occur in their lives. Ruth is a good case in point. She has accepted some of the fundamentalist ideas of her parents, which many fundamentalist-reared children adopt without becoming disturbed. But Ruth rigidly insists that she has to follow them while simultaneously demanding that she must be herself and lead a self-fulfilling, independent existence. She could easily disturb herself with either of these contradictory commands. By devoutly holding both of them, she is really in trouble! As REBT shows, transmuting any legitimate goals and preferences into absolutist "musts" usually leads to self-denigration, rage, or self-pity. Ruth seems to have all of these disturbed feelings.[1]

Assessment of Ruth

Ruth has a number of goals and desires that most therapies, including REBT, would consider legitimate and healthy: the desire to have a stable marriage; to care for her family members; to be thinner and more attractive; to keep her parents' approval; to be a competent teacher; and to discover what she really wants to do in life and largely follow her personal bents. Even though some of these desires are somewhat contradictory, they would probably not get her into serious trouble if she held them as preferences, because she could then make some compromises.

Thus, Ruth could choose to be *somewhat* devoted to her husband and children, and even to her parents, but also be determined to pursue a teaching career and to follow her own nonfundamentalist religious views and practices. She would then fail to lead a *perfectly* conflict-free and happy life but would hardly be in great turmoil. However, like practically all humans, Ruth has a strong (and probably partly innate) tendency to "sacredize" these important values. From early childhood onward, she rigidly concluded: "Because I want my parents' approval, I completely need it!" "Because I love my children, I have to be thoroughly devoted to them!" "Because I enjoy thinking for myself and doing my own thing, I have to do so at practically all times!" "Because I'd like to be thinner and more attractive, I've got to be!"

With grandiose, perfectionist fiats like these, Ruth's reasonable, often achievable, goals and standards are transmuted into absolutist "musts." She thereby almost inevitably *makes* herself—that's right, makes herself—panicked, depressed, indecisive, and often inert. Additionally, when she sees that she feels emotionally upset and is not acting in her best interests, she irrationally upsets herself about that. She strongly—and foolishly—tells herself "I must not be panicked" instead of "I wish I were not panicking myself, but I am. Now how do I unpanic myself?" She then feels panicked about her panic. And she rigidly insists, "I have to be decisive and do my own thing." Then she feels like a worm about her worminess! This self-castigation about her symptoms makes her even more disturbed and less able to see exactly what she is thinking and doing to create these symptoms. As a rational emotive behavior therapist, I assess Ruth's problems and her belief system about these problems as follows.

Ruth asks certain questions that lead to practical problems:

- How much shall I do for others, and how much for myself?
- How can I exercise and keep on a diet?
- How can I be a teacher and still get along well with my husband?
- How can I get along with my parents and still not follow their fundamentalist views?
- How can I benefit from therapy and live with the things I may discover about myself when undergoing it?
- How can I be myself and not harm my husband and kids?

Ruth could sensibly answer these questions by telling herself these things:

- If I do more things for myself, people may not like me as much as I want them to. Too bad!

- Exercising and dieting are really difficult. But being fat and ugly is even more difficult.
- If I get a teaching job, I may antagonize my husband. But I can stand that and still be happy.
- My parents will never like my giving up fundamentalism, and that's sad. But it's not awful.
- If I find out unpleasant things about myself in therapy, that'll be tough. But I can also benefit from that discovery.
- Being myself at the expense of my husband and kids is somewhat self-ish. But I have a right to a reasonable degree of self-interest.

Instead, Ruth holds these irrational beliefs that lead to unhealthy feelings of anxiety and depression and to self-defeating behaviors of indecision and inertia:

- I must not do more things for myself and dare not antagonize others.
- Exercise and dieting are too hard and shouldn't be that hard!
- If my husband hates my getting a teaching job, that would be awful!
- I can't stand my parents criticizing me if I give up fundamentalism.
- I would be a thoroughly rotten person if therapy revealed bad things about me!
- I must never be selfish, for if I am, I'm worthless.

Ruth also holds certain irrational beliefs that lead to secondary distur-bances (panic about panic, depression about depression):

- I must not be panicked!
- It's terrible if I'm depressed.
- I'm no good because I'm indecisive.

Key Issues and Themes

The key issues in most disturbed feelings and behaviors that I will look for are (1) self-deprecation, stemming from the irrational belief that "I must perform well and be approved of by significant others"; (2) the irrational insistence that "you [other people] must treat me kindly and considerately"; and (3) the irrational idea that "the conditions under which I live have to be comfortable and easy."

Ruth seems to have the first of these irrational beliefs, because she keeps demanding that she be giving and lovable, that she be thin and beautiful, that she be a good daughter, that her "badness" not be uncovered in therapy, and that she make only good and proper decisions. With these perfectionist com-mands, she leads a self-deprecating, anxious existence. She also seems to have some unacknowledged irrational beliefs that her husband absolutely must not expect her to be herself, thus making her angry at him.

Finally, Ruth has low frustration tolerance and self-pity, resulting not from her desires but from her dire needs to lose weight without going to the trouble of dieting and exercising, to have a guarantee that she won't die, to have the security of marriage even though she has a boring relationship with her husband, to be sure that therapy will be comfortable, and to need a magical, God-will-take-care-of-me solution to her problems.

Because Ruth strongly holds the three basic irrational ideas (dogmatic "musts") that REBT finds at the root of most disturbances and because some of her demands—like those that she be herself *and* be quite self-sacrificial—are quite contradictory, I imagine that she will be a difficult customer and will require intensive therapy. Within a few sessions, however, she may be able to understand some of her *musts* and *demands* and start reducing them. Because she has already taken some big risks and worked at changing herself, I predict a good prognosis despite her strong tendency to create self-defeating beliefs.

Applying Therapeutic Techniques

REBT invariably includes a number of cognitive, emotive, and behavioral methods.[2] As I work with Ruth, I use these main methods.

Cognitive Techniques of REBT   I show Ruth how to discover her rational preferences and distinguish them from her irrational "musts" and demands. Then I teach her how to scientifically dispute these demands and change them back into appropriate preferences. I encourage her to create some rational coping statements and inculcate them many times into her philosophy; for example, "I want to be a caring mother and wife, but I also have the right to care for myself." I help her do REBT "referenting"—that is, making a list of the disadvantages of overeating and nondieting and thinking about them several times a day. I also have her do reframing to see that losing some of her husband's and children's love has its good as well as its bad sides. I encourage her to use some of REBT's psychoeducational adjuncts: books, pamphlets, cassettes, lectures, and workshops. I show her the advantages of teaching REBT to others, such as to her husband, children, and pupils, so that she will better learn it herself. I discuss with her the advantages of creating for herself a vital, absorbing interest in some long-range project, such as helping other people guiltlessly give up their parental fundamentalist teachings.

Here is one way I may work with Ruth to implement the cognitive technique of helping her dispute her irrational beliefs.

Ruth: Because I love my children, I have to be thoroughly devoted to them.
Therapist: That's an interesting conclusion, but how does it follow from the observation, which I assume is true, that you really do love your children?
Ruth: Well, isn't it right and ethical to be kind and helpful to one's children?
Therapist: Of course it is. You brought them into the world without them asking to be born, and you'd be quite unethical and irresponsible if you didn't devote considerable time and energy to them. But why must you be ethical? What law of the universe says you always have to be?

Ruth: My own law says so—and that of many other people.

Therapist: Fine. But why do you have to always keep your own laws? Actually, do you?

Ruth: Well, no. Not always.

Therapist: And do other people always keep their own and their culture's laws?

Ruth: No, not always.

Therapist: So obviously, although it's highly desirable and moral for you to care for your children, is it absolutely necessary that you do so?

Ruth: No, I guess not.

Therapist: But it still is highly desirable. What is the difference between something being preferable and desirable and being utterly necessary?

Ruth: I see. Quite a difference!

Therapist: Right. And no matter how much you love them, do you always have to be completely devoted to them?

Ruth: You're questioning my desire to be completely devoted?

Therapist: Yes, I am. How realistic would complete devotion be?

Ruth: Thoroughly unrealistic. I need time for other important things.

Therapist: So your dire need to be completely devoted to your children and also to your husband doesn't stem from your love for them, doesn't follow from any law of the universe, and is impractical and unrealistic. If you strongly believe you absolutely must be completely devoted to your children, what results will you probably get?

Ruth: I'll feel very anxious about doing what I supposedly must do and depressed in case I don't.

Therapist: Yes, your *mus*turbation probably won't work.

I can have this kind of active, directive dialogue with Ruth in one of her early sessions and try to start her quickly on a new way of thinking about her demandingness.

Emotive Techniques of REBT   I will recommend that Ruth use some of the main emotive, evocative, and dramatic methods that I have found effective in REBT, such as these:

- She can forcefully and powerfully tell herself rational coping statements: "I do not (definitely not) need my parents' approval, though I would certainly prefer to have it!"
- She can tape a rigorous debate with herself, in which she actively disputes one of her irrational "musts." Then she can listen to her disputation and have some of her friends listen to it to see not only if its content is good but also if she is forceful enough.
- She can do rational emotive imagery, by imagining one of the worst things that could happen to her—for example, her father strongly berating her for her nonfundamentalist views. Then she can work on her

feelings so that she first gets in touch with the horror and self-downing she unhealthily feels and then changes it to the healthy negative feelings of sorrow and regret.

- She can do some of the famous REBT shame-attacking exercises, whereby she publicly does something she considers shameful, foolish, or ridiculous and works on herself not to feel ashamed and self-damning while doing it.
- She can learn to receive unconditional acceptance from me, no matter how badly she is behaving in and out of therapy. I can show her how to always—yes, always—accept herself, whether or not she does well.
- We can do role playing, where I play her irate father and she plays herself, to see how she can cope with his severe criticism. In the course of it we stop the role playing from time to time to see what she is telling herself to make herself anxious or depressed while reacting to my role-playing her father's criticism.
- We can practice reverse role playing, where I stick rigidly to some of her irrational beliefs and encourage her to argue me out of them.
- She can use humor to rip up her irrational beliefs, especially singing to herself some of my rational humorous songs.

In this session with Ruth I use one of the emotive techniques of REBT.

Therapist: We've been disputing your irrational belief that because you love your children you have to be completely devoted to them. You could also use one of our popular emotional techniques, rational emotive imagery. Would you like me to show you how to use this exercise?

Ruth: Yes, I would.

Therapist: OK, close your eyes—just easily close them. Now vividly imagine one of the worst things that could happen to you. Imagine that you're not thoroughly devoted to your children—in fact, that you're somewhat neglecting them. Vividly imagine that they're complaining about this and that your husband and your mother are also chiding you severely for this neglect. Can you vividly imagine this happening?

Ruth: Definitely. I can clearly picture it.

Therapist: Good. Now, how do you honestly feel in your gut and in your heart? What is your honest feeling?

Ruth: Very guilty. Depressed. Self-critical.

Therapist: Good. Really get in touch with those negative feelings. Feel them. Strongly feel them!

Ruth: I really feel them. Quite strongly.

Therapist: Good. Now, keeping the same image—don't change it—make yourself feel only sorry and disappointed about what's happening but not guilty, not depressed, not self-downing. Only sorry and disappointed, which are healthy and appropriate negative feelings, instead of guilty, depressed, and self-downing, which are unhealthy and unhealthy negative feelings. You control your feelings, so you can change them. So let me know when you're only feeling sorry and disappointed.

Ruth: I'm having a hard time getting there.

Therapist: Yes, I know. But you can do it. You can definitely change your feelings. Anyone can.

Ruth [*After a pause of 2 minutes*]: I changed them.

Therapist: And now you feel only sorry and disappointed, not guilty or depressed?

Ruth: Yes, I do.

Therapist: Good! How did you change your feelings? What did you do to change them?

Ruth: I told myself "It's too bad that my children, my husband, and my mother are chiding me for neglecting the children, but I'm not sure I am being neglectful. Even if I am, that's bad, that's wrong of me, but that behavior doesn't make me a rotten person. I'll try to be less neglectful, while not being overly devoted to my children. But if I'm still criticized, it's just too bad—not the end of the world. I can take this criticism and still have a good life."

Therapist: Excellent! Now what I'd like to see you do is to help yourself by repeating this exercise every day for the next 20 or 30 days. Remember, it only took you about 2 minutes to change your unhealthy feelings of guilt and depression to healthy negative feelings of disappointment. So repeat this every day, using the same excellent coping statement you used this time or using several other similar coping statements that will occur to you if you keep doing this rational emotive imagery. If you do this, I think you'll see at the end of 10, 20, or 30 days, when you imagine this bad event with your children happening or when some other unfortunate activating event actually does occur, that you'll tend to feel automatically—yes, automatically—sorry and disappointed about your actions, but not damning your total self for doing this.

Ruth: You think that will really help me?

Therapist: Yes, I'm fairly sure it will. So will you try it to help yourself?

Ruth: Yes, I will.

Therapist: Great. Now, if you stop doing this exercise because you think it's too hard to continue it or something like that, you can always challenge your irrational belief that it must be easy and that you shouldn't have to do it to improve. You can also use reinforcement methods to encourage yourself to keep doing it.

Ruth: How do I do that?

Therapist: Very simply. What, for example, do you enjoy doing that you do practically every day of the week?

Ruth: Uh, reading.

Therapist: Fine. No reading, then, for the next 20 or 30 days, until after you do rational emotive imagery for the day and change your feelings of guilt and depression to those of disappointment. Is that OK?

Ruth: Yes, that's OK.

Therapist: And if that doesn't work, though it probably will, you can enact a penalty when you don't practice your rational emotive imagery.

Ruth: A penalty?

Therapist: Yes. For example, what do you hate doing—some task or chore that you usually avoid doing because you don't like it?

Ruth: Well, uh, cleaning the toilet.

Therapist: Good. If, during the next 30 days, your bedtime arrives and you haven't done your rational emotive imagery exercise, you can make yourself clean your toilet for an hour.

Ruth: That would work! I'm sure I'll do the exercise every day.

Therapist: Fine!

Rational emotive imagery, like several other REBT emotive techniques, can be taught to clients like Ruth and given as homework assignments, thus making therapy effective in a relatively brief period of time.

Behavioral Techniques of REBT   As with virtually all REBT clients, I use several behavioral methods with Ruth, including these:

- I show her how to select and perform in vivo desensitization assignments, such as registering for education courses despite her anxiety about her family's disapproval.
- I encourage her to do what she is afraid to do—for example, to talk to her husband about her career goals many times until she loses her irrational fears of his disapproval.
- I encourage her to reinforce herself with some enjoyable pursuits, such as reading or music, only after she has completed her difficult-to-do homework. And if she is truly lax about doing it, I urge her sometimes to penalize (but never damn) herself with an unpleasant chore, such as getting up an hour earlier than usual.
- I plan with her and supervise her carrying out practical goals, such as arranging for help with her household tasks.
- If she starts getting over her emotional hang-ups but has skill deficiencies, I help her acquire missing skills, such as assertiveness, communicating well, or decision making.

All of these behavioral methods of REBT can be given as homework assignments to be used between sessions and checked on during the following session. Therefore, the length of therapy can be appreciably shortened for clients who do their homework and are monitored by the therapist.

In one session I show Ruth how to use one of REBT's action-oriented techniques.

Ruth: How will I deal with my panic and, as you say, my panic about panicking?

Therapist: Good question. First, let's deal with your panic about your panic. Because of this secondary symptom, you often avoid situations where you might panic, even though it would be good to participate in them. Right?

Ruth: Yes. I especially avoid seeing or talking to my father, who's critical of my handling of the children and almost everything else. So I rarely call him, and when he calls, I get my family members to say I'm out when I'm really not.

Therapist: That's a good example. When avoiding these calls, what are you telling yourself?

Ruth: If he criticizes me, I'll panic, and that would be awful!

Therapist: Right. But every time you avoid speaking to your father, you reinforce your anxiety about talking to him and being criticized. You tell yourself, "If I speak to him, I'll be very anxious." So you *increase* your anxiety!

Ruth: You're right about that. Whenever I even *think* of talking to him, I panic.

Therapist: So the first thing you can do is to say to yourself, many times and very strongly, "Panicking is very uncomfortable, but it is not *horrible*. It's only inconvenient."

Ruth: That will cure me?

Therapist: Not exactly, but it will help a lot. In addition, deliberately arrange to talk to your father more. Do, as we say in REBT, what you're afraid of doing. *Act*, as well as *think*, against your phobia of panicking.

Ruth: But won't that make me panic more?

Therapist: It may at first. But if you keep doing what you're terrifying yourself about—talking to your critical father—and convince yourself at the same time that your panic is only inconvenient, not awful, you will significantly decrease your panic about your panicking.

Ruth: Will my original panic about my father's criticism decrease too?

Therapist: Most likely it will, and it may even disappear completely. For you were originally panicked about his criticism but then made yourself so panicked about your panic that this secondary symptom became more important than your primary one and actually helped keep it alive. So if you surrender the panic about panic, your original horror of criticism may well disappear too. If it doesn't, just go back to disputing, which we previously discussed, the irrational belief that criticism makes you a rotten person and that you can't stand it.

Ruth: So I'd better think and act against my panic?

Therapist: Yes, think and act, think and act against it. Against your original panic and your panic about your panic.

Ruth: Sounds good. I'll try it.

Process Commentary   As can be seen in these typical excerpts, rational emotive behavior therapists have collaborative, Socratic dialogues with their clients and try to help them think, feel, and behave against their disturbances and, as they do so, to gain positive growth and self-fulfillment in accordance with their self-chosen goals, values, and purposes.

In using any or all of these REBT techniques with Ruth, I do not merely try to help her ameliorate her presenting symptoms (panic, guilt, and indecisiveness) but also try to help her make a profound philosophical change. The goals are for her to acknowledge her own construction of her emotional problems, to minimize her other related symptoms, and to maintain her therapeutic progress. By the time my therapy with Ruth ends, I expect that she will have strongly internalized and kept regularly using the three main insights of REBT:

1. "I mainly emotionally and behaviorally upset myself about unfortunate conditions in my life, and I largely do so by constructing rigid 'musts' and commands about these conditions."
2. "No matter when I originally started to upset myself and no matter who encouraged me do so, I'm now disturbed because of my present *must*urbatory beliefs."
3. "To change my irrational thinking, my unhealthy feelings, and my dysfunctional behaviors, I'd better give up all magical solutions and keep working and practicing—yes, keep working and practicing—for the rest of my life."

Much of Ruth's main problem is learning to be "herself" and at the same time to resist conforming too much to social rules that tell her that she must be a "good woman," must be a "thin woman," and must be a "good fundamentalist." Although she theoretically has the right to avoid following these social rules, she will tend to feel guilty and she will tend to get into some amount of trouble with her family of origin and her current family if she decides to "truly" be herself. By using REBT and trying to follow her strong preferences without turning them into absolutist demands, she can probably determine how to largely be herself and at the same time largely, but not completely, avoid antagonizing her parents, her husband, and her children. REBT encourages her to lead a balanced life in these respects. But in being an individual, she will have to select the kind of balance she desires and accept the consequences of her own choices.

After working with Ruth for several sessions, I would say that she definitely has a panic disorder and is also dysthymic. I see her as someone with a personality disorder rather than as a "nice neurotic." She is very troubled and conflicted, but she has the ability and, I hope, the determination to work through her main problems. I enjoy working with clients like Ruth because I find them to be quite open to help. If she is willing to keep trying the antidisturbance theories and practices of REBT, I have no guarantee that she will significantly change and stay changed, but I can predict that she has a good chance to change. She has already chosen not to follow some of the rigid rules of her family and her culture and is healthily sorry about the difficulties her rebellion entails. If I can help her continue to be sorry and regretful but to give up her severe guilt and self-deprecation about her rebelliousness, I think she will keep choosing her own pathways and not only she but also her close family members will considerably benefit. I sincerely hope so.[3]

A Cognitive Behavioral Approach to Family and Couples Therapy With Ruth

by Frank M. Dattilio, Ph.D., ABPP

Introduction

In the previous selection Albert Ellis demonstrates how he applies REBT, a form of cognitive behavior therapy, to individual therapy with Ruth. I have been influenced greatly by my former teacher, Aaron T. Beck, who pioneered cognitive therapy, and the late Joseph Wolpe, the father of behavior therapy. In addition to my doing individual therapy in my private practice, I have had a keen interest in applying the cognitive behavioral approach to couples and families.

There are many subtypes of cognitive behavior therapy. The two major versions that will be highlighted here are those of Albert Ellis and Aaron T. Beck. Ellis's REBT emphasizes each individual's interpretation of the events that occur in the family environment. The basic theory contends that family members largely create their own world by the phenomenological view they take of what happens to them. The focus of therapy is on how particular problems of family members affect their well-being as a unit. Throughout the course of therapy, family members are treated as individuals, each of whom subscribes to his or her own specific set of beliefs and expectations. The role of the family therapist is to help members come to the realization that illogical or irrational beliefs and distortions serve as the foundation for their emotional distress and interactional conflicts. Beck's cognitive therapy, which also balances cognition and behavior, takes a more expansive and inclusive direction by focusing in greater depth on family interactional patterns and by remaining consistent with elements derived from a systems perspective. This theory has been elaborated on by Baucom, Epstein, Dattilio, and others.[4]

Basic Concepts and Assumptions

Consistent with systems theory, the cognitive behavioral approach to families includes the premise that members of a family simultaneously influence one another. Consequently, a behavior of one family member leads to behaviors, cognitions, and emotions in other members, which, in turn, elicit cognitions, behaviors, and emotions in response. As this process continues to cycle, the volatility of the family dynamics escalates, rendering members vulnerable to a negative spiral of conflict. As the number of family members involved increases, so does the complexity of the dynamics, adding more fuel to the escalation process.

Some of the more recent cognitive behavioral approaches place heavy emphasis on *schema,* or what has otherwise been defined as a set of core beliefs.[5] As this concept is applied to family treatment, the therapeutic intervention is based on the assumptions with which family members interpret and evaluate one another and the emotions and behaviors that arise in response to these cognitions. Just as individuals maintain their own basic schemata about themselves, their world, and their future, they also maintain schemata about families. I have found in my clinical experience that emphasis should be placed both on these cognitions among individual family members and on what can be termed the family schema. This consists of beliefs held jointly by the family that have formed as a result of years of integrated interaction among members. An example of such a belief in Ruth's family of origin might be that "It is unacceptable to talk about feelings and emotions openly." Not only is this an unwritten rule, it is also a strong belief among family members.

Individuals actually maintain two separate schemata about families. The first is the schema related to the parents' families of origin, which comprises the beliefs both partners learned during their upbringing and brought to the marriage. The second and more emphasized is the schema related to families in general. These schemata have a major impact on how an individual thinks, feels, and behaves within the family setting and also contribute to the development of rules and family patterns. An example in Ruth's present family is that emotions and feelings may be discussed, but only selectively.

Schemata are thus the long-standing and relatively stable basic assumptions people hold about how the world works and their place in it and are introjected into their current family constellation. In a familial situation such as Ruth's, for example, where it is understood that the father is the head of the household, all decisions regarding the family may be suspended until he has the final word. This pattern may disempower the mother in disciplining the children, and they may perceive her, in effect, as another sibling.

The family schema is very important when conducting family therapy. It also contains ideas about how spousal relationships should work, what problems should be expected in marriage and how they should be handled, what is involved in building and maintaining a healthy family, what responsibilities each family member should have, what consequences should be associated with failure to meet responsibilities or to fulfill roles, and what costs and benefits each individual should expect to have as a consequence of being in a marriage.

It is important to remember that the family schema is shaped by the family of origin of each partner in a relationship as well as by environmental influences such as the media and peer relationships. Beliefs funneled down from the family of origin may be either conscious or unconscious, and they contribute to a joint or blended schema that leads to the development of the current family schema (see Figure 8-1 for a diagram of Ruth's family schemata).

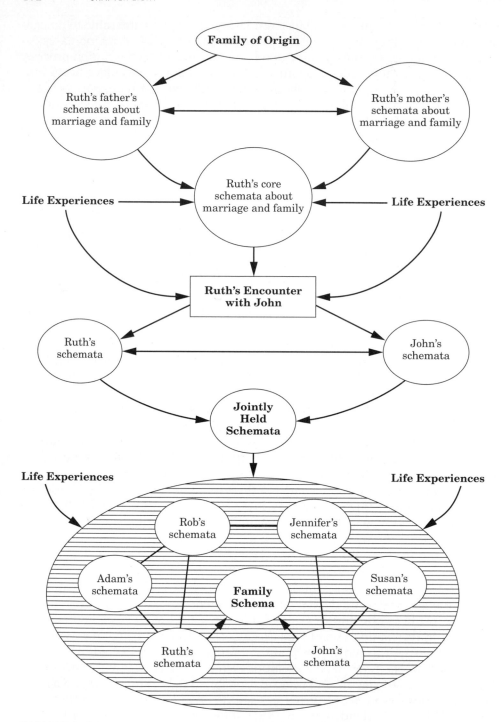

FIGURE 8-1
Ruth's Family Schemata

This family schema is then disseminated and applied in rearing the children, and, when mixed with their individual thoughts, perceptions of their environment, and life experiences, contributes to the development of the family belief system. The family schema is subject to change as major events occur (death, divorce) and also continues to evolve over the course of ordinary day-to-day experience.

As this schema begins to form, distortions may develop, contributing to family dysfunction. Ten of the more common distortions found with both couples and families are listed here:

1. *Arbitrary inference.* A conclusion is made by family members in the absence of supporting substantiating evidence. For example, one of Ruth's teenage children who returns home half an hour after his curfew is judged by the family as having been "up to no good."

2. *Selective abstraction.* Information is taken out of context: certain details are highlighted, and other important information is ignored. John fails to answer Adam's greeting the first thing in the morning, and Adam concludes, "Dad must be angry at me."

3. *Overgeneralization.* An isolated incident or two are allowed to serve as a representation of similar situations everywhere, related or unrelated. Because John and the kids have left food out from time to time, Ruth develops the belief that her family is wasteful and takes everything, including her, for granted.

4. *Magnification and minimization.* A case or circumstance is perceived in greater or lesser light than is appropriate. John demands that the children wash their hands before eating, but he fails to do so himself. When confronted by the children, he minimizes it by saying, "Well, I don't miss very often—so I'm excused."

5. *Personalization.* External events are attributed to oneself when insufficient evidence exists to render a conclusion. Jennifer blames herself for her parents' repeated arguments, saying, "Maybe I should have never been born."

6. *Dichotomous thinking.* Experiences are codified as all or nothing, a complete success or a total failure. After repeated incidences in which Adam becomes involved in trouble at school, John and Ruth conclude, "We failed as disciplinarians."

7. *Labeling and mislabeling.* Imperfections and mistakes made in the past are allowed to serve as a stereotype of all future behaviors. Ruth and John failed to follow through on their word on one occasion and are consequently regarded by the children as being unreliable.

8. *Tunnel vision.* Family members sometimes see only what they want to see or what fits their current state of mind. John holds onto the rigid belief that the man is the "head of the household," because this is the way he perceived a father to be when he was growing up.

9. *Biased explanations*. In a polarized way of thinking that family members develop during times of distress, they assume that another member has an ulterior motive. John and the children distrust Ruth because she does not always admit to depressive thoughts when she indeed is experiencing them.
10. *Mind reading*. A family member has the magical gift of being able to know what others are thinking without the aid of verbal communication. Ruth anticipates that the family views her as a failure because she is unable to stand up for herself and demand what she wants.

These distortions become key targets in family therapy. Much of the intervention in therapy involves helping family members identify these distortions and then gather evidence to aid in reconstructing their thinking. It may also include practicing alternative patterns of behavioral interaction and dealing with their negative attributions.

Cognitive behavioral theory operates on a set of assumptions that Schwebel and Fine feel are central.[6] Here is a modified version of these assumptions:

Assumption 1. All members of a family seek to maintain their environment to fulfill their needs and wants. They attempt to understand their environment and how they can function most effectively in it, even if it sometimes means testing the boundaries. (For example, Adam may exceed his curfew by half an hour.) As family members gather data about how the family operates, they use this information to guide their behaviors and to aid in building and refining family-related cognitions. This leads to the development of an individual's construct of family life and family relationships. In Adam's case, he may begin to develop the concept that he can stretch the limits and not be chastised, thus inferring that rules may be broken.

Assumption 2. Individual members' cognitions affect virtually every aspect of family life. Five categories of cognitive variables determine these cognitions: (1) selective attention (John and Ruth's focus on the children's negative behaviors), (2) attributions (Ruth's explanations for why the children act up), (3) expectations (John's expectation that Ruth and the children will do as he asks without question), (4) assumptions (Adam's view that life is not fair), and (5) standards (Jennifer's thoughts about how the world should be).

Assumption 3. Certain "obstacles" to satisfaction lie within individual family members' cognitions (for example, Ruth's rigid view of the role of a wife and mother).

Assumption 4. Unless family members become more aware of their family-related cognitions and how these cognitions affect them in certain situations, they will not be able to identify areas that cause distress and replace them with healthy interaction.

Assessment of Ruth

My differential DSM-IV-TR diagnosis of Ruth would probably include:

Axis I: (61.1) partner relational problem; (300.40) dysthymic disorder secondary to identity problem; (300.21) panic disorder without agoraphobia

Axis II: (301.6) dependent personality disorder; (313. 2) identity problem

Axis III: exogenous obesity

Axis IV: problems related to social environment

Axis V: GAF = 60 (on admission)

A family history is conducted to ascertain pertinent information about Ruth's family of origin. Although in most cases the family approach, like other modalities of family therapy, prefers to avoid "identifying a patient" and instead takes a balanced approach to dealing with family dysfunction, there are exceptions. It appears that this case is one. Ruth has already initiated individual psychotherapy, and it was decided to include her family as well. In a sense, therefore, she has already been designated as the "identified patient," and family treatment can initially center on her issues. Given her history and background, I elected to work on gaining a better understanding of her family of origin by having her invite members in for several visits. This will certainly lead toward developing a good grasp of her core schemata about herself and family life and will possibly provide me with insight into the development of her thinking style. Traditionally this should only involve Ruth, her parents, and any siblings. No other extended family members are invited—most importantly, her husband.

This session is exclusively designed for Ruth and the therapist to better understand the thinking styles of her origin and also to clear up any areas of conflict that remain from her past. If all were amenable, we could meet for three to five sessions of 2 hours each, focusing on the family schema and particularly on her emancipation from certain thinking styles that are deleterious to her. Although this is the ideal situation, such meetings are not always successful.

Ruth's family-of-origin meeting, which only included Ruth's biological parents, proved unsuccessful. Ruth's father, a very rigid man, decided to leave the family session abruptly, stating that he didn't believe in "this sort of stuff." Ruth's mother, being a rather passive individual, complied with her husband's demands to leave.

Initial Session With Ruth's Current Family

Because cognitive behavior family therapists attempt to identify both distorted schemata and maladaptive behavior patterns in family interaction, the next order of business in Ruth's case is to meet with her entire (immediate) family. As a result of the little that had been gathered from her family of origin and a separate interview with John, I now have some foundation for understanding the diverse philosophies that exist in each of their family backgrounds and can develop some insight into what schemata may have trickled down into the immediate family dynamics and affected Ruth's family schema.

During the initial family therapy session, I may ask various members of the family to describe their perceptions of the family and how things operate at home. It is often best to start with the youngest child and work up to the parents, so that the younger children are not influenced by what is said by their older siblings. As you will see in the excerpt from the initial session, I aim directly at ascertaining a solid understanding of the individual perceptions of the family and then attempt to conceptualize a joint consensus of the family schema. Once this is accomplished, the next step is to begin to educate the family in how the cognitive behavioral model of therapy works and then to begin to collaboratively identify cognitive distortions and erroneous thinking patterns that lead to maladaptive behavior patterns and dysfunction in the family.

Therapist: I appreciate everyone coming in today. The aim of this meeting is to address some of the problems that exist in the family for the family's sake. Does that sound reasonable to everyone?

Family: [*Three members nod reticently in affirmation.*]

Jennifer: It doesn't to me! I think this sucks, and I don't want to be here.

Therapist: So why did you agree to come?

Jennifer: I didn't. I was forced by my parents.

Therapist: I hear you, Jennifer, and I want you to know that I never expect people to come here against their will. So if you feel that strongly, you can leave, provided that your parents and the rest of the family agree. [*Silent pause*]

Jennifer: Well, so what do I do? Just leave now?

Therapist: Yes, I suppose you could.

Jennifer: So where do I go?

Therapist: I don't know. That's for you to decide.

Jennifer: Well that's dumb. I'm not going to just sit outside in the car—bored!

Therapist: OK, you're certainly welcome to stay if you wish, but I'm actually interested in hearing why you don't want to be here, particularly if being here would help the family.

Jennifer: Because this is all bull, and it's not my problem—it's Mom's. She just makes it everyone else's problem.

Therapist: Ah, interesting. Does anyone else view things the same way Jennifer does? [*Brief pause*]

John: No, I don't, totally. I think we all have some issues here that need to be discussed besides Mom, but Mom does have problems.

Therapist: Anyone else have an opinion?

Rob: Yes, I'd like to say something. I think our family definitely has some problems in the way we think. Everyone is, like, all over the place, and there's no sense of . . . how would you say . . .

Therapist: Family unity?

Rob: Yeah! Sort of. I mean, like, Dad is sort of off in his own world—no offense, Dad—and Mom is doing her thing and trying to do for everyone else. It's sort of crazy.

Therapist: So, I'm hearing you say that things at home are somewhat chaotic at times, and you're uncomfortable with it?

Rob: Yes, but not at times. A lot of the time.

Therapist: OK, but I want to get back to Jennifer's statement about how Mom makes her problems everyone else's. Does that seem to be true for everyone here? Are we all in agreement with Jen's statement?

John: No, I'm having a problem with Jennifer's statement. You know, Ruth and Jennifer really lock horns, and Jennifer will often take every opportunity she can to blame her mother, or anyone else for that matter—except, of course, herself.

Therapist: John, in addition to your concerns about Jennifer, you sound as though you're a bit protective of your wife.

John: Well sure, but that's also the way I really see it.

Therapist: OK, but is there any agreement with any of what the kids are saying?

John: Yeah, maybe some. I mean, look, Ruth has some problems. She's had a really rough upbringing, so I sort of see our roles as being to support her and not to give her a hard time.

Therapist: It seems to me that this is somewhat how your family has functioned for a long time until recently.

Jennifer: Yeah! Until I screwed everything up, right? Right, Mom? That's it— say it.

Ruth [*Begins to sob*]: Oh, Jennifer, stop!

Adam: I think Jennifer's problem is that she wants to grow up, and Mom won't let her, and that's why she's mad at Mom.

Susan: I sort of agree. I can see Mom starting to do a little of the same with me.

John: What? Do what?

Susan: Uh-oh! I opened my big mouth. [*Everyone chuckles*]

Therapist: No, that's OK, Susan. Say what you feel.

Susan: Well, she's starting to be kind of overprotective with me the way she has with Jen.

Jennifer: Yeah, and it's only with the girls. She's not like that so much with Adam and Rob.

Therapist: Ruth, how do you respond to everything you're hearing here today?

Ruth: Well, it's true, I guess, if I have to be honest, but it's also hard to listen to.

Therapist: OK, so you're protective of the girls, John is protective of you, and who is protective of Rob, Adam, and Dad?

Rob: Rob, Adam, and Dad. [*Everyone laughs*]

Therapist: Ah-ha! So the men take care of the men. That's interesting! Protecting one another appears to be a very important theme in your family.

John: Well sure, you've seen that with both mine and Ruth's family.

Therapist: So I guess it would be fair to say, in a way, that this line of thinking was carried down to your family here [*Everyone agrees*]. We've just identified what's called a family schema or a core belief—that we protect each other in certain ways that sometimes differ. What belief exists in your family that calls for this behavior as opposed to the idea of everyone protecting themselves? [*Silent pause*]

Susan: Is it bad that we do this?

Therapist: Well, not necessarily, but the way it has evolved in your family patterns here has caused some trouble. But let me get an answer to my question, because I think this is very important. [*Silent pause*]

John: Well, I guess as the father, I feel the blame for some of it. While I support Ruth, I've kind of dumped on her by not taking more of an active role with the kids.

Therapist: Yes, and as a result of Ruth's upbringing, she has felt compelled to assume all of the responsibility for the family, perhaps in part to compensate for you. So there are several family-held distortions, as well as individual distortions about ourselves.

Adam: What do you mean, distortions?

Therapist: Good question, Adam. Let me explain.

I then explain and review the cognitive distortions listed earlier in this chapter in a clear manner that the family members can understand, often using specific examples from their family.

Therapist: Let's try to identify some of the distortions together.

Rob: I have one that Mom does big-time.

Therapist: OK, let's hear it.

Rob: Well, it's the arbitration thing you said.

Therapist: Arbitrary inference?

Rob: Yeah, I guess that's it. Well, like if we're out past curfew, she freaks and starts accusing us of being up to no good, like we're guilty until proven innocent.

Therapist: Well, that's one that you may perceive Mom as doing, but do any of the other family members engage in the same distortion?

Adam: Yeah, Jen does!

Jennifer: Do not!

Adam: Yes, you do.

Susan: Yes, you do, Jen. You're just like Mom in that way.

Therapist: Look, guys, we're just trying to identify cognitive distortions that you all engage in from time to time. This is not meant to be an antagonizing session. Also, you want to identify those distortions that you engage in yourselves as well as those that you witness with other family members.

John: OK, I have one about myself. I sometimes find myself thinking much the way Ruth's father does, and I get annoyed when my decisions are questioned—as much as I hate to admit it. I guess I view compliance by the other members of my family as a sign of respect, yet I tend to dump a lot onto Ruth.

At this point I have attempted to uncover some of the family's schemata and also to identify cognitive distortions. At the same time the family members are being oriented to the cognitive model in a subtle but clear way in which they will eventually be able to apply some of the techniques to themselves. I am also working rather quickly with them in order to hook them into returning. The next step after identifying these distortions will be to teach them to begin to question and weigh the evidence that supports the internal statements that they make to themselves and to challenge any erroneously based assumptions.

Therapist: All right, that's a good one, John. So one of your beliefs that you're choosing to identify as being based on a distortion is that "the boss is never questioned, or it's disrespectful." In a sense, it's a matter of "do as I say, not as I do."

John: Yeah, I guess. Boy, that sounds horrible when someone else actually says it in those terms.

Therapist: Well, don't worry so much about that, John. Let's just analyze it for a moment and see if we can challenge some of the basic tenets of that belief. Now, do you have any idea why you believe in that manner— that the man should be the boss and his requests or decisions should go unquestioned?

John: Well, I know that I was closer to my father than I was to my mother. I also think that Ruthie's father had something to do with it early on. When we were first married he used to . . . sort of . . . drill me.

Therapist: Drill you?

John: Yeah, you know, like take me aside and give me his lecture about how I need to act as the man of the house and family. Also, well, this may sound odd, but I kind of get the impression that this was sort of the way Ruthie was more comfortable with also, you know—like she kind of . . . oh, I forget the word you guys use all the time. It's a popular term . . .

Therapist: Enabled it?

John: Yeah, yeah, enabled. That's it. She enabled me to be that way, subtly, I guess.

Therapist: I see. So, do you believe that you may enable Ruth as well with certain things, and perhaps you both enable the children?

Ruth and John [*In unison*]: Yes! Definitely.

Therapist: Might this be tied to the schema of taking care of one another? How does this all relate?

Rob: Well, I was thinking about that for a while when you were talking to Dad, and I think we're like a pack of wolves that sort of just look out for one another casually, and if one of us is in need, somebody will step in. But we never talk about it openly otherwise.

Therapist [*This was an interesting metaphor because wolves are animals that clearly tend to be protective of one another yet certainly are capable of protecting themselves as well.*]: OK, but how does this cause conflict?

Rob: I'm not sure.

Susan: I think that maybe the conflict comes when one person has one expectation and the other has a different expectation and it's never communicated. We just sort of . . . uh . . .

Therapist: Mind-read.
Susan: Yeah.
Therapist: OK, that's another distortion.
Adam: Wow, we're one distorted family—cool! [*Everyone laughs*]
Therapist: Well, yes, you have your distortions, but all families do. It's not so unusual!
Ruth [*In jest*]: I don't know. When I listen to it all, it makes us sound as if we're the Addams family. [*Everyone laughs*]
Therapist: Good, Ruth! That was funny!

Here I am attempting to bolster some family cohesion through levity and at the same time trying to understand the family dynamics and how each member thinks and perceives various situations. Next, I will slowly introduce the idea of restructuring some of the thinking styles to bring about change.

Therapist: I think it might be important for us to take a look at some of the distortions you frequently engage in, now that you have identified a few of them, and see whether we may be able to challenge them, particularly those that interfere the most with your family dynamics. For example, John, would you be willing to volunteer so that I can demonstrate?
John: Sure.
Therapist: You said, as I recall, that one of your beliefs is that as the father and one of the heads of the household "the boss is never questioned, or it would demonstrate disrespect"—something to that effect.
John: Right.
Therapist: OK, now how well do you believe this statement can be substantiated?
John: I don't know. It's just something I've come to know.
Therapist: So there's no substantiating evidence that renders it a sound principle. It's merely conjecture. So is it possible that it might be based on erroneous information?
John: Possibly.
Therapist: Well, what do you know about the effect of this principle? In other words, what results have you received from it thus far?
John: Well, not too good. In fact, no one obeys it, and I'm sort of scoffed at by my kids for believing it.
Therapist: All right, so perhaps you're seeing more evidence that says that it's not so effective than evidence supporting its use. So maybe it needs some modification, and you don't have to abandon the principle completely. I mean, respect is important, but to expect that no one will ever question what you say or do may be a bit unreasonable.
John: Yeah, I see your point. But then how do I get it out of my head? I mean, it's ingrained there pretty heavily.
Therapist: Good question. Cognitive therapy utilizes a great many homework assignments. The basic theory contends that you must practice challenging negative self-statements, or what we call automatic thoughts, just as

much as you have been using them in the past. One way to do this is by writing the corrected statement out each time you experience a negative self-statement, or in this case, a cognitive distortion. So, I'd like you to take a piece of paper and write across the top several headings, drawing a vertical line down the side of each to make columns like this:

Situation or Event	Automatic Thought	Cognitive Distortion	Emotion	Challenging Self-Statement	Alternative Response

Then, each time a situation occurs when you have a negative automatic thought, write it down. Starting with the left-hand column, record the situation or event in which you had the thought, and in the next column put exactly what the thought was. Next, attempt to identify what type of distortion you are engaging in and the emotional response that accompanies it. Then try to challenge that thought or belief by weighing the evidence that exists in favor of it. After that, write down an alternative response, using any new information you may have gathered. Does that make sense to you?

John: Yes, but could we run through it once so that I'm sure I have it right?

Therapist: Certainly. Let's try an example.

John: Something happened last week with Adam when he came in a little past curfew, and I said something about his being 5 minutes late. He started to, well, what I call challenge my authority by attempting to minimize what he had done, saying it had only been 5 minutes and was no big deal.

Therapist: So let's get everything down on paper.

Situation or Event
Adam arrives home
5 minutes late
for curfew.

Automatic Thought
"He's defying me. He doesn't respect my position. If I don't chastise him, I'll be a lousy father."

Cognitive Distortion
Arbitrary inference
Dichotomous thinking
Personalization

Emotions
Upsets
Angry

Challenging Self-Statement
"Just because he comes home 5 minutes beyond his curfew doesn't mean that it's aimed directly at me. It also doesn't mean that he's intending to defy me."

Alternative Response
"I could talk to him about it rather than jumping to conclusions and punishing him. Perhaps he just honestly lost track of time."

Therapist: That's excellent. Do you all see how we attempt to restructure some of our thinking?

Rob: Yeah, but what if Adam was really defying Dad? I mean, how do we know that it's correct?

Therapist: Good question, Rob. We gather information to support our alternative beliefs, and so one of the things that your dad could do is, as he said on the sheet, talk to Adam about what his intentions were in arriving home late. This could be applied to all of you at one time or the other as you recognize yourselves engaging in distorted thinking. We want to begin to examine your mode of thought and really question the validity of what you tell yourselves. This may make a monumental difference in how you interact.

From this point I begin to monitor the family members in challenging their belief statements in the fashion just demonstrated. During this process, feelings and emotions are also addressed, as well as communication skills and problem-solving strategies. Regular homework assignments are also employed to aid family members in learning to challenge their distorted thoughts more spontaneously. Eventually, I will walk each family member through this specific technique to ensure its correct use. In addition, the use of behavioral techniques, such as the reassignment of family members' roles and responsibilities, becomes an integral part of the treatment regime in this particular case. Also, homework assignments are essential in facilitating change in the process of treatment.[7] The general concept behind this is that with the change and modification of dysfunctional thinking and behaviors there will be less family conflict.

Working With Ruth and John as a Couple

Had I originally addressed Ruth and John's case from a perspective of marital counseling with couples, my approach would be somewhat altered. Most likely the extent of my work with them would remain schema focused, but more on the beliefs each partner maintains about themselves and each other as it relates to the marriage. For example, I would initially focus on the beliefs that each partner draws from his or her family of origin and how these beliefs are influencing the present marital relationship. Investigating how their current marital interaction rests on beliefs derived from their families of origin is an essential area of focus. The fact that Ruth learned that the female in the relationship absorbs the responsibility is important, as is John's belief that it is OK to shift his responsibilities onto his wife. This has caused some imbalance in the relationship, particularly after Ruth developed problems coping with stress. Reworking some of these schemas to provide more balance to the relationship is one example of a cognitive behavioral intervention. The work, of course, comes with helping each partner learn to challenge rigidly held beliefs that contribute to dysfunction and deal with the subsequent guilt that may be generalized by abandoning some of these old beliefs.

JERRY COREY'S WORK WITH RUTH FROM A COGNITIVE BEHAVIORAL PERSPECTIVE

In the *CD-ROM for Integrative Counseling* I work with Ruth from a cognitive behavioral perspective in a number of therapy sessions. Refer to the three sessions where I demonstrate my way of working with Ruth from a cognitive, emotive, and behavioral focus (Sessions 6, 7, and 8). See also Session 9 ("Integrative Perspective"), which illustrates the interactive nature of working with Ruth on thinking, feeling, and doing levels.

Basic Assumptions

In this section I combine elements from Ellis's rational emotive behavior therapy (REBT) and Beck's cognitive therapy (CT) in an integrative approach for my work with Ruth.[8] Rational emotive behavior therapy assumes that individuals are born with the potential for rational thinking but tend to fall victim to the uncritical acceptance of irrational beliefs, which are perpetuated through self-reindoctrination. Beck's cognitive therapy shares with REBT an active, directive, time-limited, person-centered, structured approach. As an insight therapy, cognitive therapy emphasizes identifying and changing negative thoughts and maladaptive beliefs (also known as schemata). According to Beck's cognitive model of emotional disorders, to understand the nature of emotional problems, it is essential to focus on the cognitive content of a client's reaction to an upsetting event or stream of thoughts. I draw on a range of cognitive, emotive, and behavioral techniques to demonstrate to my clients that they contribute to their own emotional disturbances by the faulty beliefs they have acquired. As a cognitive behavior therapist, I operate on the assumption that events or situations in life do not cause problematic emotions such as guilt, depression, and hostility. Rather, it is mainly our *evaluation* of the event and the *beliefs* we hold about these events that get us into trouble.

Initial Assessment of Ruth

As I review Ruth's intake form and her autobiography, it becomes evident that her beliefs are contributing to the majority of her problems. She has uncritically accepted certain values, many of which rely on guilt as a main motivation to control behavior. Ruth is not making clear decisions based on self-derived values; rather, she is listening to intimidating voices in her head that tell her what she should do.

Ruth has an underlying dysfunctional belief that she must be perfect in all that she attempts. If she is not perfect, in her mind, there are dire consequences. She is continually judging her performances, and she is bound to think poorly of herself because of her unrealistically high standards. Indeed, there is a judge sitting on her shoulder and whispering in her ear. What I hope to teach Ruth are practical ways to talk back to this judge, to learn a new self-dialogue, and to help her reevaluate her experiences as she changes her behavior. This will be the focus of my therapy with her.

Goals of the Therapy

The basic goal of REBT is to replace a self-defeating outlook on life with a rational and tolerant philosophy. The goal of CT is to change the way clients think by using their automatic thoughts to reach the core schemata (negative thoughts and faulty beliefs) and to begin to introduce the idea of cognitive restructuring. To do so, I will teach Ruth the A-B-C model of personality. This model is based on the premise that A (the activating event) does not cause C (the emotional consequences); rather, it is mainly B (her belief about the activating event) that is the source of her problems.

I collaboratively work with Ruth in formulating the goals for her therapy. During the initial session, Ruth indicates that she does not want to act out the rest of her life according to her parents' design. I find value in establishing a therapeutic contract with Ruth as a way to structure our working relationship.

Therapeutic Procedures

In working with Ruth as a cognitive behavior therapist, I employ a directive and action-oriented approach. Functioning as a teacher, I focus on what she can learn that will lead to changes in the way she is thinking, feeling, and behaving. Drawing on Beck's ideas from CT, I intend to focus on the inaccurate conclusions Ruth has reached by teaching her to look for the evidence that supports or contradicts her views and hypotheses. She will frequently hear the question "Where is the evidence for_____?" Through the use of open-ended questions and a Socratic dialogue, I will try to teach Ruth ways to systematically detect errors in her reasoning that result in faulty assumptions and misconceptions (cognitive distortions). After she has recognized her cognitive distortions, I will encourage her to carry out a range of homework activities, to keep a record of what she is doing and thinking, and to form alternative interpretations to replace her faulty assumptions. Eventually, through a process of guided discovery, I expect Ruth to acquire insights into the link between her thinking and the ways she feels and acts. I also expect her to learn a range of specific coping skills to deal with current and future problems.

I will ask Ruth to read literature from a cognitive behavioral perspective as an adjunct to her therapy sessions. For instance, I'll strongly recommend that she study books such as Ellis and Harper's *A New Guide to Rational Living*; Ellis's *Feeling Better, Getting Better, and Staying Better*; and Beck's *Cognitive Therapy and the Emotional Disorders.*[9]

Like any other form of learning, therapy is hard work. If Ruth hopes to successfully change her beliefs and thus change her behavior, it will be necessary for her to practice what she is learning in real-life situations. I will stress completing homework assignments, and I will ask her to fill out an REBT Self-

Help Form. This form has her analyze activating events, her beliefs about these events, the consequences of those beliefs, her disputing and debating of her faulty beliefs, and the effects of such disputing.

In working with Ruth, I attempt to integrate the cognitive and affective (feeling) dimensions. It is fair to say that I emphasize the cognitive aspects of therapy as I pull together concepts from REBT and CT. I realize that changing entails actually experiencing feelings. In my view, however, experiencing feelings alone is not enough to bring about a substantive change in behavior. Much of our therapy will focus on examining Ruth's current behavior and trying on new ways of behaving both during the therapy hour and in her daily life.

The Therapeutic Process

Elements of the Process

Working With Ruth's Faulty Beliefs   To assist Ruth in achieving a constructive set of beliefs and acquiring a self-enhancing internal dialogue, I perform several tasks as her therapist. First of all, I challenge her to evaluate the self-defeating beliefs she originally accepted without questioning. I also urge her to work toward giving up her faulty beliefs and then to incorporate functional beliefs that will work for her. Throughout the therapeutic process, I actively teach her that self-condemnation is the basis of many of her emotional problems, that it is possible for her to stop critically judging herself, and that with hard work, including behavioral homework assignments, she can greatly reduce many of her dysfunctional notions.

Ruth's *real* work, then, consists of doing homework in everyday situations and bringing the results of these assignments into our sessions for discussion and evaluation. I am concerned that she not only recognize her self-defeating thought patterns but also take steps to challenge and change them.

We explore how her fear of failing and making a fool of herself stops her from doing so many things. She then says that she would love to square dance but has not because she is afraid of being clumsy and looking like a jerk. She would love to ski but avoids it for fear that she will fall on the "bunny hill" and break a leg—and then really look like a fool. I am working with Ruth on her evaluation of events and her prediction that she will fail. I want her to see that even if she fails she can still learn to cope with the outcomes.

We continue for a couple of months, with Ruth agreeing to do some reading and also carrying out increasingly difficult homework assignments. Gradually she works up to more risky homework assignments, and she does risk looking foolish several times, only to find that her fantasies were much worse than the results. She gives her speech, and it is humorous and spontaneous. This gives her an increased sense of confidence to tackle some other difficult areas she has been avoiding.

Dealing With Ruth's Beliefs About Herself as a Mother   Ruth is feeling very guilty about letting one of her daughters down. Jennifer is having troubles at school and, Ruth says, is "going off the deep end." Ruth partially blames herself for

Jennifer's problems, telling herself that she must be a better mother than her own mother was.

Ruth: I don't want Jennifer to suffer the way I did. But in so many ways I know I'm unloving and critical of her, just as my mother was of me at that age.

Jerry: What are you telling yourself when you think of this?

I want Ruth to see that her self-defeating thoughts are getting her depressed and keeping her feeling guilty. My hope is that she will see that the key to eliminating needless anxiety and guilt lies in modifying her thinking.

Ruth: I feel guilty that I didn't help Jennifer enough with her schoolwork. If I had tutored her, she would be doing well in school. I tell myself that I'm the cause of Jennifer's problems, that I should have been a better mother, that I could have cared more, and that I've ruined her chances for a good life.

Jerry: Do you see how your line of thinking gets you into trouble? What about Jennifer's role in creating and maintaining her own problems?

Ruth: Yes, but I've made so many mistakes. And now I'm trying to make up for them so she can shape up and change.

Jerry: I agree that you may have made mistakes with her, but that doesn't mean it will be the ruination of her. Can you see that if you do so much for her and make yourself totally responsible for her, she doesn't have to do anything for herself?

I am attempting to get Ruth to dispute her own destructive thinking. She has continued this pattern for so long that she now automatically blames herself, and then the guilt follows.

Ruth: Well, I try to think differently, but I just keep coming back to these old thoughts. What would you like me to say to myself?

Jerry: When Jennifer does something wrong, who gets the blame for it?

Ruth: Me, of course. At least most of the time.

Jerry: And those times that Jennifer does well, who gets credit?

Ruth: Not me. Anyway, I dwell so much on what she's not doing that I don't often see that she does much right.

Jerry: How is it that you're so quick to place blame on yourself and just as quick to discount any part you have in Jennifer's accomplishments?

Ruth: Because problems occupy my mind, and I keep thinking that I should have been a better influence on her.

Jerry: I'd just hope that you could begin to be kinder to yourself. What I'd like you to consider saying to yourself is something like this: "Even though I've made mistakes in the past and will probably continue making mistakes, that doesn't mean I've ruined Jennifer or will. It doesn't mean I'm the same kind of mother to her that mine was to me."

Ruth: That sounds pretty good . . . If only I could say those things and mean them, and feel them!

Jerry: Well, if you keep disputing your own thinking and learn to substitute constructive self-statements, you're likely to be able to say and mean these things—and you'll probably feel different too.

Process Commentary   My major focus with Ruth is on her thinking. Only by learning to apply rigorous self-challenging methods will she succeed in freeing herself from the defeatist thinking that led to her problems. I place value on behavioral homework assignments that put her in situations where she is forced to confront her faulty beliefs and her self-limiting behavior. I also consistently challenge Ruth to question her basic assumption that she needs the approval of others to feel adequate.

 QUESTIONS FOR REFLECTION

1. What advantages do you see to the manner in which Dr. Ellis drew on cognitive, emotive, and behavioral techniques in working with Ruth's dysfunctional beliefs? any disadvantages?

2. Assume that you suggested a technique to Ruth (such as keeping a journal or reading self-help books) and she refused, telling you that what you are asking was too much to expect. What might you say to her?

3. What common faulty beliefs do you share with Ruth, if any? To what degree have you challenged your own self-defeating thinking? How do you think this would affect your ability to work with her?

4. Working with Ruth in an active, directive, and challenging manner could raise some ethical issues, especially if you attempted to impose your values by suggesting what she should value. As you review Ellis's, Dattilio's, and my work with Ruth, do you have any concerns that any of us are "pushing values"?

5. Dr. Dattilio focused on Ruth's family schemata, including beliefs from her family of origin and those in her current family. What uses can you see in working with family schemata? What are some advantages of using a cognitive behavioral approach in counseling couples? any disadvantages?

6. What might you do if Ruth came from a background where her "musts," "oughts," and "shoulds" arose out of her cultural conditioning? What if she insisted that she felt guilty when she dared to question her upbringing and that in her culture doing so was frowned upon?

7. In the example of my work with Ruth as a cognitive behavior therapist, I blended some of the concepts and techniques of Ellis (REBT) and Beck (CT). What are some aspects of REBT and CT that you might combine?

8. What ideas do you have for using cognitive behavior concepts and procedures in conjunction with Gestalt techniques? Can you think of examples in Ruth's case where you could use Gestalt techniques in working with her self-defeating thinking?

NOTES

1. For a more detailed discussion of the basic assumptions, key concepts, and practical applications of rational emotive behavior therapy, see G. Corey (2005), *Theory and Practice of Counseling and Psychotherapy*, 7th edition. Chapter 10 (Cognitive Behavior Therapy) outlines the basic elements of Albert Ellis's REBT, Aaron Beck's cognitive therapy, and Donald Meichenbaum's cognitive behavior modification.

2. For an updated work that describes the cognitive, emotive, and behavioral techniques typically employed by rational emotive behavioral practitioners, see Albert Ellis (2001), *Overcoming Destructive Beliefs, Feelings, and Behaviors*. Amherst, NY: Prometheus Books.

3. For useful self-help books that present a straightforward approach to REBT based on homework assignments and self-questioning, see A. Ellis (2001), *Feeling Better, Getting Better, Staying Better*, Atascadero, CA: Impact Publications; and A. Ellis and R. Harper (1997), *A Guide to Rational Living*, Hollywood, CA: Wilshire.

4. See See D. H. Baucom and N. Epstein (1990), *Cognitive-Behavioral Marital Therapy*, New York: Brunner/Mazel. This work offers a wealth of assessment techniques, strategies, and case vignettes with couples. Also, for a comprehensive treatment of cognitive behavioral therapy with couples and families, refer to the edited work by F. Dattilio (1998), *Case Studies in Couple and Family Therapy*, New York: Guilford Press.

5. See F. M. Dattilio (1993), Cognitive techniques with couples and families, *The Family Journal, 1*(1), 51–65; F. M. Dattilio (2000) Cognitive-behavioral strategies, in J. Carlson & L. Sperry (Eds.), *Brief Therapy With Individuals and Couples* (pp. 33–70), Phoenix, AZ: Zeig, Tucker & Theisen; and F. M. Dattilio (2001), Cognitive-behavior family therapy: Contemporary myths and misconceptions, *Contemporary Family Therapy, 23*(1), 3–18.

6. See A. I. Schwebel and M. A. Fine (1994), *Understanding and Helping Families: A Cognitive-Behavioral Approach*, Hillsdale, NJ: Erlbaum. Modifications made with permission of the authors.

7. See F. M. Dattilio (2002), Homework assignments in couple and family therapy, *Journal of Clinical Psychology, 58*(5), 535–547.

8. I do not repeat too much detail about the cognitive behavioral approaches, so it would be well to review the perspectives of Drs. Ellis and Dattilio in this chapter.

9. Here are the complete references for the books I recommend for clients such as Ruth. A. Beck (1976), *Cognitive Therapy and the Emotional Disorders*, New York: New American Library (Meridian). Beck clearly outlines the principles and techniques of cognitive therapy, giving many clinical examples of how the internal dialogue of clients results in various emotional and behavioral problems. A Ellis and R. Harper (1997), *A New Guide to Rational Living* (Rev. ed.), Hollywood, CA: Wilshire Books. The authors show how to apply the principles of REBT to problems of everyday living. A. Ellis (2001), *Feeling Better, Getting Better, Staying Better*, Atascadero, CA: Impact Publications. In this self-help book, Ellis provides practical ways to change cognitions, emotions, and behaviors.

Chapter 9

Case Approach to Reality Therapy

A Reality Therapist's Perspective on Ruth

by William Glasser, M.D.

Introduction

Before showing how I would work with Ruth, I want to provide a brief introduction to a few key concepts for what I refer to as the "new reality therapy." I continue to believe we choose all of our significant behaviors in an attempt to find happiness. Clients who are unhappy are not able to do this effectively and commonly choose what is called mental illness. If this were not so, psychotherapy would be totally ineffective because its effectiveness depends on the therapist having the skill to guide the client in the direction of making better choices. If the client were not choosing what he or she is doing, psychotherapy would be impossible, because we can't change what we don't choose.

Barring extreme poverty, physical illness, and the ravages of old age—none of which are chosen—when we are unhappy enough to seek therapy, I believe it is because we do not have a satisfying relationship. All of our chosen ineffective behaviors—neurosis, psychosomatic disease, and psychosis—are our self-destructive, often crazy, attempts to improve a present relationship or find a better one. Therefore, as you will see in the case of Ruth, reality therapy always focuses on finding the unsatisfying present relationship. This usually takes no more than a few minutes. Then, with guidance from the therapist, the client chooses ways to behave that improve the present flawed relationship or allow the client to find a new one.

We do not focus on the past because all relationship problems are in the present and must be solved in the present. We do not focus on the symptom because the symptom is always chosen to deal with the present unsatisfying relationship. The symptom will disappear when that relationship is improved. In contrast to most theoretical orientations, I believe that although we may be the product of our past we are not victims of our past unless we choose to be so. Approaching a client this way drastically shortens therapy because it quickly gets to the core of the problem, which is a present flawed or nonexistent relationship. A skilled reality therapist, using choice theory, can help most clients who are functional enough to walk into the office in about 10 sessions or less.[1]

Assessment of Ruth

Because psychological symptoms are chosen behaviors, in the description of my therapy with Ruth I use verb forms rather than nouns to describe how she chooses to behave. For example, you will see that I use "panicking" instead of "panic" to describe her symptoms. A panic disorder would be a consistent choosing of panicking behaviors as exemplified by Ruth. She will be taught to say, "I am choosing to depress" or "I am depressing" instead of saying, "I am depressed" or "I am suffering from depression." This new way of describing symptoms or disorders makes sense when you understand choice theory.

As Ruth presents herself, it is obvious that she has never been able to satisfy her basic needs except her need for survival. She does not feel that she has love, power, fun, or freedom in her life, and her choices of anxietying, panicking, and psychosomaticizing are her ways of expressing her extreme frustration. These symptoms keep her anger from bursting forth, and they scream, "Help me!"

Ruth hasn't the strength to come out and say what she wants: a relationship far better than the one she has. Her symptoms and her complaints are her only way to express her intense dissatisfaction with her life. If she does not get the counseling she needs, she will choose more and more symptoms and will ultimately become disabled by them. She will also grow fat because eating (a survival need) is her only satisfaction, and she will choose phobicking to the point where she will say she is not able to leave the house alone in a desperate attempt to keep her husband close to her.

Key Issues and Themes

First of all, Ruth needs someone who will listen to her and not criticize her for what she says. She will, however, present her story and continually ask for criticism by saying things like, "It's wrong for me to complain; I have so much; I'm acting like a baby." She will make a whole family of comments like these. She knows how to "guilt," and the counselor must not get involved in the process. My most important task as her therapist is to listen to her and tell her that she has a right to express herself without criticism.

Then, it is important for Ruth to learn about her basic needs. She needs to try to give more to her marriage and improve the relationship with her husband. I can ask over and over, "How does your being miserable help you or anyone else?" Although Ruth can be kind to her parents and others when she talks to them, it is important that she tell them firmly that she is going to do what she believes is right for her life.

I would encourage Ruth in her choice to go to work, although I would discuss with her the choice to become an elementary schoolteacher. This is a very giving role, and she may not do well at this now. She may need to work among adults and to be appreciated for her adult qualities by her peers. She needs a job where she does not have to be a "good" person to be appreciated.

Ruth's weight, diet, or symptoms should not be discussed in detail because they are not the problem. If she wants to talk about them, I will listen, but I will not encourage her to explore these topics. Talking about her problems or failures will lead Ruth to choose to guilt, because she can only solve them through a better relationship. My approach will be to focus on her getting out of the house and finding a satisfying place in the adult world. If it is satisfying enough, her complaints and symptoms will be lessened, but she will still have to work on her relationship with her husband.

Ruth's finances will be discussed. What she earns for the first several years might be spent on herself and on doing things with her husband and children that are especially enjoyable to her. I would encourage Ruth not to save her money, give it to charity, or spend it on necessities unless that is what she really wants to do. Instead, I will constantly encourage her to do what is right for her, not what is right for others or "good" for the world. I think she needs to learn to be a little selfish.

From the first session I will bring up her relationship with her husband. But this will not be to find fault with what they are doing as much as it will be to try to guide Ruth to take the initiative and do something she believes will improve her marriage. Following choice theory, she can only control her own life; she cannot control her husband's life. If John is willing to come in for marriage counseling, I will employ what I call structured reality therapy, which is described in my book *Choice Theory*.

Therapeutic Techniques

It is important that I be warm and uncritical and teach Ruth to be accepting of herself. In fact, I may say to her, "You need to realize that you are choosing your actions and only you can change what you are doing. You can't change anyone else." I will give Ruth my *Choice Theory* book to read and we will discuss it in each session until she is well aware of these concepts and how they apply to the life she has and is still choosing to live. This information, coupled with a good client–therapist relationship, should substantially reduce the time for counseling.

It is best that plans be discussed, written out, and checked off. Ruth is competent, but her competence is never used for herself. She can be asked over and over "How will satisfying your needs hurt anyone else?" and "How may doing this actually help others? Let's talk about this, because the answers to these questions are important for your life."

As much as possible, humor in the sessions will be helpful. Ruth is overdue for a laugh or two, and laughter will allow her to let go of her psychosomatic symptoms more quickly than anything else she can do. In therapy sessions I will emphasize her good points, which are many, and at each session she can be encouraged to tell what she did that was good for her and what she accomplished that she never thought she would be able to do.

It will be good for Ruth to consider the idea of inviting friends in and making a social life. She needs people. If her husband does not want to help, she can be encouraged to do this by herself. If she has a job, she might get hired help in to do the housework, which is something Ruth probably has never done or even dreamed of doing. The idea of spending money for enjoyment is worth a lot of therapy time.

Ruth can be encouraged to talk about her children and apply the ideas of choice theory to them. I will ask her what she thinks she needs to do to get along with her daughter Jennifer, and I will advise her to stop telling her daughter what to do. Also, Ruth can be challenged to stop criticizing Jennifer completely, no matter what Jennifer or any of her other children say or do. Instead, Ruth might go out with her daughter for a good time, tell her she likes her the way she is, and say, jokingly, that she should not model herself after an unhappy mother, only a happy mother.

I can teach Ruth that it is her life and that it is up to her, not anyone else, to make what she wants of it. Whenever she says that she can't do something, I can ask her why she can't, then ask her to give all the reasons why she could do it, and compare the two sets of reasons.

What Ruth needs is freedom. She has locked herself in a prison of her own making for most of her life, and there should be a discussion of who can let her out. If she is locked in, it is because she won't open the door.

A Sample Session With Ruth

I keep the sessions as light as I can. Ruth needs to learn to take her problems less seriously so it will be easier for her to convince herself that she can make better choices. Here is how I guide the therapy after about a month.

Ruth: It was really bad last night, all horrible feelings.

Therapist [*Interrupting*]: The sweats, the palpitations, the fear of impending doom, the whole kit and kaboodle of your midnight misery. I'll grant you this, if you've learned anything in your 39 years, it's how to panic. Don't you think it's time to learn something better to do at night?

Ruth: How can you talk like that? Do you really believe I'm choosing this panic, that I enjoy these attacks? How can I possibly be choosing them? They come on while I'm sleeping, and they wake me up.

Therapist: Tell me, if you're not choosing them, who is? You've read about choice theory. You choose all you do, just as I do, and just as everyone does. Of course, you're not enjoying this choice but—I know this is hard to believe—to you it's better than anything else you could choose in the middle of the night.

Ruth: You're crazy! It's not better or worse, it's what I do as I sleep. Don't you listen to me? I'm asleep; it wakes me up.

Therapist [*Not rising to the bait of arguing with her but continuing on*]: Suppose I called you in the middle of the night and woke you up before you woke up with your choice to panic. In fact, let's do it right now. Pretend you're sleeping, and I give you a call.

Ruth: I'm getting afraid to go to sleep, even to go to bed. The attacks are excruciating. You don't have any idea of how bad they are. You've never had one. If you had, you wouldn't be sitting there so smugly telling me I'm choosing this misery.

Therapist: If you want to be able to make better choices while you're asleep at night, you've got to learn to make better choices in the daytime. But, c'mon, let me call and wake you up. Will you do it, or do you have a better idea?

Ruth: Of course I don't have a better idea. If I did, would I be here listening to this nonsense? Go ahead and call me.

Therapist: OK, ring, ring!

Ruth: Hello, who is it? What time is it?

Therapist: It's me, Dr. Glasser. I got to thinking about you and your problems, and I decided to call you. Can we talk for a few minutes?

Ruth: I'm sleepy. Couldn't it wait until morning?

Therapist: Just one question—one, OK?

Ruth: OK, OK, I'm up now, so I might as well talk. What do you want to know?

Therapist: I want to know what you were thinking about tonight when you went to bed. Tell me as much as you remember.

Ruth: What I always think about—that my life is all messed up, and it's not getting better. I'm in a rut. There's nothing going on in my marriage, my body looks just awful, and my whole day is horrible. I can understand why people drink and take drugs if they feel the way I do all the time. What more is there to tell you? It's what I tell you every time we talk. That's what I think about, my awful day and my miserable life. What's the sense of repeating it now? What good will it do?

Therapist: If I call you tomorrow night, do you think the story will be the same?

Ruth: Of course it'll be the same. It's been the same for the last 10 years.

Therapist: No, it hasn't. It's different now.

Ruth: What are you talking about? How is it different?

Therapist: The panicking is new, and seeing me is even newer. That's different, a lot different.

Ruth: Yeah, it's even worse than it was. At least I didn't have the panic. And you're no bargain either. I never thought of it that way. Maybe if I get rid of you I'll get rid of the panic.

Therapist: If you want to quit, I won't try to stop you.

Ruth: Well, you don't seem to be doing me much good.

Therapist: You don't seem to be doing yourself much good either. Why don't you choose to do something for yourself? Do you want to keep going to bed afraid you're going to wake up scared to death and then come here and blame me because I'm not doing anything to help you? How's that going to help you?

Ruth: What can I do?

Therapist: You do a lot all day long, but you just don't do anything for yourself. Believe me, you'll get through the rest of the night no matter what happens. But tomorrow, even if you have what you call a panic attack, don't tell me about it. It's your choice, and I can't do a thing about it. All I can help you do is have a better day and do some different things than you've been doing. Do you want to start tomorrow, start changing the way you live, or do you want to choose to go on as you are?

Ruth [*Softening now. She's been listening. The middle-of-the-night-call technique is getting her attention.*]: But how can I?

Therapist [*With emphasis*]: How can you not? Why keep waiting? I know you're afraid. We're all afraid to try new things because they might not work out. Let's stop wasting time and start right now to make a plan for you to do something for you. You won't hurt anyone if you start to take care of yourself. If you begin feeling better, you'll be doing your whole family a favor.

After this, we make a plan to do something that, for a change, will satisfy Ruth's needs, and we're on our way.

Process Commentary   I dare not wait much longer than a month to confront Ruth's resistance. She's not a weakling; it takes a lot of strength to panic as she has. But if I don't do this, and if I let her control me with her panicking as she has been trying to control everyone else, she won't change. To gain a sense of control, she has been willing to choose the suffering she complains about. We all do it once in a while; it's just that she does it a lot. I need to intervene, for that's my job as a therapist. There is no other way. As I told her, I've seen a lot of Ruths, and they have all changed. From my experience, her prognosis is very good if she's treated this way. Once she begins to put the energy into taking effective control of her life that she puts into panicking, she will make rapid progress.

I can't tell how long therapy will take. But if we focus on the marital relationship, do not pay attention to the symptoms, teach her that the only person's behavior she can control is her own, get her to put her energy into getting closer to her husband and children, and get her to find a satisfying job, it might not take much more than 10 initial sessions. After that I might see her once a month to keep her on course.

Another Reality Therapist's Perspective on Ruth

by Robert E. Wubbolding, Ed.D.

Introduction

I will present several examples of interventions that typify the practice of reality therapy. These dialogues include specific questions that can be asked when using reality therapy. It is not my intention to imply that if the therapist merely asks a few questions the client will automatically make a rapid or dramatic change. The dialogues represent samples of the most important interventions, which are made repeatedly and rephrased in dozens of ways throughout the process of counseling.

Setting the Stage for Therapy   Because of the importance of informed consent, at the beginning of the first session or as soon as is appropriate I review with Ruth all pertinent details related to professional disclosure: my credentials, the nature and principles of reality therapy, confidentiality and its limits, her rights and responsibilities, and the general goals of counseling. I emphasize the common formulation used in reality therapy: "my job, your job, our job." "My job" is to function as an ethical professional who recognizes his limitations. "Your job" is to keep the scheduled appointments and to disclose as much as you choose. "Our job" is to work for changes in your life that will result in increased happiness (need satisfaction). I emphasize that if Ruth is willing to work hard this therapy will indeed be short term.

Exploring Ruth's Expectations   I then explore with Ruth the thoughts she had when she decided to come for counseling and the thoughts she had today before her first visit. She describes her uncertainties, her hesitancy, and her sense of failure. I encourage her to discuss her fears about counseling and about "opening Pandora's box" and becoming overwhelmed with what she might find. With empathic listening I begin to form a relationship with her. I show confidence that she can make progress, on one condition—that she is willing to work at feeling better. If she will expend some effort, she can gain a sense of control, which is now lacking.

One of my goals in the first session is to help Ruth relax about her problems. Our dialogue goes as follows:

Therapist: What thoughts went through your mind when you came here today?

Ruth: I was afraid and apprehensive. I have wondered what would happen. I often feel pain and am upset.

Therapist: How have you tried to fight off your pain, anxiety, fears, and overall upsetness?

Ruth: I have expended a great deal of energy to purge myself of my misery.

Therapist: And has this relentless effort paid off for you?

Ruth: When my efforts have not been successful, I have renewed them with more intensity and vigor.

Therapist: Is fighting your worries helping to lessen them?

Ruth: Well, I must admit that attacking my fears has not yet worked.

Therapist: If this approach is not working for you, I encourage you to think in terms of the opposite approach. Since fighting your fears does not help, now may be the time to admit to yourself, at least for a while, that you will continue to be upset. Could you consider embracing your problems? After all you've been through, it is no wonder you're upset. Who wouldn't be?

Presenting this alternative approach to clients often helps them to feel more confident in themselves. They realize that they are normal or at least handling their problems in a normal way. For Ruth, my hope is that she will begin to consider that her fear, anxiety, and overall upsetness are reactions to her problems, but not the problem itself. If she can see these reactions as normal, she has a good chance of managing them in the future.

In the initial session and in subsequent sessions, we spend a lot of time exploring her "quality world" as it relates to counseling. She goes into detail about the statement that what she wants most from therapy is to be told "what I have to do and be pushed to do it, so that I can begin to live before it's too late." I again make a significant point that she already has a tremendous advantage: even now she believes she can do something, and she wants to begin to live. I ask her to define what it means for her to "live." She describes her feeling of being a doormat at home, being overweight, being lonely and isolated, and being spiritually alienated. As she describes her pain, I express excitement that she is able to put it into words and point out that being able to articulate this pain is a major step.[2]

Ruth: To be honest, I am upset that I need to seek professional help and that I can't work out my problems on my own.

Therapist: I would be surprised if you weren't upset about seeking outside help. It's a healthy way to feel. But actually, you deserve to be congratulated for taking this first big step. It must have taken courage.

Ruth: Well, I never thought of it as a big step.

Therapist: As you sit here now, do you believe counseling can help you? Do you believe things can improve for you in a short time?

Ruth: I came because I think it will help.

Therapist: I've read your history, and we've talked here for a while, and I believe you could feel better. I make no guarantees, but I think a better life is possible. And I base that thought not on an idle wish but on four pieces of specific information: You have taken a step by coming here, and you also have at least some belief that your life can be better. Moreover, you've already set a goal: to keep living. And finally, you're very open about what hurts. In other words, you can describe your pain.

Ruth: So there's hope.

Therapist: I agree. There is hope. I also believe you can feel at least a little better quickly, on one condition.

Ruth: What is that condition?

Therapist: That you're willing to put forth some effort, even hard work. And this work, strange as it sounds, means less effort in fighting off the pain.

Ruth: I'm willing to do that.

Working With Ruth's Depression

Ruth at times resists my optimistic attitude and my emphasis on her positive steps, insisting that they are minor successes and that she sometimes feels depressed. Because of her insistence, I determine how depressed she has become. Assessing the possibility of suicide reveals there is no risk. I decide to use paradoxical techniques with Ruth. At first she schedules some time for choosing to depress herself, perhaps 10 minutes every other day. I ask her to describe in detail what she can do to make the situation worse. She enjoys this discussion and laughs heartily as she goes into detail about how she can criticize herself publicly, procrastinate even more over her plans, increase her guilt, and exaggerate her fear of death. She comes to see how such ineffective thinking holds her back from a happier and need-satisfying life. But most important, she learns through this upside-down logic that if she can make her life more miserable she can also make it more enjoyable. It is important to reemphasize that I have determined early on that she is not suicidal or depressed to the point of being incapacitated. In such cases, paradoxical techniques are to be avoided.

I then encourage Ruth to describe what she wants that she is not getting and to say what she actually is getting from her husband, from each of her children, from her religion, from school, and, most important, from herself. (She has already described what she wants from me.) This exploration takes more than one session. She gradually develops more specific goals or wants related to her family, social life, self (for example, weight), professional life, and the spiritual aspect of her life (a much-neglected area in the counseling profession).

Exploring What Ruth Wants

An exploration of one aspect of Ruth's wants as they relate to her family—more specifically, her husband—is illustrated in this dialogue.

Therapist: You've described your relationship with your husband. Describe how you would like the relationship to be. To put the question another way, what do you want from him that you're not getting?

Ruth: I want him to be understanding.

Therapist: Could you be more specific about what you want that you're not getting?

Ruth: He takes me for granted. He only wants me to be a mother for his children. He's always busy at work and doesn't think of me as an independent person. And, you know, sometimes I think he's right.

Therapist: What do you want him to feel toward you?

Ruth: I would like him to appreciate me, to like me, to be friendly.

Therapist: And if he appreciated you, what would he do differently?

Ruth: He would show me more attention.

Therapist: Ruth, if he showed you attention tonight, what would you do?

Ruth: I'd be friendly. If he would share something about himself, I'd realize that he has confidence in me and has some feelings for me.

Therapist: Would you be interested in working toward having a better relationship with him?

Ruth: Of course.

Therapist: I think you've established a goal for your counseling. We'll be talking about what you can do to make the situation better for yourself.

In this dialogue Ruth has defined one want or goal. Using similar questioning, I help her clarify her wants as they relate to her children, religion, school, and other aspects of her life. The emphasis in formulating such goals is on helping her state her own role in the desired outcome.

During these early sessions Ruth also defines what she can control and what she cannot control. I ask her to evaluate whether she can "force" others to change and how much control she can exert over her past history. I gradually help her come to believe her life will be happier if she focuses on changing her own behavior in small increments.[3]

Therapist: You've defined what you want for yourself regarding your husband, children, and school. You've said that you want to feel that your life has some spiritual purpose—that it has lasting value. Would you describe the components of your life process that you have control of and what is beyond your control?

Ruth: I've tried hard to get my husband to change, and I've also tried to lose weight, to see some purpose to my life, to get rid of the night terrors, cold sweats, and all the pain I feel, and to get a professional identity and a life of my own.

Therapist: Can you really change any of these—the people or things on the list?

Ruth: I'm not sure. I'm so confused.

Therapist: Let's take them one by one. Can you force your husband to be the kind of person you want him to be?

Ruth: No, I've tried for years.

Therapist: Have your efforts gotten the result you wanted?

Ruth: No.

Therapist: Can you control your weight?

Ruth: I've lost and gained it back so many times.

Therapist: You have lost weight! So you know how to reduce your pounds, and you've succeeded many times.

Ruth: Well, I haven't looked at it as a success. It seems to me that regaining weight is a failure.

Therapist: But you have succeeded many times. You've taken charge of your eating for extended periods.

Ruth: I suppose you're right.

Therapist: What about gaining a sense of purpose—what I would call a sense of importance—that you are somebody, that you are worthwhile? How much control do you have over specific plans to formulate this ideal and to work toward it?

Ruth: Well, the way you put it makes it sound as if I could do it and as if I do have some control.

Therapist: Ruth, in my counseling I try to translate my clients' ideas into actions—actions that they can take to fulfill their needs.

Ruth: So how do I begin?

Therapist: By taking small steps—one at a time. But let's not rush. In fact, I'd suggest that you not make any radical or extensive changes until we talk some more.

Process Commentary   I also ask Ruth to decide on her level of commitment. She is obviously not at the basic level: "I don't want to be here." For some parts of her life such as her weight she may be at the second level: "I would like the outcome, but not the effort." "I'll try," the third level, is probably characteristic of much of her life. But I want to help her see her efforts to lose weight as successes. And so I lead her to the fourth and fifth levels: "I'll do my best" and "I'll do whatever it takes." If clients are willing to be open and work hard, they can benefit in a short time from reality therapy.

The real benefit in utilizing this system is not "the words" but "the music." This questioning format, often discouraged in counselor training programs, helps Ruth develop an internal perceived locus of control and realize that she has choices. She then gains a profound belief that life can be better, that she can feel better, and that she has more control than she ever dreamed of. It should be clear that reality therapy involves more than superficial planning and problem solving.

The underlying principle is that when Ruth improves her relationships, her pain will lessen and she will be happier. I will help her in the areas of her relationships with her husband, career, and education. I will work with Ruth's gaining increased acceptance of herself as both an imperfect and a worthwhile human being.

Helping Ruth Evaluate What She Is Doing

Interspersed throughout the entire process are dozens of questions related to self-evaluation: "Did your specific activities yesterday help you to the degree that you had hoped for?" "Are your wants realistically attainable?" "Is what you want really good for you?" More specifically, "Is your boring but comfortable life what you truly want?" "Is it good for you now?" "Are you spiritually the kind of person you want to be?" "What would you be doing differently if you were the type of person you wanted to be?" And the key question, "How are you getting closer to your husband and children?" We pick up the dialogue in a subsequent session.

Therapist: Let's focus on one aspect of what you have referred to as a source of great pain, which is your relationship with your husband. You mentioned in previous sessions that he ignores you, takes you for granted, and talks only minimally to you. And I gather that you want this situation to change?[4]

Ruth: I sure do.

Therapist: And you've also decided that your own actions are the only ones that are within your control.

Ruth: Yes.

Therapist: Now I want to ask you some important questions about the choices you've been making and what you've been doing in the relationship.

Ruth: OK.

Therapist: What happened last night? Describe exactly what you did last night from the time your husband came in to the time you went to bed.

Ruth: [*She describes the entire evening in detail. I help her to be precise.*]

Therapist: What did you want from him at that time?

Ruth: [*She describes what she would have liked from him.*]

Therapist: What could you say differently from what you said last night?

Ruth: I'll say, "Hello, how was your day?" and give him a hug. Then I'll say, "Let's read the mail and then fix supper together."

Therapist: Sounds good. So you'll take charge of the only part of the relationship that's within your ability to control?

Ruth: Yes, my own actions.

Therapist: Now let's suppose he doesn't respond the way you would like. What then?

Ruth: Well, I could tell myself: "I've done what I can do, and there's no guarantee that he'll change. I choose to feel satisfaction at having made better choices than those I've made in the past."

Therapist: And, if you make this kind of effort, there is a good chance that the relationship will improve.

Process Commentary   In this session I put emphasis on helping Ruth evaluate her own behavior rather than her husband's actions. By questioning her, I indirectly reminded her that she has control only of her own actions and that if she takes action she will feel that she is doing her part. She was then helped to make short-range, attainable plans that have a high likelihood of success. In subsequent sessions she explores other choices—that is, her other unmet needs and their accompanying ineffective and effective behaviors as well as her perceptions regarding the inner sense of control she has gained and still wants to gain.

I encourage Ruth to make more attainable special plans to fulfill her need for fun. I select fun because it is the most obvious unmet need, the one she is most likely to be able to meet more effectively, and the easiest to work on. In view of the fact that she has said she wants to lose weight permanently, I encourage her to join a support group such as Weight Watchers. I suggest that she get to know the students in her classes and organize study groups. This will give her a sense of belonging and help her fulfill her need for power or achievement.

I ask Ruth to read 10 minutes a day (if she wants to) on a topic that is spiritually uplifting. A good starter is *A Set of Directions for Putting and Keeping Yourself Together.*[5] To be avoided is anything that encourages guilt, fear, or self-deprecation. She has expressed a deep need for "an anchor," and to neglect this part of her life would be unfortunate. She can at least be referred to a sensible clergyman who understands reality therapy.

Overall, I help her fulfill her needs for belonging and power and fun more effectively. This is accomplished by use of the "WDEP" system: determining wants, including level of commitment and perceived locus of control; examining the total behavior; evaluating her direction and what she is doing as well as her thinking and feelings; assisting her to make her own inner self-evaluations, especially regarding her wants and behaviors; and finally helping her develop positive and realistic plans aimed at fulfilling her needs in ways that are different from previous choices.

I feel confident in applying reality therapy with Ruth. I also feel challenged by the multitude of Ruth's problems, but my knowledge of choice theory helps me to see that when she changes any behavior the good feeling and success generalize. Thus, I am confident that picking any symptom to work on will lead Ruth to increased satisfaction with her entire life. Her obvious high level of motivation and minimal resistance facilitate relatively steady and visible progress toward the fulfillment of her wants (goals).

JERRY COREY'S WORK WITH RUTH FROM A REALITY THERAPY PERSPECTIVE

Introduction

Reality therapy is active, directive, practical, and cognitive behavioral in focus. As a reality therapist, I see my task as helping clients clarify their wants and perceptions, evaluate them, and then make plans to bring about change. My basic job is establishing a personal relationship with my clients that will give them the impetus to make an honest evaluation of how well their current behavior is working for them. Reality therapy concentrates on total behavior, which includes doing, thinking, feeling, and physiological components.

Applied to Ruth, this means that she creates her own perceived world. Because I make the assumption that changing feelings is more difficult than changing actions, the focus of therapy is on what she is doing, and to some extent, what she is thinking. Ruth will find that it is typically easier to get herself to *do* something different than to *feel* something different. Although it is acceptable to discuss feelings, this is always done by relating feelings to what she is doing and thinking.

Assessment of Ruth

Rather than focusing on Ruth's deficits, problems, and failures, I am interested in looking at her assets, accomplishments, and successes. Initially I ask her questions such as these: What do you want? How might your life be different if you had what you wanted now? What do you consider to be your major strengths? What qualities do you most like about yourself? What have you done that you are proud of? What resources can you build on? From Ruth's autobiography and intake form, I know that she has several strengths. She has graduated from college and is in a teacher education program at the graduate level. She has done this against many odds. Her parents could see no real reason why she should get a college degree. In her current situation her husband and children have not been supportive of her efforts to complete her education. She has been involved in numerous community groups and made some contributions there. Now she needs to develop a clear plan for attaining her personal objectives.

Goals of Therapy

Ruth's present behavior is not working as well as it might. She is unproductively dwelling on unfortunate events from her past, and she is paying too much attention to feelings of guilt and anxiety and not enough to those things she is doing that create these feelings. In short, she is making herself anxious and guilty by what she is doing and not doing in everyday life. I try to direct her attention toward these actions because they are the most easily controlled part of her life. I continue challenging her to make an honest assessment of how well her current behavior is getting her what she wants. Then I help her make plans to bring about change.

Therapeutic Procedures

I expect Ruth to make a commitment to carry out her plans. If she hopes to change, *action* is necessary. It is essential that she stick with her commitment to change and not blame others for the way she is or give excuses for not meeting her commitments. Thus, we will work with a therapeutic contract, one that spells out what she wants from therapy as well as the means by which she will attain her goals.

   If Ruth says that she is depressed, I will not ask *why* she is depressed, nor will I ask her to dwell on feelings of depression. Instead, I will ask what she has done that day to contribute to her experience of *depressing*. Changes in behavior do not depend on changing one's attitudes or gaining insights. On the contrary, attitudes may change, as well as feelings, once clients begin to change their behavior. I am also concerned about Ruth's present, not her past.

The Therapeutic Process

Ruth's therapeutic journey consists of my applying the procedures of reality therapy to help her meet her goals. Although the principles may sound simple, they must be adapted creatively to the therapeutic process. Although these principles are applied progressively in stages, they should not be thought of as discrete and rigid categories. Each stage builds on the previous stage, there is a considerable degree of interdependence among these principles, and taken together they contribute to the total process that is reality therapy. This process weaves together two components: the counseling environment and specific procedures that lead to changes in behavior.

Elements of the Process

Establishing the Relationship   During our initial sessions, my main concern is to create a climate that will be conducive to Ruth's learning about herself. The core of the counseling environment consists of a personal involvement with the client, which must be woven into the fabric of the therapeutic process from beginning to end. I convey this involvement through a combined process of listening to Ruth's story and skillful questioning. This process increases the chances that she will evaluate her life and move in the direction of getting what she wants.

In some of our early sessions Ruth wants to talk about occasions when she experienced failure in her childhood and youth. She quickly wants to blame past negative experiences for her fears. She seems a bit stunned when I tell her that I do not want to go over her past failures and that if we are going to talk about the past at all I am more interested in hearing what went right for her. From that topic she jumps to complaining about feeling anxiety, depression, and some physical symptoms. I ask her to describe what she would be doing if she were not depressing. This focus begins a process of redirection and gets her to think about other alternatives besides depressing. I do not encourage her to focus on feelings related to negative experiences. Part of her present problem is that she is already stuck in some negative feelings, and I do not want to reinforce her in continuing this pattern.

Challenging Ruth to Evaluate Her Behavior   After getting a picture of how Ruth sees her world, I encourage her to try something different: to take a hard look at the things she is doing and see if they are working for her. Questions that I pose to her are: "What are the things you've done today?" "What did you do this past week?" "Do you like what you're doing now?" "Are there some things you would like to be doing differently?" "What are some of the things that stop you from doing what you say you want to do?" Let me stress that I do not bombard her with these questions one after another. The early sessions are, however, geared to getting her to consider this line of questioning. Rather than looking at her past or focusing on her attitudes, beliefs, thoughts, and feelings, I want her to know that we will be zeroing in on what she is doing today and what she will do tomorrow.

I believe Ruth will change when she makes an assessment of the constructiveness or destructiveness of what she is doing. Here is a brief excerpt from a session.

Ruth: So, what do you think I'm doing wrong? There are times I want to give up, because I don't know what to do differently. [*She very much wants me to make an evaluation for her.*]

Jerry: You know how important it is for you to be the one who makes a judgment about your own behavior. It's your job to decide for yourself what is and isn't working. I can't tell you what you "should" do. [*For me to simply tell her that some of her present ways are ineffective will not be of much value to her.*]

Ruth: Well, I do want to go out and get some practice with interviews for part-time or substitute teaching. But I keep telling myself that I'm so busy I just don't have time to set up these interviews.

Jerry: And is that something you'd like to change? [*My line of questioning is to ascertain how much she wants what she says she wants. I am attempting to assess her level of commitment.*]

Ruth: Yeah, sure I want to change it. I want to be able to arrange for these interviews and then feel confident enough to have what it takes to get a part-time job.

We look at how Ruth stops herself (not why) and explore ways she might begin to change behavior that she calls "sitting back and waiting to see what happens." She says that she does not like her passivity and that she would like to do more initiating. One of the factors we talk about is how she lets her family get in the way of her doing some of these things she says she wants to do.

Planning and Action   We devote a number of sessions to identifying specific behaviors Ruth decides are not working for her. A few of these ineffective behaviors are procrastinating in arranging for job interviews; sitting at home feeling depressed and anxious and then increasing these feelings by not doing anything different; allowing her 19-year-old son, Rob, to come home after squandering money and then taking care of him; allowing her daughter Jennifer to control her life by her acting out; and continually taking on projects that she does not want to get involved in. Knowing that we cannot work on all fronts at once, I ask her what areas she wants to do something about.

Ruth decides first to line up some interviews for jobs. She makes it clear that her life is boring, stale, and without much challenge. Then she tries to convince me that everything she has to do for her family makes it next to impossible for her to get out of her boring rut. I reply, "If things are as bad as you say, do you expect them to change if you keep doing what you have been doing?"

We gradually work out some realistic plans, which include her filing applications with school districts and setting up interviews. Interestingly enough, after taking these beginning steps, she reports that she is already feeling much better.

We also develop some plans to set clear limits with Ruth's family. She has a pattern of doing things for her children and then resenting them and winding up feeling taken advantage of. Part of her plan calls for sitting down with each of her children and redefining their relationships. I suggest that it would be a good idea to have at least one session with her family. The idea both excites and frightens her. Yet she actually surprises herself when she is successful in getting John and her four children to come in for a 2-hour session of family therapy. At this session we mainly negotiate some changes in roles after Ruth has told each family member specific changes she would like and has been striving for. One of her sons and one of her daughters are not at all excited about some of the proposed changes, and they want to know what is wrong with the way things are. What I had in mind when I suggested this family session was to give Ruth an opportunity to ask for what she wants and to witness her negotiating for these changes. The session helps me see how she relates to her family, and it helps her ask for what is important to her.

Process Commentary   Functioning within the spirit of reality therapy, I do not tell Ruth what she should change but encourage her to examine her wants and determine her level of commitment to change. It is up to her to decide how well her current behavior is working for her. Once she makes an evaluation about what she is actually doing, she can take some significant steps toward making changes for herself. She has a tendency to complain about feeling victimized and controlled, and my intention is to help her see how her behavior actually contributes to this perceived helplessness. In our sessions, we focus on what Ruth does from the time she wakes up to the time she goes to bed. Through a self-observation process, Ruth gradually assumes more responsibility for her actions. She sees that what she does has a lot to do with the way she feels.

After Ruth becomes clearer about certain patterns of her behavior, I encourage her to develop a specific plan of action that can lead to the changes she desires. Broad and idealistic plans are bound to fail, so we work on a concrete plan for change that she is willing to commit herself to. Through this process, Ruth learns how to evaluate her own behavior and how to adjust her plans to experience success.[6]

 # QUESTIONS FOR REFLECTION

1. Dr. Glasser contends, "although I believe we may be the product of our past we are not victims of our past unless we choose to be so. Approaching a client this way drastically shortens therapy because it quickly gets to the core of the problem." What do you think of this viewpoint?

2. Dr. Glasser states, "All of our chosen ineffective behaviors—neurosis, psychosomatic disease, and psychosis—are our self-destructive, often crazy, attempts to improve a present relationship or find a better one." What are your reactions to this statement?

3. Both Drs. Glasser and Wubbolding seem very directive in pointing out the themes Ruth should explore, and they are also fairly directive in suggesting what she should do outside of the sessions. What are your reactions to this stance? As Ruth's counselor, would you be inclined to bring up topics for her to explore if she did not specifically mention them?

4. Do you have any concerns that reality therapy could be practiced in such a way that the therapist imposed his or her values on the client? Do you see this as potentially happening with the way Glasser, Wubbolding, or I worked with Ruth?

5. Dr. Wubbolding makes use of frequent questioning to help Ruth clarify what she wants. What are some of his questions that you most like? Why?

6. What differences do you see in the various styles and applications of reality therapy as practiced by Glasser, Wubbolding, and Corey?

7. Apply the procedures of reality therapy to what you know of Ruth. Systematically show how you would get her to focus on what she is doing, on making an evaluation of her behavior, and on helping her formulate realistic plans.

8. Assume that you are a client in reality therapy. What do you think this experience would be like for you? How would you describe your current behavior? Can you come up with a plan for changing a particular behavior you really want to change?

 NOTES

1. For a more complete discussion of Dr. Glasser's latest thinking on how choice theory applies to the practice of counseling, see W. Glasser (1998), *Choice Theory: A New Psychology of Personal Freedom,* New York: HarperCollins. See also W. Glasser (2000), *Counseling With Choice Theory: The New Reality Therapy,* New York: HarperCollins.

2. For a more detailed treatment of Dr. Wubbolding's perspective on applying reality therapy, see R. Wubbolding (2000), *Reality Therapy for the 21st Century,* Philadelphia, PA: Brunner Routledge (Taylor & Francis). This is an easy-to-read, useful, and comprehensive book that represents significant extensions of reality therapy. The practical formulation of the WDEP system of reality therapy is developed. Many excellent questions and brief examples clarify ways of using its concepts.

3. Rather than have Ruth become overwhelmed by attempting to make sweeping changes in her life, Dr. Wubbolding suggests that Ruth select small aspects of her behavior that she can change.

4. You will notice that Dr. Wubbolding uses skillful questioning as a way to help Ruth evaluate what she is doing. In *The CD-ROM for Integrative Counseling,* Session 8

("Behavioral Focus in Counseling"), you will note ways that I attempt to assist Ruth in specifying concrete behaviors that she will target for change.

5. See R. Wubbolding and J. Brickell (2001), *A Set of Directions for Putting and Keeping Yourself Together*, Minneapolis, MN: Educational Media Corporation. This is a practical and positive self-help book based on the concepts of reality therapy.

6. For an overview of the basic concepts of reality therapy, see G. Corey (2005), *Theory and Practice of Counseling and Psychotherapy*, 7th edition. Chapter 11 (Reality Therapy) describes the WDEP system that both Wubbolding and I make reference to in our work with Ruth. This chapter also contains an update on Glasser's latest formulation of choice theory and reality therapy.

Chapter 10

Case Approach to Feminist Therapy

A Feminist Therapist's Perspective on Ruth

by *Kathy M. Evans, Ph.D., Susan R. Seem, Ph.D., and Elizabeth A. Kincade, Ph.D.*[1]

Introduction

Feminist therapy grew out of the feminist movement of the 1960s and 1970s, challenging the values and assumptions of traditional psychotherapies for their focus on the individual client or family without regard to social and political context and for the androcentrism of the theories underlying psychotherapy. The origins of feminist therapy are in feminist philosophy and social action rather than in scientific psychology. Thus, feminist therapy is more similar to existential and humanistic modes of therapy than to other approaches. Individual practitioner approaches to feminist therapy vary widely from traditional talk therapy to standard cognitive behavioral techniques to social action therapy. Most feminist practitioners use a thoughtful combination of these techniques based on their interpretation of feminist philosophy and theory.

In the past, feminist therapists disagreed about whether feminist therapy was based on a series of philosophical assumptions or grounded in psychological theory. Recent literature and research suggest that feminist therapy is based on theory and not just a set of philosophical assumptions.[2]

Approaches to Feminist Therapy

Feminism holds that gender inequity exists and that this is a source of oppression to individuals and societies. In addition, this oppression is painful and harmful. This inequality is based in power, and for the most part the power balance is in favor of men. Furthermore, feminist philosophy seeks to answer the question, "What is the source of women's oppression?" Various feminist philosophies answer this question differently.

At one end of the continuum is the belief that oppression is due to patriarchy, or male domination. In this model, true change requires political and social change rather than merely individual change. At the other end of the continuum is the belief that oppression is largely caused by socialization, our internalized individual and self-replicating cultural beliefs. Within this model, individual change is possible and necessary as this forces societal beliefs and positions to change. Each version of feminism has a slightly different answer to the question, "What causes oppression?"

Liberal feminism views gender disparity as a matter of individual bias, institutional discrimination, and a matter for the legal system. This is the model most often referred to in the United States when people talk about feminism.

Cultural feminism postulates that oppression is due to undervaluing women's unique ways of being in the world. In this model, women and men are viewed as biologically and psychologically different and should be valued for their different ways of being.

Socialist feminists view the core of women's oppression as a complicated blend of economic philosophy and gender disparity. Oppression is a result of capitalism, an economic system developed within a patriarchy. In this model women are oppressed because it serves the needs of the economic system.

Radical feminists believe patriarchy is the source of women's oppression and that men's power over women in all spheres of life is so ingrained that only a total restructuring of society will bring about lasting change. Radical feminists have also postulated separate societies for men and women, as men who have been raised in the patriarchal system are too imbued with the values of the system to change.

Although underlying philosophies may differ, the basic tenets and beliefs of feminist therapy are the same: Therapist and client work together to understand and remove the psychological, sociopolitical, and cultural factors that result in client distress. Feminist therapy holds two overarching goals. The immediate goal is to relieve an individual client's distress. The ultimate goal is to alleviate sociopolitical oppression, which requires feminist therapists to take action for social change and to encourage clients to do likewise as a part of the therapeutic process.

Basic Tenets of Feminist Therapy

Feminist therapy holds a number of common tenets that cut across diverse theories. These common tenets are (a) the personal is political, (b) the importance of egalitarian relationships, and (c) privileging the female experience.

The personal is political reflects the belief that individual experiences do not occur in a vacuum. This tenet developed from the consciousness raising groups of the women's movement of the 1960s and 1970s. Many women discovered that their own private pain was, in fact, experienced by other women too. Thus, what individual women believed was their personal experience was in reality a gendered experience and thus a political and social experience. Feminist therapists operate on the assumption that the primary source of client distress lies within the social and political context, not within the individual. Pathology is reframed, and external causes are separated from internal causes. A woman is not blamed or pathologized for feeling, thinking, and behaving in ways that are a function of living in an oppressive society. However, this focus on external causes of distress does not negate the importance of examining intrapsychic factors that interact with external forces.

Feminist therapy posits that *relationships should be egalitarian*. Therefore, the counseling relationship should not replicate the power imbalance women experience in society. Most traditional therapies operate from dominant cultural values that place the counselor in the role of expert. In contrast, feminist therapy is viewed as a collaborative process in which counselor and client are considered as being of equal worth. The counselor's expertise is based on specialized knowledge; the client is an expert on herself and her experience.

Traditional psychological theory and therapies are based on androcentric norms; feminist therapy *privileges the female experience*. Historically, traditional therapy compared female experience to male experience, and females were often seen as sick or deviant. In feminist therapy, female experience is valued and is central in understanding distress. Thus, women are understood in the context of their female experience, not the male experience. This helps clients appreciate and value their own perspective on life as well as women's ways of being.

Initial Assessment and Evaluation

Although none of the three of us takes a single approach to feminist therapy, we agreed that we would each discuss Ruth's case from a different point of view. Susan will present the radical feminist perspective, Kathy the cultural perspective, and Elizabeth the socialist perspective. We will discuss our differences in conceptualizing Ruth's case when appropriate. When we agree, we will present one point of view. The final dialogue with Ruth will be a combination of our three approaches.

Traditional Diagnosis and Assessment   As traditionally practiced, diagnostic systems such as the DSM-IV-TR reflect the dominant culture's definitions of pathology and health. Many feminist therapists avoid using these diagnostic systems. However, if we as feminists were to use a formal diagnostic system to diagnose Ruth as part of her assessment, we would use the DSM-IV-TR with knowledge of its major weaknesses.[3]

The DSM-IV-TR assumes androcentric and monocultural models of mental health and functioning. Sexism, racism, classism, ableism, heterosexism, and ageism are all embedded in its descriptions. For example, overcompliance with traditional female gender-role socialization is viewed as pathological (see dependent and borderline personality disorders). Furthermore, some female gender-role stereotyped descriptors exist in certain diagnostic labels (for example, histrionic personality disorder). In contrast, diagnostic categories that have higher prevalence rates for men (such as antisocial personality disorder) have clear behavioral descriptors. Additionally, the DSM-IV-TR infers an intrapsychic focus that contradicts a political analysis. It disconnects personal experiences from the political arena and ignores the environmental context.

Traditionally, psychological distress is viewed as private and results in an individual solution rather than a social or political one. In fact few diagnostic labels locate the source of a client's problem in the environment. Misdiagnosis and blaming the victim may occur when sociopolitical factors are minimized or ignored. Moreover, counselor bias and subjectivity may influence the diagnostic process. The fact that a number of authors from different theoretical orientations arrived at a number of variant diagnoses for Ruth points to the role that clinical bias or subjectivity may play in diagnosis.

Feminist Assessment and Evaluation Historically, feminist therapists eschewed diagnosis because they could not formally diagnose internalized oppression. However, a feminist sensitivity to diagnosis can result in the use of formal diagnostic systems without replicating patriarchal assumptions and attitudes. Diagnosis, as traditionally practiced, is an act of power that exacerbates the power imbalance between counselor and client. In contrast, feminist assessment and diagnosis requires a cooperative and phenomenological approach.

After reviewing the summary of Ruth's intake interview and her autobiography, all three of us agreed that our work with Ruth would examine the multifaceted social, political, and economic context of her life. This examination would move beyond understanding Ruth within her family and seek to comprehend her personal relationships within the context of her culture and the larger society.

Ruth's exposure to sexism and other forms of oppression constitute an insidious long-term trauma. Our evaluation of Ruth consists of listening for connections between the personal and the political in her story. We work to understand Ruth as a gendered being who is assigned a subordinate status by the dominant male culture. Thus, we use gender and power as categories of analysis for Ruth and her life experience. This type of analysis creates avenues for the exploration of gender-role concerns and issues of power without punishing Ruth for participation in her socialization process and subordinate societal status.

Ruth's people pleasing, living for others, difficulty acting on her own behalf, being a superwoman, and being a good wife and good mother are viewed as evidence of her compliance with traditional female gender-role socialization and with her second-class status, not as indications of her pathology or dependency. Ruth's symptoms of panic are viewed as a result of role conflict. Women are often forced to choose between their own growth as individuals and traditional female gender-role behavior. This choice results in internal conflict that surfaces as anxiety. Ruth expresses her awareness of living for others and feeling obligated to stay in her marriage. She communicates her acute awareness of dissatisfaction with her life as it is but also clearly articulates her fear of change. Thus, Ruth's symptoms of panic, her feelings of conflict, and her identity confusion are viewed as coping strategies for or adaptations to surviving oppression, discrimination, and gender-role stereotyping. Her symptoms might also be a protest against her oppression. Ruth's behaviors and feelings are adaptive rather than pathological, and we would not give her a diagnostic label at this time.

We would also look closely at Ruth's anger. Women are not supposed to have legitimate power in patriarchal societies, and they often feel powerless. Feeling powerless often leads to feelings of rage at having little or no control over one's life. Additionally, patriarchal norms do not support and often punish direct expression of female anger. Therefore, women have learned to convert anger into symptoms that are acceptable. Based on this assumption, we explore with Ruth her feelings about being powerless. We encourage Ruth to express her anger at her treatment as a woman. We view anger as potentially positive energy and help Ruth use this energy to take either individual or social action to obtain power in her life.

We differ in our assessment work with Ruth in that Susan, working from a radical feminist perspective, pays particular attention to the meaning and presence of female gender-role compliance and noncompliance for Ruth, including past and current rewards and penalties. She examines with Ruth how her second-class status as a woman influences her psychological distress. One focus of assessment, therefore, is to identify how Ruth has internalized oppressive sociocultural forces. Kathy adds to this perspective by helping Ruth identify her stage of feminist identity development and assessing such things as anger, self-examination, acceptance, and role confusion. As a socialist feminist, Elizabeth addresses the economic issues of payment and the sociopolitical implications of a DSM-IV-TR diagnosis.

Any assessment would be done in collaboration with Ruth, and we would encourage Ruth to ask questions or pose alternative options. If, as a result of our assessment, a formal label is given, the diagnosis and its possible consequences will be discussed with Ruth. In that discussion we would share with Ruth the process by which we arrived at such a formal diagnosis. Also, Ruth would share in decisions about how this information would be used.

Therapeutic Procedures

All therapy demands a firm relational foundation, otherwise client changes tend to be ephemeral or superficial. The necessary conditions for feminist therapy are the establishment of an egalitarian relationship and a deep and thorough understanding of Ruth's story, or the narrative of her experience.

Establishing and Modeling Egalitarian Relationships   An egalitarian relationship is essential if Ruth is to achieve a sense of her own power. It is important to work with Ruth to remove artificial power boundaries in the counseling relationship. Feminist counselors consider the first contact with clients as an interview: an opportunity for counselor and client to get to know each other and make a mutual decision about whether or not they will work together. Feminist therapists work to demystify counseling. To that end, we ask Ruth why she is seeking counseling and what she wants to gain from it. We share with her that we are feminist therapists who approach counseling from a feminist perspective and explain what this means without jargon, with respect for Ruth's intelligence.

In addition, since Ruth has little experience with mutually satisfying relationships in which she is viewed as an equal participant, it is important that Ruth experience and learn how to establish egalitarian relationships in her own life. Thus it is important to model an egalitarian relationship in the counseling relationship. This modeling begins with the first session. Ruth is invited to actively participate in the assessment process, in the contracting of counseling, and in setting counseling goals. Further, feminist therapy has the goal of helping Ruth develop interdependence in relationships and enabling her to develop skills to negotiate her needs and wants in relationships.

Kathy, working from her perspective as a liberal, African American feminist therapist, acknowledges the power differential between Ruth and herself, which is based in American conceptions of race. By seeking help from Kathy, the balance of power between Kathy and Ruth shifts so that it is more equal in that Ruth (a White woman with supposedly more power in our society) needs Kathy's help (which gives Kathy more power). Kathy would explore Ruth's experiences with people of color and would tell her about herself as a professional and as a person. She would let Ruth know that if she wishes to see a counselor more similar to herself she understands.

Elizabeth, examining the case from the socialist feminist perspective also focuses on power but does so by acknowledging that clients pay for counseling and that this interferes with establishing an egalitarian relationship. In addition, as a socialist feminist she is aware of how titles are used to take power away from people. Those we call by a title usually hold economic power or social status different from our own.

All three of us hold that self-disclosure, when it is in service to Ruth, is a very powerful and important part of establishing and maintaining an egalitarian relationship. We share with Ruth our belief that although we possess expertise in counseling techniques and psychological theory Ruth has her own specialized knowledge—she is the expert in her life and experiences.

Understanding Ruth's Story   It is important that Ruth's story is accepted and validated by her therapist. Feminist therapy embraces values that may conflict with some of Ruth's cultural and religious values, and we accept this. We do not lecture Ruth about oppression; rather, we guide her through an exploration of her life experiences that involve oppression. We tell Ruth that we believe each woman experiences her gender, race, ethnicity, and culture differently, and we listen for evidence of all these factors in Ruth's story.

Further, we help Ruth understand herself in relation to her sociopolitical context. Part of understanding Ruth's story and educating her about the complex sources of her distress entails knowing her beliefs, thoughts, and feelings about being a White, 39-year-old, middle-class woman who comes from a fundamentalist religious background. We provide Ruth with information about women in general, and we self-disclose about our own beliefs and experiences when appropriate. In addition, we engage in self-examination of our own strengths and limitations, biases and prejudices, and worldview regarding this client.

Interventions and Therapy Goals

Due to the variety of feminist therapy approaches, feminist therapy is particularly amenable to a brief therapy model. Historically, feminist therapy incorporated short-term interventions such as assertion training, cognitive restructuring, and short-term dynamic models into its practice. Furthermore, feminist therapy is based on a model of egalitarianism, choice, and empowerment. These three elements produce feminist therapists who work with clients in the context of the client's environment, which includes various economic, cultural, and family situations that often preclude long-term therapy. Additionally, as one of the goals of feminist therapy is empowerment for the client, feminist therapies assume that clients will leave counseling empowered to act on their own. When and how they do this is a collaborative effort between therapist and client. This means that the therapist and client are aware of changing needs in the therapeutic relationship and negotiate for more or fewer sessions when mutually agreed upon.

To eliminate boundaries in counseling, feminist therapists share their relevant values and beliefs about society with their clients. Clients may then consciously accept or reject these values. Goals for counseling are devised collaboratively. Further, feminist therapists educate their clients about the theory and process of feminist therapy, which empowers clients to make informed choices about therapy. Therapy is demystified, and clients are taught relevant therapeutic skills. Feminist therapists model egalitarian behaviors that will help clients negotiate relationships within and outside of counseling.

Despite ideological differences in conceptualizing women's oppression, the three of us use these interventions with our clients and believe these specific interventions would be useful with Ruth. These interventions are (a) gender-role and power analysis, (b) increasing assertiveness, (c) bibliotherapy, (d) reframing Ruth's concerns and symptoms, (e) social and political action, and (f) working with weight and body concerns.

Gender-Role and Power Analysis   Gender-role analysis is used to increase Ruth's insight about how societal gender-role expectations adversely affect women and how women and men are socialized differently. Ruth needs to examine the gender-role messages (verbal, nonverbal, and modeled) she has experienced in her lifetime from society as a whole, from her family of origin, and from her religion. As a result, Ruth learns that her conflicts about her life and identity are due to the fact that she wants to step outside her traditionally defined female gender role. Ruth identifies the positive and negative consequences of following those gender-role messages. She gains awareness about her strengths and how and why these may not be valued in a patriarchal society.

With regard to power, we help Ruth recognize and value her strengths, some of which are part of her learned gender role. Ruth comes to recognize as strengths her ability to nurture and to balance a multitude of roles and a willingness to question the values and beliefs she was taught. Through therapy Ruth learns how she has internalized certain gender-role messages in conscious and unconscious ways. She is supported in developing a woman-identified sense of femininity rather than a male-identified one. Ruth is encouraged to acquire a full range of behaviors that are freely chosen rather than prescribed by gender-role stereotypes.

Working from the radical feminist stance, Susan explores with Ruth several definitions of power, resulting in a definition that best fits her. Together, Ruth and Susan explore the kinds of power to which Ruth has access. Ruth has been encouraged to exert her power in indirect and helpless ways rather than in direct and competent ways. In therapy with Susan, Ruth is encouraged to change her internalized messages about her use of power and to freely explore various ways she can use her power.

Kathy's perspective differs somewhat. As a liberal feminist therapist, her goal is for Ruth to examine her changing relationships with her husband and children, her parents, and her relationship with God. Kathy seeks to assist Ruth in realigning the balance of power in her familial relationships so that she can develop her own female style of self without subservience.

Elizabeth believes Ruth underestimates her power and is, perhaps, afraid of it. This is shown through Ruth's fears that her choices will destroy her family. As women, we are not trained to accept power or to admit that we have any. It might well be that Ruth's problems with her daughter are a manifestation of the loss of the only power she has been "allowed" to have within her dominant culture. In addition, as a socialist feminist therapist with an awareness of the economic exploitation of women, Elizabeth wonders aloud with Ruth why she is considering substitute teaching (a role that traditionally exploits married women) and has not sought to become a full-time teacher. Elizabeth would explore with Ruth whether perhaps she does not pursue full-time teaching because she fears the responsibility and freedom of her own classroom.

Increasing Assertiveness   Assertiveness training has been a part of feminist therapy since its inception. For women, assertiveness is frequently equated with aggression. Therefore, young girls do not learn how to stand up for their rights as human beings. Assertiveness training seeks to teach women how they can assert their own rights, without being aggressive. Because of the goals Ruth has set for herself, we are inclined to work with her on being more assertive.

Our analysis of Ruth is that she feels confused and guilty when she wants to step out of her prescribed gender role. Part of the goal of counseling is to help Ruth define a sense of self without taking a subservient role. As feminist therapy is based on collaboration, an assertiveness group for women is indicated for Ruth. In this group she will learn that she is not alone and that being assertive does not mean she will alienate others. She will be able to help other women as well as receive help from others in the group.

Bibliotherapy   An important goal of feminist therapy is to help Ruth begin to understand how her own situation is connected with the common experience of all women. To that end, bibliotherapy helps Ruth understand that her personal pain is not unique to her and that many women experience similar struggles. It is important that Ruth has an opportunity to discuss her reactions to the readings during counseling sessions and to explore how they apply to her life.

We suggest two types of readings to Ruth. One kind of reading is from psychologists and counselors who write about issues similar to hers. Another consists of essays and fiction by women who have explored and experienced concerns similar to hers. For example, readings in White female experience and in feminist Christianity can help Ruth retain the essence of her faith yet at the same time be more comfortable with the changes she may decide to make in her life. We suggest to Ruth several writers who explore the juxtaposition of Christianity and feminism and describe feminist and Christian ethics. These readings would help to create a sense of connection and possibilities for Ruth without overtly threatening her status quo. As feminist therapists who have benefited from the struggles and experiences of other women, we share with Ruth that reading about the lives and works of others has been a source of strength and learning for us.

Reframing Ruth's Concerns and Symptoms   Feminist therapists believe many of the symptoms women bring to counseling are symptoms of living in a male-dominated culture that does not value the female experience. Women have learned to view their experiences negatively, and Ruth is no exception. She obviously sees her symptoms as signs of weakness and believes something is innately wrong with her. Feminist therapists view Ruth's symptoms as indicative of the stress between cultural and personal conflicts. This reframing, however, does not negate her actual symptoms. Consequently, we work with Ruth to teach her how to gain control of her symptoms through cognitive and behavioral techniques such as stress and relaxation management, thought stopping, and positive self-statements. In addition, even though Ruth comes to an understanding that the cause of her problems lies within society and cultural mores, she is not absolved from taking responsibility for making changes in her life.

As a radical feminist therapist, Susan views many of the symptoms women bring to counseling as passive forms of female rebellion against femininity as defined by the patriarchy. She reframes Ruth's distress with her role in life and her family. She sees Ruth's panic symptoms as ways Ruth is trying to communicate to herself her desire to step outside the constricted traditional female gender role. Susan explores with Ruth the possibility of suppressed rage being manifested in symptoms that allow her to still be feminine yet also revolt against male-defined femininity. Ruth is encouraged to acknowledge and express her anger. Her feelings and thoughts are reframed as evidence of her revolt against being placed in a subservient role, which no longer brings her satisfaction. Susan would engage in a dialogue with Ruth about the ways in which she wants to define herself as mother and wife that might meet her need to be interdependent and nonsubservient.

The liberal feminist perspective seeks to help women understand gender roles and work toward creating a society with more equal power between the genders. Kathy works with Ruth on reframing her experience as a woman in American society and as a cultural being. Together, Kathy and Ruth explore the centuries of cultural and religious mandates regarding women and the inequities of the traditional system of marriage and family. They look at Ruth's family system and how it keeps her from taking care of herself while taking care of everyone else. Interventions include asking Ruth to listen to and identify those messages from her parents and church that are not only influenced by societal norms but also continue to be replayed in her head and cause most of her conflicts. They engage in reframing or replacing some of these internalized messages with ones that fit with her current circumstances.

Elizabeth chooses to focus on Ruth's strengths. Ruth is managing a family and is juggling various roles. Together they work to identify and honor her strengths. Ruth is asked to do some simple homework consisting of two lists: things she values about herself and things she does not value. This gives Ruth and Elizabeth a starting point for focusing on what Ruth views as important in her therapy. It helps identify what Ruth has been taught to value and not value about herself. Negative beliefs can then be gently confronted through self-disclosure, assigning readings, and presenting her with conflicting evidence of her own behavior. For instance, Elizabeth would congratulate Ruth on having raised a daughter who can stand up for herself and make her own choices, even when she knows that this will displease others.

Taking Social and Political Action   The ultimate goal of feminist therapy is to help Ruth understand how her distress as an individual woman is connected to the collective power of women as a group. Consequently, we are interested in sharing with Ruth our involvement in social action that is geared toward changing the oppressive and painful features of society. We encourage Ruth to engage in social action to reduce her sense of isolation, to help use her anger constructively and feel better about herself, and to effect some change on the structures of society. We suggest that Ruth become part of a Christian women's support group with a feminist perspective. Perhaps she could start such a group herself if one does not yet exist in her community. She could start out by attending a women's support group and getting to know something about how these groups work and branch out later.

We also recommend that Ruth engage in some sort of collective work focused on women's oppression. Social action is a way of refocusing and reframing anger. We often tell clients who doubt the usefulness of anger, or who fear their own strong emotions, that such emotions can be positive. If it were not for anger, women's shelters would not exist. If women had not been angry, sexual abuse would not have been addressed, and people would be in pain and more children abused. This puts social action in perspective. For Ruth, being involved in social action would be a way of healing past pains. We might suggest that she volunteer at the local women's shelter either on the hot line or as a support person. Being a support person would allow her to use her nurturing skills to help other women. This, in turn, would help her feel more competent. This is a potent therapeutic modality for both societal and individual change.

Working With Weight and Body Image   Western culture is unmerciful to women. We are bombarded daily with images of perfect women. Not conforming to this iconic image can severely affect self-esteem because women in our society are judged by how they look, not by what they can do. Ruth has been socialized to believe that food is comforting, and, in fact, it may be the only comfort she has when presented with emotions that women are not encouraged to express. Stuffing her emotions to conform with cultural expectations reinforces her position of powerlessness. As a result, Ruth has developed a body size that is unacceptable to that same culture. She is left in the untenable position of being punished for the only solution she could find to comply with cultural mandates. The goal of feminist therapy is to assist Ruth in discovering ways to love her body. Ruth's relationship with food is also reframed as seeking comfort, and we will help Ruth discover other ways to get her needs met.

From a radical feminist perspective, Ruth's weight is viewed as a refusal against the role of woman as body. It is a demonstration of Ruth's nonconscious wish to defy the male cultural dictate that women are to be beautiful sex objects. Ruth's weight is an obvious, but indirect, demonstration of her disallowed wish to be seen as a person, not as an object for males. Thus, Susan's work with Ruth's weight would be reframed as a protest, as a message rather than as further evidence that something is wrong with her and that she lacks willpower. Additionally, Ruth's weight may be a way to avoid seeing herself as a sexual being; it may be a way to neuter herself in her eyes and in the eyes of the males in her life. Helping Ruth to understand the power of fat would allow Ruth to make some choices about how she wants to define herself as a woman and her sexuality.

The socialist feminist perspective differs from both the radical and liberal perspectives in that it focuses on how our society twists consuming and eating into issues of power. Elizabeth believes food is a form of economic consuming. We walk into a grocery store and have a myriad of choices and it can all be ours. This is one of the few venues where women can exercise choice and be powerful. Just buying and consuming food is a way of feeling powerful. Therefore, Ruth's weight issues are related to power and maladaptive ways of gaining power. In addition, weight gain is related to depression. This is often a vicious cycle. Ruth eats to make herself feel more powerful. However, eating undermines her self-esteem because women who do not "fit" the cultural model of beauty are disparaged.

Overall, the work in feminist therapy and weight issues is aimed at increasing self-esteem and personal power, emphasizing Ruth's strengths, and increasing her repertoire of coping behaviors. We might refer her to a feminist nutrition counselor and to a weight loss support group with an empowerment focus rather than a strict weight loss focus. It is important that Ruth be referred to adjunct modalities that support her emerging sense of self. Ruth needs to be empowered to accept and celebrate her body, her mind, and her life.

Glimpses of Ruth's Therapy

Establishing and Nurturing the Egalitarian Relationship   This is the beginning of the first session. The therapist's focus on power in the relationship reinforces trust building. This discussion models a healthy relationship between peers, values Ruth's life experience, and allows Ruth to begin making healthy decisions for herself.

Therapist: You mentioned that this is your first time in counseling. Would it help you if I tell you a little about myself and about the process of counseling?

Ruth: Yeah. I guess so. I really don't know what to expect. It's a big step for me to admit that things aren't going right. Before I came in today I thought I would just ask you to tell me what to do, but now I don't know. I'm confused about what I want. Is that all right?

Therapist: I agree that it is scary and confusing when you realize that you can't solve all your problems yourself. I know this from personal experience. I can't tell you what to do because I haven't lived your life, but I do think that together we will be able to work out a counseling plan for you. I have found with other people who are anxious about counseling that a good place to start is for me to tell you how I work with my clients. Then you can tell me a bit more about why you are here, and we can talk about how we can go about counseling and what will work best for you. How does that sound?

Ruth: You mean I don't have to do all the talking right away?

Therapist: No. Not right now.

Ruth: OK. I guess I was just expecting to tell my problems and have you tell me how to solve them.

Therapist: The way I see counseling is that it's the two of us working together to find out what is best for you. You are the expert in your life. I am the expert in counseling. I work from a feminist perspective. This means two things. First, I will work hard to understand your concerns from your perspective. I value your knowledge about yourself and your difficulties. Second, I bring a social and political perspective to my understanding of you and your life. I believe the causes of the problems many women bring to counseling are external. In general women are not valued by our society, and this creates psychological distress.

Ruth [*Looking perplexed and somewhat dubious*]: I'm not sure I understand. This all sounds strange to me.

Therapist: I know when you hear this it might sound absurd. After all, if being a woman in this society is problematic, wouldn't you have noticed? I believe that you have noticed, and that is part of what your pain is about, even if you haven't recognized it yet. For example, you mentioned a concern about your weight. I know that over the decades the perfect look and weight for women has changed dramatically. Look at current fashion magazines and ask yourself who decides what looks good and if it really does look good. Then ask yourself what happens to those of us who don't fit the model. I believe that what happens when we don't fit the ideal is that we feel bad. Then, we blame ourselves for not fitting, and that leads to all sorts of negative statements about ourselves.

Ruth: I never thought that my concerns might be connected to being a woman. That's something I'm going to have to think about because all I know is that I feel scared and anxious and worried all the time about what I'm going to do, and I think something is wrong with me.

Therapist: Yes, I agree. It is scary to be here. I am not surprised that you're anxious.

Ruth: Also, I don't know if I feel comfortable working with someone who is a feminist. I know my husband will not be happy because he is always putting down feminists.

Therapist: Hmm. That's an important concern for you. It sounds like your husband is important to you, and you don't want to upset him. I am wondering, however, if you can share with me some more of your concerns about working with a feminist counselor?

Ruth: Well, I think this is just more evidence of how screwed up I am. I want someone to tell me what to do and to make this all right, but I am also afraid you will tell me that all my problems are because of my husband and that all I need to do is divorce him and leave my kids. Isn't that what feminists believe?

Therapist: I hear your concern about seeing a therapist with a strong value system that might be different from your own. It's a valid concern. With regard to feminism, I can't speak for all feminists, but only for myself as a feminist therapist. In this role, I encourage clients to take responsibility for making changes that will help them feel better about themselves. I will work with you to help you figure out what is best for you.

Ruth: So you're a feminist therapist because of your belief that a lot of women's problems are caused by the way women are treated and valued?

Therapist: Yes.

Ruth: You won't force your beliefs on me?

Therapist: No, I won't.

Ruth: OK, I guess I am willing to work with you.

Therapist: You don't sound sure.

Ruth: Yes, I am. Well, not exactly sure. I know my father says that feminists are the cause of the destruction of the family.

Therapist: It sounds like you have two concerns. One is about doing what the important people in your life think is right, and the other is that you are concerned that feminism might harm you and interfere with your relationships with those people. Does that sound right to you?

Ruth: Maybe I do want to figure myself out without others telling me what to do or how to be. This is new for me.

Therapist: You are telling me very clearly that you do not want to be influenced in ways that don't fit with who you are.

Ruth: Yes. I want to be able to figure out what I believe without others telling me what to believe.

Therapist: I think your desire to figure things out for yourself is a strength. Let me propose this: How about if we work together for four sessions. That way you can get a feel for me and how I work. We will set aside our fourth session to discuss whether or not you are feeling that I am hearing, understanding, and helping you.

Ruth: So I could leave if I wanted to?

Therapist: Yes. Although if you leave, I would like us to be able to talk about why so I can understand your decision.

Ruth: I like that. I never thought about counseling as my choice before.

Therapist: All right, it sounds like we have developed our first plan—together.

Power and Gender-Role Analysis in Family Relationships   This is Ruth's fifth session. It occurs after the therapeutic relationship has been established and Ruth and the therapist have negotiated 10 more sessions. This section reflects a melding of therapeutic influences. Elizabeth, influenced by cognitive approaches, and Susan, influenced by psychodynamic theory, collaborated on the response. Thus, Ruth is both challenged to confront dysfunctional beliefs and helped to explore emotions and relationships. This section highlights how feminist therapists integrate different styles and perspectives into their repertoire of counseling skills.

Ruth: I am so glad I am here today, I just need to talk to you.

Therapist: It sounds like something has come up for you. Last week you said you were learning to manage stress better and your episodes of panic seemed to have subsided.

Ruth: Oh, but this is different [*Pauses and looks somewhat less excited*]. My church has its own school. They know I have my Bachelor's in Education now. They want to hire me full time. How can I do that? I would be away from home all day. Even when I was going to school I was still only gone part time. Will my family think I am a lousy mother because I won't be at home? I am not even a certified teacher yet. What should I do?

Therapist: Wow, this sounds like something you are really split about. On one hand you would like to continue as you always have and not have change in your life; on the other hand you have been working toward this change for many years.

Ruth: Yeah. That's the funny thing. I didn't just go to college without a goal. I actually knew that I wanted to do something. I guessed that someday it would be real.

Therapist: The school must like you and respect you if they want to hire you for the fall.

Ruth: I have been tutoring and volunteering on and off ever since I changed churches. I like the kids and the teachers. I just thought I was lucky because they let me volunteer, but I guess I must have done well.

Therapist: So, what stops you from accepting the position?

Ruth: John and the kids. You know, John keeps telling me he wants me back like I was before I started going to school. Last week I asked him to pick up the two younger children from band practice at school while I went to a meeting. He told me that he couldn't and then was sarcastic. He said, "Maybe you'd like it better if I divorced you. Then you could go to meetings all the time."

Therapist: So you're afraid to accept the position because John talks about divorce.

Ruth: Yeah. He plays the divorce card frequently.

Therapist: So you back down from doing what you want to do when John plays the divorce card.

Ruth [*Thinks a bit*]: I guess you could see it that way. But he does have the upper hand. I don't want to lose him and the kids. I don't really dislike my life, but I'm just not satisfied. I don't know. Now I'm confused all over again.

Therapist: Let's talk about your relationship with John. I think this might help you figure out what to do about the job offer.

Ruth: OK. I think you might be right. It is my fears about my family that are confusing me. I never imagined myself as a working mother, but I really want to teach. On the other hand, I am afraid that if I teach my family will fall apart.

Therapist: Hmmm. You feel really conflicted right now and think you are responsible for keeping your family together.

Ruth: It's always been my job. I want the family together. That's probably what I am doing wrong here. By pursuing the job I am pulling the family apart.

Therapist: That certainly is a piece of what John is telling you. Even if it's not always verbal. But it is something you have learned well. And you are not alone. Traditionally this is what women do in our society. It is our job to keep the family together. This gives John a lot of power. We want to do what is best for ourselves and for others. If we do the wrong thing, people with power will tell us that we aren't good enough or even that we are deliberately bad.

Ruth: My father was like that.

Therapist: Tell me more about your father treating you that way.

Ruth: Oh, if I did something that he didn't like but I wanted to do, he would tell me I was bad or not speak to me for several days. I felt awful and so wrong.

Therapist: So when you acted on your own behalf, you felt unloved and punished by your father. Those feelings are pretty powerful, particularly to women who depend on men for their livelihood, as you have with John. Your life is changing a great deal right now, and there is much uncertainty. Your kids are getting ready to move on with their own lives in few years, so they are less invested. John implies that a divorce would be OK with him. You're scared right now and unsure if you can manage to keep the family together.

Ruth [*With anger toward the therapist*]: John would be lost without me! He still can't do the laundry. I know that's funny—and you'd probably call it stereotypical—but I have done everything for him. If he left me, he'd fall apart.

Therapist: You are angry right now. You could easily convince me that John has more invested in this relationship. What does that mean?

Ruth: That I have more power?

Therapist: That would be my guess.

Ruth: What do I do about the job?

Therapist: What do you want to do?

Ruth: I think I want the job.

Therapist: Use your power in the relationship to help John change and do the right thing for you and for your family. Your interest in teaching is an extension of being a good and caring parent. In addition, you will be setting a good model for children to follow. This is just another part of being a parent.

Working With Body Image/Acceptance   This is Ruth's eighth session. The therapist helps Ruth question the cultural definition of weight and age.

Ruth: I know it sounds silly, but I just feel old, fat, and ugly these days. I don't even try to diet anymore because it never works. Since I have trouble sleeping, I have dark circles under my eyes. I look like hell.

Therapist: You're pretty disgusted with yourself.

Ruth: Oh, I just can't stand myself anymore. I gave my full-length mirror to the girls. They are slim and trim and young; they like looking at themselves.

Therapist: They look more like how an attractive woman should look.

Ruth: Yeah, they are beautiful. What I wouldn't do to have their bodies right now!

Therapist: You know, it seems like even though we get better in so many ways as we get older, in our society the only way we are appreciated and valued is for how we look.

Ruth: You know, you're right, and it's not fair. I do think I have a lot to offer even if I'm not thin and young.

Therapist: You certainly do, but you came in here today saying that you felt old, fat, and ugly—that you look like hell. I know this is important to you because you usually don't use strong language to describe your feelings.

Ruth [*Smiles slightly*]: It sometimes seems that I feel better about one thing and then worse about something else. I guess this morning I was only thinking about how I looked in the mirror and not about how valuable a person I am. One really doesn't have anything to do with the other, does it?

Therapist: No. But that's the way we are trained to think. And if a woman looks like hell, she feels like hell because she is devalued in our society. Ruth, what do you like about yourself?

Ruth: I like that I am a loving and caring person, that I am a good mother most of the time, and that I usually get things done. I'm proud of finishing my degree and finally having taken some action on the job front.

Therapist: And what don't you like?

Ruth: That I struggle with my daughter, that I eat and can't stop, and that I'm so fat that I'm unattractive.

Therapist: We've talked about your relationship with your daughter a great deal, but we haven't really talked about your weight [*Ruth nods*]. Maybe being overweight is serving some other purpose. Maybe being fat is a way you are able to get people to recognize your strengths and protect yourself from being ogled by men. Your fat is a way of using your power. Can you think of an example of this in your life?

Ruth [*Looks dubious but thinks*]: Well, where I am teaching some of the college boys help out. They make really disgusting comments about the college girls who volunteer. I get embarrassed for the college girls when this happens. I am sort of glad that they don't even seem to notice me [*Ruth pauses*]. You know, I never would have thought about it that way in a million years. I never thought about how I might use my fat to get what I want or even to get respect. That's an interesting idea.

Therapist: Our bodies are the single most powerful asset we have in our society. We all use that power a little differently, but we often use that power to get what we want—even if we are not completely aware of it.

Ruth: It seems really manipulative to me, and I don't want to be manipulative.

Therapist: You want to become powerful in other ways.

Ruth: Absolutely.

Therapist: The way I see it you can do a couple of things to help with this problem. Let me share my ideas, and you see how they fit for you.

Ruth: OK.

Therapist: You might try to adjust your thinking about your weight by discovering ways in which being fat affords you power in your relationships and begin to love yourself just the way you are.

Ruth: That won't be easy.

Therapist: I know. It wasn't easy for me either. The hardest thing I did was to actually get a full-length mirror in my bathroom. I forced myself to look at my body and learn to love it.

Ruth: How?

Therapist: First you discover what you like and admire about your physical self. Then you look at the areas you are indifferent toward. Then think about what those areas do for you. For example, my legs support me when I stand. They get me where I am going and help me run from trouble. Many women worry about their hips and belly, which grow with each child. A way to reframe it is to think about the children they were able to nourish and protect in the uterus.

Ruth: So you just looked at your body and started to think about how each part contributes to your life instead of how fat and ugly it is [*Ruth smiles*].

Therapist: That's pretty much it.

Ruth: And it worked?

Therapist: It worked for me. I don't know if it will work for you. You're the expert on you.

Ruth as a Survivor of Sexual Assault: Another Feminist's Perspective

by Pam Remer, Ph.D.

Introduction

Given my professional focus of counseling women who are survivors of sexual assault, Jerry and I collaboratively decided to give Ruth a history that involves rape by a peer. Although rape was not identified in the description of Ruth's case, it would be consistent with the case presentation, and clients often fail to offer this information at the intake session.

In my work with Ruth, I follow an empowerment feminist therapy model that I developed with Dr. Judith Worell.[4] Although we have integrated elements of liberal, cultural, radical, and socialist feminist theories, our approach is closest in philosophy to the radical feminist theory described at the beginning of this chapter. We view both traditional gender-role socialization and institutionalized oppression as major sources of women's problems in living. Indeed, societal rape myths, traditional social roles for women and men, traditional social rules for dating situations, and the unequal distribution of power between women and men are major contributors to the existence of rape and to post-rape trauma. I am also a certified trainer, educator, and practitioner of psychodrama, and thus my counseling strategies with Ruth will reflect my integration of feminist therapy and psychodrama.

The feminist empowerment rape counseling model incorporates feminist perspectives in trauma counseling and consists of six stages. In the *pre-rape stage,* the cultural institutionalization of rape myths and gender-role socialization processes are examined for their contribution to the prevalence of rape and to the blaming of rape victims. The *rape event stage* involves the situational context variables and the victim's experience immediately before, during, and after the rape. The *crisis and disorganization stage* includes the short-term reactions to rape by both victims and society. The fourth stage, *outward satisfactory adjustment and denial,* reflects victims' needs to put the rape experience behind them by attempting to return to their former life through use of avoidance, denial, and minimization coping strategies. The fifth stage, *reliving and working through,* involves victims encountering the reality of their sexual assaults and working through the long-term consequences. In the final stage, *resolution and integration,* rape survivors find ways to make positive meaning of their traumatic experiences and to integrate positively their rape experiences into their lives.

Assessment of Ruth

Ruth's autobiography is filled with evidence of the harmful impact of traditional gender-role socialization and of institutionalized sexism on Ruth's life. Giving to others and not receiving, striving to be a "good wife and mother," being dissatisfied with her body, having panic reactions, being depressed, and being concerned with aging are very real *personal* issues for Ruth, but they also reflect typical issues for which many women seek therapy, issues that are *socially* produced by a sexist culture.

As a feminist therapist who knows about the prevalence of sexual violence in women's lives, I am also aware that many of Ruth's reactions (such as anxiety, depression, and nightmares) can be indicators of a trauma history. As a standard part of my assessment, I ask Ruth if she ever had any unpleasant or unwanted sexual experiences. In response she mentioned the "playing doctor" experience at age 6 and stated that it was her father's condemnation of her that made it negative. Although she indicated no sexual trauma history, I remained open to the possibility of her being an unacknowledged, hidden victim. I introduced her to a self-assessment tool that allowed her to be an expert on herself. She completed a Mood Rating Sheet indicating what she was thinking, feeling, and doing and what was happening around her any time she felt panicked or woke up from a nightmare. During our sixth session she reported a nightmare about a man chasing her, and some of her panic reactions have occurred when she was in a close space with a man. She was unable to connect either the dream or the panic reactions to anything specifically in her life.

Key Issues

My view of the key issues is very similar to those described earlier in the chapter. However, Judy Worell and I have added a new principle: personal and social identities are interdependent. This new principle helps therapists attend more closely to the multicultural aspects of clients' lives and to weave that diversity perspective into the other principles of feminist therapy.[5]

According to the new principle, individuals belong to interdependent social groups that are structured by cultural norms. Because these "social locations" influence people's experiences, perceptions, and others' reactions to them, assessments that include personal–social identities and their impacts on clients are important to understanding the diverse cultural contexts of our clients. Thus, early in therapy, we identified Ruth's relevant social locations: a White, heterosexual, married, middle-aged, middle-class woman who had a fundamentalist Christian upbringing. As we explored each new counseling issue, we referred back to these locations and their possible impact on the issue.

Therapeutic Process and Techniques

Identifying the Rape   Introducing Ruth to a feminist approach to therapy and forming an egalitarian relationship with Ruth is an exciting venture for me because I see so many of her counseling issues being tied to her socialization as a woman. Imagine that I have been Ruth's therapist for about six sessions during which we have built a trusting, collaborative relationship and we have used gender-role analysis to explore Ruth's introjected gender-role messages and their impact on Ruth's roles, relationships, and views of herself. By the sixth session Ruth is learning to challenge and change several of these messages (for example, "Meeting my own needs does not make me selfish nor a bad wife and mother."), and she has been experimenting with behaving congruently with these new beliefs.

In the seventh session, Ruth and I focus on the difficulties in her relationship with her 18-year-old daughter, Jennifer. In exploring Jennifer's rebellious responses to Ruth's rules, Ruth states that she is only trying to protect Jennifer because she is too young to realize how dangerous life can be for a female. Hoping to help Ruth understand the common connections she and Jennifer share as women, I invite Ruth to role-play talking to Jennifer about Ruth's fears. I explain the exercise to Ruth and my reasons for proposing it. She agrees to the exercise. I role-play from "Jennifer's chair," and I facilitate from my "therapist chair."

Ruth (*To Jennifer's chair*): I know you think I am just trying to run your life, but the truth is I'm scared for you. If you don't listen to me, you can be hurt. Someone might take advantage of you.

Pam [*As Jennifer*]: Mom, there you go, creating problems out of thin air.

Ruth [*To Jennifer's chair*]: I am not creating problems out of thin air. I know what happens if you break the rules. [*Ruth begins crying.*] If I had followed the rules, Don wouldn't have gotten the wrong idea. It was all my fault. I don't want the same thing to happen to you.

Pam [*Who has moved backed to the therapist chair*]: You've been trying to keep Jennifer safe. Sounds like you are remembering a very painful experience. If you choose to, I would like to hear what happened with Don.

In the role play, I follow Ruth's lead, and the exercise results in her reconnecting with a traumatic experience that is related to her protectiveness of her daughter. I acknowledge her desire to keep Jennifer safe, and I invite her to share with me what happened. Giving her a choice about disclosing is an important part of feminist therapy related to treating her as an expert on herself. When a woman is raped, her control is stripped from her. Therefore, I want to give her control of the disclosing process. She indicates she wants to tell me and relates the following story.

Ruth [*Haltingly*]: When I was 17 and a senior in high school—very close to Jennifer's age—I went on a church-sponsored state youth leadership retreat in a nearby city. I met a boy named Don, and we ended up working on a conference presentation together. We weren't finished at the end of the afternoon, so Don suggested we polish it up later that evening in his room. I was a little reluctant—I could hear my Dad's warnings—but Don was so nice, and I really liked him. We had fun finishing the presentation, and when I started to leave, he kissed me. It was my "first kiss," and I liked it. Then, he started to touch my breast, which surprised me. I told him I'd better go. He made some comment about my being a "goody two shoes," saying if I would just let myself, I would enjoy it. Despite my protests, he continued to touch me—on my breasts and down there. I was stunned and I froze. Even though I said "No," he overpowered me physically. The rest is a blur, but I know he pulled down my slacks and had sex with me. After he was finished, he warned me not to tell anyone. He said no one would believe me and that I wanted it. I went back to my room and didn't tell anyone. It was my fault. I led him on, and I should have fought harder. Making that presentation with him the next day was very hard.

In Ruth's sharing with me for the first time her description of what happened, I am careful to let her set her own pace and to respond empathically rather than to ask questions she may experience as an interrogation. My goal is to honor her disclosure and help her pay attention to her experience as she shares. First disclosures about traumatic experiences are huge risks for the victims because they fear being blamed and not believed. As Ruth comes to the end of her story, she looks at me with questioning eyes.

Pam: I feel sad right now about how he hurt you. I also feel angry with him for his violation of your trust and of your body. I am honored that you trusted me enough to risk telling me.

Ruth: But it was my fault. I shouldn't have gone to his room. My dad warned me what would happen if I didn't follow his rules.

Pam: I hear that you are blaming yourself for what happened. And I want you to know that I do not think you were to blame. I believe what Don did to you is connected to some of your counseling issues—your nightmares, your panic attacks. In therapy we can explore what happened and your reactions to it. You will be able to heal from this experience.

Ruth: I'm not sure I want to talk about this anymore. I feel ashamed and scared.

Pam: We can start by exploring your feelings about working on this issue. I hear how afraid and embarrassed you are feeling. As I have told you before, you always have the choice about what we will focus on here. I want to share with you some information about trauma and healing from trauma so that you can make an informed decision.

Ruth: OK. I would like to hear about what we might do. But I'm still not sure. I can't believe I told you. I've never told anyone. I feel relieved and scared.

Pam: I'm guessing you are pretty overwhelmed right now with all kinds of feelings.

Ruth [*Nods*]: But I do feel sort of safe with you.

Pam: I'm glad. I want you to know something about me that I haven't mentioned before. I am a rape survivor. I didn't tell anyone for a long time about what happened. I can remember feeling both relieved and scared the first time I told someone.

Process Commentary   At this early point in feminist trauma counseling, I work to strengthen my relationship with Ruth. I connect her present day concerns to the effects of trauma as I am beginning to negotiate a therapeutic contract with her to address the rape in our sessions.

Sharing my here-and-now reaction to hearing Ruth's disclosure fits with the egalitarian relationships principle of feminist therapy. I am letting her see my reactions so she will not have to wonder what I am thinking. My reactions in the first two responses also represent a different perspective of what happened as not her fault. However, I do acknowledge her perspective with my empathic response. I also introduce the idea that counseling can help her heal from her trauma, but that the choice about addressing it is hers.

Although I do refer to her experience as traumatic, I do not use the word *rape* because she has not labeled it as such. Part of her healing process will be to examine her definition of rape and to challenge her rape myths. As a result of that work, she will probably decide to use the label, but for now I want to stay in her frame of reference.

Diverging from many traditional rules against therapist self-disclosure, in my last response I share with Ruth that I am a rape survivor. When feminist therapists disclose about the issues they share with their clients as women, clients learn directly about how the "personal is political" and the egalitarian relationship principle is also honored. While I do not disclose to all my sexual assault survivor clients, I do disclose to most. I believe Ruth has demonstrated a lot of resiliency and can handle and benefit from my disclosure. She will know directly from me that she is not alone and that rape is not an uncommon occurrence in women's lives. She will see that healing from rape is possible. Notice that I use the word *rape* to label my own experience; in so doing, I am acting as a role model for her.

After giving Ruth information about the feminist trauma counseling approach I would use and after exploring Ruth's ambivalence about addressing the trauma, she makes a commitment to work on what happened with Don. With this commitment we move into the *reliving and working through stage.*

Challenging Cultural Perspectives of Rape   To help Ruth understand how her personal experience with sexual assault has social causes, she and I will analyze the cultural components of rape. A cultural analysis of rape requires examining and challenging rape myths perpetuated by society, identifying and restructuring gender-role socialization messages that support the existence of rape for both women and men, and understanding how power differentials between men and women contribute to rape. Rape myths, gender socialization, and the power accorded to men in a patriarchy interact to produce a rape victimization process. In this process women are held responsible for their victimization and rape is legitimized. The cultural context of rape is the core of the *pre-rape stage,* but it is explored in therapy early in the *reliving and working through stage.* For Ruth to view her experience within its cultural context, she and I need to review her lessons about rape, lessons learned and that continue to be reinforced from many different societal sources. To review her "lessons," Ruth and I participate collaboratively in the following psychodrama exercise. I place an empty chair in the middle of the room to represent Ruth as a tiny girl maturing into a woman. Standing around the chair, Ruth and I role-play all the socializers from whom she learned about rape. We teach "the chair" about rape.

Pam: Women can prevent rape if they really want to. You can't put a pencil in a moving bottle.
Ruth: It's a woman's fault if she gets raped.
Pam: Be aware of strangers, they are the ones who rape.
Ruth: You should not wear short skirts or low tops unless you want to get raped.

After we have exhausted the rape messages she has learned, I invite her to add any gender-role messages related to rape, especially ones about the rules for women's and men's sexual and relationship behavior.

Ruth [*To the chair*]: You should be in charge of a man's sexual behavior. If you start something, he will get so turned on he can't stop.
Pam: Women should not be strong physically.

Ruth: Men are the bosses and women should do what they say.
Pam: Women should always be polite. Don't make a scene.
Ruth: Women should be virgins until they marry.

Although in earlier sessions Ruth and I had explored her gender-role messages, an important part of a feminist approach to rape therapy is to examine her gender-role messages specifically related to rape and to identify her socialization about rape. Myths about rape permeate our society's socialization of both males and females, which leads to self-blame in victims. An example of one of these myths is that rape victims want to be raped and that women are responsible for such acts. From the feminist perspective of the personal is political, victim self-blame must be explored by challenging its cultural context. For example, Ruth's socialization as a White woman in a fundamentalist Christian church taught her to be polite, to take responsibility for men's sexual behavior, and to believe women are at fault if they are raped. In addition, the exercise Ruth and I enacted illustrated experientially for Ruth how her beliefs about rape were culturally learned and how her learned beliefs about rape and women's roles are connected to blaming herself for her rape.

To effectively challenge her rape myths, Ruth also needs accurate information about rape. For example, I tell her that the majority of rapes are acquaintance rapes, not stranger rapes. Using bibliotherapy techniques, I encourage her to read about rape, especially about other women's acquaintance rapes.

As Ruth learns facts about rape and challenges her gender-role messages related to rape, she revises her definition of rape to include her own experience, and she blames her perpetrator for raping her instead of blaming herself. She is also learning to trust her own perceptions.

Ruth: The homework you gave me to write a paragraph about what I think "rape" is really hit me hard. I'm beginning to see rape as "nonconsensual sex," and as soon as I wrote that sentence down, I felt afraid. I realized that what Don did to me fits that definition. I think I was [*Ruth takes a deep breath*], I was raped.
Pam: I can see how terrifying applying the word *rape* to yourself is. I would like you to pay attention to what you are feeling right now.
Ruth: My face is hot, my palms are sweaty, I am having an urge to bolt out of here. I guess I would like to run away from the word *rape*. And at the same time I "know" here [*She places her hand on her heart*] that I was raped.
Pam: Your heart knows you were raped. What does it mean to you to acknowledge that you were raped?

Process Commentary   Ruth's acknowledgment to herself and me that she was raped is a very important step in her healing. By asking her to pay attention to her here-and-now feelings, I am inviting her to use her emotional responses as important sources of information about herself. Valuing women's perspectives includes encouraging women to self-define themselves and to learn to trust their feelings and intuition as legitimate sources of information, as women's ways of knowing.

Expressing the Unexpressed   The heart of most trauma therapies includes some type of recapitulation or detailing of the trauma event. I believe the recapitulation must be done within the safety of a trusting relationship in which the client is believed and not blamed. Further, the therapist should be emotionally and empathically present. Therapists who counsel rape survivors must have first explored and confronted the effects of their own traditional gender-role and rape myth socialization processes. They also need to identify and work through any sexually traumatic experiences from their own lives. Being present with clients who have been raped while they recount the details of their victimization requires therapist clarity and courage. I could not be an effective therapist for clients who have been raped until I had achieved a substantial amount of healing myself.

Ruth recounts the details of her assault in several different sessions with increasing detail and feeling. As a feminist therapist, I am careful on each occasion to have Ruth pay attention both to how she is responding internally, which increases her knowledge and trust of herself, and to what is going on outside her, which helps keep the rape placed in its situational and cultural contexts. The following dialogue is a brief excerpt from one of Ruth's later recapitulations. I have asked her to recount the rape event using present tense verbs to increase her awareness and expression of feelings.

Ruth: He is pulling down my slacks, and then he had sex with me.
Pam: I'm aware you switched from the present to the past. What are you feeling right now?
Ruth: I'm scared.
Pam: He has you pinned, and he's taking off your clothes. Your genitals are exposed, and you are feeling scared. If you can, stay with your feelings of being scared, and tell me what is happening.
Ruth: I'm saying "No," and he isn't stopping. I'm not strong enough to stop him [*Ruth pauses*]. I'm frozen, I can't move.
Pam: What are you thinking?
Ruth: There is nothing I can do to stop him. [*Ruth's hands are trembling and tears are rolling down her cheeks.*]
Pam: You are feeling absolutely terrified and frozen. You are powerless to keep him from raping you.
Ruth: Yes.

Later in the session, after we close down the recapitulation, I ask Ruth what she learned from her feelings and awareness during the account.

Ruth: I've never really let myself feel before how powerless and exposed I felt when he yanked my slacks down. The terror I felt lets me know I really was raped.

Pam: If you still had doubts about whether what he did was rape, the fear you felt today clears away those doubts.

Ruth: Yes, and I realize how rough he was with me. I might have been more physically hurt if I had fought any harder.

Process Commentary
Detailed recapitulation is a painful process, but it facilitates healing. By having Ruth describe in detail what Don did to her, she provides herself and me with evidence for refuting her self-blame (for example, how roughly he pinned her and tore her clothes from her). Her feelings during the rape (and in session) give her emotional validation that she was raped, and she is able to integrate that emotional knowledge into cognitive awareness ("I know I was raped").

Ruth's recapitulation also allows us both to become more aware of how the rape was played out in and on her body. Rape usually adds to a woman's relationship problems with her body. She will hold her body responsible for the rape because of its attractiveness or because of its physical powerlessness. If she had an orgasm during the rape, she may feel betrayed further by her body. Subsequent sexual difficulties and weight problems are common for rape survivors. A part of my subsequent work with Ruth centers on her understanding about orgasm as an involuntary physical response and about the normality of physical and psychological freezing when flight and fight are not effective or possible. In this work she learns to forgive her body and to have a more positive, nurturing relationship with her body.

Positively Integrating Rape   Defining the last stage of healing from rape is difficult. Survivors have many different perspectives on what constitutes healing, and part of the therapist's job is to facilitate the client's defining what resolution means to her. I define the last stage as beginning when the most important negative impacts of the rape have been worked through. Thus, the last stage is one of finding positive ways to integrate the rape experience into one's own new and emerging identity. In this stage, survivors search for and create meaningful answers to existential questions about why the rape happened to them and modify pre-rape schemas about the world always being a just one where bad things do not happen to good people. They become more aware of the personal strengths they possess that allowed them to survive their attacks and to have the courage to engage in the healing process. They also find ways to create positive meaning for the trauma. For example, they might work for changes in their state's rape laws or volunteer at their local rape crisis center. In this way the *resolution and integration stage* of healing comes full circle back to the *pre-rape stage*. That is, the survivor's creation of positive meaning for a rape becomes a prevention strategy for future victims. Many feminist therapists believe that part of their role is to become involved in social change, and both the survivor and the therapist often participate in this. Toward the end of therapy, Ruth shares the following imagery with Pam.

Ruth: I am standing on the top of a hill after a tiring and arduous climb. Other women are on the hill with me, and I recognize them as sister survivors who have made journeys similar to mine. In my imagery, we have at one moment joined hands in a cheer of shared victory and in the next moment have extended our hands to those who are still climbing the hill.

JERRY COREY'S WORK WITH RUTH FROM A FEMINIST PERSPECTIVE

Introduction

The *CD-ROM for Integrative Counseling* is especially useful as a demonstration of interventions I make with Ruth that illustrate some principles and procedures of feminist therapy. In Session 1 ("Beginning of Counseling") I demonstrate ways to engage Ruth as a collaborative partner in the therapeutic venture. Session 2 ("The Therapeutic Relationship") highlights the importance of creating a good working relationship and demystifying the therapy process. In Session 3 ("Establishing Therapeutic Goals") I show how I work collaboratively with Ruth in formulating clear and personal goals that will guide the course of therapy. Clearly, Ruth is the expert on her own life and my job is to assist her in attaining the goals we jointly identify as a focus of therapy. In Session 4 ("Understanding and Dealing With Diversity") Ruth brings up gender differences, but she also mentions our differences in religion, education, culture, and socialization. Together we explore how any of our differences might affect our therapeutic task. Such open exploration is essential if therapy is to be effective.

Basic Assumptions

The basic assumptions, goals of therapy, and therapy strategies of feminist therapy have been spelled out in detail earlier in this chapter by Drs. Evans, Seem, Kincade, and Remer. In my description of counseling Ruth from a feminist perspective, I will emphasize how I would enlist her as a collaborator. I'll also describe working with Ruth and John in conjoint counseling. In working with Ruth from a feminist perspective, it is essential that the interventions I make be done within the context of her social and cultural world, and that I attend to the environmental factors that are contributing to the problems that bring Ruth to therapy.

Assessment of Ruth

I strive to include Ruth in the assessment and treatment phase. Collaborating with Ruth in all aspects of her therapy will provide a rich therapeutic experience. I am not eager to give Ruth a diagnosis, for I don't see how a diagnostic category will assist her in formulating a picture of what she wants from therapy. Assessment will be an ongoing process in which the two of us will consider what is the most appropriate focus of our work together. (For a detailed discussion of the feminist perspective on assessment strategies, refer to the selection at the beginning of this chapter.)

Goals of Therapy

Functioning within a feminist therapy model, my primary goal is to intervene with Ruth in ways that increase the chances of her recognizing, claiming, and embracing her personal power. After the first few sessions, Ruth and I collaboratively establish these goals to guide the therapy process:

- Trusting her own intuition rather than relying on outside experts
- Learning that taking care of herself is as important as taking care of others in her life
- Accepting her body rather than punishing herself for not having the perfect body
- Identifying internalized gender-role messages and replacing them with her own constructive beliefs
- Acquiring skills to bring about changes at home and school
- Defining for herself the kind of relationship she wants with her husband and her children

Therapeutic Procedures

I spend time talking with Ruth about how therapy works, and I enlist her as an active partner in our relationship. As a part of the informed consent process, we discuss ways of getting the most from the therapy process, clarifying expectations, identifying Ruth's goals, and working toward a contract that will guide her therapeutic journey. This educational process assists Ruth in being an informed client and is the basis for evaluating how useful the therapy is in terms of reaching her personal goals.

The Therapeutic Process

Elements of the Process   Ruth says that she loves reading, and she is very open to reading selected books on topics that are directly pertinent to therapy issues. As a supplement to our sessions, I encourage Ruth to keep a journal and talk with her about bibliotherapy. Ruth and I explore a range of possibilities for extending the therapeutic value of our sessions. She also agrees to join a women's support group that is available through the Women's Center at her college. Although at first she was reluctant to take the time for herself to join this group, she is finding that she can identify with other women in her group.

Ruth is able to bring her experiences in her support group, her reading, and her journal writing into her therapy sessions.

The Therapeutic Relationship   Guided by the principle that the therapeutic relationship should be egalitarian, I take three steps to reduce the power differential between us. Certainly I do not want to misuse the power that is inherent in being a therapist.

First, I monitor the ways I might misuse my power in the professional relationship, such as by diagnosing unnecessarily, by giving advice too freely, by staying aloof behind an "expert" role, or by discounting the impact of the power imbalance between Ruth and myself.

Second, I call to Ruth's attention the power that she has in this collaborative relationship. I expect her to take responsibility for herself, to become aware of the ways she relinquishes her power in her relationships with others, and to take increasing charge of her life.

Third, I consistently attempt to demystify the counseling process. I do this by sharing with Ruth my own perceptions about what is going on in our relationship, by making her an active partner in determining any diagnosis, and by engaging in appropriate and timely self-disclosure.

Role-Playing Ruth's Marriage   In one session Ruth and I do some role playing in which I stand in for John. She tells me (John) how frightened she is of making demands on me for fear that I might leave. Out of that session Ruth begins to be aware of how intimidated she has allowed herself to become. She continues to set John up to punish her by giving him the power to make her feel scared and guilty. As a homework assignment I ask her to write a letter to John saying all the things she really wants him to hear, but not to mail it. The writing is geared to getting her to focus on her relationship with her husband and what she wants to be different. (In an earlier session I gave her a similar assignment of writing a detailed letter to her father, which she agreed not to send to him but to bring in for a session with me.) I make the observation to Ruth that in many ways she is looking to John for the same things she wanted from her father as a child and adolescent. Further, she assumed the role of doing whatever she thought would please each of them, yet she typically ended up feeling that no matter how hard she tried she would never succeed in gaining their approval. I try to show her that she will have to change her own attitudes if she expects change in her relationships, rather than waiting and hoping her father or her husband might change. This is a discovery for her, and it represents a different direction for her life.

Holding a Joint Session With John   Ruth expresses her interest in having John come to a few counseling sessions with her, yet she is ambivalent about the prospects of getting him to agree. Initially she gives a list of reasons why she is sure that he will never come to any kind of counseling. After some discussion with me, she does agree to ask him to attend at least one session (which we will also role-play first). To her surprise, John agrees to join her. Here are a few excerpts from this initial joint session:

Ruth: I brought John here today even though I don't think he really wanted to be here. [*Notice that she speaks for him.*]

Jerry: John, I'd like to hear from you about what it's like for you to be here today.

John: When Ruth asked me, I agreed because I thought I might be of some help to her. I know I don't need therapy for myself, but I couldn't see any harm in giving it one shot.

Ruth: Now that he's here, I don't know what to say.

Jerry: You could begin by telling him why you wanted him here.

Ruth: It's that our marriage just can't go on this way much longer. Things are no longer satisfactory to me. I know that for many years I never complained—just did what was expected and thought that everything was fine—but the truth is that things are not fine by me.

John [*Turning to me*]: I don't know what she means. Our marriage has always seemed OK by me. I don't see the problem. If there's a problem, she's got it.

Jerry: How about telling Ruth this?

I want Ruth and John to talk to each other directly rather than talking about each other. My guess is that at home they are very indirect. By having them speak to each other in this session, I get a better sense of how they interact.

Ruth: See, that's the problem. Everything is fine by John—I'm the one who's crazy! Why is he so content while I'm so discontent?

Jerry: Tell John. You're looking at me. He needs to hear from you, not me.

Ruth: Why, John, am I the only one who is complaining about our marriage? Can't you see anything wrong with the way we're living? Do you really mean that everything is just fine by you? Why is everything on me?

Jerry: Ruth, let me make a suggestion. You are asking John questions. Instead of asking him these questions, tell him what it is like for you to be in this relationship with him.

Ruth [*Again turning and addressing me*]: But I don't think he ever hears me! That's the trouble—I just don't think he cares or that he listens to me when I talk about our life together.

Jerry: So here is an opportunity to test out your assumptions. I hope you are willing to hang in there with him and keep on talking.

Ruth [*With raised voice and a great deal of emotion*]: John, I'm tired of being the perfect wife and the perfect mother, always doing what's expected of me. I've done that for as long as I can remember, and I want a change. I feel that I'm the only one holding together our family. Everything depends on me, and all of you depend on me to keep things going. But I can't turn to any of you for emotional support. I take care of everybody and everything, but nobody takes care of me.

Jerry: Tell John what that does to you and what you want from him.

Ruth: I'm very tired of the way things are with us [*Pause*]. There are times that I need to know that I matter to you and that you appreciate me.

John: Well, sure—and I appreciate your hard work. I know you do a lot in the home, and I'm proud of you.

Jerry: How does it feel to hear John say that to you?

Ruth: But you never say that—you just don't tell me that you appreciate me. I need to hear that from you. I need to feel your emotional support.

Jerry: Yet right now he is telling you that he appreciates you and is proud of you. So, how is it for you to hear what he just said?

I am calling to Ruth's attention that in this brief interaction, for one short moment, her husband responded to her in a way that she says she would like him to. Yet she does not acknowledge what he did say, which is what she says she'd like to hear more of.

Ruth: I like it when you tell me that you appreciate me. It means a lot to me.

John: I'm just not used to talking that way. Why say a lot of useless words? You know how I feel about you.

Jerry: John! That's just the problem. You don't often tell Ruth how you feel about her and what she means to you, and she is not very good at asking for that from you.

Ruth: Yeah, I agree. It hurts me that you think I want to hear useless words. I'm missing affection from you. It's so hard for me to talk about my life with you—about you and me—about our family—oh! [*Ruth's eyes grow moist, she lets out a sigh, and then she grows quiet.*]

Jerry: Don't stop now, Ruth. Keep talking to John. Tell him what your tears and that heavy sigh are about.

My hunch is that Ruth often feels defeated and stops there, seeing herself as misunderstood. I am encouraging her to stay with herself and continue to address John. Even though John is looking very uncomfortable at this point, he sounds receptive.

John: Sometimes I find it hard to talk to you because I feel I can never do enough. How can I be sensitive when you don't tell me what you want?

Jerry: John, she is telling you right now what she wants. How is it for you to hear what Ruth is saying to you?

John: Maybe she is right. I should listen more often.

Jerry: So, are you willing to listen to Ruth a bit more right now?

John: Sure.

Ruth: You may not know how important going to college really is for me, John. I so much want to finish and get my credential. But I can't do that and be responsible for the complete running of our house. I need for the kids to pitch in and do their share instead of always expecting me to do everything. I need some time to myself—time just to sit and think for a few minutes—when I'm at home. And I'd like to be able to sit down with you after dinner and just talk for a bit. I miss talking to you. The times we do talk, the topic is household maintenance.

Jerry: What are you hearing, John, and how does this sound to you?

John: Well, we have to talk about chores. I just don't understand what she wants me to say.

John continues for a time with a very critical voice. Yet eventually he does admit that the children don't help as much as they could and that he might be willing to do a bit more around the house. He adds that the way he grew up men were supposed to work outside of the house and women were supposed to stay home and take care of the family. He admits that he doesn't know how to begin making changes to these well-established patterns.

Ruth: Well, I'd really like your help at home. And what about spending time with me? Do you want to talk with me?

John: Yes, I do, but too often I just want to relax after working all day. I want it to be positive at home after a long day.

Jerry: It sounds as if both of you would like to talk to each other. Would you be willing to set aside some time during the next week when you can have some uninterrupted conversation?

Together we develop a realistic contract that specifies when, where, and how long they will spend uninterrupted time with each other. John agrees to come in for another joint session. I let him know that it will be important that we explore messages that he has embraced unthinkingly and determine if there are ways he might modify his version of what constitutes a "natural" role for women and men. I point out to both of them that they have bought into a fixed vision of whose responsibility it is to maintain the family. This is expressed when Ruth requests that John and the children help her with household chores, for instance. When Ruth asks for help, it is implied that household maintenance is exclusively her job. They may want to begin to question these stereotyped gender-role expectations and consider redefining their roles. At a future session we will focus on what both John and Ruth have learned about roles and division of responsibilities, deciding if these values are functional in their marriage.

In the meantime I ask Ruth to monitor what she actually does at home for 2 weeks and to keep these notes in her journal. I suggest that she write down a specific list of the changes she wants at home. We pursue our individual sessions, working mainly on what she wants in her life for herself, and at times what she wants in her family situation.

Process Commentary Ruth and I spend several sessions working with her part in creating and maintaining the difficulties she is experiencing in her marriage. I challenge her to stop focusing on John and what he can do to change and, instead, to change her own attitudes and behaviors, which may lead to changes in her relationship with him. Ruth begins to see how difficult it is for her to make requests of John or to ask him for what she needs emotionally. Although she initially resists the idea of telling him directly what she wants with him and from him, she eventually sees some value in learning to ask for what she wants. Ruth has decided in advance that he (and others) will not take care of her emotionally, and with this expectancy she has blocked off possibilities of feeling emotionally nourished by others. She often becomes aware of slipping into old patterns, many of which were developed as a child, yet she becomes increasingly able to avoid these traps and to behave in more effective ways.

Ruth and I spend considerable time in our sessions talking about messages she received about gender roles. Up to this time she had not really given much thought to the impact her socialization continues to have on her, nor had she reflected on how she (and John) have uncritically accepted stereotyped gender roles. Much time is devoted in our sessions to reviewing and critically examining decisions she made about herself as a woman. Ruth is realizing that her definition of herself is rather restricted, and now she is beginning to think about how she wants to expand her options.

 ## QUESTIONS FOR REFLECTION

1. How might you integrate concepts and techniques from the other therapy orientations you've studied with feminist therapy? Are there any theories that you think would not fit with a feminist perspective? If so, which ones, and why?

2. What themes from the feminist approach would you most want to incorporate in counseling Ruth?

3. Feminist therapists believe in the value of educating clients about the therapy process and stress the importance of an egalitarian relationship. What other counseling approaches share this orientation? What are your thoughts about demystifying therapy and establishing a collaborative relationship with a client such as Ruth?

4. Feminist therapy takes a dim view of traditional diagnosis and assessment. What other therapies share this view? At this point, what are your thoughts about the use of the DSM-IV-TR as a basis for making an assessment and arriving at a diagnosis? To what extent do you think that traditional diagnosis contributes to blaming the victim?

5. Feminist assessment and diagnosis requires a cooperative and phenomenological approach. If you accept the feminist perspective on assessment and diagnosis, what problems might you expect to encounter in an agency that required you to come up with a diagnosis during an intake session?

6. What would you say to Ruth if she is enrolled in a managed care program that permits only six therapy sessions, and then only if a suitable diagnosis is submitted to the health provider program?

7. Feminist therapy focuses on gender-role and power analysis. What ways might you employ these interventions in your work with Ruth and John during a conjoint session? To what degree have you thought about how your gender-role socialization has influenced your views of what it means to be a woman or a man? How might your views influence your work with a client like Ruth?

8. Assume that Ruth were to say to you: "I know I am dependent on my husband, and that he wants me to give up my professional ambitions as long as our children still live at home. I really don't want to make waves in our marriage, so what I want from you as a counselor is to help me to be happy in doing what is expected of me." How might your own values work for or against you if Ruth tells you she is seeking adjustment more than change in her life?

9. As you read about the basic tenets of feminism, to what extent do you think it is appropriate for a therapist to teach clients ways of challenging the status quo and a patriarchal system? What modifications, if any, might you make in applying feminist therapy to clients who embrace cultural values that keep women in a subservient role?

10. Ruth's weight and her body image are of central concern to her. Contrast the psychoanalytic view with the feminist perspective of the meaning of Ruth's overweight condition. Do you see any way to integrate these two perspectives in working with Ruth's concern about her weight?

 NOTES

1. We made a commitment to feminist collaboration in writing for this chapter and the order of our names holds no meaning. This is truly a collaborative piece with each of us contributing equally to its content and effort.

2. A more detailed description of feminist therapy can be found in G. Corey (2005), *Theory and Practice of Counseling and Psychotherapy* (7th ed.), Chapter 12 (Feminist Therapy).

3. The source for making a traditional diagnosis is the DSM-IV-TR. American Psychiatric Association (2000), *Diagnostic and Statistical Manual of Mental Disorders* (4th ed., text revision), Washington, DC: Author.

4. For more information on this model, see J. Worell and P. Remer (2003), *Feminist Perspectives in Therapy: Empowering Diverse Women*, New York: Wiley.

5. A discussion of the principles of feminist therapy can be found in G. Corey (2005), *Theory and Practice of Counseling and Psychotherapy* (7th ed.), Chapter 12 (Feminist Therapy).

Chapter 11

Case Approach to Postmodern Approaches

A Social Constructionist's Perspective on Ruth

by Jennifer Andrews, Ph.D.

Introduction

Most traditional counseling models rely on the notion that the therapist is an expert about the client. The models presented in this chapter represent a change in the attitude of therapists toward their clients. The postmodern approaches are based on the assumption that the client is the expert on his or her life and the therapist is a consultant who encourages and assists the client in clarifying and achieving his or her goals. My expertise in the case of Ruth is used to construct questions in our interviews that will assist her to discover more choices and to develop a sense of being in charge of her life.

Basic Assumptions

Social constructionism proposes that reality is created in language between people, and the expertise I offer Ruth has to do with language and meaning. Thus, when Ruth tells me that she has just accepted a job as a substitute teacher, I want to know what this means to her. I do not know the correct path for Ruth in her life. I do not make assumptions about substitute work or insert my values into her decisions. Rather, I focus on her expertise about teaching. I try to use ordinary everyday language in a conversational style while remaining curious about Ruth's situation and her ideas about it.

Prior to any assessment, I read Ruth's autobiographical notes and her intake summary. After reflecting on this material I had the following thoughts:

What an amazing woman. With four adolescents, approaching launching, she had the foresight to start an alternative life plan for herself 4 years ago. She is rehearsing her new life in her mind's eye while her current life is demanding and very much in progress. How did she manage to break away from her church 9 years ago? How did she decide to become a teacher? I wonder if the same process is at work in this situation where she sees herself perhaps outgrowing a situation and she needs for something to be different. Her concerns about her husband seem to be legitimate. If she is accurate about his wanting her to remain the way she was, then her changes are probably difficult for him to support. I wonder if he would join her for some couples work. Her complaints about anxiety and panic need to be addressed. I need to listen to her very carefully. It seems that she has made some relationships through her college program. I wonder how she perceives some of her new friends seeing her. I am likely to ask her what they would tell me about her. If she is able to have multiple voices in her head instead of just the ones that diminish her, she may experience some support for her changes. I wonder what actions she has taken about her weight problem.

Many other thoughts occur to me as I anticipate my first interview with Ruth.

Assessment of Ruth

I am therapeutically interested in how people describe their lives. Frequently the stories people tell about their problems and the meanings they attribute to their stories are a reflection of how others value them. For instance, when Ruth describes herself as a "superwoman who gives and gives until there is little left to give," I become curious about how she came to believe she is a superwoman and ask her how that description helps or hinders her in achieving her goals. If I ask her if a "superwoman" gives to herself, she may give some thought to what self-care means to her. Furthermore, the meaning of "superwoman" can change, and subsequently, her reality of giving to herself can change.

Operating from a social constructionist perspective, I experience a dilemma when I am required to assess and diagnose clients. As part of the community of therapists, I understand the need to speak a common language, and I use the *Diagnostic and Statistical Manual* (DSM-IV-TR), which classifies mental disorders in a language that is common to other mental health practitioners.[1] In communicating with insurance companies or creating case notes, I am required to use the DSM-IV-TR. My assessments and provisional diagnoses are generally arrived at in collaborative conversation with the client. I explain the use of the diagnostic manual and the requirement for diagnoses for record keeping and reimbursement. Because Ruth will be using her husband's health care insurance for reimbursement, I read the descriptions from the DSM-IV-TR to her and ask her which she thinks is a better description of her complaint: "Would you say that you are more depressed or more anxious?

Or do you think you are experiencing a combination of these moods? How long would you say this has been a problem?" With this therapeutic approach, a written record is never a surprise to a client, and, generally, the client appreciates becoming an informed participant in creating his or her records.

Traditionally mental health workers are concerned with the first two sections of the DSM-IV-TR, which help them diagnose the client with clinical disorders or personality disorders. For example, Ruth could be described as having a dependent personality disorder (301.6), a panic disorder (300.01), or an eating disorder (307.50). A social constructionist would regard these diagnoses as having been derived from an expert posture and as disrespectful of the client. The third section of the DSM-IV-TR is concerned with medical conditions such as heart condition, diabetes, or a broken leg.

The DSM-IV-TR also offers two more sections that are descriptive of subjects that are compatible with my thinking. Axes IV and V are concerned with psychosocial and environmental problems and the overall ability of the client to function in his or her daily life. It is in Axis IV that we can truly experience ourselves as having systemic lenses. I show Ruth the Severity of Psychosocial Stressors Scale and ask her where she sees herself regarding the severity of the stressors in her life over the last year. I then show Ruth Axis V, the Global Assessment of Functioning (GAF), and we go through the ratings until she arrives at the code she feels most closely describes her situation. I respect her opinions and stay out of the "one-up" position of knowing more about her than she knows about herself. We continue to discuss this at different times during the course of therapy to monitor gains she is making.

After discussing the assessment criteria, we agree on some provisional diagnosis. I include Ruth in this formal process as fully as possible. We agree to a diagnosis of Generalized Anxiety Disorder with panic attacks (293.83) on Axis I. At my suggestion we consider a V-code (62.89) Phase of Life problem, and she agrees to include this too. She wonders about a V-code (61.20) for the parent–child relationship problem with her daughter but then says it isn't serious enough to list here. She also declines listing her relationship with her husband as a problem. I explain Axis II, but Ruth doesn't think that an Axis II diagnosis applies to her. We agree to list the weight problem on Axis III, and she comments that she wants to take this up with her medical doctor, to treat it seriously. On Axis IV she creates a list that includes problems related to the social environment, adjustment to life cycle transition (for example, launching children, graduation from BA program, seeking credentials), self-concept, self-esteem, and related concerns about aging and health. On Axis V she locates herself between a 60 and 62 because she is having panic attacks.

Key Issues

Traditional therapeutic approaches have assumed the presence of some internal structure that we have called the "self." More recent ideas claim that the self is relational, fluid, and ever changing depending on what we are doing and with whom we are doing it. We do not have scientific evidence supporting either position, but the latter view is a more optimistic one for therapists. If the self is mutable and relational, change can be accomplished more easily than if we see the self as a permanent structure that is relatively unchangeable. It makes sense to me that Ruth is having a hard time knowing who she is at the moment. She is in a transitional stage of development, moving from the identity of wife and mother to a new identity she hasn't yet fully articulated. How interesting that she is having this crisis at 39 years of age. She tells me there is something about becoming 40, which says that she is at midlife, no longer a youth with all of her potential ahead of her. She says that she hasn't achieved her goals, and she feels like a failure.

Times of transition can be characterized by feelings of confusion, despair, humiliation, and shame. The person in transition is no longer certain about having a place of belonging, or a place in the world. In primitive societies people in this state become invisible; they cover themselves in ashes and have out-of-body and hallucinogenic experiences. They truly do not know who they are. The identity crisis is over when they reincorporate into the community. Usually this happens with ceremony and ritual. At this time they step into changed identities, new commitments, and new descriptions of who they are and what they will become. The community welcomes them back with this new identity and supports the changes.

Ruth is not living in a primitive community; here the transition is unofficial and the rituals are partial. For example, even though graduation and credentialing are formal rituals that herald her new identity, she does not experience a major change in her life. Through conversation about her new relationships with colleagues and new friends, Ruth can expand her sense of what she has accomplished. Our exchange may go as follows:

Therapist: If one of your colleagues were here right now and I asked her how she sees your teaching ability, what would she say?

Ruth: My friend Carole would say that I am a good teacher and a wonderful team member. Carole can count on me, and she admires my ability to be a mom to four kids and be the kind of student I have been.

This is an example of how I work to situate new behaviors and punctuate Ruth's competencies. As Ruth gives herself compliments through these imagined conversations, she begins to accept the credit she so richly deserves. Therapy can become a ritual space where having these conversations connects her with her developing ideas about her own future.

I believe that "reality" is not objective, not "out there." It is very much a result of individual experience, which includes all of Ruth's past experiences. Her ideas about religion, marriage, personal appearance, and parenting can be seen as internal filters through which all of the current situations are experienced. I can only learn about Ruth's unique experience by asking her about it and listening carefully to what she says.

The Therapeutic Process

At our first session I am very interested in what it is that Ruth wants for her future. The conversation proceeds:

Ruth: I want to become a teacher. My children are getting older and I can see that they will all be off on their own in only a few years. So I started to think about what will happen to me when they leave home.

Therapist: So you started to make plans for your own future?

Ruth: Yes, but it isn't that simple. I feel guilty about taking so much time for myself. I wish I could do this without feeling guilty.

Therapist: You would like to feel more comfortable about realizing your personal goals.

Ruth: That's true, but it is more complicated because my own goals also involve my marriage and my relationship with my husband.

Therapist: Your marriage is important to you.

Ruth: Yes, very important. My relationship with John needs some work, as well as my relationship with Jennifer, my daughter. She is 18, and this is a crucial time. She'll be leaving home soon, and I want her to remember that we had a good home life.

Therapist: Ruth, what other goals do you have for yourself?

Ruth: I would like to lose a significant amount of weight. I would like to be seen as a good-looking teacher, not an overweight, middle-aged wannabe. I have tried over and over to lose weight, but rather unsuccessfully.

Therapist: I wonder if you can tell me about anything that you undertook where you were successful?

Ruth: Yes, 9 years ago I decided to leave the church that my parents belong to.

Therapist: How did you do that?

Ruth: Oh, it was very difficult. It took years of planning and trying and failing repeatedly before I finally left for good.

Therapist: I am interested in how you knew that last time was "for good."

Ruth: The last time I left, it was irreversible. I knew in my bones that I could not go back. I am no longer a member of that church.

Therapist: I hear that a time came when you could not return to the church of your childhood. I am still curious about how you knew that you had outgrown the church.

Ruth: I knew for years before, but I didn't have the courage to stand up to my mother and father.

Therapist: So you finally got the courage to stand up to your parents and that made the separation permanent?

Ruth: Yes, but you know, I still hear them inside my head. They continue to protest in my mind, but it doesn't matter now. There's no turning back at this point.

Therapist: I guess that we all have voices that continue to talk to us. I agree that the voices from our childhood can remain powerful and resonant even when we have outgrown their authority.

Ruth: Well I sure have those voices!

Therapist: Your parents were good teachers. Their lessons took root. Do you think the lessons have outlived their usefulness to you?

Ruth: I haven't thought about it that way. I guess those early lessons come at a time when we are the most impressionable. Hard lessons to shake off.

Therapist: What did you learn from your parents that is likely to influence your teaching methods?

Ruth [*Laughs*]: I have already employed some of those methods with my own children.

Therapist: If you think of these internal voices as early lessons, do you suppose you might feel less guilty?

Ruth: Thinking about it as early lessons, rather than the truth, makes it easier already.

Therapist: Is there anything in this example that will make current changes you are considering a bit easier for you?

Ruth: I will really think about that one.

At our first session I ask Ruth to think about the fact that we have limited sessions from her insurance plan. Therefore, it would make sense to prioritize what to work on. As a part of prioritizing her goals, I ask her who in her life would support the changes she is wanting to make.

Ruth [*Without hesitation*]: John would support me in the changes that I want. He would be happy for me that I finished school, and he would like my new friends.

Therapist: So John's responses to you are very important when you think about the future.

Ruth: Definitely.

Therapist: I don't know what I can do to help John change. I wonder whether we should invite John to join us for a session or two. Think about what would be the pros and cons of such a meeting. Perhaps you can talk with John about it too.

Ruth: I'll for sure consider this and probably bring it up to John.

Therapist: Ruth, what would you like to consider here that you can work on without needing anyone else to change?

Ruth: I wish that I didn't need so much approval from other people. It would be nice to be comfortable when I make a decision and not have to worry about what everyone else thinks about it.

Therapist: Ruth, there are probably other things that may come up during the week that we can add to your goals. We can talk more about them next week.

A week passes, and Ruth returns. She tells me that the disadvantage to having John attend a meeting would be that she would have to share the time and she was just getting to want more for herself. On the other hand, she could have a safe forum to deal with many of her concerns about her future and their future. When she brought this up with John, they began to talk about some of the issues that concern her. Ultimately she thought that having him attend was preferable and that she could share her time for one or two sessions. We continue to talk about her priorities for change, and we planned to have John attend the next session.

The next week Ruth and John appear in my office. Ruth introduces John, and after some polite socializing and getting acquainted, I reflect on an exercise that many couples have found to be useful for their relationship. I describe how I can be driving home alone in my car and having a rather accurate conversation with my husband. After many years I have incorporated a version of him and our relationship that is fairly reliable, and I can rehearse a conversation with him. I further point out that when working with a couple in therapy, I often reflect upon what different interests and ideas he might be considering if he were in conversation with this couple. I ask for permission to interview the "Ruth inside John" and the "John inside Ruth." I explain that they may "pass" on any question they prefer not to answer, and I assure them of my intention of being respectful. Ruth offers to go first. I suggest to John that he listen in a way that a good friend would be listening, and I provide reassurances that the person who is in the listening position will have ample opportunity to talk before the session is over.

Therapist: Hello John inside of Ruth. Is it OK with you if we chat for a short while with you responding as-if you are John?

Ruth [*Answering as John*]: Yes.

Therapist: John, I was wondering what your ideas are about the plans Ruth is making for a teaching career?

Ruth [*As John*]: I know that Ruth has been working really hard to become a teacher, and I think that probably she is a good teacher. But I don't care for the commitment of time that she has to put into this thing, and it doesn't stop. And now she is talking about getting a job, and we'll see less of her.

Therapist: John, are you telling me that you would like to see more of Ruth?

Ruth [*As John*]: Yes, I feel like she has run out on our agreement about our family responsibilities.

Therapist: What other thoughts do you have about Ruth's plans?

Ruth [*As John*]: I don't see where she has put me into her schedule. I can't tell you when the last time was that we were intimate. She is always writing papers.

Therapist: Thank you John in Ruth. I would like to ask John a few questions now [*Speaks directly to John*]. John, as you listened to Ruth's version of you talk about how she believes you feel about her plans, what occurred to you? What percent was she accurate?

John: I would say that she was about 50% accurate.

Therapist: Really? What part did she get right, and what part perhaps did not quite fit?

John: Well, I do want to see more of her. And I do feel that she sort of changed the rules about how we participate in the family. But she totally doesn't get that I am really proud of her. At first I wasn't too upset about school because I didn't seriously think that she had it in her. But then as the years went by I could see that she was going to do it. I felt proud of her, yet I also felt angry that she traded us in for a degree. Sometimes I'm worried that she will leave me.

Therapist: Ruth, as you hear John tell us his thoughts and feelings about your plans, what occurs to you?

Ruth: I knew he was upset and not supportive of my returning to school, but it was upsetting to hear him say I traded him and the children in for a degree.

Therapist: Was there anything else that he said that surprised you, and why was it surprising?

Ruth: I never had the sense that he was proud of me because he never gave me any indication of being proud.

Therapist: What did you hear that made you feel most hopeful?

Ruth: At first it was sad to hear him say he was afraid I would leave him, but then it felt good to know that he does still care about me and our marriage.

Therapist: Now, John, I am inviting you to talk with me as if you were Ruth [*After a nod of consent from John*]. What effect did you think continuing your education and mapping out a teaching career would have on the family and your relationship with John?

John [*As Ruth*]: I thought improving myself through education would be a way to improve the relationship [*Pause*]. We would be more equal, and I would be able to contribute more income for the family's future.

Therapist: So some people might agree that you had honorable intentions. What would you say is most important for you and the future of the marital relationship now?

John [*As Ruth*]: That my husband would stop trying to stop me from being the kind of person that has become important to me.

Therapist: How has he contributed to your becoming this way or taking this position?

John [*As Ruth*]: Small things. Like, there was a time he kissed my neck when I fell asleep reading my textbook at night or when he brought me coffee and hugged me early in the morning.

Therapist: What are some of the small things you do that you know John appreciates?

John [*As Ruth*]: When I come into the den to watch television with him.

Therapist: I'm curious, what was it about these times that was important?

John [*As Ruth*]: He knows that I think watching television is a waste of time. But the other night I came in and snuggled next to him, and we both talked about how we felt connected.

Therapist: What else have you tried to do to help the situation so far?

John [*As Ruth*]: I have made special efforts to express my appreciation for John's extra help at home and with the children.

Therapist: What difference do you think his experiencing that appreciation has on the relationship now and perhaps promises for the future?

John [*As Ruth*]: That's a tough question. I would hope that he realizes that I still love him. Early in our relationship, he used to tell me that I looked at him with loving eyes. We were intimate and had fun together.

Therapist: Can you imagine the difference it will make when you are both appreciating one another and seeing each other through your loving eyes?

John [*As Ruth, with tears in his eyes*]: I would really like to have that happen.

Therapist: Is it OK if we stop at this point and allow Ruth to comment? [*John agrees, and I then turn to Ruth.*] How well would you say John performed being you? For example, on a scale of 1 to 10, where 1 would indicate he was completely off base and 10 would mean he was 100% on target, where would you rate John's internalized experience of you and the relationship?

Ruth: I am having a very strange reaction to what John imagined that I would say. I haven't really thought about it, but as he spoke I thought, "Yes, that is what I would like to say." It is almost like John has answered from the best part of me. I would like to have John come back again and have both of us continue to talk here with you together. [*John expresses his interest in returning.*]

Therapist: I want to thank you both for the special way you each were willing to participate in this relational exercise. From what you have both said, it seems that each of you has had a struggle during this difficult time of so many changes. And I am pleased to be a witness to what your relationship may look like as you continue your conversations and struggle together. Thank you again for this opportunity. When would you prefer to meet again?

Process Commentary   During the initial interview, I want to hear at least a few things about people's lives that are not related to the presenting problems—their interests, their living situation, and so forth. I want to be as clear as possible as to what Ruth expects from our meeting together. I want to be able to provide a unique kind of listening, what has been referred to by some colleagues as "generous listening." This is not listening for symptoms that will help provide a diagnosis, for surface clues to deep meaning or underlying themes, for couple or family dynamics, for self-defeating cognitions, or for so-called facts related to some theory of personality. This kind of listening attempts to open up more possibilities rather than close possibilities. In my inquiry and responses, I attempt to utilize Ruth's and later John's vocabulary and worldview rather than mine. I am interested not only in how the problems affect Ruth's life and relationships but in how her personal values, abilities, accomplishments, and possible resources affect her life and relationships.

I often recall an old saying attributed to Native American meetings that reflects important aspects of this therapeutic process: First, "Show Up"; next, "Be Present"; then, "Tell the Truth"; and finally, "Don't Be Attached to Outcomes." I attempt to connect and cultivate a genuine curiosity in the present. I am interested in both Ruth's and John's lived experience and realities ("truths") that evolve in conversations external to and within our meetings. I attempt to be aware of how certain ideas and practices that are found in our society may have some influence on Ruth and her relationships. In couples therapy I listen particularly for things Ruth tells herself that may be associated with pressures from the culture in which she was brought up. I strive to avoid leading either Ruth or John to any predetermined resolution of problems or preferred way of being in the world.

During the later phase of therapy, I am concerned about the multiple voices that Ruth experiences about her future. This includes voices about gender, culture, self-limitations, and assets available to her. The internalized dialogues that she has carried from the past and her present relationships are important ideas to bring into the therapy. These multiple voices enhance the possible choices that Ruth can make.

The session in which John joined us was valuable because Ruth could experience John's ideas directly instead of the version of John that is her internalized reality. In this exercise I am trying to be more client-focused than theory-focused and therefore I feel free to use therapeutic interventions that may be particularly helpful to Ruth.[2] There were a number of possible advantages of introducing "an internalized other" exercise in this couples session:

- Each partner has a greater opportunity to understand and appreciate the other's personal perspective and story.
- An attitude of reflection and contemplation is fostered and escalating, more-of-the-same interactions are avoided or minimized.
- Each partner can eavesdrop on the other's "best self," and defensiveness is minimized.
- Each partner has the opportunity to experience what it is like to "stand in the other's shoes."

I feel optimistic about Ruth's future. It is to her credit that she is already involved in a process of change. Therapy is just another tool she is using to assist herself in the endeavor that she began years ago. She is on a path to change that is irreversible. Ruth's case is a good example of a client taking charge of her life and developing new choices or possibilities for her future and relationships.

A Solution-Focused Brief Therapist's Perspective on Ruth

by David J. Clark, Ph.D.

Introduction

Ruth called for an appointment and told me that she was interested in working with me because she had read about brief therapy in her class work. She had never been in therapy and was concerned that it would take a long time and interfere with her family life. We set an appointment for the following week.

Solution-focused brief therapy is based on the notion that there are times when a person's particular problem has not been an issue. This exception to the problem is called "a solution," and it is considered to be happening already in the client's life. My task as a therapist is to be a detective who looks for these exceptions. My tools for this investigation are my questions within a collaborative relationship with the client.

Basic Assumptions

The solution-focused approach represents a different perspective from most of the traditional therapy approaches with respect to thinking about and doing brief therapy. Applied to the case of Ruth, this model assumes that she has the internal and external resources she needs to make the kind of changes she wants to make. My work with Ruth is not a problem-solving approach but one that helps her to discover her internal strengths and the external resources to utilize them. Here are some basic assumptions underlying my approach and interrelated guidelines I use in counseling Ruth from a solution-focused perspective.

1. I strive to keep the conversation nonpathological and to redescribe problems in such a way as to open up possibilities. When Ruth describes herself and her life with a problem focus, these descriptions continue to reinforce her beliefs about herself, keeping her stuck in old actions. I find it helpful to offer a new description that invites Ruth to think about the exceptions to her problems.

As Ruth describes the situation that brings her to therapy, I kindly and respectfully suggest a new description that employs hope. Suggesting a new perception does not change the diagnosis or minimize the problem. It simply normalizes and redefines the presenting problem so that Ruth may begin to perceive solutions to it. Problems are not viewed as pathological manifestations but as ordinary difficulties and challenges of life. I view diagnosis as being important and a sign of the underlying fact that something has gone off track.

2. There is a focus on looking for exceptions to the problems that Ruth brings up for discussion. I tend to ask, "What is different about the times when you do not feel quite as depressed?" Changing the direction in therapy from a problem focus to a solution focus can dramatically change Ruth's beliefs about her life situation.

3. This approach does not highlight Ruth's deficits, problems, and failures. Instead, emphasis is on her strengths, assets, accomplishments, abilities, competencies, skills, and successes. When a strength becomes evident in the therapy session itself, I comment on it as a method of reinforcement. Compliments are often perceived as real when they relate to here-and-now interactions. Ruth provides some evidence of her strengths in her autobiography and intake form.

4. Rather than trying to promote insight, I focus on Ruth's ability to survive a problem situation. For me, it is important to refrain from urging Ruth to engage in totally unfamiliar activities. She is more likely to take on activities that she has some degree of comfort with and that fit within her realm of experience.

5. I view Ruth as a person who has complaints about her life rather than as a person with symptoms. In solution-focused therapy, empathy, compassion, and genuine concern are essential for establishing a therapeutic partnership. In addition, it is especially important to help Ruth understand that she has strengths and coping styles that have been successful in dealing with troublesome situations in the past. This provides Ruth with a positive message that can translate into productive actions.

6. I operate on the assumption that complex problems do not necessarily require complex solutions. I invite Ruth to think in simpler ways. Ruth's life situation tends to appear the most complicated when she truly believes that her problem will be solved only when someone else changes his or her behavior. Here are some questions I am likely to pose to Ruth:

- What would it do for you when the behavior of _____ changes?
- Suppose that happened. What would you be doing on the day the change occurs that could be different from what you did yesterday?
- Suppose _____ never changes but you are ready to step back into life on a small scale. What behaviors would others see as they watched you go through your day that would tell them you were getting back into life?

In some situations Ruth may feel overwhelmed by how complicated her problems are. Her beliefs may seem to center around the need for a problem to be totally solved in order for her life to move forward. I am likely to answer by saying, "I understand how hard it is to envision this happening and how easy it is to imagine how it might not ever happen. But I'm still interested in what you would like to be doing instead."

7. It can be helpful to temporarily adopt Ruth's worldview to lessen her resistance. I reframe resistance by considering certain behaviors as doing something important for Ruth, and I assist her in the discovery of actions and behaviors that would be less dangerous and interfering than the ones she currently uses. Asking Ruth to discuss how her present behaviors offer support, relief, and gratification can help resolve resistance.

8. I assist Ruth in viewing her problem (such as depression) as external to herself and to her life. This can help her see the problem as a separate entity that influences but does not always control her life. I might ask Ruth, "Consider a scale from 1 to 10, where 1 indicates depression has total control of you and your life and 10 indicates you are in control of it. Where would you say you are today?" By asking how the problem has been affecting Ruth's relationships, she can feel more capable of intervening in her own life. This may increase her self-rated level of confidence and her degree of hopefulness. Ruth can learn to think of her new actions as giant steps that move her away from her problem's influence on her life, which will empower her.

9. I focus only on what is possible and what Ruth is able to change. I assist Ruth in thinking about and establishing useful goals in therapy: ones that are realistic, attainable, meaningful, and measurable. When Ruth states, "I just want to be happier," I respond with, "When you are happier, someday, what would _____ be seeing you do differently?"

10. My tendency is to go slowly and encourage my clients to ease into solutions gradually. An effective method of measuring small amounts of success efficiently is one that suggests a need for change on the basis of a client's reported position on a scale. I ask, "What needs to happen between now and the next time we meet for you to maintain the 3 and or to move up a little bit to, say, a 3.5?" I want to teach Ruth to see how each new strategy is an experiment rather than a technique that guarantees success. Whatever happens as a result of a new strategy is simply part of an experiment toward change.

Assessment of Ruth

When Ruth arrived at my office, an early intervention was to get her thinking about what kind of changes she most wanted in her life.

Therapist: Have you thought about how you would know that therapy was no longer needed?

Ruth: I am not sure I understand. Could you ask that question another way?

Therapist: Ruth, if we were to work together for 2 or 3 months and if therapy went really well, what would be happening that would make you say, "It was a really good thing that I went to see Dave"?

This is a typical beginning of a first solution-focused therapy session. I immediately start to work toward a goal. Asking Ruth to focus on what positive difference therapy could make starts her thinking in the direction of a goal. As she focuses on the future and constructs positive outcomes, she is inventing and rehearsing these events.

Ruth thinks a while and answers, "I would be getting along better with my husband and with my daughter, Jennifer. I would be confident in going forward in my teaching career. I would be losing weight sensibly and feel better about myself." She pauses and adds, "I would be more sure of my decisions." Ruth's enthusiastic answer is important to me because in solution-focused brief therapy we see the work as interactional. In having a specific and positive vision for what she can achieve through therapy, Ruth communicates her willingness and interest in having change occur.

If Ruth presents a request for third-party payment by her health care provider, I may have specific paperwork responsibilities, which include the DSM-IV-TR diagnosis.[3] Solution-focused brief therapy tends to eschew formal diagnosis, yet this is typically a requirement for third-party payment. These issues would be discussed with her. We agree that Axis I would be an Adjustment Disorder with mixed anxiety and depressed mood (309.28). To acknowledge her concern with her weight problem, I agree to a provisional diagnosis on Axis I of an Eating Disorder (NOS: 307.50). For the distress with her husband and daughter, we choose V-codes for relational problems: Parent-Child Relational Problems (V61.20) and Partner Relational Problem (V61.10). I defer diagnosis on Axis II and III. Axis IV, Psychosocial and Environmental Problems, highlight the transition Ruth is going through, including the decisions about work, completing her credentials, and making peace with John about these changes.

The DSM-IV-TR also has a fifth axis. This is called the Global Assessment of Functioning (GAF). This scale gives an overall description of how the client is functioning. The GAF describes the general functioning of the individual regarding his or her psychological, social, and occupational pursuits. The range of the GAF scale is from a low of 1, which indicates that the client is persistently suicidal or homicidal, to a high of 90, which indicates that the client is free of any symptoms. Ruth has bouts of anxiety and depression as described on the scale, and we estimate that her score would fall between 70 and 75. Here again, Ruth and I collaborate to find the score that we agree is a description of her situation.

The Therapeutic Process

A key concept of solution-focused brief therapy is that we are always looking for positive exceptions or difference. We call these positive exceptions "news of difference." When we find news of difference, we ask many questions about the difference, because we believe that this information can lead to change. Consequently, we are not as interested in hearing about the problem as we are in hearing about times when the problem is not a problem—the exceptions.

Most of the time clients want to talk about their problems, which we call "problem-talk." This is rarely helpful in bringing about change. Only when we ask questions about difference do clients shift to focus on that. We call the resulting conversation about difference or exceptions to the problem "change-talk." It is through change-talk that clients are able to co-create real and enduring change. Once we are having this kind of conversation, we ask important questions to create opportunities for change, such as "What has to happen for that (the change) to happen more often?" Here is an example of a conversation with Ruth aimed at having her think about changes.

Therapist: The day people call for an appointment is usually a day that they feel low. They have decided that they cannot solve their problem on their own, and they are ready to invite a stranger to help.

Ruth: Well, yes, I was really at a loss to know how to deal with my problems by myself.

Therapist: On a scale of 1 to 10, where 1 represents how you were feeling when you made the call for an appointment and 10 represents how you will be feeling when you are done with therapy, where would you say you are right now?

Ruth: I'm about a 3 today.

Therapist: If we assume that you were a 1 when you called, how did you move from a 1 to a 3?

Ruth: When I made the appointment, I started to focus on what I would say when I got here, and when I got clearer about that, I felt better.

Therapist: What difference do you notice in yourself when you are at a 3?

Ruth: I feel a little more sure of myself, and I feel hopeful that I can get better.

Therapist: What does your husband notice when you are at a 3?

Ruth: He notices that I am less wishy-washy. I sound more definite when I say something.

Therapist: How is that helpful? [*Another way of asking about difference*]

Ruth: Well, he takes me more seriously when I sound focused.

Therapist: And what difference does that make?

Ruth: I want to continue in getting my teaching credential. John wants me to stay home. I don't think he believes I am competent. When I sound focused, I think he sees me as more competent.

Therapist: And when he sees you as more competent, does he treat you differently?

Ruth: John seems to respect me more when I feel more sure of myself. I think he starts to take me seriously.

Therapist: When you are at a 3, how does your relationship with your daughter change?

Ruth: Jennifer acts less confrontational when I feel better.

Therapist: What difference does that make to your relationship?

Ruth: It is a lot easier for us to be around each other? We are less irritable.

These questions I am posing to Ruth are called relational questions because they punctuate the effect that different behaviors have on other people and, reciprocally, how their changes influence her responses. During the therapeutic process I continue with questions that look for differences. I want to know if Ruth responds differently to John when he sees her as more competent. I point out the fact that change is reciprocal and interactional. When Ruth changes, John changes in his reactions to her, and she then changes in reaction to his response to her. I never think of the person as an individual. I believe people are always in relationship to themselves (internal dialogues), other people, a life context, a community context, or a cultural context.

An acronym, EARS, outlines the therapeutic process I follow: *Elicit, Amplify, Reinforce, Start over.* I listen to the client and elicit news of difference by inquiring about what is different. I amplify the difference by asking more questions about the difference: "How was that helpful?" or "What difference does that make?" I reinforce the difference by letting the client know that I am impressed. This may be by a nod of the head or a simple expression like, "wow" or "really," and then I start over: "What else is different?" Although this process is simple, it is not easy. With certain therapeutic models, counselors are lured into asking questions about the problem or engaging in discussions about feelings. This line of inquiry tends to distract from the direct path of learning what differences will have an impact on clients and what has to happen for those events to happen more often.

The format of a solution-focused session, which I employ with Ruth, involves a reliable pattern with which she will become familiar. The first part of the session, about 35 minutes, is spent in change-talk conversation such as this.

Therapist: What will be signs to you that changes are happening, even in small ways? [*The questions I pose to Ruth lead to news of difference.*]

Ruth: There would be less tension at breakfast.

Therapist: What would be there instead of tension?

Ruth: John and Jennifer would be having a pleasant conversation, and they would be friendlier to me.

Therapist: How do you explain that these changes would happen?

Ruth: I think that they would see that I was more relaxed and would follow my lead.

Therapist: When was the last time something like that happened, even a little bit?

Ruth: Last Sunday morning we all had brunch together, and it was less tense.

Therapist: How do you explain that things were better last Sunday?

Ruth: We all had plans to go to church together, and we had separate events planned for the afternoon. We were looking forward to the day.

Therapist: What has to happen for these kinds of differences to happen more often?

Ruth: I guess if we really start to make more separate plans for ourselves, then the kids could be more independent and the tension would lessen.

Therapist: When these better experiences continue to happen, what difference will this make in your life?

Ruth: My life would start to look more like what I'm hoping for, and I could get on with my teaching career without worrying so much about the family.

After this we take a break during which time I leave the room for about 5 minutes to think about the session and to develop some compliments, a bridging statement, and a homework task. The compliments must be genuine and represent something that Ruth can feel good about. A second benefit of the break is that it sets an expectancy. Ruth will eagerly wait for me to return, and she is anxious to hear my comments. I take notes during the session and survey my notes for the compliments. When I decide what they are, I write them down and read them to Ruth. I generally select only two or three of the many potential compliments that I have listed.

Frequently, when I give compliments, clients nod their head in agreement with me. This subtle agreement puts the client into a "yes set." In other words, the client is starting to agree with me. Doing this with Ruth makes it more likely that when I assign a homework task she will follow it. I look at my notes to see where desired changes are already occurring, and I am likely to assign something Ruth is already doing as a homework task. Homework is also linked to the original assessment of Ruth's position with me. When I return from the break, the message and homework assignment could sound like this:

Therapist: Ruth, I am impressed with your ability to take charge of your life. Not many people are able to do what you did 10 years ago. It took a lot of courage to leave the church in which you were brought up. And more recently, your decision to go to school and become a teacher shows courage and determination. Now you are completing your education to launch another big change in your life. In view of the fact that last Sunday was a better morning because you all had plans for the day, I am wondering if you might do some homework?

Ruth: What do you have in mind?

Therapist: Between now and the next time we meet, could you, on two separate occasions, deliberately plan for a meal when everyone has some different plans and notice if the better mood is still present? Next time we meet we can discuss what you noticed.

Ruth: I can certainly give that a try.

Therapist: OK! I'll plan to see you again at this time in 2 weeks.

In this case, I looked for something Ruth told me about in the session that worked and built an introduction to the homework task. This introduction makes sense of the task and is called a bridging statement, or segue. An alternative homework assignment might be: "Ruth, since you find yourself at a 3 and you feel better at a 3, I'm wondering if you can intentionally notice how you rate yourself on days when you are feeling good about an interaction with John or Jennifer. I suggest that you make some notes about your ratings and what was happening at the time that you rated it. Next time we meet we can discuss your experience with this task." Because I am asking her to do something, I call this a "rehearsal task."

One procedure that is part of solution-focused brief therapy is the "miracle question." There may be times when Ruth cannot think of any exceptions to a problem she is experiencing. She might report that a certain problem is always there. In these instances, I look for "hypothetical solutions." These are solutions that have not yet happened, but because I ask the question, Ruth is likely to think of an exception. Even though it hasn't happened in Ruth's daily life, it can happen in her consciousness as she invents it in her mind. Typically the miracle question sounds like this:

Therapist: Suppose that after we finished here and you went back to your life and finished your day, that tonight while you were asleep a miracle happened and the problem that brought you here was solved. Wouldn't that be nice? Tomorrow morning when you wake up you don't know that the miracle happened because you were asleep when it happened. Now, what would be the first clue to you that would make you think that a miracle must have happened? What would be the first indication that the problem was solved?

Ruth: In the morning when I first see John, he will smile at me and say "good morning."

Ruth comes up with a response to the miracle question, and I regard this response as news of difference. I can use this in our conversation or in homework assignments. The response is an exception to the problem even though it is only hypothetical, and it is Ruth's material, not mine.

Process Commentary   Solution-focused therapy is typically completed in less than six sessions, and outcome research demonstrates that 78% of clients are satisfied with the results of the therapy.[4] With Ruth, sessions four through six are essentially maintaining and reinforcing gains or achieved solutions. My major focus with Ruth is on her lived experience (thinking, feeling, behaving, and relational context). We work together in a collaborative relationship, setting useful goals for the course of therapy. The purpose of asking questions about exception periods, coping strategies, and pretreatment change is to initiate conversations about client-based strategies, strengths, and resources. All of this is referred to as *solution-talk*. I operate from a relational, pragmatic, and minimalist perspective. My primary emphasis is on describing what Ruth and others did differently during the exceptional period. I then prescribe more of what she has found that works. I place value on related observational and behavioral homework tasks with an emphasis on the so-called common factors of outcome research.[5] At times, I utilize outcome–process measurements such as those discussed by Duncan and Miller.[6]

A Narrative Therapist's Perspective on Ruth

by Gerald Monk, Ph.D.

Introduction

Ruth is a highly motivated person who wants the pain to stop. She teeters back and forth between relishing the excitement of what ongoing life changes may bring into her life in one moment and being disturbed by the fear of what these life changes may bring in the next moment.

Ruth contacted me because she has heard that I work from a narrative perspective, which she thinks might be a good fit for her. Ruth wants me to help her get clarity about what she might do with her life. What she wants most of all is certainty about what will make her happy without cost to others. She wants to know whether she should continue to stay married to John. She wonders whether she will survive without him at worst, or be miserable on her own at best. She is not sure that John will survive without her, and that worries her.

Ruth is fearful of the judgment that she will incur from God, her father, and her children if she were to live a life that is not influenced by servitude, compliance, and emotional caregiving toward her husband and her soon to be grown children. She is frightened by attacks of anxiety, periods of depression, the prospect of dying and going to hell, her aging body, and her weight gain.

Ruth wants me to take the pain away, give assurances that all will be well, and give her clarity that whatever decisions she makes will be the right ones. She wants to develop more courage and feel in charge of her life.

Basic Assumptions

A narrative approach involves entering a therapeutic situation with a range of specific assumptions. These assumptions have been largely pieced together into what is called narrative therapy by Michael White and David Epston.[7] These individuals have drawn principally from the work of Gregory Bateson[8] (biologist and systems theorist), Edward Bruner[9] (ethnographer), Jerome Bruner[10] (psychologist), and Michel Foucault[11] (French historian). From these sources, a coherent practice has been formulated.

At the heart of this practice is the notion that we live our lives according to the stories that people tell about us and the stories that we tell ourselves. The story is not merely viewed as a means by which real experiences are accounted for. Rather, the story constructs "real experiences" and actually shapes our reality. Narrative practitioners contend that we construct what we see as well as describe what we see.

Significant therapeutic importance is placed on how people story their experiences and perform these stories in their lives. Narrative therapists work from the premise that narratives do not encompass the full richness of our lives. Rather, particular lived experiences, or narratives, are not selected out for expression. These lived experiences are often overlooked, never noticed or understood, and are overshadowed by dominant problem-saturated stories. It is these overlooked lived experiences that are the material of interest in the narrative approach. Although a client is often strongly positioned by a problem-saturated story, a narrative therapist recognizes that this person will also have desirable lived experiences. These experiences are viewed as the basis from which an alternative, more preferred story line can be developed.

Narrative therapists maintain that problems are identified within sociocultural and relational contexts rather than existing within individuals.[12] The therapeutic endeavor concentrates on the socially constructed dialogue and the narrative accounts that clients present. Narrative practitioners maintain that one's identity or personhood is developed, sustained, and transformed in and through relationships, both immediate and within the society at large. Their recognition of sociocultural contexts and language in generating problems invites narrative therapists to challenge traditional Western psychology, which defines adjustment in terms of dominant cultural values. Therefore, although traditional psychotherapy privileges Western, White, middle-class values as the "valid" means to mental health, narrative approaches recognize the potential negative effects of therapies that pathologize and categorize human beings when they do not conform to stereotypical health standards. Instead, they hold knowledge tentatively and assist people to identify resources to attain preferred outcomes.

Consistent with its opposition to models of health, narrative approaches employ a nonexpert stance in relation to clients. Narrative therapists seek to understand clients' lived experience and avoid efforts to predict, interpret, or pathologize. Within this process, narrative practitioners are committed to collaborating with clients in assisting them to experience a heightened sense of agency or ability to act in the world.

Narrative therapists consider problems through a political lens, whether an overt cultural problem such as racism or a more covert pressure such as "healthy" relationships. This sociopolitical conceptualization of problems invites the exploration of cultural practices that produce dominant, oppressive narratives. In other words, this approach encourages us to reflect on where we get our restrictive notions and how these ideas produce a negative effect on us or others. Accordingly, narrative therapists "deconstruct" or "unpack" the cultural assumptions that contextualize client problems to demonstrate the effects of oppressive social practices on their clients. This practice invites narrative therapists to identify how dominant cultural practices or certain mainstream belief systems attempt to define and regulate people.

Narrative Techniques

Narrative techniques are constructed on the assumptions just described. I will discuss the techniques of externalizing, mapping the effects, deconstruction, co-authoring alternative stories, several kinds of questions, and building an audience as a witness to the emerging preferred story.

Externalizing Conversation   "The person is not the problem. The problem is the problem." This catch phrase, coined by Michael White, is associated with narrative therapy because of its emphasis on separating the problem from the person rather than demanding that the person own the problem. This is perhaps narrative therapy's most distinctive feature. The method employed to separate the person from the problem is referred to as *externalizing conversation*. Externalizing conversations create space between clients and problems to counteract oppressive, problem-saturated stories, thereby altering clients' relations to problems. Externalizing requires the therapist to identify discourses (cultural ideas and beliefs) that are problematic and oppressive and to identify the effects of these discourses on clients. This externalization allows clients to locate problem stories within a community context rather than within themselves.

Although externalizing descriptions are typically developed in consultation with clients, narrative practitioners actively contribute in this process by identifying externalizing descriptions that fit with the problem's central themes and the wider sociocultural milieu. In fact, narrative practitioners use externalizing conversations to interrupt the tendency of the community or individuals to pathologize people into positions of helplessness, guilt, and shame. For example, a therapist's externalizing language is captured in these questions: "To what extent is this notion of the perfect wife contributing toward the distress that you currently feel?" "How do you manage to fulfill all of the demands placed upon you when fear continues to undermine your confidence?"

Mapping the Effects of the Problem Story   The full effects of the problem story have seldom been grappled with by the person seeking help. Clients often fear that they might be overwhelmed by their difficulties. When externalized descriptions of problems are embedded in the conversation, their effects on clients are examined in a more dispassionate light. Clients feel less shamed and blamed. When the problem influences are examined in a systematic fashion, people feel listened to and that their concerns are taken seriously. They become more mindful of the burden they have been operating under, and after hearing and using externalized descriptions, they are more motivated to move away from the harmful effects of the problem. The externalized problems are understood in terms of the length of time they have been around (length), the extent to which they have had an impact on the person's life (breadth), and the strength and intensity of their influence (depth).[13]

Here are some examples of questions exploring the length, breadth, and depth of the problem-saturated story:

Length Questions
- How long has this problem been around?
- When did it start?
- If things keep going like this, what length of time do you think you might be wrestling with this problem?

Breadth Questions
- How widely spread is this difficulty?
- To what extent is it troubling you on a day-to-day basis?
- How are your present difficulties affecting your mental health, relationships with yourself, friends, children, husband, wife, siblings, physical well-being, your work, leisure time, spiritual well-being, plans for your future, ability to have fun?

Depth Questions
- What level of distress has this problem been causing you?
- At what times is this problem most difficult to handle?
- When is it less difficult?
- On a scale of 1 to 10, how impactful is the problem right now if 10 indicates the problem is in charge of you and 1 indicates that you are completely in charge of it? What score would you give it at its worst? at its best?

Deconstructive Practices   Frequently, people are unaware of how discourses restrict their knowledge, volition, and ways of being in the world. Alternative, more preferred ways of living may remain out of reach, unavailable, or unattainable. Deconstruction questions provide opportunities for the client to examine the cultural restraints that hold them back. Deconstruction questions involve challenging taken-for-granted assumptions about how life must be lived, feelings that must be felt, and behaviors that must be performed. Here are some examples of deconstruction questions:

- What ideas do you have about being female that explain why you acted that way?
- Where and how did you learn these ideas?
- Who in your life keeps reminding you that you should continue to live by these ideas?
- What areas of your life keep reinforcing these ideas about how you should think, feel, and act?[14]

Co-Authoring a Preferred Story   The biggest challenge in constructing a non–problem-saturated story, or what is called an "alternative story," lies in the contrast between the fragility of the emerging story and the intensity and strength of the problem story. Problem stories typically take hold over a long period of time. Clients often experience problem stories as true accounts of what is taking place in their lives. Just as the problem story has grown in strength, so must the alternative story develop sufficient plot strength to be vibrant and potent enough to challenge and stand up to the authority of the problem-saturated story. A range of specific questions designed to elicit the alternative story open up new possibilities for clients who have lost sight of the competencies and abilities that have once been expressed but are often eclipsed by chronic problem issues. The alternative story needs to be fleshed out in sufficient detail in the counseling sessions so that it remains compelling and strong. The alternative story has a beginning in the early life of the client. It is the task of the practitioner to rediscover with clients their demonstrated abilities and strengths in their early life. These rediscoveries are essential to the process of making desirable changes in their present life.

A narrative practitioner makes notes of these competencies, or makes a mental note to return to these later when a preferred client narrative will be constructed. These lived experiences provide the material for the emerging history of the preferred story. Moments of creativity, capacity, and capability are woven together into a story that will endure in the face of the problem-saturated stories that are ready to reconsume the client. Unique outcome, unique account, redescription, and unique possibility questions are all examples of questions that help elicit the client's preferred story.[15]

Unique Outcome Questions   Client competencies are the unique outcomes (sparkling moments that stand apart from the problem story) that provide the material that can be storied into an enlivening narrative. In other words, in collaboration with the client, the practitioner locates desirable experiences the client can reflect on that can be used to assemble a new plot for the alternative story. For example:

- Tell me about moments recently where this anxiety and distress has subsided even for a short time.
- Have you had any brief flashes of clarity amidst the confusion? Tell me about these momentary insights.
- In our interview together, are there things you are saying to me that hint at some possible creative solutions to the dilemma that you face? Say more about this.

Unique Account Questions   These questions assist clients in giving an account of how they were able to accomplish the desirable, favored moments. These questions provide opportunities to promote encouragement and optimism and help to build a sense of competence and capacity for people struggling with issues that attempt to incapacitate them. Here are two examples:

- How were you able to speak out and stand up for yourself when it seemed like everything and everybody else were wanting you to go along with their ideas for you?
- What is it about you that gives you the strength to ask for new possibilities for your life when you have been instructed to conform to certain prescriptions of how to be a woman?

Redescription Questions   Redescription questions invite people to reflect on new emerging or submerged preferred identities. Another way of saying this is that redescription questions provide an opportunity for clients to explore other ways of being in the world that are in contrast to the ways they are currently adopting. They get at people's preferences for their personal development and the kinds of new relationships they are establishing. Here are some examples:

- What does this action, series of thoughts, or feeling responses tell you about yourself that you have not previously been in touch with?
- Now that you are prepared to question and reexamine the direction your life is taking, what does this behavior suggest to you about the personal qualities and abilities you are exhibiting right now?

Unique Possibility Questions   Unique possibility questions move the focus into the future. They encourage people to reflect upon what they have currently achieved, and based on these successes, they invite people to consider what their next steps might be. Here are some examples:

- Given your present discoveries and understandings, what do you think your next steps might be?

- When you are acting from this preferred identity, what actions will it lead you to do more of?
- Now that you have observed people responding in a supportive manner to your self-caring, what plans do you have for yourself to not let go of your ability to nurture yourself?

Building an Audience   Identities or ways of being are not performed in a vacuum. We are forever presenting ourselves to an audience. An audience is those significant others in families and communities whose opinions and viewpoints have immense influence on a client. Sometimes this audience is critical and scathing. When significant others are consistently negative, they act as powerful definers of how we perceive ourselves and the dominant stories we carry about our lives. Thus, dominant problem stories are often cultivated under the gaze of scornful or judgmental observation.

Emerging alternative stories that carry with them the possibility of a preferred self-description must be nurtured by an audience of significant others who will notice and take delight in this desired self-depiction. An appreciative audience can verify the changes being made as real and sustainable. A common form of narrative questioning might begin with the request that the client identify a person in his or her life who would be least surprised to learn of the changes he or she is now making. Clients can be asked what this valued person might say or do if informed about the emerging new story.[16]

Preparing for a Therapeutic Conversation With Ruth

Narrative therapy is essentially a therapy of questions conducted by persons who work from a nonexpert position of respectful and persistent curiosity and naive inquiry. Ruth will be asked if it is OK to ask her a series of questions about her life circumstances. Ruth will be given the assurance that she does not have to answer any questions she finds intrusive or distressing. I view Ruth as the senior author in the therapeutic conversation. She is the expert on her own life and will be consulted in regard to what she would like to achieve, how long she would like to attend sessions, and who she would like to include in future meetings. Therapy is generally a playful and optimistic activity where Ruth is viewed as somebody who already has a variety of resources, abilities, and insights that she can capably bring to bear on her problem concerns. Together we discover her talents and capacities, which provide the basis for storying narratives of strength and resiliency, and we seek to understand the problem-saturated stories that restrain Ruth from attaining the level of personal satisfaction she would like to achieve.

In working with Ruth I am attentive to learning about the problem-saturated stories that are shaping her troubles. Through a systematic process of careful listening and curious and persistent questioning, the therapeutic task is to co-construct enlivening alternative client narratives with Ruth. This is done within a spirit of partnership and collaboration. In the narrative conversation, I address seven domains in assisting Ruth with her concerns, although in practice they may not be followed in a specific order. I want to assist Ruth in some of the following ways:

- Story the problem-saturated narratives that feature prominently in her life.
- In a focused and systematic way, consider and experience the effects of the problem narratives on her life.
- Determine the extent to which she would like something different than her present circumstances.
- Deconstruct discourses that have a negative impact on her.
- Story a range of preferred alternative narratives that lie outside the problem-saturated stories.
- Reflect on how preferred narratives invite Ruth to construct new, more preferred identities.
- Build an audience to the emergence of Ruth's preferred identities.

Like many other narrative therapists, I view Ruth's concerns within the context of her life. I see us as two cultural beings doing the best we can to sustain ourselves in the face of a world that is challenging, fast changing, and unpredictable. As we work together, we are both making sense of our lives and producing meanings that take us forward, whatever they might be.

Initial Assessment and Evaluation

I begin my interview with Ruth by inviting her to tell me the concerns she has and what she is hoping to accomplish in our meetings together. I want to understand what help she would like from me. I explain the philosophy and practices underpinning narrative therapy because I want to be as transparent as I can be about what I am here to do. From a narrative perspective, I am not at all invested in producing a DSM-IV-TR diagnosis to guide my work with Ruth. I am concerned about the inadvertent effects of labeling Ruth's experience in this way, and I am opposed to the pathologizing tendencies that the DSM-IV-TR promotes. The DSM-IV-TR focuses on inadequacy and personal failure rather than on solutions and attention to resources and competence. It is seldom useful in helping me know what to do. I believe that Ruth is in a continual state of reinventing her identity, and such labeling invites a static perspective about her future directions. It also fails to address the significance of interpersonal and cultural factors that shape Ruth's experience.

However, if I worked under a managed health care system requiring a DSM-IV-TR diagnosis, we would look at Axes I, III, IV, and V only, and I would explain that this may or may not be helpful to Ruth. I would not engage in an Axis II diagnosis because of its totalizing descriptions of people. In a collaborative manner, we would probably choose what I would call a "cultural description" (what others may call a diagnosis) that Ruth was comfortable with. I would emphasize to Ruth the somewhat subjective, arbitrary nature of the exercise and the significant variation in diagnoses that are made by practitioners using this system.

Therapeutic Processes and Procedures

Telling Problem-Saturated Narratives   Ruth tells me about a number of her concerns including her feelings of confusion, depression, inadequacy, distress, and anxiety. While Ruth still has concern with the panic attacks, the yoga class she is taking has decreased their frequency. Ruth also expresses concerns about her weight problems. However, right now Ruth is requesting very specific help—she wants advice about what she should do in relation to her marriage. She doesn't want martial counseling, but she wants to explore her own feelings about whether "she still loves John." She wants to get as clear as possible about whether she should try and salvage her marriage with John or leave him. She thinks some of the difficulties she is having with Jennifer (her daughter) relate to her current lack of communication and cooperation with John.

Despite entering into counseling, Ruth can barely believe she is asking herself these questions, let alone telling somebody else. Ruth feels like she is really letting John down by exploring her confusion, uncertainty, and ambivalence about their relationship. She wants lots of assurance that what she is doing is not evil and full of betrayal.

Ruth: I can't believe I am telling you about my inner thoughts about my future. It is scary to say these things out loud.

Therapist: Tell me more about that.

Ruth: Well, I felt like I would always be married to John. Even though we have had some terrible times together I have never, until very recently, faced the prospect that I could leave John. The fear of judgment from my children, from John, from my father, and fear of some kind of divine punishment—that I would go to hell—has stopped me from even considering anything but staying together. But right now I have been honest enough to accept the fact that I hate the kind of life I have been living and shudder to think that I may continue to live this life until the day I die.

Therapist: Ruth, tell me about your life right now and how it got to be this way. [*An invitation to tell the problem-saturated story*]

Ruth talks about how desperately unhappy she is. She talks about the fact that while John was OK about her pursuing a teaching credential, he has continued to be somewhat resentful about her developing her own professional interests. She feels like she can't really talk to John about how alone she feels. She lies alone at night wishing she were living somebody else's life. She talks some more about how scared she is to make any life changes. She is worried that things could get even worse.

I ask Ruth to tell me the story of her relationship with John from when they first met. She described the euphoria of falling in love and the profound sense of security she felt being with him. Ruth felt protected from the world. John was so strong, so secure within himself, so confident. He was also a good provider. Their relationship worked well for her for the first 15 years, but in the last 5 years things have started to deteriorate. She described feeling taken for granted by John and the children as they reached adolescence. Ruth feels like a chauffeur, a housemaid, a cook, a counselor, a financial planner, and a caregiver/nurse. She reports feeling unfulfilled and unsupported. Ruth talks about her fear of speaking honestly to John about the depth of the despair she feels.

Therapist: What's stopping you from speaking to John about your present feelings?

Ruth: I really don't know. I guess I am just terrified that my world is going to come crashing around my ears if I tell people how I really feel.

Therapist: How long do you think fear and terror has stopped you from expressing your heartfelt thoughts? [*I introduce externalizing conversation into the interview.*]

Ruth: When I think about it, I have always been scared of speaking out. From as early as I can remember, I have been frightened about so many things.

Ruth speaks at length about how fear has silenced her in many different areas of her life on so many occasions. I am very curious about Ruth's relationship with fear. I enter the next phase of the narrative conversation.

Exploring the Effects of the Problem Narratives on Her Life   I begin by exploring with Ruth the effects of being silenced by fear. I ask Ruth what contributions fear and terror have made to her life. What has it added? What has it taken away? What has the fear cost her? What has the impact of fear had on her health? her relationships? her career? her spirituality? her ability to enjoy her life? Theses questions help us map the effects of the problem.

Ruth speaks about how she is having no fun in her life right now. She fears that there is nothing inside her if she were to speak about what she cares for. She speaks about having so much doubt about whether she should keep pursuing her career. She feels that the fear she is feeling stops her from taking risks to build new friendships. Ruth speaks about being afraid of what Jennifer might do if she is more honest with her daughter. Most of all, fear is causing her misery because she feels she can't speak openly with John about how she is feeling about her life. Ruth agrees that this state of affairs is far from ideal!

Therapist: Do you think there might be a relationship between being silenced and living with fear and the depression, anxiety, panic attacks, and confusion you speak of? [*Exploring themes and plot connections within the problem story*]

Ruth: I think there is a relationship between these feelings and being able to speak openly about what is going on.

Therapist: Ruth, tell me how big you think fear is right now as you think about talking to John about what is really going on. Out of 10, how much do you think fear is silencing you from sharing your thoughts and feelings with John? [*Further mapping the effects of the problem according to depth*]

Ruth: I guess it's just about 10 because I just feel so terrible. I feel so unhappy. He has no real idea about how unhappy I am.

Making a Decision to Create an Alternative Narrative   At this stage, I encourage Ruth to begin creating an alternative narrative.

Therapist: Ruth, you have been speaking fully about the kind of life you have led with fear, and at times terror, dominating the quality of your relationships with your family and friends, your career, and diminishing your ability to play, have fun, and create a life of your own design. I am wondering if you feel ready to take on this pervasive fear, or do you feel that fear might still be serving you well?

Ruth: I know that being so afraid has closed in on my life in so many ways. I feel ready to take this on, but it would be too overwhelming to become so honest with myself and everybody else in lots of areas of my life all at once.

Therapist: So you would like to challenge fear and express yourself more openly, but you want do so in small steps. Is that right?

Ruth: Sure.

Understanding the Discursive Constraints   As Ruth is motivated to diminish the fear and anxiety that has dominated so much of her life, I ask her if she is willing to explore some of her life experiences that have contributed to the fear and anxiety she has felt. Ruth has made a link between the desire to step outside of her duties as a wife and a mother and the fear of doing so. She remembers the consequences as a young child of wanting to play and have fun, and the tensions and judgments that arose in the family if she participated in activities that weren't related to caring for others.

Therapist: Ruth, where did you learn how to be a woman, a wife, a parent?

Ruth: I don't know. I haven't really thought about it.

Therapist: Well, I am just wondering where you got the ideas of being very caring and putting your own needs aside to focus on other people's needs, sometimes at the expense of your own.

Ruth: I guess I mainly got the ideas from my Mom and the way my Dad treated my Mom, and the way he still treats her.

Therapist: Do you think you live your life according to the ways your Mom modeled how you should be a woman, mother, and wife?

Ruth: I'm not sure. I don't think I have really examined whether I live the same kind of life that my mother does. I know she would never have considered developing a career or going to college. In that way, we are quite different.

Therapist: Yes, that does seem to be a real difference. I am wondering if you can identify areas where you are the same?

Ruth: Well, I think Mom sees relationships in pretty traditional terms. The man is the head of the household, the primary income earner, the protector, if you like. The woman's job is to rear the children, to look after and take care of the house, and I guess to take care of the husband.

Therapist: How many of these ideas have you taken on board that your mom trained you in?

Ruth: Well, I guess for the first 15 years I've followed in Mom's footsteps. That is the kind of woman I have been for virtually all my married life. Now, this is the problem. I feel like I want to stop doing that. I don't want to keep feeling responsible for John's happiness at the expense of my own. I don't want to keep living my life through John. But this is what I hate. I feel so guilty for wanting to establish my own career. And yet I feel really resentful of John when he doesn't support me and help me with the kids. I am also sick of being some kind of domestic slave. Sometimes I feel really clear about wanting a very different life, and then I start feeling really guilty and bad. I get so confused, and then I get depressed again.

Therapist: What areas of your life keep reinforcing these ideas about how you should think, feel, and act?

Ruth: Well, I think my Mom and Dad sure reinforce the kind of mother I should be. Dad has been really opposed to me training as a teacher. He feels it is taking me away from my duties as a parent. Mom is asking me whether I still cook for John and the children since I started my teacher training. I guess those are some obvious examples. There are lots of other subtle ones. Anyway, I just get this really yuk feeling when I am wanting to do career stuff, develop new friendships, and want John to get more involved in helping with the kids and around the house.

As Ruth and I work together, we mutually identify a number of cultural influences that are shaping Ruth and her experiences. My task here is to work with her to deconstruct some of the cultural discourses that might play a central role in producing the conflicts, depression, anxieties, tensions, ambiguities, and fears Ruth experiences. On the white board, Ruth and I work together and identify the following cultural discourses as being influential in her defining herself as a woman:

- As a woman, you are a worthy person if you live your life to serve others.
- As a woman, you are a selfish and unworthy person if you consider your own needs and want to have a lot of fun in your life.
- It is a woman's job to dedicate her life to being the socioemotional caregiver to her husband and children.
- A wife can gain her sense of pleasure and satisfaction through the achievements of her husband.
- A woman's job is to stand by her husband no matter what the cost.
- A woman should put aside her own career aspirations to fulfill the needs of a man.

As Ruth looks at this list, she agrees that these are the very beliefs held by her husband, and by her to some extent. These are also common cultural ideas about women that circulate in many societies.

Therapist: Ruth, do you think there is any relationship between the fear and anxiety you experience and the efforts you are making to continue to fulfill these prescriptions about the kind of life you should be leading?

Ruth: Oh, yes, there is. I guess I have believed that these ideas about womanhood were true and it was my job to fulfill them. I have really started to question these beliefs in the last 5 years. I think I have been faithfully living by these ideas for virtually all my life. But I really don't know whether this is going to help. I guess I want some specific advice about what I should do.

Therapist: OK, let's figure out what you are already doing to challenge these beliefs before I give you any suggestions. Is that OK with you?

Ruth: Sure, but I don't see what I am doing to challenge these beliefs. I feel like a complete weakling living the kind of life I am leading. I wish I were more courageous.

Therapist: Ruth, I would really like to ask you some questions about your ability to challenge others and speak about things that you care about.

Ruth: OK, but I really don't think there is anything much to say about courage. I don't have any.

Building the Alternative Story   At this point, we turn to the storying of Ruth's preferred narrative.

Therapist: Ruth, I am really intrigued that you are not aware of the occasions where you have been courageous and have challenged the kind of fear that had closed in so much on your life. I am really excited to start making some connections with you about the many moments you have mentioned already in this session where you are being an active participant in your life. For example, tell me about what it was like to make a decision to come to counseling.

Ruth: What do you mean?

Therapist: Well, you knew you were going to start examining your life in a way you haven't done before, and that must be pretty scary.

Ruth: You're right. I was terrified to make the appointment. I was thinking to myself, "What if I find out things about myself that I don't like?" You know, I am still really scared about where this is going to go.

Therapist: Would it be true that last year you would have been seriously challenged by fear and not made an appointment, and yet recently you decided you could make an appointment and start talking with me as openly as you have? [*An identified unique outcome*]

Ruth: Yeah, but I have been feeling so desperate, I just had to go ahead and do something. I have been feeling like I am going crazy.

Therapist: OK, I hear that. However, despite feeling desperate, how did you prepare to face fear so directly and start talking about your life so openly with me? [*Unique account question*]

Ruth: I dunno, I just said to myself one day, "I can't stand this anymore, I have got to do something."

Therapist: What do you think you might have said to yourself in the face of "Oh, my God, my life could completely change in ways I can't predict. I have got to do something." Did you say, "I can do this?" What did you say?

Ruth: I really don't know. I think I just said, "Ruth you have got to do something." I don't want to keep doing what I have been doing.

Therapist: OK, you knew you wanted something more, and you were prepared to go for it in spite of the fear.

Ruth: Yes, I guess so.

Therapist: OK, so we have one example of your ability to demonstrate courage and face fear. You were saying earlier that you feel like fear is about 10 and that you are almost completely silenced by it. Is that right?

Ruth: Yes.

Therapist: Well, as I am having you reflect more on these issues, I am wondering if there are even just a few occasions where you speak up about feelings you are having in day-to-day interactions with John.

Ruth: I usually don't tell John what I am feeling, and frankly I don't think he is interested most of the time.

Therapist: Can you think of an occasion in the last week where you have said to John something you feel strongly about and you didn't let fear silence you?

Ruth: Well, I guess there was an occasion on Tuesday when I said to John I needed his support when the children are rude. I told him in no uncertain terms that I wanted him to speak up and challenge the children when their tone of voice is rude.

Therapist: What was it like to tell him that?

Ruth: It felt good, but I'm not sure it made much difference.

Therapist: In that moment, how much were you in charge of yourself, and how much was fear in charge?

Ruth: I felt pretty confident saying that. It is more difficult to talk about my feelings for him and about our marriage.

Therapist: What would you rate fear in that moment?

Ruth: Oh, about a 3.

Therapist: Earlier you said you were excited about what could be in your life even though fear was really huge. You have been willing to talk openly and honestly with me to gain more understanding of yourself.

Developing the Alternative Story   In this phase of the narrative interview, I am storying lived experiences with Ruth about her courage, her ability to be decisive, to take risks in the face of not knowing, and being willing not to be controlled or stifled by fear. We speak together about a number of unique outcomes, occasions when Ruth has demonstrated courage in the face of serious fears. These include making a decision to train as a teacher, completing university studies, taking huge risks by leaving her parents' fundamentalist church, the courage to speak about shaming experiences about playing doctor when she was a child, her ability to care for her siblings when she was a child, and her ability to reflect now on her right to have fun and joy in her life.

We speak about the strengths and abilities required to raise four children, to "make a marriage work," and her ability to know that she has a right to be excited about her life. All of these lived experiences are linked together into a narrative of resilience and strength. To thicken the plot of the story of risk-taking, courage, determination, having the right to enjoy life, I need to story with Ruth the courageous events that had recently happened and link them to events featured throughout her life. This includes eliciting occasions from as early as she can remember when Ruth displayed acts of courage. These memories are folded into the narrative that honors her own journey throughout her life. Ruth feels very excited and more potent as she reflects on these events.

It is not enough just to construct a lasting preferred narrative of strengths and abilities. We also need to reflect on how these actions influence Ruth's evolving and changing identity. In other words, I am interested in assisting Ruth to revise her understandings of herself as she reflects on these preferred narratives. I continue to move into exploring the unique account questions to further thicken the plot of this emerging story.

Therapist: Ruth, we have spent some time reflecting on the many, many instances when you have demonstrated courage in the face of fear and the unknown. What explanation do you give of your ability to have a history of courage, determination, and a willingness to take risks? [*Unique account question*]

Ruth: Well, to tell you the truth, it comes as a bit of a shock to think that I have been kind of brave at different stages in my life. It is surprising to put all of those experiences together and realize there really is something to all of this.

Therapist: What does this say about the kind of person you are?

Ruth: Well, I guess it says that I can be gutsy sometimes.

Therapist: Do you like that description about yourself?

Ruth: I do, but it still feels a little strange to describe myself in these terms.

Therapist: OK, I understand that. You want to get used to that?

Ruth: Yeah, I do.

Therapist: What title would you give this story of courage that we have been exploring together? [*A question to concretize the alternative story*]

Ruth: It is really hard for me to think of this. I am not really creative in that way.

Therapist: Would you like to have a name for this story? The story tends to be much more present for you when you name it. Are you willing for us to name it together?

Ruth and I go back and forth, and we eventually come across a title that is fitting for Ruth. We call it "Ruth's coming out." I then explore with Ruth the impact of the redescribing questions.

Therapist: What does it mean for you now to think of yourself as gutsy when you consider facing John and telling him what is honestly going on for you?

Ruth: Well, I think it helps. I will still feel scared, but I really want to be more honest with John. I think I am prepared to face him. We keep getting stuck in an argument, and I keep ending up feeling blamed. So often I feel like I have done something wrong, and I end up feeling guilty. To tell you the truth, I don't feel very hopeful for our relationship. All he really wants me to do is to go back to the kind of person I was before.

Recruiting an Audience   I explore with Ruth the possibilities of recruiting an audience who will provide support for her as she moves more fully into her preferred story of "Ruth's coming out." Depending on how our work goes together with Ruth, John, and their children, it might be possible for Ruth's own family to appreciate her growing confidence, stronger voice, and ability to take more risks and be more honest. What is more realistic at this juncture is to engage Ruth to consider people in her life now who can support her, applaud her efforts, and cheer her on.

Therapist: I have been wondering as we have been working together, who would be least surprised to hear your "Ruth's coming out" story? You know, if they were to hear about this whole story of you who takes risks, challenges others, faces fear, who might say, "Sure, I'm not the least surprised to hear that Ruth did that"?

Ruth: Well, the only person I can think of now is my maternal grandmother. She would not be surprised by my "coming out story."

Therapist: What would your grandmother say to you if she were sitting in the room with us now?

Ruth: Well, she might say, "Ruth you have got what it takes. Trust yourself. It will all work out."

Therapist: What is it like to hear that?

Ruth: It is really good. It encourages me.

Ruth and I talk some more about the people in her life and what they would say to her if they listened in on our conversation. Ruth identifies two of her friends that she would like to bring into the loop and be much more open with about what is going on in her relationship with John. She thinks she will get some support from these friends.

Future Challenges

In future sessions, we will come back to these cultural ideas that have been so influential in producing anxiety, depression, and confusion in Ruth's life. Ruth is coming to awareness that many of the troubles she is experiencing are not caused by personal deficits or difficulties in communicating. Rather, they are about the discursive clashes that invade her world. These culture clashes pull men and women in different ways. Here are a few examples of discursive clashes:

- It is a woman's job to dedicate her life to being the socioemotional care-giver to her husband and children, versus men and women sharing the family responsibilities for providing for the emotional and psychologi-cal needs of its members.
- A woman's job is to stand by her husband no matter what the cost, versus men and women have the right to an equitable and respectful relationship.
- A woman should put aside her own career aspirations to fulfill the needs of a man, versus a woman has a right to develop her own career aspira-tions within a marriage and be supported by her partner.

There are flashes of awareness in Ruth that John is not a bad person in-tent on thwarting her plans. Rather, she is beginning to see that John is sub-ject to cultural messages about how to be a man and a husband just as much as she is shaped by the cultural messages about how to be a woman and a wife. Knowing this doesn't mean it is going to be easy for Ruth to accept John's traditional beliefs about important familial matters when they are in opposi-tion to her changing viewpoints. The difference for Ruth involves her know-ing that the challenges she is experiencing with John aren't about her going crazy. It is about something much bigger than her.

Concluding My Work With Ruth

Ruth is already changing her sense of herself, and she knows a little more about what is possible in her life. She is connected more with her ability to take risks and express herself more openly and honestly, and she is more un-derstanding about her confusion and anxieties about what she wants and what she is to do. There is also a qualitative shift in the extent to which she feels frightened. She is more trusting of herself in the face of the consequences of her decisions. However, there is a lot more to do.

Ruth doesn't know for sure whether she should continue to stay married to John, but she is now prepared to explore what it will mean to stay together as intimate partners. She is more confident in her ability to survive and less burdened by worrying about John's future. Issues about her relationship with the children remain a concern to her. She is more trusting of herself to handle her father's reactions to her, including blaming and judgment, and recognizes that this relationship will always be a struggle for her. Our work together has provided a strong foundation to address these ongoing concerns. Her story, "Ruth's coming out," is important to her and reminds her of her new emerg-ing identity as a gutsy Ruth. Ruth is motivated to do more in future counsel-ing sessions. For instance, she wants marital counseling, she wants a closer yet more respectful relationship with her children, and she wants to address her problems with body image and weight.

Ruth and I have established a strong collaborative partnership, and she is beginning to believe in her own expertise. She feels more sure of herself, knowing that many of the struggles she faces are less to do with some kind of personal deficits, malfunctions, and dysfunctions occurring within her and more to do with the clash of cultural expectations required of her as a woman, mother, and partner. As she enters into the next stage of her personal work, she is becoming less willing to internalize inadequacy and more willing to externalize and challenge the cultural prescriptions that have constrained the kind of life she wishes to lead.

At this point, Ruth doesn't have all the answers to her questions, nor may she ever have such answers. She still doesn't know whether she will leave John, defy the God that her father introduced to her, change her body shape, or ever be completely free of sadness and anxiety. However, she is certain that whatever she is yet to come up against, she has the strength and courage to step forward into the unknown.

JERRY COREY'S WORK WITH RUTH: A COMMENTARY

Introduction

In this chapter three different contributors have presented postmodern approaches to counseling with Ruth: Dr. Andrews (social constructionist), Dr. Clark (solution-focused brief therapy), and Dr. Monk (narrative therapy). Because of these detailed descriptions, I will deviate from the usual format of discussing at length my particular approach within this theory and will make only brief mention of a few aspects of working with Ruth from the solution-focused and narrative perspectives. Then I will show how I might build on earlier work from these theories in thinking about Ruth's case.

Basic Assumptions

Narrative therapy emphasizes the value of devoting time to listening to clients' stories and to looking for events that can open up alternative stories. I make the assumption that Ruth's life is inhabited by powerful cultural stories. Her life story influences what she notices and remembers, and in this sense her story influences how she will face the future. Although I am somewhat interested in Ruth's past, we will certainly not dwell on her past problems. Instead, our focus will be on what Ruth is currently doing and on her strivings for her future.

I make the assumption that many of Ruth's problems have been produced by the contradictory cultural messages she has received from society about what kind of person, woman, mother, and partner she should be in the world. Part of our work together will be to look for personal resources Ruth has that will enable her to create a new story for herself. In short, from the narrative perspective my commitment is to help Ruth rewrite the story of her life. The collaboration between Ruth and me will result in her reviewing certain events from her past and rewriting her future. Drawing on contributions from solution-focused brief therapy and narrative therapy, I am more concerned about Ruth's strengths than I am in discussing her problems. A problem-focused approach to therapy is likely to cement unhelpful modes of behavior.

Many of the various theories stress the central role of a working relationship and a collaborative spirit in therapy (Adlerian therapy, the humanistic approaches, the cognitive behavioral approach, and feminist therapy). Working within a postmodern approach, I am influenced by the notion that our collaboration will be aimed at freeing Ruth from the influence of oppressive elements in her social environment and empowering her to become an active agent who is directing her own life.

The Therapeutic Process

In the first instance, the heart of the therapeutic process from the postmodern perspective involves identifying how societal standards and expectations are internalized by people in many ways that may constrain and narrow the kind of life that they might otherwise lead. Second, it focuses on how identifying a client's resistances to limiting cultural restraints provides the basis for the construction of an alternative story. Ruth's preferred story will be constructed based on her ability to embrace what she might regard as desirable cultural meanings and her ability to resist limiting cultural prescriptions. Ruth's autobiography provides me with significant clues to the unfolding story of her life.

Narrative therapy and solution-focused brief therapy can help Ruth feel motivated, understood, and accepted. A method of supporting Ruth with the challenges she faces is to get her to think of her problems as external to the core of her selfhood. A key concept of both solution-focused therapy and narrative therapy is that the problem does not reside in the person. Even during the early sessions, I encourage Ruth to separate her being from her problems by posing questions that externalize her problem. I view Ruth's problems as something separate from her, even though her problems are influencing her thoughts, feelings, and behaviors. Ruth presents many problems that are of concern to her, yet we cannot deal with all of them at once. When I ask her what one problem most concerns her right now, she replies, "Guilt. I feel guilty so often over so many things. No matter how hard I work at what is important to me, I generally fall short of what I expect of myself, and then I feel guilty." Ruth feels guilty because she is not an adequate daughter, because she is not the mother she thinks she should be, because she is not as accomplished a student as she demands of herself—when she falls short of "perfect performances" in these and other areas, guilt is the result.

My intention is to help Ruth come to view her problem of guilt as being separate from who she is as a person. I ask Ruth how her guilt occurs and ask her to give examples of situations where she experiences guilt. I am interested in charting the influence of the problem of guilt. I also ask questions that externalize the problem, such as "What is the mission of this guilt, and how does it recruit you into this mission?" "How does the guilt get you, and what are you doing to let it become so powerful?" "How has guilt dominated and disrupted your life?" "What does guilt whisper in your ear?"

In this narrative approach, I follow up on these externalizing questions with further questions aimed at finding exceptions: "Has there ever been a time when guilt could have taken control of your relationship but didn't? What was it like for you? How did you do it?" "How is this different from what you would have done before?" "What does it say about you that you were able to do that?" "How do you imagine your life would be different if you didn't have this guilt?" "Can you think of ways you can begin to take even small steps toward divorcing yourself from guilt?"

My questioning is aimed at discovering moments when Ruth hasn't been dominated or discouraged by the problem of guilt. When we identify times when Ruth's life was not disrupted by guilt, we have a basis for considering how life would be different if guilt were not in control. As our therapy proceeds, I expect that Ruth will gradually come to see that she has more control over her problem of guilt than she has believed. As she is able to distance herself from defining herself in terms of problematic themes (such as guilt), she will be less burdened by her problem-saturated story and will discover a range of options. She will likely focus more on the resources within herself to construct the kind of life she wants.

Process Commentary   In close alliance with the work of Drs. Andrews, Clark, and Monk, my approach places emphasis on Ruth's assets rather than her liabilities. Looking at her strengths is not unique to the postmodern approaches, for other theories also emphasize the resources of the client. Building on a client's strengths is part of Adlerian therapy, the humanistic therapies, cognitive behavioral therapies, feminist therapy, and reality therapy. Likewise, most of these approaches pay primary attention to what is happening currently and the client's future strivings rather than exploring the past. However, postmodern approaches to working with Ruth are distinct to the extent that they encourage her to create a richer life story by exploring new cultural meanings that are desirable to her. In this sense, therapy is a new beginning.

 ## QUESTIONS FOR REFLECTION

1. In reflecting on the separate contributions of Drs. Andrews, Clark, and Monk, what are some basic assumptions that all of these therapists share?

2. What are some of the main differences you notice in reviewing each of the therapeutic styles in this chapter?

3. What are your thoughts about the manner in which diagnosis is viewed by the postmodern approaches? What do you think about working with Ruth to collaboratively establish a diagnosis?

4. What are some of your reactions to the specific techniques used by each of the therapists in this chapter? What are some of the techniques that you would want to incorporate into your therapeutic style? What kind of questions do you find particularly useful?

5. What are some of the advantages to the approach of externalizing the problem from the client? How might you attempt to do this with Ruth? Are there any disadvantages to this approach?

6. To what degree might you want to incorporate solution-talk as opposed to problem-talk? How would you deal with Ruth if she insisted that she come to see you so she could talk about her problems?

7. Asking clients to think of exceptions to their problems often gets them to think about a time when a particular problem did not have such intense proportions. What are some of the advantages you can see in asking Ruth to talk about a time when she did not have a given problem? How might you build on times of exceptions?

8. What are some ways that Gerald Monk's narrative therapy with Ruth shares common ground with the feminist approach?

9. In what ways are some of the basic ideas of narrative therapy compatible with a multicultural perspective on counseling practice? What applications do you see for using narrative therapy with culturally diverse client populations?

10. In considering all of the therapists in this chapter, what fundamental differences separate postmodern approaches from some of the traditional therapies?

 NOTES

1. American Psychiatric Association. (2000). *Diagnostic and statistical manual of mental disorders* (4th ed., text revision). Washington, DC: Author.

2. Anderson, H., & Goolishian, H. (1992). The client is the expert: A not-knowing approach to therapy. In S. McNamee, & K. J. Gergen, (Eds.), *Therapy as social construction* (pp.25–39). Newbury Park, CA: Sage.

3. American Psychiatric Association. (2000). *Diagnostic and statistical manual of mental disorders* (4th ed., text revision). Washington, DC: Author.

4. DeShazer, S. (March 23, 2002, personal communication). Teaching and training of solution-focused behavioral therapy with Steve DeShazer. Family Studies Center at Purdue University, Calumet, Indiana.

5. Miller, S. D., & Duncan, B. L. (2000). Paradigm lost: From model-driven to client-directed, outcome informed clinical work. *Journal of Systemic Therapies, 19,* 20–31.

6. Duncan, B. L., & Miller, S. D. (2000). *The heroic client* (Appendix V, pp. 237–240). San Francisco: Jossey-Bass.

7. Michael White and David Epston are the principal founders of Narrative Therapy. See M. White & D. Epston (1990), *Narrative Means to Therapeutic Ends*, New York: Norton.

8. Bateson, G. (1972). *Steps to an ecology of mind.* New York: Ballentine Books.

9. Bruner, E. (1986). Ethnography as narrative. In V. Turner & E. Bruner (Eds.), *The anthropology of experience.* Chicago: University of Illinois Press.

10. Bruner, J. (1990). *Acts of meaning.* Cambridge, MA: Harvard University Press.

11. Foucault, M. (1980). *Power/knowledge: Selected interviews and other writings.* New York: Pantheon Books.

12. See an excellent overview of these ideas in J. Freedman & G. Combs (1996), *Narrative Therapy: The Social Construction of Preferred Realities*, New York: Norton. See also G. Monk, J. Winslade, K. Crocket, D. & Epston (1997), *Narrative Therapy in Practice: The Archaeology of Hope*, San Francisco: Jossey Bass.

13. Winslade, J., & Monk, G. (1999). *Narrative counseling in schools: Powerful and brief.* Thousand Oaks, CA: Corwin Press.

14. White, M. (1992). Deconstruction and therapy. In D. Epston & M. White (Eds.), *Experience, contradiction, narrative & imagination* (pp. 109–152). Adelaide, Australia: Dulwich Centre Publications.

15. White, M. (1989). The process of questioning: A therapy of literary merit? In *Selected Papers* (pp. 37–46). Adelaide, Australia: Dulwich Centre Publications.

16. See Recruiting an Audience, in M. White (1995), *Re-authoring Lives: Interviews and Essays*, Adelaide, Australia: Dulwich Centre Publications.

Chapter 12

Case Approach to Family Therapy

A Family Systems Therapist's Perspective on Ruth

by Mary E. Moline, Ph.D.

Introduction

Family therapy perspectives call for a conceptual shift from practicing individual therapy, for the family is viewed as a functioning unit that is more than the sum of the roles of its various members. The family provides a primary context for understanding how individuals function in relationship to others and how they behave. Actions by any individual family member will influence all the others in the family, and their reactions will have a reciprocal effect on the individual. The transactions that occur between the individual and other family members shape the person's concept of self, relationships with others, and worldview.

For a family with members who demonstrate a poor sense of self, a developmental approach might be integrated with a systems model. In the case of Ruth a systemic family approach requires an assessment of her family system, including her husband, her children, and her parents. An even more comprehensive systemic assessment could include examining her relationships (interactions) with other important units such as church, work, and friends. No rules dictate how much of her system of relationships the therapist must work with; rather, this will depend on the therapist's clinical judgment. Conceptually (or symbolically), however, the therapist will make interventions with Ruth that will enable her to deal with her husband, children, and parents, even though they may not be physically present in the therapy session.[1]

Confidentiality and Dealing With Secrets

A decision family therapists often make prior to a client's first visit is whom they will see. Many insist that a client's entire family be seen during the first visit. Given the variety of systemic approaches available, the therapist may decide to see only the concerned client in the beginning and later invite others in his or her system to attend therapeutic sessions. In that case, the matter of confidentiality must be addressed. The therapist needs to decide if what a client reveals in an individual session will be kept secret. It should be noted that many systems therapists avoid seeing the concerned client first, partially because of the problems involved with deciding how to deal in family therapy with this client's disclosures.

In my view, a safe rule in working with couples or families is not to keep secrets. This definitely applies in those situations where the law mandates that the therapist reveal information indicating that clients are likely to harm themselves or others and in child abuse cases. Even in those situations where the law does not mandate revealing a secret, it is advisable to inform clients of any policies that apply to dealing with secrets. If secrets are kept, the therapist will certainly have a difficult time doing effective therapy with various parts of a family system. Therapists can easily forget what they may not say when the entire family gets together. For this reason many family therapists refuse to become entangled in keeping secrets, and they let this be known from the outset.

If you decide to work within the framework of refusing to keep secrets, I suggest that you have this policy in writing and that you encourage your clients to discuss its ramifications. This contract informs your clients of the risks involved with the therapy process. Of course, clients in family therapy should be clearly informed about the legal limits of confidentiality from the beginning, just as would be the case for individual therapy.

Cultural Perspective

Family therapists are concerned about how the family is influenced by their ethnic and cultural perspective. What might be observed as an ineffective hierarchical structure in a White, middle-class family may be quite normal if observed in a Latino, middle-class family. For example, in a Latino family, having the grandmother take on the parent role for the grandchildren may be culturally normal. However, a grandmother in Ruth's family taking on the parent role might create problems in the system. If the grandmother in Ruth's family is Ruth's mother-in-law and she is forming a coalition with Ruth's husband regarding the rearing of their children, this might disempower Ruth's role as the parent. Thus, it is important to consider the family's cultural perspective before determining if certain behavior is to be considered a problem. What might be considered enmeshment in one family may be normal for another family.

Key Themes and Issues

Ruth's problems could be viewed from a developmental approach, with the theme of family stages becoming central to the treatment process. Or Ruth's family could be assessed from a structural perspective, in which case the boundaries of the system (rules for communicating) are also quite important. It may even hold true that the themes or issues to be examined determine the theoretical approach. In Ruth's case I would approach treatment from a structural intergenerational model, which is my integration of models developed by Murray Bowen and Salvador Minuchin. My rationale for working from this integrated perspective is that Ruth's primary concern regarding change is how her going back to school and seeking a teaching job are likely to affect her husband and children.

I view treatment in three phases. I approach the first two phases from an intergenerational (Bowen) model. The first phase involves having Ruth's husband, John, attend sessions, and the second phase includes assessing John's and Ruth's families of origin. The third phase entails bringing Ruth's entire family in for assessment and intervention. I approach these family sessions from a structural model. A more detailed explanation of these models is given in the section that deals with an assessment of Ruth.

Ruth appears to be unable to define herself separately from her husband and her children. Her struggle with her identity leads me to examine her process of *differentiation* (identity) as a central issue. Other key issues that I would assess and treat pertain to the ways in which anxiety is perpetuated through rigid (inflexible) patterns of three-person systems (known as *triangulated interaction*) across multiple family generations and to the ways in which her current family structures communication. I borrow the concepts of differentiation and triangulation from Bowen's approach to family therapy.[2]

Differentiation Ruth appears to be struggling with developing a sense of self that is separate from her family and possibly from her family of origin. Her decision to develop an identity separate from her parents, husband, and children is known in Bowen's terminology as the process of differentiation. The less differentiated people are, the more they invest their energies in relationships to the degree that they do not have a separate identity. Ruth is so concerned about what her husband and children will think if she pursues her own goals that she becomes immobilized. The goal for Ruth from a systemic perspective is to increase her level of differentiation. This does not mean that she will selfishly follow her own directives; rather, it implies that she can determine the direction of her life.

What keeps Ruth from having a sense of self is that she usually interacts with others by triangulation. This is a process by which a person (A) does not directly communicate information with another person (B) but goes through another individual (C). Gossip is a form of triangulation. It is an indirect and often ineffective form of communication. For example, Ruth may wish to communicate that she is upset with her father, but she chooses to tell her mother instead. In turn, her mother relays the message to father and adds, "How dare you make my daughter angry!" This results in a confused and poorly delivered message. Ruth needed another person to deliver her thoughts to her father because she was unable to do so herself. Her indirect communication is a manifestation of her lack of differentiation. Her style of communication keeps her emotionally fused to others, such as her parents, husband, and children. In her case, the more fused she has become with others, the less she has been able to understand what she values and believes. To some degree, her value system has become identical to those of the people with whom she is fused. Fortunately, it appears that she is at least examining a desire to become a separate individual from John and that she is considering what the consequences will be if she does acquire a new sense of identity.

Anxiety   Ruth's fused relationship with John gives her a sense of well-being. When she attempts to change her relationship to others in her system (parents, husband, and children), however, the level of stress (anxiety and emotional distress) increases in the system. Her inability to reduce anxiety and emotional distress is exhibited by physical symptoms such as panic attacks, difficulty in breathing, and inability to sleep. Her referring physician has determined that there is no organic or physical causation. Depending on the outcome of her medical evaluation, she may be given medication as a way to control her symptoms so that she will be more amenable to psychotherapy. Generally, I do not recommend medication for removing anxiety symptoms because of my belief in the value of working through the issues that are leading to panic attacks rather than merely numbing these symptoms.

Ruth is anxious that her movement away from homemaking to teaching may threaten her family. Such anxiety is typical of clients who exhibit little clear sense of self. A differentiated person makes decisions confidently about the direction of his or her life and is willing to face the consequences of those decisions as necessary. The anxiety that is manifested in Ruth's family system pertains to the intensity, duration, and types of tensions that are occurring between the members. Anxiety is occurring because John and the children fear the possible changes taking place with Ruth. They may assume that her changes imply that she no longer loves them. One way of examining this anxiety and how it is manifested is to work with Ruth from a natural systems (Bowen) perspective. The goal is to explore the processes within the family system that bring about Ruth's symptoms, including the manner in which family members form triangles.

Transgenerational Patterns of Interaction   A triangle (three-person relationship), according to Bowen's theory, is the smallest stable unit of human relations. Triangulation consists of redirecting a conflict between two people by involving a third person, which stabilizes the relationship between the original pair. In other words, if two people are threatened by conflict, a third person is introduced in an attempt to create an overt appearance of togetherness. Actually, the conflict and the focus on the third person serve the purpose of reducing the tension between the two people.

This concept can be applied to Ruth's case. To assess her panic attacks and determine her level of differentiation, the therapist can assess the patterns of interaction in her current family as well as the relational patterns that have occurred in previous generations and have been transmitted from generation to generation. As mentioned, this involves examining the triangular process.

Looking at the situation between Ruth and John provides examples of triangular relationships. Because this couple is not able to discuss emotionally charged issues, there has been a tendency to focus on a particular child within the family. Jennifer, who is seen as the rebel, gets considerable attention. John may not have learned how to share the feelings of loneliness that he experiences when he considers Ruth working outside the home. Likewise, she cannot share how angry she feels about his not accepting her need for a career apart from her role in the family. Instead of dealing directly with each other about their concerns as a couple, they argue about their daughter Jennifer.

Consider this example as yet another illustration of the nature and functioning of triangles. Jennifer comes home and tells her mother she is angry that there is no food on the table. She also begins to complain about all the time her mother spends at school and accuses her of neglecting the children. If Ruth allows herself to become anxious about Jennifer's response, she may not be able to sit her down and tell her about her need to go to school. If her identity (self) is influenced strongly by Jennifer's values, she may go to John and say, "Jennifer is at it again. She doesn't appreciate me at all." Then she may begin to experience physical symptoms, including shortness of breath. In his attempt to reduce her anxiety, John may approach Jennifer and say, "You've made your mother very upset. You will stay home tonight."

This example provides a further illustration of the nature of interlocking triangles. These indirect relationships do not solve family problems; rather, they increase the chances that symptoms will be maintained. Ruth and Jennifer do not discuss their upset feelings toward each other; instead, John takes on their anxiety.

Every family system forms triangles, but when one triangle becomes the consistent or persistent pattern of communication, symptoms arise. Ruth's symptoms include panic attacks. Jennifer may not be allowed to have peer relationships, and any of her attempts to define herself separately from the triangle will lead to anxiety among key family members. Jennifer may be rebellious and act out or may turn her angry feelings inward and become depressed. It is likely that she will develop psychosomatic symptoms because that is her mother's pattern of relieving stress.

I am particularly interested in observing Ruth's relationship with John. To help her attain her goal of determining her own direction without experiencing anxiety, I want to observe and understand the patterns that characterize their relationship. How and why do they avoid emotionally charged topics? With whom in the family do they form alliances? How are triangular relationships in Ruth's current family a manifestation of patterns that go back over one or two generations in Ruth's and John's families?

Whatever the marital relationship patterns are, it is most likely that they will become apparent by studying patterns that have been passed on over several generations. This method of interacting and relating is often referred to as the family emotional system. An exploration of both John's and Ruth's families of origin may determine patterns of closeness, conflict, and distance that emerge from generations of interaction. I would work with those themes that emerge from an intergenerational perspective. The goal of therapy from this perspective, which is the reduction of anxiety expressed in the system so that all the members of the family can improve their sense of self, fits Ruth's case well.

Rigid Boundaries   Observed from a structural paradigm, a theme in Ruth's case is that the family structure appears to have rigid boundaries. Boundaries are the rules that define who participates and how members of a family interact with one another and with "outsiders." Ruth says on the phone that she is concerned about "losing" her children. They are appropriately trying to join peer groups outside the home, which worries her. They are at an age (16 to 19) when it is time for them to gain an identity outside of the family.

It appears that Ruth's family does not have mutually agreed-upon rules that would help it through this developmental stage. This is understandable, for her family of origin was characterized by rigid rules. Now her current family may be struggling with making the transition from a family with children to a family with adolescents and adults. Thus, the rules may be: "Adolescents will not challenge their parents." "The parents will decide what adolescents do with their time." These rules may be appropriate for children but not for adolescents. If a family keeps these rules and adolescents agree to abide by them, the family has rigid boundaries. Its rules for communication are closed. They do not change, even when the need to do so is appropriate to a developmental stage.

In working with Ruth's family I want to ascertain who is interacting with whom and by what rules. I will be raising this question: Are coalitions of two people who join together against another occurring in this family? If Ruth is having a difficult time defining herself within this system, perhaps her children and her husband are having the same difficulty. I want to ascertain whether rules for communication are closed (no opportunity for change) or open (constantly changing) and whether relationships are distant or enmeshed. It is probable that it is not just John who is having difficulty with Ruth's need to change but that her children are having the same trouble. If she is having a hard time defining herself outside this system, it may be that her children and her husband are having the same struggle. I will examine her family system from a structural family therapy perspective, mainly founded by Salvador Minuchin. Structural family therapists focus on the interactions of family members to determine when, how, and to whom individuals presently relate as a way to understand the organization or structure of a family. The structural approach pays particular attention to concepts such as the family as a system, boundaries, power, and transactional patterns. For a detailed account of structural family therapy, see Minuchin's book, *Families and Family Therapy*.[3]

Assessment of Ruth

Family therapists bring to the therapeutic process their own perceptions and interactive processes, which have been influenced by their family's intergenerational system, as does the client. Together they form a new system. As within any system, a change in one part will influence the other. Therefore, a treatment approach that comprehensively addresses the family as well as the "identified" client is required. Because a family is an interactional unit, it has its own set of unique traits. It is not possible to accurately assess an individual's concern without observing the interaction of the other family members, as well as the broader contexts in which the person and the family live. To focus primarily on studying the internal dynamics of an individual without adequately considering interpersonal dynamics yields an incomplete picture. Ruth is embarking on a journey that will affect those closest to her: her husband, her children, her family of origin (parents and siblings), her peers, and her therapist. In addition, assessments made about her will evolve and change as the therapeutic process progresses.

The assessment and treatment process has three phases. In Phase 1, I will have John accompany Ruth for the first visit. I will ask him to assist her in assessing her presenting problem by asking them about their marital history and about their children. My decision to include him is based on my limited phone conversation with her, in which she said she was aware not only that it frightened her to think of making changes in her life but also that he was resisting her changes and preferred that she remain her "old self."

It is my goal to assess Ruth and John's relationship and try to determine what influence each has on the other. What kind of relationship do they have that prevents her from changing and him from wanting change? Do they lack the ability to negotiate a different relationship, and if so, why? To address these questions and as a means of enhancing their relationship, I will encourage John to become interested in couples therapy and in therapy with the entire family. If he chooses to become involved in the process, I will continue to work with both Ruth and John and examine their families of origin (Phase 2). To assess patterns that affect the presenting problem, it is necessary to assess a client's family over a span of three generations.

Phase 3 entails bringing the entire family in for assessment. If there are changes in Ruth and John, I predict that other parts of the system will react. In our telephone conversation, Ruth indicated that she was concerned that her professional involvement would threaten her family. From my perspective it is important to include John and, later, the entire family, because they appear to be part of the reason Ruth's changes have been difficult. There are many ways to approach this case from a systemic perspective.

Establishing a Diagnosis

In addition to the descriptive assessment of Ruth's family, I might be asked to provide a formal diagnosis for Ruth, depending on the setting in which I work. Just as the assessments made about Ruth are subject to change as the therapeutic process progresses, any diagnosis should be considered tentative at the initial phase of therapy. Using the DSM-IV-TR framework, I would assign these diagnoses to Ruth:

300.01: panic disorder without agoraphobia

V61.20: parent–child relational problem

V61.1: partner relational problem

301.6: dependent personality disorder

Ruth was referred to me because of her general anxiety symptoms, which interfered in many areas of her functioning. I justify her diagnosis of panic disorder without agoraphobia on the ground that her anxiety is not due to direct physiological effects of a substance or a general medical condition. She said that she had concerns about having additional anxiety attacks and that she sometimes felt that she was "going crazy."

Although Ruth's main reason for seeking therapy was her generalized anxiety, her relationship problems with her parents and with her spouse could certainly be underlying factors contributing to the symptoms of anxiety and panic. The diagnoses of parent–child relational problem and also partner relational problem seem appropriate due to a number of her behavioral patterns. Her relationships with her parents are characterized by impaired communication, rigid discipline, and overprotection, all of which are associated with clinically significant impairment of the way she functions as an individual and in her family. Likewise, her relationship with her husband is marked by ineffective communication and fear of losing his support, which also affect her functioning.

I gave the diagnosis of dependent personality disorder because Ruth has exhibited many of the traits associated with this condition since her childhood. The following criteria confirm this diagnosis:

- She has difficulty making decisions without a great deal of advice from others.
- She expects others to assume responsibility for major areas of her life.
- She has difficulty disagreeing with significant others because of her fear of losing their approval.
- Because of her lack of self-confidence in her judgment, she has trouble initiating projects and following through with them (such as completing her teaching credential and getting a teaching position).
- At those times when she is alone, she is anxious because of her insecurities in taking care of herself.

These traits, which were passed down from several generations, will, I hope, be reduced through family therapy. My initial assessment and tentative diagnosis of Ruth logically lead to several specific treatment goals.

Treatment Goals

The individual goal for this case is the reduction of Ruth's symptomatic behaviors (panic attacks). The family system goals include (1) reducing triangles that have prevented her and others from obtaining a confident position in the system; (2) restructuring her immediate system so autonomy by all family members will be encouraged; (3) changing patterns of interaction, not only among family members but also between her and John, so that the relationship can become more flexible and able to cope with changes as the family moves to the next developmental stage; (4) reducing the presenting symptoms; and (5) creating an environment in which all members of the system feel secure and, indeed, are reinforced as they make needed changes.

Phase 1: Session With Ruth and John

My goals for our first session are (1) to obtain a working and therapeutic relationship with Ruth and John (or "join the family" in Minuchin's terms); (2) to assess John's willingness to be involved in the treatment process; (3) to encourage John's participation as a critical actor in this family act; and (4) to explore family-of-origin dynamics to shift the focus from symptoms (Ruth's panic attacks) to process (who says what to whom and under what circumstances). This shift will help put Ruth's problems in a larger context, minimize blame, and thereby reduce anxiety, especially hers. Another goal is to confirm or refute my stated hypotheses (described in the section on themes and issues).

After introductions, I begin with Ruth's and John's concerns regarding this session. I address them individually.

Therapist: How were you feeling before you got here, and how is it to be here?
Ruth: I'm a little nervous to have John here with me.
Therapist: Could you explain what you mean by a little nervous?
Ruth: I guess I'm afraid that he may be here to make sure I continue to do things his way.
Therapist: What do you mean by "doing things his way"?
Ruth: That he'll be upset if I talk about wanting to make changes such as going to work. And that he'll try to pressure me not to.
Therapist: John, to what degree do you think Ruth's concerns are realistic?
John: Well, to some degree her concerns are realistic. At first when she asked me to come here, I was angry because I thought she was inviting me because I was the one with a problem. Then I decided that I'd give it a try.

I am interested in their answer to the question "How were you feeling before you got here?" This question brings out in the open each person's reactions and gets dialogue going that makes it possible to discover what each needs to be more relaxed before treatment can begin. Their answers to this question tell me that John and Ruth are willing to be honest with each other. Neither hesitated, and yet both were nervous in sharing their concerns. His honesty and her willingness to share their reactions are signs that the prognosis for change in their relationship is good. Her anxiety may be reduced as they learn to negotiate a new relationship.

Other questions I pursue during the beginning of the first session are (1) "Who said what to whom to convince you both to come to this session?" and (2) "What do you both hope to have happen during this session, and what do you expect from me?" These questions help me ascertain how each sees the meaning of their being here. If it appears that John has a desire to be a part of the therapeutic relationship, I continue to gather background information on both of them. This is done in the form of a genogram.

A *genogram* is an organized map, or diagram, that demonstrates one's family over three generations. It is a method by which therapist and client shift from examining a symptomatic individual (Ruth) to a family system conceptualization of the problem, and it often gives an indication of a solution. In obtaining this transgenerational history, I acquire a history of the nuclear family (Ruth and John's family), a history of her extended family, and a history of his extended family.

One goal in developing a genogram is to determine the following: (1) *relationship patterns* that have been repeated from one generation to the next, which explain the context in which the presenting problem or symptoms developed; (2) the occurrence, if any, of *emotional cutoffs,* which are a means by which people attempt to distance themselves from a fused, or overclose, relationship; (3) *triadic relationships* (triangles), which denote conflict, fusion, or emotional cutoffs; and (4) *toxic issues* such as religion, gender independence, money, politics, and divorce, which create in the client emotional reactivity with other parts of the system.

In doing the genogram work with Ruth and John, I will gather the following information about their current family, their family of origin, their mother's family, and their father's family: occupations; educational background; date of births of self and present children; dates of marriage, separation, or divorce; names of former spouses and children; miscarriages, stillbirths, and adopted and foster children; where all children now live; dates and types of severe illnesses; passages such as promotions and graduations; demographic data; cultural and ethnic data; socioeconomic data; military service; religion; addictions such as drugs, alcohol, and sex; abuse of old people, children, or adults; and retirement or unemployment dates. This information forms a database that will be used to demonstrate family interaction patterns. After gathering this information I prepare a summary that gives useful information in understanding Ruth and John's relationship.[4]

Summary   Through the process of using the genogram to understand the family system, I learn that John has unresolved feelings toward his mother. It is my new assumption that John's triadic relationship (fused with his father and emotionally cut off from his mother) has kept him from forming a healthy individuated relationship with Ruth or with any other woman. His parents were unable to resolve their conflicts, and so one parent moved closer to him, just as the other was emotionally cut off in an effort to reduce the stress and anxiety in the marital dyad. John and Ruth discovered that they were continuing the same pattern that was evident in John's family of origin. Their identities were blended (fused) to the extent that they were unable to discuss the emotionally laden issue of gender independence, and therefore they chose not to relate to each other. In an attempt to dissipate their anxiety, they triangled Rob into their relationship (see Figure 12-1). John, like his father before him, chose to tell his son about his unresolved feelings toward his wife. Rob began to distance himself from his mother, most likely for reasons he cannot completely understand. This triangle left Ruth feeling isolated and without support. She felt that her family really did not appreciate her. But an emotional revelation during therapy helped give Ruth and John a new perspective on the family's problems.

In addition, a new option for interacting was opened up. John found he was able to break the *family rule* of not discussing emotionally charged issues, especially with a woman, a rule that prohibited Ruth from exploring with him how each of them felt as she was trying to become a more independent person within this system. When she decided to make some changes, she inadvertently influenced him to change. This is a good example of how change in one part of the system will result in other parts of the system being changed.

Phase 2: Ruth's Genogram

I assign Ruth to gather information from her parents and siblings and any other family member willing to discuss her family's story. I ask John to collect the same information from his family. I tell them that the purpose of gathering

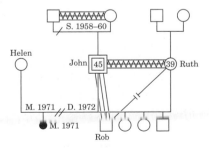

FIGURE 12-1   Multigenerational Triangles, Showing Repeated Structural Patterns With Emphasis on John's Family

such data is not to help them change others in the system but to assist them in making individual changes that can also result in a healthy relationship. After Phase 1, both John and Ruth say they feel a strengthened sense of commitment to their marriage.

Ruth finds in going to her parents' home and separately approaching each of them that her mother is freer to discuss the family and their issues than her father. However, her father does give her some illuminating details about himself. The process of gathering information is an intervention within itself. Ruth is breaking the family taboo about asking questions of her superiors and also is inquiring about their own feelings in regard to others.

Mother's Family   Ruth discovers that her mother is relieved to tell her about the family. Her mother, Edith, says she is the eldest of three siblings. She explains that she felt burdened by the role of caretaker for her brother and sister. She also says her father was abusive toward her and punished her severely if she did not obey him. He was not a religious man and was a heavy drinker. Edith decided at an early age not to try to relate much to her father. Her family members never discussed their feelings about one another. Conflict arose when religion was brought up or when she talked of going on to college. Her father and mother sat down with her and explained that they could not afford to send her (but they did send her brother) and that she would not be permitted to bring the subject up again.

Edith tells Ruth that she never heard a supportive word from any member of the family. Also, there was a rumor that Edith's mother had been sent to a hospital for what was known then as a nervous breakdown. This incident was never discussed among family members, and Ruth had never heard about it. She asks why her mother never spoke about this incident, and Edith weeps, saying that she was never allowed to discuss it. This is the first time Ruth has seen her mother cry, much less express emotions. In addition, her mother shares that she sees Ruth as the most stable person in the family. This is the first positive remark Ruth can remember receiving from her mother.

Father's Family   Ruth's father, Patrick, is less cooperative. He asks her a number of questions about her need to know family information. I advised her it was best not to tell the family that her questions were part of a therapeutic process. She chooses to say that they are part of an educational experience, which is true. Her father begins by saying that he is uncomfortable with giving her any information about his family. This is the first time he has admitted a feeling to her. When she asks about his reasons, he says families should keep their lives private. He believes only God should know what really goes on inside a family. Ruth does not react to her father but simply accepts whatever he feels comfortable revealing.

Patrick goes on to tell her that his older brother died at birth and that his youngest sister committed suicide. Her death left him as the only child of a fundamentalist minister and a mother that he knew little about. This is the first time her father has ever shared anything about himself. It allows Ruth to see her father in a different light. She also gains a sense about herself that she never had before. She discovers that she can handle discussing emotionally laden issues with her father. In the past she would never have permitted herself to do so. She also feels more grown up with her father. It is as if he is treating her as an equal for the first time. Her genogram evolves as shown in Figure 12-2.

Ruth's Interpretation of Her Genogram   Ruth develops her own insight regarding her place and process in the family. Here are some of her discoveries:

- A toxic issue in this system over the years is a female notion of independence from the family.
- Over three generations the eldest daughters have been emotionally cut off from their fathers and have remained distant with their mothers, and the mothers and fathers have stayed in conflicted marriages.

One hypothesis regarding this pattern is that what controls anxiety in this couple's relationship is for the husband and wife to deflect their attention to the eldest daughter. The toxic issue that evokes the process is the desire of the eldest daughter to move physically and emotionally away from the fused triad (mother/father/daughter).

Ruth begins to understand that when she became the focus of attention in her family, her parents' communication with each other increased. When she tried to move out on her own (emotionally and physically), her parents would focus on her. They were unable to work out their personal conflicts and instead chose to argue about her. When Ruth complied and the family appeared calm, her mother and father approved of her and had little more to say to each other.

In a therapy session we discuss Ruth's understanding of patterns carried on from one generation to the next:

Therapist: Ruth, what are you learning from the work you're doing with your family?

Ruth: I'm beginning to realize that whenever I made an independent move, I began to feel guilty. My movement created a great deal of reactivity from my parents, and in my desire to reduce their anxiety I decided not to have a career. In some ways, I believe, I was keeping them together.

Therapist: Do you see any correlations between what you did in your family of origin and what you're currently doing in your own family?

Ruth: I'm seeing that I've continued the pattern. If John even hints at being uncomfortable with my making decisions independently from the family, I feel guilty, and I feel responsible for reducing his stress. Also, I'm continuing this pattern with my children. I make them feel guilty if they try to become independent from the family.

Therapist: Do you still believe John doesn't want you to become your own person?

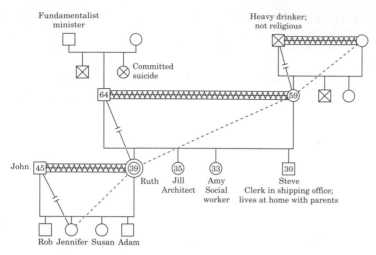

FIGURE 12-2   Multigenerational Triangles and Repeated Structural Patterns in Ruth's Genogram

Ruth: Not anymore. It is becoming clearer to us how we've brought the patterns of our own families of origin into our marriage. We're getting along much better. In fact, John has actually encouraged me to take courses next semester.

Therapist: Have your panic attacks continued during this time?

Ruth: I still get anxious, but now that I'm beginning to see what this is all about, I haven't had a panic attack for quite a while now.

This work accomplished with John and Ruth is a condensed example. It could take months before someone would come to these conclusions. For a time I might meet weekly with the family, and then at a later time meet less frequently.

Phase 3: Presenting Ruth With the Idea of Family Therapy

Ruth reports that since she and John began to come to therapy, Adam has been acting out more at home and at school. He and Ruth are having more arguments, usually centering on her request to have him clean up his room or do his homework. Before she entered treatment, they were very close, going to the movies and attending school events. John is frustrated with Adam, who has been having trouble at school. According to John, Adam does not clean his room when asked.

I recommend to Ruth that she consider bringing her entire family into the therapeutic process. She and John, having explored their intergenerational dynamics in depth, have made some significant changes. According to both of them, their relationship has improved, and she is feeling far less guilt and anxiety about her decision to return to school. However, she complains that their children are still resisting change, and especially her changes. Adam and Jennifer have told her that they prefer the "old Mom" and do not want their lives to become unsettled.

Based on our discussion, Ruth decides to ask her family to join her in therapy. The entire family is asked to attend the first session. All of the children agree to participate, which can be considered a good sign. But Rob, the elder son, is reluctant. He feels that he does not have any problems, and he does not understand why he should attend.

With the family's permission, I ask Jerry Corey to attend the meeting as my co-therapist. The luxury of having female and male co-therapists can be most therapeutic. Because I have been working with John and Ruth, we have a relationship that the children might perceive as a coalition, with their parents against them. Having a neutral person as part of a therapeutic team can counterbalance this situation. Choosing a co-therapist of the opposite gender allows for working with transference and also provides opportunities for the co-therapist to model behaviors during the session.

The First Session   Jerry asks the family members to be seated wherever they want. I thank the family for coming and address each member by first name. I say that the purposes of this first meeting are to establish the goals for treatment and to assess with them whether further sessions might be helpful to the family. We also discuss the limits of confidentiality and the reporting laws for the state.

The Presenting Complaint   It is apparent that there is some confusion over why everyone needs to be present. Therefore, we ask Ruth to explain her concerns to the family and her hopes for these sessions.

Ruth: Since John and I have been in therapy, I've seen this family change. Adam, you've been more moody. We've been arguing more, and you seem unwilling to take any suggestions of mine to get your homework done or to clean your room. I believe our marriage is improving, but my relationship with the children, especially Adam, is getting worse.

Jerry and I observe that Ruth and Adam sit next to each other. John sits next to me, and Jennifer sits between Adam and Susan. Rob, who is 19, sits away from the rest of the family. Jerry and I ask each member for his or her observations regarding the family. We also ask them: "If you could get something from this session for yourself, what might that be? Would you like to have a different relationship with anyone in your family?"

The Family Interaction   Here are some excerpts of a dialogue among the family members, Jerry, and myself during this first session with the family. Those present in the family include Ruth, John, Rob, Jennifer, Susan, and Adam.

John: Since Ruth and I began to improve our relationship through counseling, Adam has become less obedient and cooperative, especially with

Ruth. Yesterday, Adam yelled at Jennifer, and when I tried to punish him, Ruth told me to leave him alone and let them work it out by themselves. I disagree with her new idea of how to discipline these children.

Rob [*Interrupting and in anger*]: You should listen to Mom. She knows more about what is going on in this family than you.

Jerry Corey: Rob, you sound angry at your father. If that is true, can you tell him why you are upset, and would you share that directly with your father? [*Jerry has Rob face his father.*]

Rob [*Looking at Jerry as if he was odd, but he faces Dad directly*]: You are on everyone's case, and you don't have a clue as to what is going on in this family. Mom is more reliable and has backed off from telling us continually what to do. She's not on my case as much as she was before.

Jerry: Rob, would you tell your mother what you mean by "being on your case"?

Rob: Mom would always want to know where I was going and what I was doing. She would clean my room without my permission.

Jerry: Rob, you're talking about your mother as though she weren't in the room. How about talking directly to her over there?

Rob: You're asking me to do something I'm not comfortable with. Why can't I just explain myself to you?

Jerry: You have said you're uncomfortable with the way things are in this family. You would like more of a voice in how you are treated in your family. One way for that to happen is to talk directly to your parents so they receive clearly the messages you want them to understand. Try this out and see if it doesn't give you a stronger position in the family.

Rob: That's kind of hard for me to do. It's not something that I usually do.

Mary Moline: I can understand that, Rob. But I believe you are up to the task. Jerry and I are not just asking you to deal directly with your family, but for each of you to talk directly to one another. It also helps Jerry and me to better understand your position in this family.

Rob: OK. I also want to say something about Dad. I feel he's too hard on Adam.

Jerry: So, Rob, there sits your dad. Can you tell him directly what you mean by your statement that he's too hard on Adam?

Rob [*Reluctantly*]: Dad, you're always upset when Adam starts arguing with his sisters or me. And you're getting on my case lately. If I'm not home by 10, you get all bent out of shape, just like Mom used to do.

Jerry: John, how is it for you to hear what Rob is saying to you?

John [*Looking to Jerry*]: I don't believe I have to take this. I never corrected my father.

Mary: John, would you please sit closer to Rob and tell him directly how it is for you to hear what he is saying to you?

John [*Moves his chair closer to Rob*]: Well, it does make me upset. Don't you know how much your mother and I care for you?

Rob [*Facing his father and looking surprised*]: No, I don't know you care.

Mary: It seems that the two of you have more to talk about. I'm hoping that you two will continue this dialogue before the next session. Is that possible?

Both agree to meet outside and before the next session. They agree to go out for lunch and discuss their relationship. They agree to report at the next family session what occurred.

Mary: I would like to make sure that we get to each person in the family before this session is over. [*She turns to Jennifer.*] What would you like to say about being here and what you would like for yourself in these sessions?

Jennifer [*Looking to Ruth and Susan*]: Susan and I like the idea of coming here, because the family seems so different since Mom and Dad went to counseling. But we feel that Mom has abandoned the family.

Jerry: Would you tell your mother what you mean by "abandoning the family"?

Jennifer: Well, Mother, you don't do our wash anymore. We have to make our own lunches. You're arguing more with Adam and me. I want to stay out of the house when the bickering begins, especially between you and Adam.

Mary: Ruth, how do you respond to what Jennifer just said to you?

Ruth: It's hard to hear Jennifer disapproving of my going to college or my wanting her and the children to become more independent from me. I think that's why it's so difficult for me to get a job outside the home. I'm torn between making myself happy or my family happy.

Mary: How do you respond to what your mother just said, Jennifer?

Jennifer: I'd rather not respond right now.

Mary: That's OK, you don't need to answer now. I hope we can get back to what's going on between you and your mother later in this session. [*She turns to Susan.*] How, specifically, would you like things to be different for yourself with each member of your family?

Susan: Jennifer and I would like more of Mom's time.

Jerry: Instead of talking for Jennifer, perhaps you could talk for yourself. Later Jennifer can say what she would like to be different.

Mary: Susan, is there anything that you want to add?

Susan: Well, I'd like to say that I agree with Rob that Dad is not as nice as he used to be since Mom got into counseling. He's nicer to Mom but seems more upset with all of us and . . .

John [*Interrupting*]: How can you say that I'm not nice to you? I do the best I can, and nobody appreciates that!

Jerry: Is that what you were trying to tell your father, Susan? Did he hear you right?

Susan [*Turning to Jerry*]: No.

Jerry: Would you mind telling your father what you'd like from him?

Susan [*With tears in her eyes*]: Dad, it's not that we don't appreciate how hard you work. It's just that I don't hear anything nice from you anymore.

Mary: Susan, if you could have one thing different with your father, what would that be?

Susan: That we could do something together without getting into a fight.

Mary: How would that be for you, John?

John: Well, if I could find the time, I'd like to do more with Susan. But I don't know what a father does with a 17-year-old.

Mary: Why don't you ask her?

John [*Looking at Susan, after a long pause*]: Well, what do you think?

Susan: We could go to a movie.

Mary: Is that something you'd like to do with Susan?

John: Yeah, if we could ever agree on a movie.

Mary: It sounds good, and I hope the two of you will make the time to talk with each other about what both of you want. [*She turns to Adam.*] Adam, what would you like to say about yourself?

Adam: I think it's unfair that my family picks on me.

Mary: Who in this room picks on you, and would you tell them directly?

Adam: Susan, you've been picking on me. And Jennifer just sits around and smiles. And, well . . . [*Fidgeting and looking to the floor*] Dad and Mom have been upset with me a lot lately and . . .

John [*Interrupting*]: When have I been upset with you that you didn't deserve it?

Ruth [*Interrupting and turning to John*]: I think you ought to let Adam finish.

Mary: Ruth, how about letting John speak for himself. [*She looks to John.*] What would you like to say to Adam?

John: I feel that everyone is picking on me, and it's getting me mad!

Jerry: John, I can understand that you might feel as if you're being picked on. But another way to look at this is to consider that what they're telling you is a sign that they trust you enough to be open and honest with you about their feelings. Maybe these are things that they haven't been able to express to you until now.

John: Well . . . I don't know . . . But I do want my kids to be able to talk to me.

Jerry: If you could be more open with them, that would allow them to be more open with you. A short time ago Adam said some things to you, and you seemed to be very emotionally moved. Is there anything you'd like to say to Adam?

John: It's very difficult to hear what you had to say, Adam. [*He turns to Jerry laughingly.*] Did I do it right this time?

Jerry: I hope you'll continue to talk. [*He addresses all the family members except Ruth.*] Several of you have mentioned that your mother's counseling has affected your lives. Some of you have even said that you felt abandoned by her. Would each of you be willing to talk to your mother?

Susan: Mom, it's hard to see you being different. I was so used to you taking an interest in us, even though at times I complained. You did so much for us, but I guess you have a life of your own too.

Rob: I think you're right on, Susan!

Adam: Mother, I miss you not sticking up for me more. I don't like fighting with you, but at times I find myself starting a fight with you.

Mary: Do you think the fighting and missing your mom are related?

Adam [*Thinking for a while*]: Maybe!

Jennifer: I like talking like this. We never do this at home, and we're not even fighting right now.

Mary [*Turning to Ruth*]: How is it for you to hear that?

Ruth: It feels good to see my family talking about themselves and realizing that I don't have to take so much care of them anymore.

Jerry: Our time is almost up, but before we close I'd like to ask each of you if there are reasons you might want to return.

All of the family members feel that it is important to return because they like what has happened during the session. They are agreeable to attending another session the following week. Jerry then explains to them the value of doing some homework before the next session. Because the family members are open to this idea, he suggests the following assignments:

- For Ruth: Avoid interfering when one of the children is attempting to interact with John.
- For Susan and John: Decide on an activity that you're willing to do together before the next session.
- For Rob and John: Take some more time to let your father know what you'd like with him. You agree to go out together and talk. Rob, it's important that you don't tell your father how he should be different, but instead talk about yourself with him.
- For Jennifer: Take the initiative to ask your mother to do something with you before next week, such as going shopping or spending 20 minutes together.
- For Ruth and John: Continue to discuss what you would like to do with each other and what you would like to do separately. When you do start to focus on the children, try to talk instead about yourselves.

The family members are asked if they have any objections to these assignments and if they would be willing to follow through with them by the following week, at which time they will meet again with both therapists. All feel that they can complete the assignments.

It is important that families work on issues outside of therapy as well as during therapy. In this way they can observe that they have the strength to make their own changes. By taking this responsibility they empower themselves. The only family member not given an assignment is Adam. This is an attempt to keep the other family members focusing away from him and keep him from continuing to be identified as a "patient" in this family.

Process Commentary   The co-therapists set out to observe the structure of the family by (1) allowing the members to sit where they wanted to and (2) attempting to get a clearer picture of the family's transactional patterns. We assume, in observing the structure of this family, that Ruth's change has produced stress among the siblings. There was stress between Ruth and John, but including John in the beginning session reduced it. Ruth appears to have rigid boundaries with Adam. Her ability to make changes has strengthened her boundary with Adam, and he is reacting to those changes. No longer does she feel the need to give in to his demands. But conflicts have increased in their relationship. Her changes are resulting in new strains on this relationship. If Adam can have a closer relationship with his siblings or other peer groups, he may be able to better adjust to this change. Jennifer also appears to be having difficulty with the changes, not only with Ruth but also with the fact that the spousal subsystem is becoming stronger. We repeat: If change occurs in any one part of the system, change will occur in the other parts. In other words, changes in Ruth and changes in Ruth and John's relationship have affected the equilibrium of this family. Whenever possible, therefore, it is important to have the whole family enter treatment so that the changes that occur are productive for the system as well as each individual within it.

In this family there is an enmeshment among members. They lack a clear sense of their individuality and roles in the family. Families such as this one are prone to conflict and confusion, and the behavior of one member or unit, in this case both Ruth and John, immediately affects the other members of the family.

Through a Bowenian process, Ruth and John are learning new behaviors. She is learning not to maintain her role as peacemaker, and he is learning to be more supportive of her. As a result, the other family members are being forced to learn to deal with one another. Up to this session they have been increasing the conflict among themselves and with Ruth to bring her back into her previous role as mediator. In family therapy terms this is known as an attempt to maintain homeostasis, which involves prompting a return of the family to the former status.

This system (family) is relatively functional. Its members were able to make some strides in communicating in the session, especially considering that they generally have not expressed their own feelings with one another. John and Ruth's exploration of transgenerational patterns has assisted them in learning how to express these feelings, and that change helped them facilitate the children's flexibility, difficult as it has been at times. Intergenerational patterns of not expressing feelings and allowing independent thought are not likely to continue. Because these patterns do not change overnight, the family still has considerable work to do. The committed effort aimed at modifying these patterns will not only free this family to be more honest and open but will benefit future generations.

The family has an excellent chance of making these structural changes:

- Becoming more direct with one another
- Taking the focus off of Adam as a problem
- Reducing the coalition that Adam and Ruth have against John
- Reducing the enmeshed (overclose) relationship Ruth has with Adam so she can have a closer relationship with John and so Adam can have appropriate closer relationships with his siblings and other peers

The chances are that the entire family will not always be included in future therapy sessions. Instead, therapy may include parts of the system (John and Rob), the spousal subsystem (Ruth and John), or the sibling subsystem (Rob, Jennifer, Susan, and Adam). Ruth and John will need to continue strengthening their independence from each other and their togetherness.

 ## QUESTIONS FOR REFLECTION

1. What differences do you see between working with Ruth in individual counseling and using family therapy? Do you think that including her family in a few sessions will promote or inhibit her progress in individual therapy? Do you see any disadvantages in not meeting with her individually in therapy?

2. What possible ethical issues are involved if you do not suggest family therapy for Ruth, given clear indications that some of her problems stem from conflicts within her family?

3. If you were conducting family therapy in this case, whom would you consider to be your primary client? Would your client be the family as a system? Ruth? John? Jennifer? Adam? Susan? Rob? Can you see any ethical binds if you develop an alliance with certain members of this family?

4. How do you think your own relationships in your family of origin might either help or hinder you in working with this family? Can you see any possible sources of problems or potential countertransferences? If you become aware that you have unfinished business with either your family of origin or your present family, what course would you probably take?

5. If you were working with Ruth's family, with whom might you be most inclined to form an alliance? With which person do you think you would have the most difficulty in working, and why?

6. If you and Ruth were from different cultures, what factors would you as a family therapist want to address with both her and the members of her family? What role might cultural factors play in understanding the structure of this family? How might the interventions you make vary depending on the cultural background of the family involved in the therapeutic process?

7. Do you have any bias toward Ruth because of her desire to change her role within the family? Does her thinking fit with yours regarding female roles in the family? regarding male roles in the family?

 ## NOTES

1. As a basis for understanding the guest contributors' presentations of family therapy perspectives on working with Ruth, refer to G. Corey (2005), *Theory and Practice of Counseling and Psychotherapy*, 7th edition. Chapter 14 (Family Therapy)

contains a comprehensive overview of the approaches to family therapy along with a comprehensive list of references and recommended readings on family therapy.

2. Bowen, M. (1978). *Family therapy in clinical practice*. New York: Jason Aronson.

3. Minuchin, S. (1974). *Families and family therapy*. Cambridge, MA: Harvard University.

4. For detailed information about constructing genograms, consult M. McGoldrick, R. Gerson, & S. Shellenberger (1999), *Genograms: Assessment and Intervention* (2nd ed.), New York: Norton.

Chapter 13

Bringing the Approaches Together and Developing Your Own Therapeutic Style

This chapter focuses on how to work with the themes of Ruth's life from a variety of therapeutic perspectives. I want to reemphasize that no one approach has a monopoly on the truth. There are many paths to the goal of providing Ruth with insight and mobilizing her resources so that she can take constructive action to give new direction to her life. These therapeutic perspectives can actually complement one another. Before demonstrating my own integrative style with Ruth, I will discuss counseling her from a multicultural perspective.

 ## WORKING WITH RUTH FROM A MULTICULTURAL PERSPECTIVE

I discussed Ruth's cases with Jerome Wright, Ph.D., a colleague and a friend who teaches social work practice and cultural diversity courses at Savannah State University in Georgia. Dr. Wright conceived of a way to encourage his students to appreciate the subtle aspects of working with cultural themes in the lives of clients. He gave Ruth's case to his students and asked them to form small study groups to research the cultural variables that would apply to her if she were from each of these ethnic groups: Asian American, Latino, African American, and Native American. The students were also asked to think of issues that would be involved if she were being counseled from a feminist perspective and special issues to consider if she were a lesbian. Each of the study groups had the freedom to present its findings in any way it saw fit, as long as the members did so as a group. I attended my colleague's class to hear each of the group presentations. Some did role-playing situations, others invited guest speakers who represented the group they were studying, and others found interesting ways to involve the class in their presentation. I was impressed with the value of this approach in teaching multicultural awareness to counseling students. Issues such as race, ethnicity, gender, age, socioeconomic status, religion, lifestyle, and sexual orientation are crucial when establishing a therapeutic relationship with clients.

Becoming immersed in the study of cultural diversity is not without its dangers, however. Accepting stereotypes and applying general characteristics of a particular group to every individual within that group is problematic. Indeed, the differences among individuals within a given ethnic group can be as great as the differences between populations. What is important to keep in mind is that knowledge about the client's culture provides counselors with a conceptual framework that can be used in making interventions. But knowledge of a client's cultural values is only the beginning. Counselors need to be aware of how their own culture influences their behavior. It is especially important that counselors be aware of their assumptions and biases and how these factors are likely to influence the manner in which they work with clients who differ culturally from them. Counseling across cultures is personally demanding, but it can also be exciting.

A guiding principle of my practice is that I allow my client to teach me what is relevant to our relationship. It would be impossible for me to have comprehensive and in-depth knowledge of the cultural background of all of my clients. However, it is not unrealistic to expect clients to teach me about those aspects of their culture that are important for us to attend to in our work together. I have become convinced that universal human themes unite people in spite of whatever factors differentiate them. Regardless of our culture, we have a need to receive and give love, to make sense of our psychological pain, and to make significant connections with others. Besides these universal themes that transcend culture, we need to be aware of specific cultural values as we counsel people from various backgrounds. Any difference that has the capacity to create a gap in understanding should be explored, including differences such as age, gender, lifestyle, socioeconomic status, religion, and sexual orientation.

The Many Faces of Ruth

Let's assume that Ruth is an Asian American. Depending on her degree of acculturation, I want to know something about the values of her country of origin. I may anticipate that she has one foot in her old culture and another foot in her new one. She may experience real conflicts, feeling neither fully Asian nor fully American, and at some points she may be uncertain about the way to integrate the two aspects of her life. She may be slow to disclose personal material, but this is not necessarily a reflection of her unwillingness to cooperate with the counseling venture. Rather, her reluctance is likely to reflect a cultural tradition that has encouraged her to be emotionally reserved. Knowing something about her case and about her background, I am aware that shame and guilt may play a significant role in her behavior. Talking about family matters is often considered to be something shameful and to be avoided. Furthermore, in her culture stigma and shame may arise over experiencing psychological distress and feeling the need for professional help.

As another example, consider the importance of accurately interpreting nonverbal behavior. Let's assume now that Ruth is a Latina and that she is cautious in attempting to maintain eye contact because her therapist is a man. I would probably err if I assumed that this behavior reflected resistance or evasiveness. Instead, she is behaving in ways that she thinks are polite, for direct eye contact could be seen as disrespectful. Also, I would need to be patient while developing a working alliance with her. As is true of many ethnic groups, Latinos have a tendency to reveal themselves more slowly than do many Anglo clients. Again, this does not mean that Ruth is being defensive, but it can reflect different cultural norms. She may not relate well to a high level of directness, because in her culture she has learned to express herself in more indirect ways.

If Ruth were a Native American and if I were unfamiliar with her culture, I could err by interpreting her quiet behavior as a sign that she was stoic and unemotional. Actually, she may have good reason to be emotionally contained, especially during the initial meeting with a counselor of a different cultural background. Her mistrust does not have to be a sign of paranoia; rather, it can be a realistic reaction based on numerous experiences that have conditioned her to be cautious. If I did not know enough about her culture, it would be ethically imperative either that I learn some of its basic aspects or that I refer her to a counselor who was culturally skilled in this area. I don't burden myself with the unrealistic standard that I should know everything. It would be acceptable to admit to her that I lacked knowledge about her culture and then proceed to find a way to remedy this situation. Openness with a client can certainly be the foundation for a good relationship. Ruth can provide me with some information regarding what would be important for me to know about her cultural background.

If Ruth is a member of a minority group, she is likely to have encountered her share of discrimination based on being different. This factor will need to be addressed if her counselor is of a different ethnic or racial group. As an African American, Latina, Native American, Asian American, or Pacific Islander, Ruth will share the experience of institutional oppression. She will know what it means to struggle for empowerment. Chances are that being both a woman and a member of one of these minority groups she will experience a compounding of the problems that have previously been described in her case. This experience is bound to be reflected in the dynamics of our therapeutic relationship. I will need to somehow demonstrate my good faith and my ability to enter her world and understand the nature of her concerns. If I ignore these cultural realities, chances are that Ruth will not stay in therapy with me very long. However, I cannot emphasize enough the guiding principle of letting her provide me with the clues for the direction of therapy. In our initial encounter I will want to know what it was like for her to come to the office and why she is there. Rather than having prior conceptions of what we should be doing in this venture, I will ask her what she wants and why she is seeking help from me at this time in her life. If cultural issues are present, I expect that they will emerge very soon if I am listening sensitively to her and attempting to understand her world. As you read about the themes in Ruth's life in the following pages, be aware of how cultural variations could easily be woven into the fabric of the counseling process.

 QUESTIONS FOR REFLECTION

1. If your cultural background and life experiences are very different from Ruth's, will this present any particular problems in establishing a therapeutic relationship? If you do differ from her on any of these dimensions—race, culture, ethnicity, socioeconomic status, value system, religion, or sexual orientation—would you feel a need to discuss these differences with her? From your perspective might any of these differences incline you to refer her to another therapist? What are the ethical considerations in referring Ruth to another therapist?

2. In examining your own belief system and life experiences, do you think you would have any difficulty working therapeutically with any particular racial, ethnic, or cultural group? If you expect that you might have difficulty, what are your concerns, and what might you do about them?

3. What specific aspects about each culture do you feel a need to understand to develop a therapeutic alliance and work effectively with a client? If you do not have this knowledge, how could you go about acquiring it?

4. From your perspective how important is it that you be like your client in each of the following areas: age, gender, race, ethnicity, culture, socioeconomic status, religion, values, sexual orientation, education, marital status, and family status?

5. Are you aware of referral sources for clients from various ethnic and cultural backgrounds? If so, what are they? If not, how could you find out about such referrals?

JERRY COREY'S INTEGRATIVE APPROACH TO WORKING WITH RUTH

In this section I work toward an integration of concepts and techniques from the various schools of therapy by demonstrating the progression of Ruth's counseling. I will then ask you to work with her by drawing particular aspects from each of the models and applying them to her. For an illustration of my work with Ruth, see Session 9 ("An Integrative Perspective") of the *CD-ROM for Integrative Counseling*.[1]

Each therapy approach has something unique to offer in understanding Ruth. I will use a combination of approaches to work with Ruth on a thinking, feeling, and behaving basis. Table 13-1 shows what I am likely to borrow from each of the therapies as I conceptualize Ruth's case. As I describe how I would proceed with her based on the information presented in her autobiography and the additional data from the 11 theory chapters, I make parenthetical comments that indicate from what theoretical orientations I am borrowing concepts and techniques in any given piece of work. Thus, in addition to seeing a sample of my style of working with Ruth, you will have a running commentary on what I am doing, why I am using particular techniques, and what direction I am going in. As you read, think about what you might do that is similar to or different from my approach.[2]

TABLE 13-1 Major Areas of Focus in Ruth's Therapy

Orientation	Areas of Focus
Psychoanalytic Therapy	My focus is on ways in which Ruth is repeating her past in her present relationships. I have a particular interest in how she brings her experiences with her father into the session with me. I concentrate on her feelings for me because working with transference is a major way to produce insight. I am also interested in her dreams, any resistance that shows up in the sessions, and other clues to her unconscious processes. One of my main goals is to assist her in bringing to awareness buried memories and experiences, which I assume have a current influence on her.
Adlerian Therapy	My focus is on determining what Ruth's lifestyle is. To do this, I examine her early childhood experiences through her early recollections and family constellation. My main interest is in determining what her goals and priorities in life are. I assume that what she is striving toward is equally as valid as her past dynamics. Therapy consists of doing a comprehensive assessment, helping her understand her dynamics, and then helping her define new goals.

(continued on next page)

TABLE 13-1 *(continued)*

Orientation	Areas of Focus
Existential Therapy	My focus is on challenging the meaning in Ruth's life. What does she want in her life? I am interested in the anxiety she feels, her emptiness, and the ways in which she has allowed others to choose for her. How can she begin to exercise her freedom? I assume that our relationship will be a key factor in helping her take actual risks in changing.
Person-Centered Therapy	I avoid planning and structuring the sessions because I trust Ruth to initiate a direction for therapy. If I listen, reflect, empathize, and respond to her, she will be able to clarify her struggles. Although she may be only dimly aware of her feelings at the beginning of therapy, she will move toward increased clarity as I accept her fully, without judgment. My main focus is on creating a climate of openness, trust, caring, understanding, and acceptance. Then she can use this relationship to move forward and grow.
Gestalt Therapy	My focus is on what is emerging in Ruth's awareness. I am guided by the shifts in her awareness, and together we create experiments that grow out of her awareness and her struggles. The emphasis is on our dialogue and the quality of our contact in the therapy sessions. I ask Ruth to bring her feelings of not being accepted into the present by reliving them rather than by merely talking about past events. I am mainly interested in helping her experience her feelings fully, not in developing insight or speculating about why she behaves as she does. The key focus is on how Ruth is behaving and what she is experiencing.
Behavior Therapy	My initial focus is on doing a thorough assessment of Ruth's current behavior. I ask her to monitor what she is doing so that we can have baseline data. We then develop concrete goals to guide our work. I draw on a wide range of cognitive and behavioral techniques to help her achieve her goals: stress reduction techniques, assertion training, role rehearsals, modeling, coaching, systematic desensitization, and relaxation methods. I stress learning new coping behaviors that she can use in everyday situations. She practices these in our sessions and elsewhere.
Cognitive Behavior Therapy	My interest is focused on Ruth's internal dialogue and her thinking processes. I uncover the ways in which she is creating her problems through self-indoctrination and retention of beliefs that are not rational or functional. By use of Socratic dialogue I try to get her to detect her faulty

TABLE 13-1   *(continued)*

Orientation	Areas of Focus
	thinking, to learn ways of correcting her distortions, and to substitute more effective self-statements and beliefs. I use a wide range of cognitive, behavioral, and emotive techniques to accomplish our goals.
Reality Therapy	Our focus is guided by the principles of choice theory. Key questions are "What are you doing now?" and "Is this behavior helping you?" Once Ruth has evaluated her own current behavior and has decided what she wants to change, we collaboratively make plans. I get a commitment from her to follow through with these plans.
Feminist Therapy	My interest is to provide a context for Ruth to evaluate how oppression may be operating in her life today. As a woman she has learned to subordinate her wishes to care for her family, which makes it difficult for her to identify and honor what she wants out of therapy. Because oppression profoundly influences Ruth's beliefs, choices, and perceptions, we will examine the cultural context of her gender-role socialization and how that is influencing her behavior now.
Postmodern Approaches	Rather than focusing on problems, I ask Ruth to look for exceptions to her problem or for times when she functioned without a specific problem. I also strive to get her to externalize her problem from the person that she is. The crux of Ruth's therapy is to conceive of the kind of life she would like to have, a life without the problems that are bringing her into therapy. The emphasis is on finding solutions rather than talking about problems.
Family Systems Therapy	My focus is on the degree to which Ruth has become differentiated from her significant others. We also examine ways in which anxiety is perpetuated by rigid interactional patterns and by her family's structure, and ways in which she can balance her role as a mother with taking care of herself.

Initial Stages of Work With Ruth

I read Ruth's autobiography before our initial session, and I am interested in working with her. I like her ability to pinpoint many of her concerns, and the data she provides are rich with possibilities. From these data alone I do not have a clear idea of where our journey together will take us, for a lot will depend on *how far* Ruth wants to go and what she is willing to explore. From the data alone, though, I do have many ideas of how I want to proceed.[3]

Our Beginning   I assume that Ruth, too, has some anxiety about initiating therapy. I want to provide her with the opportunity to talk about what it is like for her to come to the office today. That in itself provides the direction for part of our session. I surely want to get an idea of what has brought her to therapy. What is going on in her life that motivates her to seek therapy? What does she most hope for as a result of this venture? I structure the initial session so that she can talk about her expectations and about her fears, hopes, ambivalent feelings, and so forth. Because Ruth's trust in me will be an important part of the therapy process, I give her the chance to ask me how I will work with her. I do not believe in making therapy into a mysterious adventure. I think Ruth will get more from her therapy if she knows how it works, if she knows the nature of her responsibilities and mine, and if she is clear on what she wants from this process. (This way of thinking is typical of Adlerian therapy, behavior therapy, cognitive behavior therapy, reality therapy, feminist therapy, and postmodern approaches.)

The Contract   I begin formulating a working contract that will give some direction to our sessions. As a part of this contract, I discuss what I see as my main responsibilities and functions, as well as Ruth's responsibilities in the process. I want her to know at the outset that I expect her to be an active party in this relationship, and I tell her that I function in an active and directive way (which is characteristic of most of the cognitive, behavioral, and action-oriented therapies).

I see therapy as a significant project—an investment in the self, if you will—and I think Ruth has a right to know what she can expect to gain as well as some of the potential risks. I begin by getting some sense of her goals. Although she is vague at first, I work with Ruth to help her define her goals as specifically and concretely as possible. (This process is especially important in Adlerian therapy, behavior therapy, cognitive behavior therapy, reality therapy, and the postmodern approaches.) I will come back to goals in a bit.

Ruth's Self-Presentation   As a way of beginning the counseling process, I see value in first letting Ruth give her presentation of self in the way she chooses. How she walks into the office, her nonverbal language, her mannerisms, her style of speech, the details she chooses to reveal, and what she decides to relate and not to relate provide me with a valuable perspective from which to understand her. I am interested in how Ruth perceives the events in her life and how she feels in her subjective world. (This is especially important in the existential and person-centered models and in the postmodern approaches.) If I do too much structuring initially, I will interfere with her typical style of presenting herself. So I give everything to listening and letting her know what

I am hearing (something that person-centered therapists put a premium on, and something I especially value in the initial stages of therapy).

I want to avoid the tendency to talk too much during this initial session. Being fully present in the therapy session and giving Ruth my sincere attention will pay rich dividends in terms of the potential for therapy. If I listen well, I will get a good sense of what she is coming to therapy for. If I fail to listen accurately and sensitively, there is a risk of going with the first problem she states instead of waiting and listening to discover the depth of her experience.

Gathering Data   I did not begin the session by asking Ruth questions pertaining to her life history, but after Ruth talks about what brought her to therapy at this particular time I ask questions to fill in the gaps. This method gives a more comprehensive picture of how she views her life now, as well as events that she considers significant in her past. Rather than making it a question-and-answer session, I like the idea of using an *autobiographical approach*, in which Ruth writes about the critical turning points in her life, events from her childhood and adolescent years, relationships with parents and siblings, school experiences, current struggles, and future goals and aspirations, to mention a few. I ask her what she thinks would be useful for her to recall and focus on and what she imagines would be useful to me in gaining a better picture of her subjective world. In this way she does some reflecting and sorting out of life experiences outside of the session, she takes an active role in deciding what her personal goals will be for therapy, and I have access to rich material that will give me ideas of where and how to proceed with her. (This unstructured, or open-ended, autobiography could fit into existential, person-centered, and Gestalt therapy models, in which the emphasis is on the subjective world of the client. Also, psychoanalytic and Adlerian therapists would want to know a lot about her developmental history.)

Therapy Proceeds

I favor integrating cognitive work into therapy sessions and recommend some books to Ruth to supplement her therapy. These may include novels, books that deal with central areas of concern to her personally, and something on the nature of therapy. For example, I suggest that she read some books about women facing midlife crises, about parent–child relationships, about enhancing one's marriage, about sex, and about special topics related to her concerns. (This is consistent with behavior therapy, reality therapy, and, especially, rational emotive behavior therapy.) I find that this type of reading provides a good catalyst for self-examination, especially if these books are read in a personal way—meaning that Ruth would apply their themes to her life.

Clarifying Therapy Goals   During the beginning stages, I assist Ruth in getting a clearer grasp of what she most wants from therapy, as well as seeing some steps she can begin to take in attaining her objectives. Like most clients, Ruth is rather global in stating her goals in her autobiography, so I work with her on becoming more concrete. When she looks in the mirror, Ruth says she does not like what she sees. She would like to have a better self-image and be more confident. I am interested in knowing specifically *what* she does not like, the ways in which she now lacks confidence, and what it feels like for her to confront herself by looking at herself and talking to me about what she sees.

Ruth reports that she would like to have more fun in her life. She can be helped to pinpoint specific instances in which she is overly serious and not having fun. We can further define what she would like to be doing that she considers to be fun. We consistently move from general to specific; the more concrete she is, the greater are her chances of attaining what she wants. (It is from behavior therapy that I have learned the value of specifying goals.)[4]

Importance of the Client–Therapist Relationship   I am convinced that one of the most significant factors determining the degree to which Ruth will attain her goals is the therapeutic relationship that she and I will create. (This element is given primary emphasis in the person-centered, existential, Adlerian, feminist, Gestalt, and postmodern approaches.) Therapy is not something the therapist *does* to a passive client, using skills and techniques. Although I am the expert on making therapeutic interventions, Ruth is clearly the expert on her own life. I operate on the premise that therapy will be productive to the extent that it is a collaborative venture. Furthermore, Ruth will get the most from her therapy if she knows how the therapeutic process works. I strive to demystify the therapy process by providing information, securing her informed consent, sharing with her my perceptions of what is going on in the relationship, and by making her an active partner in both assessment and treatment phases. I am concerned with the potentially harmful uses of power dynamics in the client–therapist relationship, and I strive to build mutuality and a sense of partnership into the therapeutic endeavor. (This reflects the emphasis on equality characteristic of feminist therapy.)

Therapy is a deeply personal relationship that Ruth can use for her learning. The person I am is just as important as my knowledge of counseling theory and the level of my skills. Although I must use techniques effectively and have a theoretical base from which to draw a range of techniques, this ability becomes meaningless in the absence of a relationship between Ruth and me that is characterized by mutual respect and trust. (I am influenced by the existential, feminist, person-centered, and postmodern approaches, which emphasize the personal characteristics and attitudes of the therapist.) To what degree can I be real with Ruth? To what degree can I hear what she says and accept her in a nonjudgmental way? To what degree can I respect and care for her? To what degree can I allow myself to enter her subjective world? To what degree am I aware of my own experiencing as I am with her, and how willing am I to share my feelings and thoughts with her? An authentic relationship is vital at the initial stages of therapy, and it must be maintained during all stages if therapy is to be effective.[5]

Working With Ruth in Cognitive, Emotive, and Behavioral Ways

My eclectic style is a blend of concepts and techniques from many therapeutic approaches. As a basis for selecting techniques to employ with Ruth, I look at her as a *thinking, feeling,* and *behaving* person. Although I may have to describe the various aspects of what I am doing separately here, keep in mind that I tend to work in an integrated fashion. Thus, I would not work with Ruth's cognitions, then move ahead to her feelings, and finally proceed to behaviors and specific action programs. All of these dimensions would be interrelated. When I am working with Ruth on a cognitive level (such as dealing with decisions she has made or one of her values), I am also concerned about the feelings generated in her at the moment and about exploring them with her. And in the background I am thinking of what she might actually *do* about the thoughts and feelings she is expressing. This *doing* would involve new behaviors that she can try in the session to deal with a problem and new skills that she can take outside and apply to problems she encounters in real-life situations. (As a basis for this integrative style, I am drawing on the cognitive and emotional insight-oriented approach of psychoanalysis; on the experiential therapies, which stress the expression and experiencing of feelings; on the cognitive therapies, which pay attention to the client's thinking processes, affecting behavior and beliefs; and on the action-oriented therapies, which stress the importance of creating a plan for behavioral change.)[6]

Exploring Ruth's Fears Related to Therapy   Ruth begins a session by talking about her fears of coming to know herself and by expressing her ambivalent feelings toward therapy:

Ruth: Before I made the decision to enter therapy, I had worked pretty hard at keeping problems tucked away neatly. I lived by compartmentalizing my life, and that way nothing became so fearsome that I felt overwhelmed. But this reading that I'm doing, writing in my journal, thinking about my life, talking about my feelings and experiences in here—all this is making me uncomfortable. I'm getting more and more anxious. I suppose I'm afraid of what I might find inside of me if I keep searching.

From an existential perspective, I see this anxiety as realistic, and even useful. I surely do not want to merely reassure Ruth that everything will turn out for the best if she will only trust me and stay in therapy. I want to explore in depth with her the decision she must now make. Looking at her life in an honest way is potentially frightening. There are risks attached to this process.

Although she has security now, she is paying the price in terms of boredom and low self-respect. Yet her restricted existence is a safe one. The attractions of getting to know herself better and the possibilities for exercising choice and control in her life can be very exciting, yet also frightening. At this point I hope Ruth will look at this issue and take a stand on how much she wants for herself and the risks she is willing to take in reaching for more.

Ruth Decides to Continue   Being in therapy is a series of choices. Not only does therapy open Ruth up to new possibilities by expanding her awareness and thus widening the brackets of her freedom to choose, but she makes choices all during the therapy process itself. I respect her choices, and I support her when she is struggling with difficult ones. I also push her gently and invite her to ask for more and to take more risks. Ultimately, she is the one who decides many times during our sessions the depth to which she is willing to go. (This is very much an existential concept.)

Ruth Works to Become Free   In one session Ruth expresses her desire to be liberated.

Ruth: All my life I've felt unfree. I've had to be the person that my parents wanted me to be, I've had to be the wife that John expected me to be, and I've had to be what my kids expected as a mother. I'd like to be free and feel that I can live for me, but so far I don't seem to be able to.

Jerry: Between now and our next session, I'd like to suggest that you do several things. In your journal let yourself imagine all the ways you've felt unfree in your life. Just write down phrases or short sentences. It might help if you could write down messages you've heard from your parents. What have they said they wanted of you? It might help if you actually imagine that you are for a time your father and just write as fast as you can all the things he might say about all he expects. Then let yourself write to Ruth as your mother. Again, without thinking much, just let her words and thoughts come to the paper. If you do that several times this week, we can pursue it more next week.

Here is the idea of "homework assignments" (borrowed from the cognitive and behavioral therapies), only I am stressing the feelings that go with such an exercise. In this way Ruth can review some earlier experiences, and I hope she will stir up some old feelings associated with these memories, which we can deal with in future sessions.

At the following session Ruth brings her journal and says she would like to talk about what it was like to write herself letters (as her father and as her mother), saying all that was expected of her. I ask her to share what this was like, and I pay attention to her body as well as her words. (Like the Gestalt therapist, I think the truth of one's messages is conveyed in voice inflections, postures, facial features, and the like. If I listen only to her words, I am likely to miss a deeper level of meaning. Like the person-centered therapist, I value listening to what she is feeling and expressing.) Although I think it is important that I reflect and clarify (a person-centered technique), I deem it crucial that I bring myself into a dialogue with Ruth. If I am having reactions to what she is saying or if she is touching something within me, sharing my present experience with her can facilitate her work. (This is valued in existential, person-centered, Gestalt, and feminist therapies.) My own disclosure, at timely and appropriate moments, can lead to a deeper self-exploration on Ruth's part. I must take care not to disclose merely for its own sake; nor is it well to take the focus off of her. But even a few words can let her know that I understand her. (This is valued especially in feminist therapy.)

Ruth is talking about her mother's messages to her. As I listen to her, I notice that there is a critical tone and a sharpness to her voice, and she makes a pointing gesture with her finger. I get an idea that I want to pursue.

Jerry: Would you sit in this red rocking chair? Actually rock back and forth, and with a very critical voice—pointing your finger and shaking it—deliver a lecture to Ruth, who is sitting in this other chair.

Ruth: I want you to work hard and never complain. Look at how I've slaved, and look at how moral I've been. Life is hard and don't forget that. You're put on earth here to see if you can pass the test. Bear all your burdens well, and you'll be rewarded in the next life—where it counts!

There are many possibilities of places to go from here. (So far I have been using a Gestalt technique of asking her to "become" her mother in the hope that she can actually feel what this brings up in her as she relives the scene.) I ask her to sit in the other chair and be Ruth and respond to her mother's lecture. The dialogue continues with exchanges between Mother and Ruth, and finally I ask her to stop and process what has gone on. This technique can also be done with her father, and will likely be done in further sessions because her relationship with her father continues to have a powerful influence in her way of being and behaving.

I give Ruth a different kind of journal assignment at this session. Earlier I had suggested that she write about all the ways she has felt unfree in life. Her personal writing was a catalyst that stimulated some useful exploration in her therapy sessions. Now I ask Ruth to think about the times in her life when she felt the most free. I ask her, "If you were to awaken and a miracle happened when you were asleep, what would your life be like if you were really free?" By using this *miracle question*, a solution-focused technique, I am inviting Ruth to design the kind of free existence she would hope for. As an alternative, I might use the Adlerian "acting as if" approach: "Ruth, I know that you experience yourself as being unfree most of the time, but I'd like you to try an experiment. For one week I would like you to consciously act as if you were free. For this period of time operate on the assumption that you are the free person now that you'd like to be. Let me suggest that you write in your journal about your experience when you are acting as if you are really free."

I assume that it is not a matter of Ruth feeling completely unfree or completely free, rather her sense of freedom may exist on a continuum. When she describes a time when she felt relatively free, I would then pursue with her what she did to contribute to feeling free. What's more, I will ask her to come up with small steps she can take and is willing to take to move in the direction of increasing her sense of freedom. The various journal assignments are useful for helping Ruth carry out her own therapy at home; she can then bring into her therapy session topics she wants to pursue.

We Work on Ruth's Cognitions   Gestalt techniques are very useful for assisting Ruth to get an experiential sense of what might be called "toxic introjects." These are the messages and values Ruth has swallowed whole without digesting them and making them her own. My goal is to help her externalize these introjections so that she can take a critical look at them. I have an investment in getting her to look at this process and make her values truly her own. (This is very much an existential notion. From my perspective, authenticity consists of living by values one chooses rather than living blindly by values given by others.)

I ask Ruth to identify as many family rules as she can that she recalls having grown up with as a child. She recollects parental messages such as these: "Don't think for yourself." "Follow the church obediently, and conform your will to God's will." "Never question the Bible." "Live a moral life." "Don't get close to people, especially in sexual ways." "Always be proper and appropriate." We spend time identifying and dealing with gender-role messages Ruth still struggles with such as these: "Your main concern should be your family." "Don't put your career needs before what is expected of you as a woman." "Defer to what men want." "Always be ready to nurture those who need care and attention."

In addition to working with Ruth's feelings, I find it essential to work with her *cognitive structures*, which include her belief systems, her thoughts, her attitudes, and her values. (In behavior therapy attention would be given to beliefs and assumptions that have an influence on her behavior; in rational emotive behavior therapy attention would be paid to irrational beliefs and self-indoctrination; in Adlerian therapy we would look at her basic mistakes; in reality therapy the focus would be on values; and in feminist therapy we would do an assessment of the impact of gender-role messages.) I focus on the underlying messages Ruth pays attention to now in her life. I assume that her self-talk is relevant to her behavior.

Ruth Brings Up Her Spirituality   Although I do not have an agenda to impose religious or spiritual values on Ruth, I do see it as my function to assess the role spirituality plays in her life currently and to assess beliefs, attitudes, and practices from her earlier years. Several times Ruth initiated a discussion about the void she feels in the area of religion. She was brought up with a strict fundamentalist religion and was taught that she should never question the religious and moral values that were "right." Eventually Ruth rejected much of the guilt-oriented aspects of her religion. However, even though she cognitively confronted many of the religious beliefs she was taught, on an emotional level she still feels a sense of unease and has yet to find what she considers a viable alternative to the religion of her parents.

Ruth lets me know that mainly what she remembers from her church experiences is feeling a sense of guilt that she was not good enough and that she was always falling short of being the person that her church and parents thought she should be. Not only was she not enough in the eyes of her parents, but she was also not enough for God.

Ruth is engaged in a struggle to find spiritual values that will help her find meaning in her life. Although formal religion does not seem to play a key role for Ruth now, she is struggling to find her place in the universe and is seeking spiritual avenues that provide her with purpose. She is floundering somewhat and realizes that this is a missing dimension in her life. Ruth also lets me know that she is pleasantly surprised that I am even mentioning religion and spirituality, because she was not sure that it was appropriate to bring matters such as religion and spirituality into counseling. She lets me know that it was good for her to be able to initiate a discussion about her past experiences with religion and her present quest to find a spiritual path that has meaning to her. Ruth informs me of her intention to further explore in her sessions ways that she can enhance her spiritual life.

Ruth Brings Up Her Father   We devote several sessions to discussion of how Ruth's father played a central role in the moral and religious values that she believed she had to accept to stay in his "good graces." Eventually, Ruth gets the insight that she does not want to live by the religious dogma that her father preached, nor does she want to accept for herself the messages he continues to give her about the "right path for living."

As we explore the messages that Ruth was reared with, one theme seems to emerge. She has lived much of her life in ways that were designed to get her father's approval. She feels that unless she gets her father's acceptance and approval, she will never have "arrived." She reasons that if the father who conceived her could not love her, then nobody ever could. If this man does not show her love, she is doomed to live a loveless life! I proceed by using cognitive behavioral concepts and techniques to get her to critically evaluate some invalid assumptions she continues to make.

As much as possible, without pushing Ruth away, I challenge and confront her thinking and her value system, which appear to be at the root of much of her conflict. I am not imposing my values on her; rather, it is a matter of getting her to look at beliefs and values she has accepted to determine if she still wants to base her life on them. Does she want to spend the rest of her life in a futile attempt to "win over" her father? Does she want to continue making all men into her father? What will it take for her to finally gain her father's acceptance and love—if this is possible? What might she think of the person she had to become to gain his acceptance? I take this line of questioning in an attempt to get her to *think*, to *challenge* herself, and to *decide* for herself her standards for living.[7]

Dealing with Ruth's Past in Understanding Her Decisions I have been talking about some of the early decisions Ruth made in response to messages she received from her parents. I very much value the exploration of a client's early childhood experiences as a basis for understanding present pressing issues. (The psychoanalytic approach emphasizes a reconstruction of the past, a working through of early conflicts that have been repressed, and a resolution of these unconscious conflicts. Family approaches encourage clients to work through conflicts with their parents.) I accept that Ruth's childhood experiences were influential in contributing to her present development, although I do not think these factors have *determined* her or that she is fixed with certain personality characteristics for life unless she goes through a long-term analytic reconstructive process. (I favor the Gestalt approach to working with her past.) I ask her to bring any unresolved conflicts from her past into the here-and-now through use of her imagination and role-playing experiments. In this way her past is being dealt with in a powerful way as it is being manifested in her current problems.

In Ruth's attempt to face her past I expect some *resistance*—hesitation, defenses, and barriers—at certain anxiety-provoking points. (Psychoanalysis has resistance as a central concept; Gestalt therapy mentions the "impasse.") In working with resistance, I attempt to respect it. In other words, I see that Ruth's resistance is an inevitable part of how therapy proceeds. To some extent it is healthy for Ruth to be cautious. Her reluctance shows that she is aware of the risks of changing and the anxiety that coming to terms with unknown parts of herself brings up. I do not see resistance necessarily as conscious defiance or as an unwillingness to cooperate. (Behavior therapists often assume that "resistance" is an excuse on the therapist's part for poor management of techniques. They see it as a function of failure by the therapist to make a correct assessment and apply an appropriate treatment plan.)

Overall, Ruth is a willing and motivated client. She is insightful, courageous, able to make connections between current behavior and past influences, willing to try risky behaviors both in the session and out of the session, and willing to face difficult issues in her life. Even under such favorable (and almost ideal) circumstances, I still think Ruth will experience some resistance. She debates about whether to continue therapy; at times she blames her parents for her present problems; and at other times she chooses to stay comfortable because of her fear of plunging into unknown territory. In short, I work with whatever resistance she shows by pointing out its most obvious manifestations first and encouraging her to talk about her fears and explore them. An effective way to deal with resistance is to recognize it and deal with it directly. This can be done in a gentle yet confrontational way, along with providing support to face issues that she might otherwise avoid.[8]

Working Toward Redecisions   I try to structure situations in the therapy session that will facilitate new decisions on Ruth's part. Her redecisions have to be made on both the emotional and cognitive levels. (In encouraging Ruth to make new decisions, I draw on cognitive, emotive, and behavioral techniques. I use role-playing procedures, fantasy and imagery, assertion-training procedures, Gestalt techniques, feminist therapy social action strategies, solution-focused therapy techniques, narrative approaches, and family systems therapy methods, to mention a few.) She can spend years getting insights into the cause of her problems, but I think it is more important that she commit herself to some course of action aimed at changing herself and also bringing about environmental change. (Here I like the Adlerian and reality therapy emphasis on getting the client to decide on a plan of action and make a commitment to carry it out.)

Encouraging Ruth to Act   In many ways I look at therapy as a place of safety where clients can experiment with new ways of being to see what behavioral changes they really want to make. The critical point consists of actually taking what is learned in the sessions and applying it to real-life situations. I consistently encourage Ruth to carry out homework assignments geared to having her challenge her fears and inhibitions in a variety of practical situations. Thus, if she says that she is yearning for a weekend alone with her husband yet fears asking for it because she might be turned down and the rejection would hurt, I challenge her: "If you don't bother to ask, chances are you won't have this weekend you say you want with John. You've often brought up in your sessions that you don't ask for what you want, and then end up feeling depressed and unloved. Here's your chance to actually *do* something different."

At various times I gently ask Ruth to decide if she *really* wants to make changes in her life or merely wants to *talk about* making changes. Because she sincerely wants to be different, we use session time in role playing and behavioral rehearsal, and then I ask her to experiment with her new learning in different life situations, especially with her family. For me, translating what is learned in the sessions into daily life is the essence of what therapy is about.[9]

Evaluating Ruth's Therapy Experience

My style of counseling places emphasis on continuing assessment by both the counselor and the client from the initial to the final session. In my work with Ruth I bring up from time to time the topic of her progress in therapy. We openly discuss the degree to which she is getting what she wants from the process (and from me). If she is not successfully meeting her objectives, we can explore some factors that might be getting in the way of her progress. I could be a restricting factor. This is especially true if I am reacting to her strictly from a technical approach and am withholding my own reactions from her. If I am being inauthentic in any way in the sessions, I am certain this will show up in a failure on her part to progress to the degree to which she might have.

I also explore with Ruth some of the circumstances in her life that may be contributing to what appears to be slow or nonexistent progress. She has done a lot of changing, which may itself be creating new problems in her home relationships, and she may feel a need to pull back and consolidate her gains. There may be a plateau for a time before she is ready to forge ahead with making other major life changes. Still another factor determining her progress or lack of it lies within her—namely, her own decision and commitment of how far she wants to go in therapy. Is she willing to make some basic changes in her personality and create a new identity for herself? Is she willing to pay the price that changing entails? Does she merely want to solve some pressing problems on the surface while remaining personally unchanged? These are but a few of the factors we have to consider in understanding any failure in the therapy process.

How do Ruth and I determine the degree to which she is progressing? What criteria do we use to make this determination? (Behavior therapy is built on the assumption that assessment and evaluation are basic to the therapy process. Techniques must be continually verified to determine if they are working. Behavior changes in the client are a major basis for making this evaluation.) I look at Ruth's work in the sessions and what she is doing outside of them as a measure of the degree to which therapy is working. Another important index is our relationship. If it is one of trust and if she is dealing with difficult personal issues in her therapy and also working on these issues outside of the sessions, then therapy is working. Also, her own evaluation of how much progress she sees and how satisfied she is by the outcomes is a major factor in assessing therapeutic results.

When is it time for Ruth to terminate therapy? This, too, is a matter that I openly evaluate at appropriate times and we explore in a collaborative way. Ultimately, I see termination as her choice. My hope is that once Ruth attains a degree of increased self-awareness and specific behavioral skills in meeting present and future problems, she might well be encouraged to end formal therapy and begin to become her own therapist. (This is a cognitive behavioral approach.) To keep her beyond this point could result in needlessly fostering her dependence on me, which is not too unlike the problem that brought her to therapy in the first place.[10]

How Would You Work With Ruth Using Your Own Approach?

Try your hand at achieving some synthesis among the 11 approaches by drawing on each of them in a way that seems meaningful to you—one that fits your own personality and your view of people and the nature of therapy. Here are some questions to help you organize the elements of your approach.

1. What would you be thinking and feeling as you approach your initial session with Ruth? Use whatever you know about her from the material presented about her and her autobiography in the

first chapter, from the 11 chapters on her work with various therapists, and from my integrative approach in working with her in this chapter.

2. Briefly state how you see Ruth in terms of her current dynamics and most pressing conflicts. How would you feel about working with her as a client? How do you view her capacity to understand herself and to make basic changes?

3. How much direction do you see Ruth needing? To what degree would you take the responsibility for structuring her sessions? Where would you be on a continuum of highly directive to very nondirective?

4. If you were applying brief therapy with Ruth, what kinds of interventions would you most be interested in making?

5. What major themes do you imagine that you would focus on in Ruth's life, especially if you were working within the context of short-term therapy?

6. In what ways might you go about gathering life-history data to make an initial assessment of her problems and to determine which therapy procedures to use?

7. How might you help Ruth clarify her goals for therapy? How would you help her make her goals concrete? How would you assess the degree to which she was meeting her goals?

8. How much interest would you have in working with Ruth's early childhood experiences? her current issues? her future aspirations and strivings? Which of these areas do you favor? Why?

9. What value do you place on the quality of your relationship with Ruth? How important is the client–therapist relationship as a determinant of therapeutic outcomes?

10. Would you be more inclined to focus on Ruth's feelings? her thought processes and other cognitive factors? her ability to take action as measured by her behaviors?

11. How supportive might you be of Ruth? How confrontational might you be with her? In what areas do you think you would be most supportive? most confrontational?

12. How much might you be inclined to work toward major personality reconstruction? toward specific skill-development and problem-solving strategies? toward social action strategies?

13. How might you explore Ruth's major fears, both about therapy and about her life?

14. What life experiences have you had that would most help you in working with Ruth? What personal characteristics might hinder your work with her?

15. How might you proceed in dealing with Ruth's parents and the role she feels that they have played in her life? How important would it be to focus on working through her attitudes and feelings toward her parents?

16. To what degree would you strive to involve Ruth's current family in her therapy?

17. How much might you structure outside-of-therapy activities for Ruth (homework, reading, journal writing, and so forth)?

18. What specific techniques and concepts might you derive from the psychoanalytic approach? from the experiential approaches? from the cognitive, behavioral, and action-oriented approaches? from the postmodern approaches? from systemic approaches?

19. Would you orient Ruth's therapy more toward insight or toward action? What balance might you seek between the cognitive aspects and the feeling aspects?

20. How might you make the determination of when Ruth was ready to end therapy?

 AN EXERCISE: THEMES IN RUTH'S LIFE

A few of the major themes that have therapeutic potential for further exploration are revealed in these statements that Ruth made at one time or another:

1. You seem so distant and removed from me. You're hard to reach.
2. In spite of my best attempts, I still feel a lot of guilt that I haven't done enough.
3. I just don't trust myself to find my own answers to life.
4. I'm afraid to change for fear of breaking up my marriage.
5. It's hard for me to ask others for what I want.
6. I feel extremely tense, and I can't sleep at night.
7. All my life I've tried to get my father's approval.
8. It's hard for me to have fun. I'm so responsible.
9. I've always had a weight problem, and I can't seem to do much about it.
10. I'm afraid to make mistakes and look like a fool.
11. My daughter and I just don't get along with each other.
12. I give and give, and they just take and take.
13. I've lived by the expectations of others for so long that I don't know what I want anymore.
14. I don't think my marriage is the way it should be, but my husband thinks it's just fine.
15. I'm afraid to tell my husband what I really want with him, because I'm afraid he'll leave me.
16. I fear punishment because I've given up my old religious values.
17. I wear so many hats that sometimes I feel worn out.
18. There's not enough time for me to be doing all the things I know I should be doing.
19. I'm afraid of my feelings toward other men.
20. When my children leave, I'll have nothing to live for.

Look over this list of Ruth's statements and select the ones that you find most interesting. Here are three suggestions for working with them. For each of the themes you select, (1) show how you would begin working with Ruth from each of the 11 perspectives; (2) take only two contrasting approaches and focus on these; or (3) combine several therapeutic models and work with Ruth using this synthesis.

Attempt to work with a few of Ruth's statements after reading about my integrated way of working with her in this chapter. This would make interesting and lively material for role playing and discussion in small groups. One person can "become" Ruth while others in the group counsel her from the vantage point of several different therapeutic perspectives. Practicing a variety of approaches will assist you in discovering for yourself ways to pull together techniques that you consider to be the best.

 ## CONCLUDING COMMENTS

Developing a counseling style that fits you is truly a challenge. It entails far more than picking bits and pieces from theories in a random and fragmented manner. As you take steps to develop an integrated perspective, think about these questions. Which theories provide a basis for understanding the *cognitive* dimension? Which theories help you understand the *affective* dimension? Which theories address the *behavioral* dimension? As you are aware, most of the 11 therapies you have studied focus primarily on one of these dimensions of human experience. The task is to wisely and creatively select therapeutic procedures that you can employ in working with a diverse population. Knowing the unique needs of your clients, your own values and personality, and the theories themselves is a good basis for beginning to develop a theory that is an expression of yourself.

It requires knowledge, skill, art, and experience to be able to determine what techniques will work best with particular clients and with certain problems. It is also an art to know *when* and *how* to use a particular therapeutic intervention. Because building your personalized approach to counseling is a long-term venture, I do hope that you will be patient with yourself as you continue to grow through your reading, thinking, and experience in working with clients and through your own personal struggles and life experiences.

 ## NOTES

1. In addition to the video, see Chapters 15 and 16 of Corey (2005), *Theory of Counseling and Psychotherapy*, 7th edition, which address the topic of an integrative perspective in more detail.

2. My book, *The Art of Integrative Counseling*, consists of parallel topics and will be a useful source if you want a more in-depth presentation of how to develop an integrative approach.

3. The *CD-ROM for Integrative Counseling* provides a demonstration of my work with Ruth during the initial stage of counseling (Session 1, "Beginning of Counseling").

4. Refer to Session 3 ("Establishing Therapeutic Goals") in the *CD-ROM for Integrative Counseling* for a demonstration of ways I assist Ruth in identifying concrete goals that will guide our work together.

5. Refer to Session 2 ("The Therapeutic Relationship") in the *CD-ROM for Integrative Counseling* for a demonstration of some issues that are essential to developing a therapeutic alliance.

6. In the *CD-ROM for Integrative Counseling*, Session 6 deals with the cognitive focus, Session 7 deals with the emotive focus, and Session 8 deals with the behavioral focus.

7. In the *CD-ROM for Integrative Counseling*, Session 11 ("Understanding How the Past Influences the Present"), Ruth explores her feelings toward her father via a role play.

8. In Session 5 ("Understanding and Dealing With Resistance") in the *CD-ROM for Integrative Counseling*, Ruth expresses some resistance toward continuing counseling.

9. In Session 12 ("Working Toward Decisions and Behavioral Change") in the *CD-ROM for Integrative Counseling*, Ruth explores some of her early decisions and begins to make new decisions.

10. In Session 13 ("Evaluation and Termination") in the *CD-ROM for Integrative Counseling*, Ruth and I review what she has learned in counseling and also discuss future directions after terminating counseling.